SEMEIA 50

PARAENESIS: ACT AND FORM

Guest Editors:
Leo G. Perdue and John G. Gammie

©1990
by the Society of Biblical Literature

Semeia 50

ISSN 0095-571X
ISBN 1-58983-113-6

Printed in the United States of America
on acid-free paper

CONTENTS

PART THREE: RESPONSES

CONTRIBUTORS TO THIS ISSUE

Harold W. Attridge
  Department of Theology
  University of Notre Dame
  Notre Dame, IN 46530

Claudia V. Camp
  Department of Religion Studies
  Box 30772
  Texas Christian University
  Ft. Worth, TX 76129

John G. Gammie
  Faculty of Religion
  The University of Tulsa
  Tulsa, OK 74104

Amy-Jill Levine
  Department of Religion
  Swarthmore College
  Swarthmore, PA 19081

Leo G. Perdue
  Brite Divinity School
  Texas Christian University
  Ft. Worth, TX 76129

†Jerome D. Quinn

†James M. Reese

Vernon K. Robbins
  Department of Religion
  312 Physics Building
  Emory University
  Atlanta, GA 30322

Raymond C. Van Leeuwen
  Calvin Theological Seminary
  3233 Burton Street SE
  Grand Rapids, MI 49506

James G. Williams
  Department of Religion
  501 Hall of Languages
  Syracuse University
  Syracuse, NY 13244–1170

INTRODUCTION

With this issue of *Semeia*, authors with expertise in the Old and New Testaments explore the process and form of moral exhortation (paraenesis) in the ancient Near East and the Graeco-Roman world. Professor Perdue in his opening essay has carried forward his earlier studies on paraenesis in the attempt to compose a programmatic study on the types of social groups out of which moral exhortation came and of the kinds of social function moral exhortation has performed (using the categories in particular of Victor Turner).

Professor Gammie in his opening essay has also sought to make a programmatic statement on the larger secondary genre, Paraenetic Literature, into which he argues the moral exhortation called paraenesis must be placed as a division or sub-genre. Other component parts of this larger, complex or composite genre are also examined.

After the initial essays had been composed and revised, they were circulated to contributors to utilize in their own analysis of moral exhortation in specific works: Proverbs 1–9 (van Leeuwen), the Q Document (Levine), the Sermon on the Mount (Williams), the Pastoral Epistles (Quinn), and the 'Epistle to the Hebrews' (Attridge). Each one of these authors, in varying degree of detail, has either engaged in direct discussion with the opening essays in an inquiry on the nature of the moral exhortation in the respective work(s) under investigation, or the authors have sought to apply the approach of the opening essays for corroboration of, or musings upon, their own findings and explorations.

In each of the above-mentioned studies in the second part, a distinctive concern or concerns is apparent. Van Leeuwen seeks for the dominant cluster of metaphors in Proverbs 1–9 and finds it in the notion of "limit." Levine assesses the nature and kind of feminist sensitivities in the common source of Matthew and Luke. Williams probes the proper generic designation of the Sermon on the Mount as well as the nature of the genre Gospel. Quinn expounds the notion of "irrefutability" which he avers inheres in a surprising number of instances of the terms *parainein* and *parainesis* and carries over to the Pastoral Epistles. Attridge sees a need to expand the data base employed by Perdue and Gammie and ventures that in the 'Epistle to the Hebrews' another kind of sub-genre of moral exhortation, homily or λογός παρακλήσεως, is to be found.

The first essay in the second section by one of the editors is of a slightly different sort. Professor Perdue's study, "The Death of the Sage and Moral Exhortation: From Ancient Near Eastern Instructions to Graeco-Roman Paraenesis," is in a sense an expansion of his interest in the social location of moral exhortation, and it also fills in some of the social and historical circumstances surrounding the works which Gammie has examined in his opening essay on form.

The third section of the volume is devoted to responses. Professor Reese finds both Perdue's and Gammie's methodologies wanting and advocates a third way of analysis of ancient texts by way of semiotics and the encyclopaedic approach to definitions. Professor Camp takes on all of the writers in the volume—including Professor Reese—whose focus of analysis resides in texts which emerged before the common era. Professor Robbins, on the other hand, has concentrated on those whose focus of analysis is in texts produced in the common era.

PART ONE:

THE SOCIAL CHARACTER AND MORPHOLOGY OF PARAENESIS AND PARAENETIC LITERATURE

THE SOCIAL CHARACTER OF PARAENESIS AND PARAENETIC LITERATURE

Leo G. Perdue

ABSTRACT

Paraenesis as process reflects two models of social organization: order and conflict. At the level of *Gesellschaft*, the paradigm of order, traditional and conservative, regards duty and obedience as the motivation for most actions, and seeks to preserve the existing social order. The primary occasions for moral exhortation are entrances into new stages of life, social roles, and social groups. The social functions of moral instruction are the act of protrepsis (conversion), the procedure of paraenesis (confirmation), socialization, and legitimation. At the level of *Gemeinschaft*, moral exhortation is based more on intimacy.

The paradigm of conflict seeks to subvert the institutional values of the *Gesellschaft*. Paraenesis based on this model may be pessimistic, doubting any real change may be initiated. Or the outlook may be optimistic, hoping that a new social order will emerge. Normally, the experience of *communitas* emerging from a variety of *Gemeinschaften* provides the stimulus and values for moral existence.

0   *General Introduction.* The paraenetic literature of Judaism and early Christianity drew heavily from two major cultural spheres: the ancient Near East (especially Israelite and Jewish wisdom influenced by the sages of Egypt and Mesopotamia) and Graeco-Roman civilization (notably the moral philosophers).[1] The extant literary corpora of moral instruction produced by these cultures are rather extensive. And, as might be expected, the content of this literature is diverse. This is due in part to cultural particularity, including the specific form of social organization at a given period. But diversity also results from the presence of paraenesis in many different institutions and groups within the same society. Moral instruction was found in such different contexts as schools, royal courts, governmental bureaucracies, households, and markets, in places public as well as private. The teachers, audiences, and tradents who shaped, practiced, and transmitted paraenesis included males and females in a variety of social classes and roles, including rulers, nobles, scribes, rhetors, teachers, students, priests, soldiers, and parents. The forms of presentation were oral, e.g., paraenetic speeches and various types of oration which

included paraenesis, and written, including especially letters, instructions, and collections of sayings.

Whether oral or written, one overriding purpose characterized all forms of paraenesis: the providing of guidance for the moral life. Regardless of how the moral life may have been defined by a culture or a sub-group, paraenesis was designed to provide general and practical guidance for human behavior within a previously shaped, comprehensive understanding of social reality. Moral guidance could confirm the validity of a prescribed way of life or seek to convert the audience to a new manner of existence (Burgess: 229–31, n. 2). Or it could seek to subvert an existing social structure and provide for the formation of a different one. And while the content of moral instruction varied widely from culture to culture and age to age in regard to specific virtues, there were typical social features common to the literature and the oral traditions which lay behind it.

The purpose of this essay is to construct a paradigm for describing and interpreting the social character of paraenesis in the cultural worlds of the Eastern Mediterranean from the Early Bronze Age through the formative beginnings of early Christianity. This paradigm contains four major categories: models which best describe and interpret the types of society and social groups among which paraenesis flourished, social features common to Paraenetic Literature, social and anthropological settings in which paraenesis was used, and the social functions of moral instruction.

1   *Social Models for Interpreting Paraenesis.* Paraenesis is an element of social thought which may be placed within the two major models for understanding the nature, organization, and functioning of human societies and communities: order and conflict. Each of these models makes important assumptions about the cosmos and the character of society.[2] These models are not simply the theoretical constructions of modern sociology, but are also reflected by the societies, communities, social groups, and individuals who produced and used paraenesis as an important segment of their own social thought.

1.1   *The Paradigm of Order.*[3] Traditional paraenesis represents a primary level of knowledge in those societies of the Eastern Mediterranean world which were modelled on the paradigm of order (Perdue, 1977).[4] In its ideal form, this social model projects a world order as originating at creation and continuing to categorize and regulate all existing elements into a harmonious whole (Perdue, 1990). Accordingly, everything has its place, norms, time, and function. A divine council (allowing for the freedom of the gods) or natural law (a more deterministic view) maintains this order, often through a system of retribution which sustains life and grants wellbeing for those who live in harmony with cosmic norms, but brings punishment and destruction to violators (Koch). For example, Egyptian instructions reflect the conception of a cosmic order, Ma'at ("justice," "righteousness," "truth") which originated at creation and continues to permeate every sphere of reality, including nature and the major institutions of society (kingship, state religion, family, occupations, etc.). The goal of the wise was to live in harmony with the social and cosmic spheres of Ma'at and to experience its beneficence. Thus Ptahhotep instructs his son:

> IF THOU ART A LEADER commanding the affairs of the multitude, seek out every beneficial deed until it may be that thy (own) affairs are without wrong. Justice[5] is great, and its appropriateness is lasting; it has not been disturbed since the time of him who made it, (whereas) there is punishment for him who passes over its laws. It is the (right) path before him who knows nothing. Wrongdoing has never brought its undertaking into port (ANET: 412).

In its broad sweep, Egyptian society was a *Gesellschaft*, conceived ideally as a microcosm, with its basic institutions, classes, and laws grounded in and reflective of the structure of the cosmos (Toennies). Social inequities based on class, gender, and position were projected as part of the natural order or due to the will of the gods. Individuals were to accept their fate, normally determined at birth, and to behave according to their place and its norms in the social order. Grounded in the order of creation and enforced by the power of the state, laws (whether embodied in the person of the king, transmitted orally, and/or written down in lawcodes) were authoritative and required obedience. State religion legitimated social institutions, patterns, and laws, and its festivals and rituals were designed through mythic enactment to sustain the natural and social order. Conformity to social rules and obligations of the *Gesellschaft* was required, while variance from the laws and customs of the prevailing order was considered deviant behavior, threatening the wellbeing of both the individual and society. Change was viewed as disruptive and consequently was resisted by both political power and social custom.

In general, human nature was regarded as selfish, with a tendency to be dominated by passions and driven by desires. If left uncontrolled, individual selfishness and reckless passion would lead to social chaos. Salvation from the dangers of passion was provided by the gods and/or the use of human reason in establishing the social order and controls necessary for society and community to survive.[6] To this end, political institutions held the power and authority necessary to maintain the integrity of the social order, combat the threat of anarchy, and insure the society's survival in its present form.

Paraenesis which reflects this type of model has the tendency to control by ideology powerless groups. The appeal to nature, the gods, and tradition may well be used to support the privileged status and position of those who possess power and wealth. Thus moral exhortation became a powerful means of ideological control in the process of social formation.[7]

Social relations of a more intimate variety, including those of the family, extended kinship groups, clubs, and religion based on personal piety, were also considered to be part of the natural and/or divine order. This type of smaller, more personal society is a *Gemeinschaft*, or community (Toennies, 1963), where social custom and religious precepts defined responsibilities and obligations for group and individual behavior. Authority was also more personal, usually grounded in recognized heads of the communities. Motivations for ethical action were based on intimacy, honor, compassion, and the will of the personal gods of these smaller groups and associations.

Social knowledge derived primarily from the observation of natural laws and divine revelation. Natural and divine law tended to be equated and were authoritative, requiring unquestioning submission from community members. Societal myths were created, not only to explain the origins of the community and its basic institutions, but more importantly to legitimate its present form. As a type of social knowledge, traditional paraenesis encompassed the features of this projected cosmic, social, and anthropological order (*Gesellschaft*) and exhorted the community's members on the basis of duty and self-interest to follow and conform to its expectations. Obligations and behavior for the more personal social existence (*Gemeinschaft*), also often reflected in paraenesis, appealed more to personal relationships (e.g. the authority of the parent) and feelings of intimacy. Ethical action produced well-being within nature, the larger society, the community, and the individual, sustaining their ongoing existence. Immoral behavior produced chaos in every sphere and was viewed as a threat to communal and individual life.

1.2   *The Paradigm of Conflict.*[8] A second model of society is conflict.[9] This model also makes major assumptions about the cosmos and society. In its ideal expression, this model projects a world which is not a harmonious order, but rather an arena of opposing forces which struggle for domination. Gods or forces of order and chaos are in conflict, vying for control. Struggle, not harmony, characterizes social life in the *Gesellschaft*. Viewed from below, that is by social groups denied access to power and status in the larger society, the ruling group is often considered coercive and oppressive. Within these groups of the powerless, paraenesis took on the significant role of undermining traditional teaching in order to destabilize the oppressive institutions controlled and ordered by the power elite. This is the function of the poetry of Job and more especially the subversive sayings of the early Jesus tradition preserved in Q (L. Perdue, 1986). The content of the teaching of the early Jesus movement emphasized the egalitarian nature of the table community which welcomed all groups, including especially the marginals and the oppressed, to equal participation (Fiorenza, 1983: 105–59).[10]

Some powerless groups and individuals in antiquity considered substantial social change to be impossible, and found meaningful existence in a variety of more intimate communities (families, clubs, friendships, and/or religious groups). This is true, for example, of Qoheleth and Seneca. Others (e.g., apocalyptic seers) considered social change at the level of the *Gesellschaft* possible, but only by radical action, usually in the form of divine intervention, supplemented perhaps by nonconformist human behavior, including at times revolution. In either case, however, society and human beings were capable of eventual redemption.

As an element of their social knowledge, paraenesis within communities adhering to a model of conflict could be subversive in two senses (L. Perdue, 1986: 28–32). First, subversive paraenesis assumes the forms of its traditional counterpart, but gives it new content. The intent is to subvert the conventional understanding of reality by undermining its social knowledge and bringing into question its legitimacy (Beardslee). This would include the paraenesis of the order-model which attempts to legitimate the power and position held by the normally male aristocracy. Indeed, among groups which considered change possible, there is at times a call for destabilizing behavior designed to bring about the disintegration of the prevailing order. Second, paraenesis may also be subversive in positing a new, though not fully realized, social order which calls for its own code of behavior (e.g., the "Kingdom of God" in Q and Luke). The new order is either to be more egalitarian or to grant power and position to certain social groups previously denied them (Gager, Fiorenza, 1983). Wellbeing and harmony are to characterize the new order, once it comes into existence. The critical wisdom tradition in Israel was characterized by subversive paraenesis in the first sense, while apocalyptic was characterized at times by subversive paraenesis in both the first and second meanings.

1.3   *Structure—Anti-Structure.* If paraenesis reflects both a paradigm of order and of conflict, what is needed is a social model which takes into account both forms of social organization. One such model is provided by Victor Turner. A dynamic, bipolar social and anthropological model which embodies both paradigms of order and conflict is the one of structure and anti-structure developed by Turner (1967a, 1967b, 1972, 1974a, and 1974b).[11] He develops a dynamic, processual model in which society represents the continuing movement back and forth between structure (*societas*) and anti-structure (*communitas*). These two poles operate within both the larger society and the smaller social communities.

Turner begins with A. van Gennep's *rites de passage*, "rites which accompany every change of place, state, social position, and age (1967a: 94)." These rites contain three temporal and spatial phases: separation, margin (*limen*, "threshold"), and aggregation (reincorporation). In the first phase, individuals or groups are detached from a fixed place in the social structure and leave behind all prior cultural conditions. They then enter the second phase, liminality, a state of "betwixt and between" devoid of structure's laws, customs, and ceremonies. During liminal situations, ritual actions and symbols have two phases. In the first phase novices experience the death of their previous social identity and its governing norms (their situation is metaphorically described as death, the tomb, the womb, wilderness, darkness, eclipse, etc.). Paraenesis in this first phase is subversive, designed to undercut the validity of the prior social world and to produce anomy, at least temporarily. Rituals and symbols associated with the second phase imitate the experiences of birth (metaphors include light, fertility, new creation, etc.). This is the dangerous time for proponents of the order model when liminals question and may come to repudiate the values and norm of the *Gesellschaft*. During this phase of the liminal experience, "ritual leaders" construct for the novices a new social reality and instruct the novices in the roles and responsibilities they are to assume, once aggregation (reincorporation) occurs. The design of the liminal experience is ontological as well as instructional: the initiates are reduced to *prima materia* out of which new beings are created, capable of living transformed lives with different behavior patterns. Recreated, they then reenter society, completing the cycle with the third stage.

Turner distinguishes two types of liminality: status elevation and status reversal. In the former the novice moves to a higher position in the social structure. It is this type of experience that provides the context for much traditional paraenesis. In the latter the person or group who occupies low status positions exercises authority over superiors during the liminal experience. After reincorporation, the superiors reassume their normal positions, but duly chastened by the experience of ritual abuse. Yet in regard to social groups of marginals, this superiority may be located within the societal mythos and organization constructed by liminals, e.g., the preaching of itinerant charismatics in the Jesus movement, or the "poor" marginals represented by the community at Qumran which developed its own alternative social structure and hierarchy (cf. Turner, 1972). Within their own social world these marginal groups became the chosen who are to rule over their unrepentant oppressors. Anti-traditional paraenesis, designed to subvert the existing social structure and produce a new social reality, is a feature of this type of "permanent" liminality.

Turner's own interests are primarily in the second stage, liminality, in which all behavior is temporarily at least nonconformist. During this phase, egalitarianism (*communitas*) may develop among the initiates because of common status and shared suffering. Even alienation towards the social structure may develop, leading to either chaos or constructive change in the form of alternative social arrangements. Proponents of the existing social order recognize the dangers of these liminal periods, so that they attempt to build limits and controls into these times of passage. Thus traditional paraenesis functions within these liminal periods to lessen the danger of *communitas* and to stabilize the social order. For example, students passing through a course of study undergo a liminal experience in which their moral instruction is designed to mold character and provide codes of behavior for their expected social roles.[12] This is evidenced in royal and official installation rituals and the accompanying instructions (e.g., "The Instruction of Ptah-hotep," "The Instruction for King Meri-ke-Re," "The Instruction of Amen-em-het"; cf. Faulkner). However, all liminal periods were considered dangerous by those committed to maintaining the social order and were to be controlled by various means, including the conformity created by traditional paraenesis. By contrast subversive paraenesis could take shape within these liminal occasions and appeal especially to groups which were denied access to power and status. A new order of egalitarianism or social inversion could be envisioned and constructed.

2.   *General Social Features of Paraenesis.* In terms of its social character, literature may be broadly conceived as conservative, critical, or radical in response to a society's traditional values and beliefs and those institutions and roles which are formed for their realization. Except for nihilism which seeks to negate all meaning, the broad social functions of literature are to preserve, question, transform, or replace social values and beliefs on the basis of an existing or envisioned view of human society. This comprehensive view of society provides the context within which paraenesis comes to assume meaning. Thus the argument by some ancient writers (e.g. Libanius, ἐπιστολμαῖοι χαρακτῆρες 1,5f.) that paraenesis, by definition, is universally true and irrefutable is not correct. To be sure, those with a strong penchant for preserving the existing social order sought to legitimate their moral instruction by claiming universal validity and unquestioned authority. It is here that paraenesis becomes ideology

and seeks to control oppressed groups who are denied privileged social positions.

2.1 *Paraenesis as traditional and unoriginal.* Much paraenesis is traditional and unoriginal (Vetschera; Malherbe, 1987). Even among diverse cultures there are strikingly similar sayings, admonitions, and other forms of paraenesis.[13] While some of this is due to cultural borrowing, it is more often the case that much of the Paraenetic Literature from the Eastern Mediterranean world reflects a societal model of order which sought to preserve existing forms of social institutions and roles.[14] Thus, Pseudo-Isocrates tells Nicocles:

> And do not be surprised that in what I have said there are many things which you know as well as I. This is not from inadvertence on my part, for I have realized that among so great a multitude both of mankind in general and other rulers there are some who have uttered one or another of these precepts, some who have heard them, some who have observed other people put them into practice, and some who are carrying them out in their own lives. But the truth is that in these discourses it is not possible to say what is paradoxical or incredible or outside the circle of accepted belief, but, rather, we should regard the man as the most accomplished in his field who can collect the greatest number of ideas scattered among the thoughts of all the rest and present them in the best form (*Ad Nicoclem*: 40–41).

Classical Egyptian instructions also transmitted traditional knowledge to preserve the social order.[15] Thus the vizier Ptah-hotep in nearing the end of his instruction affirms:

> An obedient son is a follower of Horus. It goes well with him when he hears. When he becomes old and reaches a venerable state, he converses in the same way to his children, by renewing the instruction of his father. Every man is *as (well) instructed as he acts.* If he converses with (his) children, then they will speak (to) their children... (ANET: 414).

This and other Egyptian instructions draw on both the sense of duty and loyalty to the larger society and the sense of obligation, grounded in emotional bonding, to the more personal communities.

In similar fashion the appeal to and reverence for tradition, what the "ancestors" have taught, is often made to validate the correctness of the teaching in paraenetic literature. Thus Job's opponent, Eliphaz, underscores his own authority by declaring that his teaching contains

> what the sages have revealed,
> and their fathers have not hidden (Job 15:18).

Similar appeals in Paraenetic Literature are made to state religion, the natural order, human nature, and personal relationships (human and divine).

2.2   *Non-traditional.* There are paraenetic texts which criticize or even reject traditional values. As noted above in §1.2., these are subversive or "aphoristic" in the sense James Williams uses the latter term, i.e., they may use the language of traditional paraenesis, but the content and function disassemble the prevailing social order. This type of subversive paraenesis is often connected with an individual, at least in its origins, rather than being the anonymous product of traditional society (Crossan). In this regard, it is more like the chreia than the proverb. However, the critical, subversive teachings of individuals may often extend to social groups which develop around them (e.g., the Cynics and the early Jesus movement). These texts derive from individuals or groups who call into question the prevailing view of the social order promulgated especially by those in positions of wealth and power. The ruling aristocracy originates and transmits important social knowledge to maintain the system that gives them advantages and to insulate themselves from the threats of change. Untraditional values, at odds with those of the power elite, create a counterlifestyle followed by a social group which may seek social change. Paraenesis of this type reflects a social model of conflict. In the context of this type of group, paraenesis has the twofold purpose of subverting the prevailing social paradigm and establishing and maintaining the contours of its own patterns of life.

An important example of subversive paraenesis which calls into question many traditional values and institutions is Qoheleth. Written during the early period of Hellenization (first half of the third century, B.C.E.), this reflection begins with a poem on nature and human toil. The objective of this poem is not to discover sapiential values and their required human institutions which are grounded in the order of creation, but rather to submit that human activity is analogous to the predetermined, tedious, cyclical movements of elements in nature. Nothing "new" ever really occurs. And unlike the earth that continues forever, human generations and the products of their activity appear for a time and then pass into the oblivion of death and forgetfulness. Neither humans nor their institutions are eternal. While "the God" is creator, this divine power resides in mystery, acting capriciously and in secret when dealing with humans. There is no righteous order permeating creation which may be incorporated into human behavior and society, and no human freedom to shape a new social reality. Rulers are likewise capricious and maintain their positions through the brutal use of power. Similar appeals to religion and tradition are negated by this sage.

Without the traditional anchoring of sapiential values and social institutions in the order of creation, the moral instruction of Qoheleth, while not debilitating skepticism that leads to a denial of all meaning, centers on the capacity to experience the one divine gift to humanity, "joy," which derives extemporaneously from simple human activities and family relationships. While regarding the larger society as hopelessly corrupt and impervious to improvement by human efforts, Qoheleth derives meaning from the intimacy of smaller communities (friendship and the family, *Gemeinschaften*).

There is some evidence from the epilogue (12:9–14) that Qoheleth's teachings led to the development of a social group (perhaps a "wisdom school" of Jerusalem intelligentsia during the early period of Greek political control) who transmitted his teachings. While Qoheleth's teaching brought into question traditional values and institutions, there is no evidence that he thought social change, either through human or divine action, was at all possible.[16] Hence, Qoheleth's teaching is subversive in removing the variety of forms of legitimation, but not constructive in envisioning a new social order. A system of tyranny, upheld by the divine despot, will continue in spite of the loss of its integrity.

A later example of subversive paraenesis, associated with the social experience of liminality, is the sayings source Q, produced by an early Christian community prior to the fall of Jerusalem. Incorporating both prophetic and sapiential features, the form of the document is best understood as a wisdom instruction seeking to subvert the prevailing social order of Roman Palestine and to construct a new social reality (Kloppenborg). Traditional paraenesis, including proverbs and beatitudes, is often recast into sayings intended to subvert the values and institutions of a paradigm of order supported by the prevailing power structure (e.g. Q's = Luke's formulation of the beatitudes in the "Great Sermon," Matt. 5:3f.=Luke 6:20bf.; cf. Perdue, 1986: 16–18). The subversive teachings of Jesus in Q are coupled with a wandering, mendicant lifestyle (Jesus and some early Christian prophets) that is decidedly anti-structural (Turner, 1974: 73; Theissen). The extent of Q's feminist sensitivities is examined below by Levine in Part II of this volume.

The intent of this more radical type of Christian paraenesis, unlike Qoheleth's, was not simply to subvert the dominant social order, but also to usher in a new, egalitarian one, the "kingdom of God," in which righteousness would prevail. Change was possible, but only through divine intervention, supplemented by human action. A beneficent social order of peace and wellbeing was soon to be established after the return of the rejected Lord to judge the world (Gager).[17]

2.3   *Teacher-Student.* While the settings and occasions vary, both traditional and subversive paraenesis point to several common features involving teachers and their students. First, the one who instructs the recipient is the moral superior, generally because of a higher social position and greater knowledge. Thus Ben Sira, a learned sage of substantial reputation,[18] issues an invitation to the "unlearned" to come and "lodge in his school," thereby taking up a course of study that would lead to the variety of occupations and roles mentioned in 38:24–39:11 (scribe, teacher, diplomat, counsellor, etc.). A similar invitation is issued by Woman Wisdom, personified as a teacher and royal figure in Prov 1:20–33 and 8:1–36 (Lang). Similarly, the Greek rhetor Isocrates is credited with three paraenetic texts (written discourses) which exhort an audience, presumably of young officials and youth aspiring to governmental office, to loyal and virtuous service (Fiore 55f.).[19]

In traditional paraenesis, the relationship between teacher and student is often described in terms of parent and child (Prov 1:8; Sir 3:1; "The Instruction of Ptah-hotep,").[20] These titles may be due in part to the familial origins of some traditional paraenesis.[21] Yet, while the use of these titles may at times reflect actual social roles (Fontaine), they more often suggest a social bond between student and teacher imitative of familial relationships.[22] For example, Quintilian argues that the teacher should act *in loco parentis* for students who are learning under his direction (*Institutio* 2. 1–8).

The recipient of the teaching is usually young, inexperienced, and either has entered or is about to enter a new stage of life and/or social role involving new responsibilities. Clear examples are found in "royal instructions" issued to kings coming to the throne. Two Egyptian texts, "The Instruction of Amen-em-het" and "The Instruction for King Meri-ka-Re," are presented as coming from deceased kings who speak to their successors during the ritual passage of the coronation festival (Perdue, 1983: 85–89).[23] These instructions are designed to provide guidance for inexperienced kings in the tasks of successful rule.[24] In similar fashion, Isocrates instructs Nicocles in matters of kingship after he has recently come to his father's throne (*Ad Nicoclem*).

This does not mean that paraenesis is intended only and always for inexperienced youth. Even experienced sages were exhorted to continue their efforts, for the search for wisdom was a lifelong task. In the prologue (Prov 1:2–7) to the collection, "The Sayings of Solomon" (Proverbs 1–9), both the purpose of the instruction and its intended audience are listed. In addition to humans in general and the "unlearned," Prov 1:5 mentions the "wise one" and "the one of understanding," who may also "increase in learning" and "obtain guidance."

2.4   *Dialogical*. The relationship between teacher and student points to the personal character of much paraenesis, whether traditional or non-traditonal. Indeed, most paraenesis was originally spoken, and oral tradi-

tion was a major means for the continuation of the material (Thyen: 85).
Literary collections and instructions were also produced, some of which
demonstrate a high degree of literary skill (Van Leeuwen, 1988).[25] However, even paraenetic texts were not monologues or dull collections,
meant solely for memorization by industrious students, though memory
work was one of the learning techniques in the variety of schools in the
ancient world. Rather, these texts were enlivened by the personal relationship between teacher and student, taking on a dialogical character, even
in letters and instructions. In addition to familial roles used to
characterize the relationship, friendship is often mentioned as the basis
for the instruction (Cicero, *De officiis*, 1.58; Seneca, *Ep.* 3, 6, 9; see Cancik:
58–66; Hadot: 165f.; Thraede: 125–46).[26]

2.5   *Examples.* The use of *paradeigmata* follows from the teacher-
student relationship described above. In using examples, the teacher
points to noteworthy humans whose lives and actions are portrayed as
incorporating either the virtues or vices of the larger social order under
discussion at a given point. Legendary, historical, and contemporary examples of virtue or vice are presented, as well as ideal types (Aristotle,
Ars rhetorica, 2.20.2; cf. Fiore; Gaiser; and Price). For example, Pseudo-
Isocrates says to Demonicus:

> Thus it is easy to learn from the labors of Heracles and the exploits of
> Theseus, whose excellence of character has impressed upon their exploits so
> clear a stamp of their glory that not even endless time can cast oblivion upon
> their achievements (*Ad Demonicum* 8).

In pointing to the tragic end of those corrupted by vice, Dio Chrysostom
mentions the sons of Iocasta who killed each other in their lust for the
throne, the destruction of Troy precipitated by the passion of Paris for
Helen, the dissolution of the Persian empire occasioned by the desire of
Xerxes to conquer Greece, and the greed of Polycrates of Samos that led to
his impalement. The teacher then writes, "These instances, in order that
they may be warning examples to you, I have taken not only from exceedingly ancient, but also from subsequent times (*Or.* 17.16)."

     However, those usually considered the best examples for emula-
tion were the student's family members, teachers and friends, i.e., those
from the more intimate communities. Pseudo-Isocrates underscores the
example of the recently dead father of Demonicus:

> I have produced a sample of the stature of Hipponicus, after whom you
> should pattern your life as an ensample, regarding his conduct as your law,
> and striving to imitate and emulate your father's virtue... (*Ad Demonicum*,
> 11).

Meri-ka-Re's royal father points to his many accomplishments during his reign (as well as his failures) in articulating a policy for the new ruler to emulate (*ANET*: 416; cf. "The Instruction of Amenem-het," *ANET*: 418–419). The woman of worth in Prov 31:10–31 points to an ideal model of rather prominent aristocratic women in Israelite society (cf. Camp), while an aristocratic Judith embodied the desired virtues of courage, wisdom, piety, and faithful dedication to the liberation of the oppressed. Isocrates points to his own example for emulation (*Adv. soph.* 16–18) as does Paul and Seneca (*Ep. 6; Ep. 71. 7;* cf. Cancik: 48f.).[27]

The examples of moral virtue found in traditional paraenesis reflect the values and behavior of the prevailing social order. They incorporate in ideal fashion those individuals who established and maintained social stability through their illustrious lives. Paradigms of vice, of course, are usually portrayed as those who met destruction for offending the social order, or in the worse cases threatened its stability and continuance. Imitation of virtuous *paradeigmata* leads to the continuance of the social order and the mythos which supports and sustains it. More personal examples (family, teachers, and friends) may also be used to support the traditional values of the larger society, but are especially presented to incorporate the virtues of the intimate communities (families, philosophical and religious groups, and friendships).

Subversive paraenesis, by contrast, may present examples or types of morally noble people whose virtue fails to produce the desired results. Qoheleth tells of a poor, wise man (probably an ideal type, not an historical figure) whose counsel saved a city from a great king. Yet he is not remembered and therefore "immortalized" by human memory for his deeds (9:13–16). And subversive paraenesis often points to cases of the wicked who succeed in the *Gesellschaft* either in spite of or because of their vile deeds (e.g., Ecc 7:15, 8:10). However, critical wisdom may also envision an order of society at variance with the prevailing one and presents models who incorporate "counter-culture" values for imitation (e.g., Diogenes for the cynics, John the Baptist and Jesus in Q and Luke). These "antihero" models subvert the social order and may also be used as models for a counter-culture group (even a *Gemeinschaft)* seeking to establish a new social identity.

2.6   *Literary Collections.* As Gammie observes in the following essay, paraenesis may be found in every variety of primary literature. However, in my judgment, two secondary genres were used in the ancient Near East for the collection and preservation of paraenesis: Instructions and Sayings Collections. I prefer the term "Sayings Collections" to Gammie's "Paraenesis," although the nature of the collections both of us have in mind is obviously very close. School handbooks and letters supplemented these secondary genres in the Graeco-Roman world. Both traditional and subversive collections were shaped, preserved, and transmitted by communities who continued to use them as the primary source of moral knowledge. Collections did eventually reach a "canonical" or fixed status in their communities for a variety of reasons (antiquity, use, presumed authorship, and content), though prior to reaching this static level redactional features involving rearrangement, additions, subtractions, and rewriting of individual pieces may be reconstructed in part (Rosenkranz: 108–9).[28] This process of shaping demonstrates that social formation, even in traditional and conservative communities, involved the dynamic interaction of texts and communities (Sanders). Indeed many texts may well have been "canonized" only when the communities that preserved them in a fluid state were faced with the threat of dissolution. The prohibition against changing the text and especially the hesitation to create new social knowledge in the form of dynamic collections suggest that the traditional forms of a society have either died, faced the imminent danger of discontinuance, or become stagnant. Societies and communities refusing to continue the dynamic process by creating new collections along with other types of social knowledge eventually stagnate and die. Living communities may preserve their own canonical texts from earlier eras along with those created by other groups, but both are used primarily as resources in the generation of new and vital knowledge.

2.7   *Repetition.* The need to be reminded of expected behavior and to be exhorted to continue the path to virtue also points to the social character of paraenesis. Thus Seneca explains to Lucilius: "I am exhorting you for too long, since you need reminding rather than exhortation (*Ep.* 13, 15)." Elsewhere, Seneca speaks of precepts which both "refresh the memory" and exhort to virtuous action:

> Advice is not teaching; it merely engages the attention and rouses us, and concentrates the memory, and keeps it from losing grip. We miss much that is set before our very eyes. Advice is, in fact, a sort of exhortation. The mind often tries not to notice even that which lies before our eyes; we must therefore force upon it the knowledge of things that are perfectly well known (*Ep.* 95, 21, 25).

Dio Chrysostom explains the necessity of repetition by vivid and concrete examples:

> Just as we see physicians and pilots repeating their orders time and time again to those under their command, although they were heard the first time—but still they do when they see them neglectful and inattentive—so too in life it is useful to speak about the same things repeatedly, when the majority know what is their duty, but nevertheless fail to do it (*Or.* 17. 2).

Later he takes an example from ritual settings:

> For just as in the Mysteries the initiating priest more than once explains beforehand to those who are being initiated each single thing they must do, in like manner it is profitable that the words concerning things beneficial be repeated often, or rather, all the time, just like some sacred admonitions (*Or.* 17. 5).

The continuing need for a moral guide underscores the dialogical character of moral exhortation. Paraenesis is not literature merely meant for private reflection.

3   *Social Contexts of Paraenesis*. Malherbe points to the variety of social contexts in which paraenesis was issued (Malherbe, 1986; 23–29).[29] Existence in complex societies, including those of the ancient world, involved the diversification of roles and tasks defined by various factors, including age, gender, class, occupation, family, legal status (e.g. citizen or slave), and membership in organizations, clubs, and groups. Therefore, even in the same society moral behavior was defined in different ways, depending on the particular combination of these factors. Further, the same individual could be expected to follow a variety of moral codes, depending on the number and types of social roles held. Obviously, tensions between the differing requirements of the *Gesellschaft* and *Gemeinschaft*, as well as between various social roles, could and did arise. Indeed the task of moral philosophers was to integrate the competing expectations of life into a comprehensive and systematic whole. Paraenesis provided the content for shaping and integrating the moral life.

If one takes the common social and biological development of individuals as pivotal, the occasions for paraenesis may be placed within three distinct, though often interlinking categories: the biological stages of life (birth, puberty, marriage, parenting, retirement, and death), roles (determined by age, gender, marriage, legal status, class, and occupation), and memberships in groups and associations.[30] Paraenesis was often issued to addressees in a liminal setting, either at the actual point or at least the anticipation of entrance into these stages, roles, and groups (thus possessing a protreptic function in the broadest sense of the term). The moral exhortation was then often repeated, both to remind recipients of expected behavior associated with the stage, role, or group and to reconfirm the validity of the guidance (thus a paraenetic function). In reminding recipients of their moral responsibilities and duties, they were compelled to reflect upon that "threshold" experience of entrance into the stage, role, or group when paraenesis provided the new nomos for expected behavior. Duly reminded, they were then urged to continue to actualize that order within their daily existence.

3.1   *Stages of Life.* Societies and groups develop complex sets of rituals and instructions designed for each stage of an individual's life: birth, puberty, marriage, parenting, retirement, and death (Turner, 1967b). The paraenesis associated with each of these times of passage points to the future responsibilities and behavior expected of an individual in both society and community. While paraenesis was issued in anticipation of movement into these new stages and then reiterated at the actual point of entrance, its repetition by moral guides would continue long afterwards.

An example of this context for paraenesis is provided in the following essay by Quinn. He argues that elements of 1 Timothy, particularly 2:11–15, reflect the instruction issued by a bishop or presbyter to a Christian bride during the ritual occasion of marriage. The instruction, says Quinn, "reaches its apogee in its promise that the husband and wife...will find salvation in parenthood, provided 'they continue in faith and love and holiness, with self-control.'" I would add that the Pastorals reflect an order model in which the author attempts to bring the social life of the community into conformity with the norms of Graeco-Roman society, including the patriarchal household (cf. Fiorenza, 1983, 1984). The submission of wives in marriage is a case in point. In following a "hermeneutics of suspicion," the vision "beneath" the Pastorals may well reflect some Christian women who, having experienced the *communitas* of the Gospel, question and at times refuse to submit to male domination and even renounce traditional female roles in the family (cf. The Acts of Paul and Thecla). The anti-traditional nature of early Palestinian Christianity, grounded in a conflict model of society and the liminal experience of *communitas*, is being suppressed by conformity to the patriarchal household.[31]

3.2   *Social Roles.* The multiple social roles held by an individual at various points in life were formed and supported by traditional paraenesis. Paraenetic Literature contains many examples of the instruction of students, rulers, bureaucrats, parents, children, and spouses, to name some of the most common roles.

Introductions to several paraenetic texts represent the occasion of the teaching as a liminal one: the entrance into new social roles and their incumbent responsibilities. For instance, the "Instruction of Khety," an Egyptian text dating from the Middle Kingdom or earlier (ca. 2,000 B.C.E. [*ANET*: 432–34], is counsel given to a student entering his course of studies. The setting created by the brief introduction, devoted to the exaltation of the scribal profession over other, less appealing trades, is a boat trip up the Nile. Khety instructs his son, Pepy, as they are journeying southward to the Residence City where the youth is to enter the scribal school for royal service. While contrasting the superior merits of scribal service and life with those of less noble professions, the father also teaches his son the proper behavior and industry necessary for success at school and later, after professional life begins. The primary motivation for becoming a successful scribe is personal wellbeing, including promotions accruing from obedient service acknowledged by the king. Yet there is also the honor brought to the family by a successful child.

The legendary narrative attached to the "Instruction of Ptah-hotep" (*ANET*: 412–14) sets the teaching at the time the aged vizier, desiring to retire from royal service, instructs his successor. The instruction covers a wide range of topics relating to the specific roles and responsibilities of the vizier and other, less exalted royal positions, as well as more general ones of parenting, friendship, and marriage. The instruction was intended for the entire range of Egyptian officials during the period of the Old Kingdom, not simply the vizier. It was also copied and preserved along with other instructions in the schools, becoming an important text in the social formation of Egyptian students training to become bureaucrats (R. J. Williams, 1990).[32]

Royal instructions from Egypt,[33] Israel,[34] and Greece[35] are often placed at the beginning of a new king's reign or official's appointment (Perdue, 1983:85–96). The original social setting for the "Instruction of Amen-em-het" and the "Instruction for Meri-ke-Re" appears to be the installation ceremony when new kings were ritually installed. In both texts the deceased fathers of the new rulers address their sons on matters of successful rule. These texts presumably were reused in subsequent New Year's festivals during the kings' lifetimes to remind them of royal duties and their subjects of the importance of loyal service. The Deuteronomic redactors placed the instruction of Solomon shortly after his ritual installation as co-regent, but immediately before David's death. While edited to include standard Deuteronomic concerns with the law of Moses and the covenant with David (1 Kgs 2:3–4), there is a fragmentary, earlier instruction in *Realpolitik* embedded in vv. 5–9 which counsels Solomon to reward the dynasty's loyal supporters and to execute its enemies.[36] The frequency with which paraenesis finds its setting upon the death of the sage is extraordinarily prominent and long lived from early ancient Near Eastern through Graeco-Roman times. I examine this subject more fully in the opening essay of Part II of this volume.

From Graeco-Roman civilization, a variety of paraenetic texts point to similar instructions of kings and officials at the time of entrance into their offices. The paraenetic section in Isocrates' "Nicocles" (48–62) follows one (10–47) defending the superiority of monarchic government. This discourse, placed in the mouth of the King of the Cyprians, is designed for royal officials who are exhorted to render faithful service to their rulers (Fiore, 53).[37] "To Nicocles" is presented as coming at the time the young king has just assumed the position of king. Plutarch's treatises on statecraft also offer counsel to the ruling class on wise and virtuous behavior in a wide variety of social situations, not simply political matters. For example, in his *Praecepta gerendae reipublicae* he gives guidance in all affairs of political and private life (*Gesellschaft* and *Gemeinschaft*) to the young Menemachus at the time of his entrance to public service as a magistrate at Sardis. Even so this paraenetic text had a much broader appeal and could be adapted to officials in any particular city (Renoirte: 69f.).[38]

Paraenesis, however, was not limited to the social formation of only the aristocracy during periods of liminality. The well-known "Instruction of Amen-em-opet" (*ANET*: 421–25) is represented as coming from an official in the administration of royal estates who instructs his son, Hor-em-maa-kheru, a young priestly scribe active in the temple of Min. Even more telling is "The Instruction of 'Onchsheshonq," written by a priest of Re in Heliopolis for Egyptian peasants, not officials and courtiers (Glanville, Gemser). The content of the text mainly covers the assortment of social roles and their responsibilities (family, friends, neighbors, landlord, and religion) held by rural folk living in the country and small villages in Egypt of the fifth and fourth centuries, B.C.E.

Many paraenetic texts are general enough to include instruction in the variety of social roles which the recipients either presently hold or may expect to assume. Training in schools in Egypt (Brunner, 1957), Mesopotamia (Kramer), Israel (Crenshaw, 1985; Lemaire), Greece, and Rome (Lang; Malherbe, 1986 and 1987) included moral instruction using paraenetic texts collected and preserved as a part of the school curriculum. In Judaism and early Christianity, religious and moral instruction in the synagogues and churches was provided, leading to the eventual compilation of paraenetic texts (testaments, letters, instructions, and Sayings Collections or, to use Gammie's term, Paraeneses).

In addition to school instruction, appropriate segments from these collections could be selected and then adapted for particular occasions: marriage, the birth of a child, death, entrance into school, the start of a professional career, and so on. The large book of Ben Sira is one example of a compilation of a variety of paraenetic texts. This book consists of selections from the paraenetic materials issued to Ben Sira's students who studied in his school. However, the fragments of Ben Sira's text at Masada two centuries after its composition, the extensive use of the Greek translation in Hellenistic Judaism and early Christianity, the translation of the Greek text into Latin possibly as early as the second century C.E., and the Ben Sira scrolls found in a Cairo synagogue dating a millennium after his death point to the book's widespread use for religious and moral training for many centuries. Teachers continued to use these texts for instruction and homilies both before and after these stages and roles had been entered. Many of the paraenetic materials compiled in Ben Sira pertain to a variety of social roles and their associated duties and responsibilities: parent, child, spouse, citizen, and occupation. These were the normal roles Jewish students who trained under Ben Sira could have expected to fill in Jerusalem of the second century, B.C.E.

3.3   *Social Groups and Communties.* In addition to family and occupation (scribes, farmers, etc.), paraenesis was used by groups and communities within the larger society for the instruction of their novices and members. The instruction would be given in preparation for entrance into the group or community and repeated later, especially during important ritual occasions. While part of the content of paraenesis could have almost a universal appeal, there are many examples of paraenetic materials which are designed for specific groups or communities. The development and existence of philosophical schools in Greece and Rome, Jewish sects during the Hellenistic and Roman periods, and early Christian communities provide clear examples of the presence and use of paraenesis by communities within their larger societies.

4   *Social Functions of Paraenesis.* Paraenesis has a variety of social functions which may be summarized under the headings of protrepsis, paraenesis, socialization, legitimation, and conflict.

4.1   *Protrepsis (Conversion) and Paraenesis (Confirmation).* One should begin to speak of the social functions by reference to the Greek terms protrepsis and paranaesis.[39] While often used interchangeably by certain writers, the terms may be differentiated primarily on the basis of social functions, not content or literary form. Paraenesis refers not only to the traditional content of moral instruction, but also to the process of confirming the validity of the moral life undertaken and exhorting the audience to continue in this path (Stowers: 92–93). As Gammie has demonstrated, the need for precepts is greater, once the journey is underway. Protrepsis refers to the process of converting the audience to a new way of life, or exhorting one to take up the responsibilities and virtues required of a new stage or social role (Stowers: 92; see Prov 1:20–33, 9:1–6, Sir 51:23–30, and Matt 11:28–30 as examples of protrepsis in biblical texts). Thus, as Gammie has correctly argued, protrepsis presents a more sustained argument than paraenesis, since the attempt to convince the audience to turn from their present course to launch into a new one requires more persuading. The already converted generally accept the validity and authority of the teaching, but are in need of guidance regarding specific application and reassurance that both the social world and the definition of behavior for their situation are legitimate.

Protrepsis and paraenesis refer then, to two distinct, but connected stages along the way to virtue: entrance to the path of life and continuance in the course undertaken. Even when a text is explicitly protreptic in function (conversion), it may be used paraenetically, i.e., by those who reflect upon their earlier entrance into a particular stage of life, role, or group.

4.2   *Socialization.* The primary function of traditional paraenesis, at home within an order paradigm, is socialization. Berger and Luckmann define socialization as "the comprehensive and consistent induction of an individual into the objective world of a society or sector of it" (130). Primary socialization occurs during childhood when the teachers are parents and their surrogates, most often those who make up the immediate kinship group (grandparents, uncles, aunts, etc.). This reflects the formative nature of family life. The common occurrence of family titles— father, mother, son, and daughter—in paraenetic texts may occasionally point to the actual kinship structure which introduces children to the larger social reality. The kin as teachers assume the role of "significant others," those with whom the children have strong emotional ties. Their attitudes, beliefs, norms, and behavior provide examples for children to learn and acquire as their own (Berger: 130). During the process of socialization, children develop a "generalized other," i.e. a social reality in which these beliefs, customs, and patterns of behavior are abstracted and given the status of self-evident reality. Through internalization a "symmetrical relationship" is formed between the reality "out there" and the subjective reality within (Berger and Luckmann: 127).

Once weaned from their primary teachers, students begin the process of "secondary socialization" with a view to entering new social roles, the adult stages of life, and various social groups (Perdue, 1981b: 251). In liminal occasions, paraenesis helps to construct a nomos for individuals and groups entering a new level of social existence. This is the type of socialization in both society and community which is reflected by most traditional Paraenetic Literature. Teachers who induct individuals into these more specialized and responsible areas may also assume the role of the significant other, as evidenced by cases of personal relationships revealed by many paraenetic texts (e.g. Seneca's correspondence to Lucilius).[40] Once socialized at this higher level, a generalized other (social reality) abstracted from the values and behavior of significant others is constructed and internalized so that one's place and function within society (*Gesellschaft*) and community (*Gemeinschaft*) are understood. A variety of "subworlds" is created involving special knowledge about roles, stages of life, and group behavior, but normally subordinated to the overall symbolic world of the larger society. Repetition, of course, continues in order to remind people of the authenticity of the constructed social reality and their places and responsibilities within its structure.[41] Conversation and dialogue, especially with significant others, recreate the subjective reality of the social order. Paraenesis plays a vital role in this process of inducting individuals into a social reality.

4.3   *Legitimation.* Legitimation is "socially objectivated knowledge that serves to explain and justify the social order (Berger: 29)." This is necessary when the structure and symbolic world of a society are transmitted to a new generation not considering them to be "self-evident." Thus explanations, justifications, and rituals of confirmation are necessary. Different kinds of knowledge are used, including the common sub-forms of paraenesis (proverbs, admonitions, etc.), at what Berger and Luckmann call the "second level of legitimation." Paraenesis contains the rudimentary, theoretical propositions related to concrete actions (Berger and Luckmann: 94). These actions are oriented to a social world which is eventually internalized by its participants.

In the paradigm of order, paraenesis is presented as irrefutable by some ancient teachers (Libanius, ἐπιστολιμαῖοι χαρακτῆρες, 1, 5.). It speaks of institutions and behavior grounded in the natural order and undergirded by tradition. This does not mean that all paraenesis is universally valid, but within a particular social system it presents knowledge that is generally accepted as true, for it appeals to reason, knowledge, experience, nature, religion, tradition, and authority-figures (including the teacher).[42] The danger of traditional paraenesis is that it may become ideological and used to keep the powerless "in their place." Crisis in the form of the death of significant others, suffering, and the demands for justice by oppressed groups can threaten the validity of the social world and lead to anomy. However, there is the potential for the formation of a new social order that is either egalitarian or an inversion of the old one.

Legitimation becomes more difficult in pluralistic societies where a variety of social worlds compete for adherents. Different social realities may be reflected explicitly in paraenetic texts intending to reject "false" alternatives and to accept the "true" one. For example, involved in the contrast between Woman Wisdom and Woman Folly in Proverbs 1–9 is the competition of Israelite and Canaanite cultures for the loyalties of Israelite youths (Böstrom). Likewise, the threat to Judaism posed by Hellenization was the primary motivation for producing the Wisdom of Solomon, as its teacher sought both to convert apostate Jews and to reconfirm the validity of Judaism.[43] Subverting the alternative social reality became necessary in order to reduce its attraction to potential converts and members. Thus in the Wisdom of Solomon the refutation of competing groups, including those who practiced nature religion, idolatry, and the mysteries, is a serious undertaking .

Finally, when crisis threatens the social reality constructed by a society or community, legitimation becomes all the more imperative, though increasingly difficult. Indeed the more strident and authoritarian the paraenesis becomes, the more likely it is that its social reality is undergoing serious challenge and threat. This is the case with the instruction given to Job by his three opponents whose rigid theory of retribution was used to substantiate a view of history and society in which pious morality had its rewards. Indeed as the dialogue continues into its later stages, the tone becomes increasingly belligerent, and the opponents' views of retribution all the more inflexible. Job's appeal to friendship and the understanding of his specific situation would have necessitated their repudiation of the paradigm of order constructed by traditional wisdom. This they were not prepared to do. If a socio-political crisis is present, it is not easily identified. However, the collapse of Judah during the early sixth century B.C.E. is certainly plausible. In any case, when the prevailing social reality no longer commands acceptance, traditional paraenesis loses its power to convict. Indeed, as was the case with the Book of Job, the subversive paraenesis of disputation may challenge and threaten to overturn the prevailing order and its moral life. Anomy, at least for a time, may occur, but eventually a new social world emerges in which the moral life takes on transformed meaning. For instance, in the Joban world where the deuteronomic dogma of retribution became bankrupt, the struggle for justice and the inevitable experience of suffering became constituent parts of an anticipated new social reality.[44]

4.4   *Conflict.* Anti-traditional paraenesis undermines the legitimacy of the prevailing order of the society and competing communities by calling into question the social knowledge undergirding their symbolic universe.[45] Fragmentation and disintegration of the larger society or communities may be the objective of subversive paraenesis, though in some instances there was the realization that the impact would be negligible. More importantly conflict with the *Gesellschaft* and other communities was designed to shape identity by establishing social boundaries. The common social functions of socialization and legitimation in originating and continuing the group would also be present, though its lifestyle and values may differ widely from the society at large. By withdrawal within this *Gemeinschaft*, a different social reality is constructed and efforts are undertaken to protect it from the threat of outside worlds. A good example of this sectarian position is the Epistle of James (Perdue, 1981 b).

5   *Conclusions and Summary.* We have argued that paraenesis reflects two models of social organization: order and conflict. The social character of the order model is traditional and conservative, for it seeks to transmit accepted forms of institutions and values. Duty and obedience are the motivations for moral actions, with the expectation that wellbeing for the individual and society will result. Exemplary models of human conduct (*paradeigmata*) incorporate traditional virtues in their behavior, and collections transmit those values which constitute and preserve the social order. In the process of social formation, individuals receive moral instruction at the point of entering new stages of life, social roles, and social groups. While the instruction may often be repeated after entrance, these three "threshold" (liminal) contexts are the primary occasions. Consequently, social formation and legitimation are the key social functions.

While much of the content of paraenesis reflects the virtues and institutions of the larger society (*Gesellschaft*), some paraenesis reflects the character of smaller, more intimate associations, including family, friendship, and club (*Gemeinschaften*). Thus, moral acts in these groups are tied to emotional bonds. Teachers become "parents" and students are their "children," titles which often reflect the same personal character revealed by the dialogical and repetitive features of paraenesis. Teachers, friends, and family members are esteemed as *paradeigmata*, worthy of emulation.

Liminal periods in the societal model of order are those points of transition for individuals and groups which are the most potentially disruptive. These periods include times of entrance into new stages of life, social roles, and social groups. Anti-traditional paraenesis may be issued to subvert the prior social world of novices, before traditional moral instruction is issued in order to create a new nomos (standard of behavior and social order) to be internalized.

Some paraenetic texts reflect a second social model: conflict. While sharing most of the same features of its more traditional counterpart, anti-traditional paraenesis seeks to subvert the institutions and values of the larger *Gesellschaft*. This type of paraenesis may reflect a pessimistic outlook in doubting that any real change may be brought about in the larger structures of society. Or the perspective may be more optimistic, looking to initiate significant change that will lead to a new social order. In either case, *Gemeinschaften* (families, clubs, or friendships) may well provide the important context and values for a moral life.

NOTES

[1] In addition to Gammie's introduction which follows, other assessments of the literary and formal features of paraenesis are provided by K. Berger, Bultmann, Dibelius,

Küchler, Malherbe (1986, 1987), L. Perdue (1981b, 1986), Thyen (85–116), Vetschera, and Wendland.

[2] For an introduction to the major paradigms of social thought, cf. W. D. Perdue (1986). Fiorenza (1983) examines the clash between the specific expressions of these two social models (egalitarianism and patriarchy) in the early Christian movement.

[3] Plato's *Republic* is the classic example of the paradigm of order. Modern sociological theorists representing this model include Emile Durkheim, Robert K. Merton, and Talcott Parsons.

[4] While characteristic of most cultures in the ancient Near East, Egypt of the Old Kingdom is the best example of this idealized social model (Schmid, Gese). Paraenetic Literature belonging to this paradigm includes the classical Egyptian Instructions, much of the Book of Proverbs, Ben Sira, the Wisdom of Solomon, and the Pastoral Epistles.

[5] *Ma'at*.

[6] Sages of ancient Egypt contrasted "the heated man," driven by passions and folly, with the "silent or cool man," able to control desire and live according to wisdom (Leclant).

[7] Fiorenza (1983, 1984) has noted that many biblical texts function ideologically to legitimate the androcentrism of patriarchal society. Because of its prominent position in social formation, paraenesis plays a dominant role in shaping values and character. Following a hermeneutic of suspicion, Fiorenza argues that a feminist interpretation looks beneath androcentric texts for the egalitarian vision that is being suppressed .

[8] Examples of this paradigm include the critical wisdom tradition expressed mainly in reflective essays (the poetic book of Job, Qoheleth, Agur [Prov 30: 1–9]; "A Song of the Harper" [ANET: 467], "A Dispute over Suicide," [405–7], "The Dialogue of Pessimism" [600–601], "The Babylonian Theodicy" [601–4], the literature of the Cynics, apocalyptic, the aphoristic strata of Q, and James). Some of this literature reflects the understanding that while human society is corrupt, it may be changed for the better. Other texts are more pessimistic, believing that society is incapable of improvement.

[9] Modern conflict theorists include Herbert Marcuse, Karl Marx, and Juergen Habermas.

[10] Fiorenza (1983: 140) states: "As a conflict movement within Palestine, Syria, Greece, Asia Minor, and Rome, it challenged and opposed the dominant patriarchal ethos through the praxis of equal discipleship." Fiorenza also points to the important participation of women, even some of wealth, in the early Christian missionary movement (1983: 160–204).

[11] Turner notes: "...if we see that there is a constant interplay between these on various levels and in various sectors of sociocultural fields, then we will begin to avoid some of the difficulties inherent in systems of thought which recognize only structurally positive values, rules, and components; and they are only 'positive' because they are the rules recognized as legitimate by the political and intellectual elites at a given time (1974b: 80)."

[12] Turner argues that the great religions are those which harmonize, or hold in a field of legitimate tension, structure and *communitas* (1974b:80). They recognize that a human being "is both a structural and an anti-structural entity, who *grows* through antistructure and *conserves* through structure (83)."

[13] See, for example, the study of the "Golden Rule" in the so-called popular ethics of Judaism, early Christianity, and the sophists (Dihle).

[14] Egyptian instructions were preserved for centuries as an important part of school curriculum for teaching students both ethics and the more practical skills of reading and writing (R. J. Williams, 1972).

[15] See Hellmut Brunner, 1980: 964–68. Brunner notes that the content of Egyptian instructions are "political in the broad meaning of the term, in that they introduce the students to Egyptian society and its rules of behavior" (1980: 966).

16 The eventual canonization of the sayings of Qoheleth does testify, of course, to the existence of a social group which transmitted and edited them. Conservative sages sought to refute some of Qoheleth's teaching, as evidenced by the epilogist in 12:9–14. Indeed, some of the efforts of Ben Sira seemed to be designed to challenge the teachings of Qoheleth.

17 The Epistle of James by contrast seeks inversion of the present order. Thus the poor and oppressed will come to possess power and status in the new order, whereas the wealthy and powerful who do not join the new community of the righteous poor will be condemned (Perdue, 1981b). Inversion is, of course, a common apocalyptic theme growing out of prophetic eschatology.

18 See the adulation of Ben Sira's wisdom by his grandson in the "prologue."

19 "Nicocles," "To Nicocles," and "Demonicus." "Nicocles" is presented as a treatise on kingship (ending with a paraenetic section in 48–62) by King Nicocles himself. However, the text was written by Isocrates and presumably uttered by Nicocles, one of his former students, at the early stage of his reign in order both to validate the royal office and to instill loyalty in young officials.

20 Brunner, 1980: 965–66.

21 Non-traditonal wisdom is less inclined to use the social titles of "father" and "son," preferring none at all (Qoheleth's impersonal tone is reflected here) or titles of equality ("brother" in James). This practice points to the liminal nature of certain groups seeking either to subvert social institutions or to present alternative social arrangements.

22 Note that in the royal instructions, the teacher is the actual father (or in the case of Lemuel the queen mother, Prov 31:1-9).

23 The "Testament of David" (2 Kgs 2:1-11) has a similar form and function. Here the dying David instructs the young Solomon in "wise" and pragmatic rule (Perdue, 1983).

24 These "royal instructions" are politically motivated in helping to legitimate rulers and their royal policies and in attempting to incorporate loyalty within royal courtiers and the citizenry (Perdue, 1983; Volten; R. J. Williams, 1964).

25 In his dissertation, Van Leeuwen rejects the view that paraenetic texts demonstrate a lack of system and beauty.

26 Thraede notes that friendship is a common topos of Graeco-roman letters. For a discussion of this style of address in paraenetic texts, see Thyen: 88–90.

27 Fiore notes that "Nicocles" is a political brochure written by Isocrates, though placed in the mouth of Nicocles, the Cyprian King, with the purpose of exhorting royal officials to faithful service to the king (53). In this discourse, the king becomes the premier example for officials to emulate.

28 Van Leeuwen demonstrates that the redactional process was not haphazard, but followed rhetorical patterns.

29 Thyen notes that paraenesis, as oral instruction, found its Sitz im Leben in the synagogue homily, the instruction of the philosophical schools, the Stoic-Cynic diatribes, and the preaching of the different mystery religions (85).

30 One must caution against the common argument (Thyen: 86) that paraenesis may not be used to describe the specific elements of the teaching of the speaker (writer) or the situation of the hearer. This view is based on the erroneous notion that traditional paraenesis is often transmitted within texts in a loose, unedited fashion, without careful coordination to the religious perspectives of the authors or the actual situation of the hearers. It is the case that later editors on occasion inserted contrasting paraenetic materials into literary texts (e.g. the epilogue to Qoheleth and the speeches of Elihu in Job), and collections were often compendia designed to cover the wide-range of social roles, stages, and responsibilities. However, the assumption that teachers drew on

paraenetic texts indiscriminately, without adjustment to their own teachings or the situation of the audience is unfounded and misleading.

31 Fiorenza (1983: 109) notes: "As a rule, prescriptive injunctions for appropriate 'feminine' behavior and submission increase whenever women's actual social-religious status and power within patriarchy increase."

32 Cf. "The Instruction of Ahikar" (*ANET*: 427–30). The accompanying legend also presents the occasion for the instruction as the time when the aged royal official chooses his nephew Nadin to replace him at court.

33 "The Instruction of Amen-em-het" (*ANET*: 414–18) and "The Instruction for King Meri-ka-re" (*ANET*: 418–19).

34 "The Testament of David" (1 Kgs 2:1–11)

35 Isocrates, *Ad Nicoclem*, and Dio Chrysostom, *Or.* 17.

36 Cf. "The Instruction of King Lemuel," given to the young king by the Queen mother at the time he is beginning public rule (Prov 31:1–9).

37 Compare the Egyptian "Instruction of Sehetep-ib-Re," which is a panegyric exalting the godlike qualities of King Ni-maat-Re of the Twelfth Dynasty (Middle Kingdom). Its intent is to elicit dedicated service to the king from his royal officials.

38 A wide assortment of letters to subordinate officials contains general paraenesis on proper behavior (cf. Welles). Commenting on one letter written to a recently appointed official, Fiore remarks: "Letters of this sort, then, are outlines of the scope of the office and hortatory reminders for the new officials as well as communications to the communities of what would be expected of them under the new regime (83).

39 Burgess notes that παραινέω and προτρέπω are often used interchangeably without clear definition. However, he adds that in its specific meaning προτρεπτικὸς λόγος "is an exhortation to some general course-philosophy, rhetoric, virtue. It gives a comprehensive view setting forth the advantages and removing the objections....The παραίνεσις is practically without formal definition....In distinction from the προτρεπτικὸς λόγος the παραίνεσις presents a series of precepts which will serve as a guide of conduct under fixed conditions. The παραίνεσις...may have a restricted and personal application, *e.g.*, how to manage servants; or it may be more general, *e.g.*, how to live well." In the following essay, Gammie notes that moral exhortation to a "dual audience" (the converted and unconverted) brings into question the tendency to make clear distinctions between paraenesis and protreptic. However, he does add that one formal distinction between the two is that paraenesis tends to list precepts, while protreptic makes a more sustained argument.

40 Even at this higher level of socialization, intensely personal language and relationships characterize paraenesis. The tendency of paraenesis in clubs, religious groups, apprenticeships, and schools is to imitate the intimate social relationships of the family in order to create what Toennies describes as a *Gemeinschaft*.

41 The modern emphasis on the creation of a symbolic universe through language and non-verbal communication is found in the work of symbolic interactionism (Mead, 1934; Blumer, 1969).

42 Berger and Luckmann point to four levels of legitimation. The first level attempts to make sense of the "totality of the institutional order" to its participants. They come to understand the motives and reasons for the existence and nature of this order. At the second level, the order becomes "subjectively meaningful" to the participants in relation to their own lives. They see themselves as members of this order. The third level involves the origin and transmitting of "explicit theories" about the order—its origins and operation. Finally, at the fourth level, the participants come to create and live with the "symbolic universe" or world view in which the social system is located (85–118).

43 Hence this work functions as both protrepsis and paraenesis. This view is nearly shared by Gammie in the next essay but challenged by Reese in his response. Reese prefers the classification of protreptic; for his reasons see §8 of his response.

44 Rainer Albertz has attempted to demonstrate that the Book of Job, like its Mesopotamian counterpart *Ludlul bel nemeqi*, reflects the crisis of competing social classes. In post-exilic Judah, the former ruling aristocracy of Judah is represented by the character Job, and the nouveau-riche is represented by the three opponents (1981, 1990).

45 In the establishment and maintenance of group identity, boundaries, and cohesion, conflict with other communities and their social realities is necessary (Coser, 1956).

WORKS CONSULTED

Albertini, E.
   1923   *La composition dans les ouvrages philosophiques de Sénèque*. Bibliothèque des Écoles Françaises d'Athenes et de Rome 127. Paris: Thorin et Fontemoin.

Albertz, Rainer
   1981   "Der sozialgeschichtliche Hintergrund des Hiobbuches und der 'Babylonischen Theodizee'." Pp. 349–72 in *Die Botschaft und die Boten*. Ed. Jörg Jeremias und Lothar Perlitt. Neukirchener Verlag.

   1990   "The Sage and Pious Wisdom in the Book of Job: The Friends Perspective." Forthcoming in *The Sage in Israel and the Ancient Near East*. Ed. John G. Gammie and Leo G. Perdue. Winona Lake, IN: Eisenbrauns.

ANET   See Pritchard.

Aristotle   See Freese.

Beardslee, William
   1979   "Saving One's Life By Losing It." *JAAR* 47: 57–72.

Berger, Klaus
   1977   *Formgeschichte des Neuen Testaments*. Heidelberg: Quelle & Meyer.

Berger, Peter
   1967   *The Sacred Canopy*. Garden City, NY: Doubleday.

Berger, Peter and Thomas Luckmann
   1966   *The Social Construction of Reality*. Garden City, NY: Doubleday.

Blumer, Herbert
   1969   *Symbolic Interactionism: Perspective and Method*. Englewood Cliffs: Prentice-Hall.

Boström, Gustav
1935   *Proverbiastudien.* Lunds Universitets Årsskrift, N. F. Aud. 1.
        Bd. 30, Nr. 3. Lund: C. W. F. Gleerup.

Brunner, Hellmut
1957   *Altägyptische Erziehung.* Wiesbaden: Harrassowitz.
1980   "Lehren." *Lexikon der Ägyptologie* 3: 964–68.

Bultmann, R.
1910   *Der Stil der paulinischen Predigt und die Kynisch-Stoische Diatribe.*
        Göttingen: Vandenhoeck & Ruprecht.

Burgess, Theodore L.
1902   *Epideictic Literature.* Pp. 89–261 in *Studies in Classical Philology*
        3. Chicago: University of Chicago Press.

Burk, August.
1923   *Die Pädagogik des Isokrates als Grundlegung des humanistischen
        Bildungideals im Vergleich mit den zeitgenössischen und den
        modernen Theorien dargestellt.* Studien zur Geschichte und
        Kultur des Altertums 12. Würzburg: E. Drerup.

Butler, Harold E.
1920   *Quintilian. Institutio oratio.* 4 vols. LCL. Cambridge, MA:
        Harvard University Press.

Camp, Claudia V.
1985   *Wisdom and the Feminine in the Book of Proverbs.* Bible and
        Literature Series II. Sheffield: Almond/JSOT.

Cancik, H.
1967   *Untersuchungen zu Sencas Epistulae Morales.* Hildesheim: Georg
        Olms.

Cicero.   See Miller.

Clark, Donald L.
1957   *Rhetoric in Greco-Roman Education.* New York: Columbia.

Cohoon, James W. and H. Lamar Crosby
1925   *Dio Chrysostom. Discourses.* 5 Vols. LCL. Cambridge, MA:
        Harvard University Press.

Coleman, R.
1974   "The Artful Moralist: A Study of Seneca's Epistolary Style."
        Classical Quarterly 24: 276–89.

Colson, F. H.
  1921   "Quintillian 1,9 and the 'Chria' in Ancient Education." *Classical Review* 35: 150–54.

Coser, Lewis
  1956   *The Functions of Social Conflict.* Glencoe, Illinois: The Free Press.

Crenshaw, James L.
  1974   "Wisdom." Pp. 225–64 in *Old Testament Form Criticism.* Ed. John H. Hayes. San Antonio: Trinity University Press.
  1985   "Education in Ancient Israel." *JBL* 104: 601–615.

Crossan, John Dominic
  1983   *In Fragments: The Aphorisms of Jesus.* San Francisco: Harper & Row.

Dibelius, M.
  1936   *A Fresh Approach to the New Testament and Early Christian Literature.* New York: Charles Scribner's Sons.

Dibelius, M. and H. Conzelmann.
  1972   *The Pastoral Epistles.* Hermeneia. Philadelphia: Fortress.

Dihle, Albrecht.
  1962   *Die goldene Regel: Eine Einführung in die Geschichte der antiken und frühchristlichen Vulgärethik.* Göttingen: Vandenhoeck & Ruprecht.

Durkheim, Émile
  1933   *The Division of Labor in Society.* New York: Macmillan.

Emminger, Kurt.
  1902   "Ps-Isokrates *pros Demonikon* (1)." *Jahrbücher für Philologie und Pädagogik,* supp. B. 27: 373–442.

Faulkner, R. 0.
  1955   "The Installation of the Vizier." *JEA* 41: 18–29.

Fiore, Benjamin
  1986   *The Function of Personal Example in the Socratic and Pastoral Epistles.* 105. Rome: Biblical Institute Press.

Fiorenza, Elisabeth Schlüssler
  1983   *In Memory of Her.* New York: Crossroad.
  1984   *Bread Not Stone.* Boston: Beacon.

Fontaine, Carole
1990   "The Sage in Family and Tribe." Forthcoming in *The Sage in Israel and the Ancient Near East*. Ed. John G. Gammie and Leo G. Perdue. Winona Lake, IN: Eisenbrauns.

Freese, John Henry
1975   *Aristotle: The "Art" of Rhetoric*. LCL 22. Cambridge, MA: Harvard University. First printed 1926.

Frey, J.
1946   *Studien zur dritten Rede des Isocrates*. Ph. D. Dissertation, Freiburg .

Funk, R. W.
1967   "The Apostolic Parousia: Form and Significance," Pp. 246–68 in *Christian History and Interpretation: Studies Presented to John Knox*. Ed. W. R. Farmer, *et. al*. Cambridge: Cambridge University Press.

Gager, John
1975   *Kingdom and Community*. Englewood Cliffs: Prentice-Hall.

Gaiser, Konrad
1959   *Protreptik und Paränese bei Plato*. TBAW 40. Stuttgart: Kohlhammer.

Gemser, Berend
1960   "The Instructions of ʿOnchsheshonqy and Biblical Wisdom Literature." VTSup 7: 102–45.

Gese, Hartmut
1958   *Lehre und Wirklichkeit in der alten Weisheit*. Tübingen: J. C. B. Mohr (Paul Siebeck).

Glanville, S. R. K.
1955   *The Instructions of ʿOnchsheshonqy*. Catalogue of Demotic Papyri in the British Museum. London: British Museum.

Gummere, Richard M.
1917   *Ad Lucilium epistulae morales*. 3 Vols. LCL. Cambridge, MA: Harvard University Press.

Habermas, Juergen
1970   *Toward a Rational Society*. Boston: Beacon Press.

Hadot, I.
1969   *Seneca und die griechisch-römische Tradition der Seelenleitung.*
        Berlin: de Gruyter.

Hijmans, B.
1976   *Inlaboratus et facilius: Aspects of Structure in Some Letters of
        Seneca.* Leiden: Brill.

Isocrates.   See Norlin.

Kloppenborg, John
1984   *The Literary Genre of the Synoptic Sayings Source.* Ph. D. Disser-
        tation, University of St. Michael's College, Toronto.

Koch, Klaus
1955   "Gibt es ein Vergeltungsdogma im Alten Testament?" *ZThK*
        52: 1–42.

Kramer, Samuel Noah
1990   "The Sage in Sumer." Forthcoming in The Sage in Israel and
        the Ancient Near East. Eds. John G. Gammie and Leo G.
        Perdue. Winona Lake, IN: Eisenbrauns.

Küchler, Max
1979   *Frühjüdische Weisheitstraditionen.* OBO 26. Göttingen: Vanden-
        hoeck & Ruprecht.

Lang, Bernhard
1975   *Frau Weisheit.* Düsseldorf: Patmos.

Leclant, Jean
1963   "Documents nouveaux et points de vue récents sur les
        sagesses de l'Égypte ancienne." Pp. 5–26 in *Les sagesses du
        Proche- Orient ancien.* Ed. Jean Leclant. Paris: Universitaires de
        France.

Leeuwen, Raymond van
1988   *The Problem of Literary Context in Proverbs 25–27.* SBLDS.
        Atlanta: Scholars.

Lemaire, André
1979   *Les écoles et la formation de la Bible dans l'ancien Israël.* OBO 39.
        Göttingen: Vandenhoeck & Ruprecht.

Malherbe, Abraham J.
1986   *Moral Exhortation. A Greco-Roman Sourcebook.* Library of Early Christianity. Ed. Wayne A. Meeks. Philadelphia: Westminster.
1987   "Hellenistic Moralists and the New Testament. *"In Aufstieg und Niedergang der römischen Welt.* Part 2, Vol. 27. Ed. W. Hasse and Hildegard Temporini. Berlin: de Gruyter.

Marcuse, Herbert
1954   *Reason and Revolution.* New York: Humanities Press.

Marx, Karl
1967   *Capital: A Critique of Political Economy.* 3 vols. New York: International Publishers.

Mead, George Herbert
1934   *Mind, Self and Society.* Chicago: University of Chicago.

Merton, Robert K
1968   *Social Theory and Social Structure.* New York: The Free Press.

Miller, Walter
1913   *Cicero. De officiis.* LCL. Cambridge, MA: Harvard University Press.

Norlin, George
1928   *Isocrates.* 3 Vols. LCL. Cambridge, MA: Harvard University Press.

Parsons, Talcott
1937   *The Structure of Social Action.* Glencoe, IL: The Free Press.

Perdue, Leo G.
1977   *Wisdom and Cult.* SBLDS 30. Missoula: Scholars.
1981a   "Liminalilty as the Social Setting of Wisdom Instructions." *ZAW* 93: 114–26.
1981b   "Paraenesis and the Epistle of James." *ZNW* 72: 241–56.
1983   "The Testament of David and Egyptian Royal Instructions." Pp. 79–96 in *Scripture in Context II.* Ed. William W. Hallo, James C. Moyer, and Leo G. Perdue. Winona Lake: Eisenbrauns.
1986   "The Wisdom Sayings of Jesus." *Forum* 2: 1–34.
1990   "Cosmology and the Social Order." Forthcoming in *The Sage in Israel and the Ancient Near East.* Ed. John G. Gammie and Leo G. Perdue. Winona Lake, IN: Eisenbrauns.

Perdue, W. D.
1986   *Sociological Theory*. Palo Alto: Mayfield.

Peter, H.
1901   *Der Brief in der römischen Literatur: Literaturgeschichtliche Untersuchungen und Zusammenfassungen*. Leipzig: B. G. Teubner.

Plato   See Shorey.

Plutarch. See Babbitt.

Price, Bennet J.
1975   *Paradeigma and Exemplum in Ancient Rhetorical Theory*. Ph. D. Dissertation, University of California, Berkley.

Pritchard, J. B., ed.
1969   *Ancient Near Eastern Texts*. 3rd. ed. with Supplement. Princeton: Princeton University.

Renoirte, T.
1951   *Les 'Conseils politiques' de Plutarque*. Louvain: Publications Universitaires.

Rosenkranz, B.
1966   "Die Struktur der Ps-lsokrateischen Demonicea." *Emerita* 34: 95–129.

Sanders, James A.
1984   *Canon and Community*. Guides to Biblical Scholarship. Philadelphia: Fortress.

Schmid, H.-H.
1968   *Gerechtigkeit als Weltordnung*. BHT 40. Tübingen: J. C. B. Mohr (Paul Siebeck) .

Stowers, Stanley K.
1986   *Letter Writing in Greco-Roman Antiquity*. Library of Early Christianity. Ed. Wayne A. Meeks. Philadelphia: Westminster.

Shorey, Paul
1930-35 *Plato. Republic*. 2 Vols. LCL. Cambridge, MA: Harvard University Press.

Theissen, Gerd
1977   *Sociology of Early Palestinian Christianity*. Philadelphia: Fortress.

Thraede, K.
1970   *Grundzüge griechisch-römischer Brieftopik.* München: C. H. Beck.

Thyen, H.
1955   *Der Stil der jüdisch-hellenistischen Homilie.* Göttingen: Vandenhoeck & Ruprecht.

Toennies, Ferdinand
1963   *Community and Society.* New York: Harper & Row.

Trillitzsch, W.
1912   *Senecas Beweisführung.* Berlin: Akademie.

Turner, Victor
1967a   *The Forest Of Symbols.* Ithaca: Cornell University.
1967b   *The Ritual Process.* Ithaca: Cornell University.
1972   "Passages, Margins, and Poverty: Religious Symbols of Communitas." *Worship* 46: 390–425.
1974a   *Dramas, Fields, and Metaphors.* Ithaca: Cornell.
1974b   "Metaphors of Anti-Structure in Religious Culture." Pp. 63–84 in *Changing Perspectives in the Scientific Study of Religion.* Ed. Allan W. Eister. New York: John Wiley & Sons.

Vetschera, Rudolf.
1911-12 *Zur griechischen Paränese.* Smichow/Prague: Rohlicek and Sievers.

Volten, Aksel
1945   *Zwei altägyptische politische Schriften.* Analecta Aegyptiaca 4. Kopenhagen: Einar Munksgaard.

Weichert, Valentine, ed.
1910   *Demetrii et Libanii qui ferunter. Tupoi Edistolikoi et Epistolimaioi Charakteres.* Leipzig: B. G. Teubner.

Welles, C. Bradford.
1974   *Royal Correspondence in the Hellenistic Period: A Study in Greek Epigraphy.* Chicago: Ares.

Wendland, Paul
1895   *Philo und die kynisch-stoische Diatribe.* Beiträge zur Geschichte der griechischen Philosophie und Religion. Berlin: Georg Reimer.

Williams, James G.
1981   *Those Who Ponder Proverbs.* Sheffield: Almond Press.

Williams, R. J.

1964   "Literature as a Medium of Political Propaganda in Ancient Egypt." Pp. 14–30 in *The Seed of Wisdom*. Ed. W. S. McCullough. Toronto: University of Toronto.

1972   "Scribal Training in Ancient Egypt." *JAOS* 92: 214–221.

1990   "The Sage in Egyptian Literature." Forthcoming in *The Sage in Ancient Israel*. John G. Gammie and Leo G. Perdue. Winona Lake, IN: Eisenbrauns.

PARAENETIC LITERATURE: TOWARD THE MORPHOLOGY OF A SECONDARY GENRE

John G. Gammie

ABSTRACT

Genre analysis is potentially heuristic and useful for determining works to be studied in common. It strives for clarity and a thorough awareness of classical rhetorical categories. This essay expounds Paraenetic Literature as one of the two main branches of Wisdom Literature. It seeks to determine the main sub-genres of Paraenetic Literature and especially to clarify the differences between paraenesis and protreptic, admonitions and exhortations, precepts and observations. Neglected sub-genres and devices are also treated—notably encomia (praises) and synkrisis (comparison). A chart showing the sub-genres shared by Apocalyptic Literature and Paraenetic Literature is also included, as is a Glossary.

0.1   In the previous essay, Professor Perdue examines the varying ways in which moral instruction in antiquity functioned to convert, confirm, socialize or legitimize diverse types of social groups. His exposition focuses on Paraenesis as "act". The present essay focuses on Paraenesis as "form". My interests here are taxonomic. That is, I attempt to define and locate Paraenesis as a literary genre or type. Investigation soon proved that Paraenesis, however, cannot be properly classified as a major literary type or even as a secondary genre. It seems rather to be best identified as one of the two main subdivisions of a larger composite and secondary genre, Paraenetic Literature. Accordingly, properly to understand the place of Paraenesis as a sub-genre it became obvious to me that it is necessary to set forth the contours and component parts of Paraenetic Literature as a secondary literary genre. Hence, as the title of my essay indicates, this essay deals with the larger whole, Paraenetic Literature, with its various components—including Paraenesis.

As will become obvious, Professor Perdue and I are not always in full agreement in our use of terms, but the differences should not be exaggerated for his focus is upon the *process* and *social settings* of moral exhortation in antiquity. My concern is to attempt to bring some clarity to the definition of the diverse *literary components* of the Paraenetic Literature.

0.2   The geographic and temporal boundaries of materials examined in this essay, as in this volume, will extend from the ancient Near Eastern

world of Egypt, Sumeria and Babylonia to the Mediterranean world of the
Roman Empire.

0.3   The contents of this essay will be set forth as follows:

    1. Underlying Principles of Genre Analysis
        1. Productive or Heuristic purpose
        2. Curricular usefulness
        3. Desirability of definitional clarity
        4. Relation to past rhetorical analyses
    CHART ON THE SECONDARY GENRES OF WISDOM LITER-
ATURE
    2. The Main Divisions of Paraenetic Literature
        1. Instructions
        2. *Paraeneses*
    3. The Component Sub-Genres of Paraenetic Literature
        0. *Synkrisis*
        1. Protreptic
        2. Admonitions
        3. Exhortations
        4. Precepts
        5. Praises or *encomia*
        6. *Měšālîm*
        7. Wisdom Sayings
        8. Fables
        9. Riddles
        10. Didactic Tales
    4. Summation
        1. Clarification of terminology and relationships
        2. Distinctiveness of present study
        3. Paraenesis and protreptic
        4. The usefulness of identification of sub-genres
        5. The usefulness of taxonomy

1   Several underlying principles with respect to genre analysis and
definition may be set down at the outset.

1.1.1   The purpose of genre analysis should not simply be taxonomic
but should be, as David Tracy has recently urged, productive or heuristic
(263). That is to say, the task of classification should not be conceived as
an end in itself but rather to set forth the typical so that the student may
be led to make fresh discoveries with respect to individual author's messages and intentions. This topic will be addressed briefly below in § 4 and
contributors to the volume also have been invited to explore it.

1.1.2   A frequently overlooked, but heuristically important, function of genre-analysis is to lend guidance as to which works may or may not fruitfully be included in a given curriculum or course of study. If like works are studied together they are frequently illuminating. Fresh insights may be in the offing when relevant works previously excluded from a curriculum are studied together.

1.1.3   It is a worthy goal to attempt to bring clarity to vexed issues in the definition of sub-genre and in particular of closely related genres. This essay will be devoted to that end, but an illustration of the problem may be given now with respect to two hortatory sub-genres: paraenesis and protreptic.

(a)   Benjamin Fiore has recently shown—contrary to the position held by Burgess earlier in this century (Burgess, 1902: 229-232, n. 2)—that protreptic and paraenesis are not equivalent terms (Fiore: 41). Paraenesis, he shows, is a more inclusive term than protreptic (Fiore: 41). The extent to which this claim bears up under examination will be explored below in § 2.2.2

(b)   The target audience of *paraenesis* may be, as Stowers has recently argued, *primarily* the converted, that is, those already convinced of the appropriateness of the goals and virtues being exhorted. Stowers may also be correct in holding that *protreptic* has as its *primary*, target audience the unconverted, the potential disciple, the undecided such as an ancient rhetor appealed to in an inuugural lecture (Stowers: 91-96; Resse, 1970: 117-121). But this claim also needs scrutiny. Accordingly we shall examine below in § 2.2.2, is Stowers' distinction a bit too neat? How helpful is it in instances where a probable *dual audience* comes into question as it does not infrequently in the Bible, e.g., Deuteronomy, Daniel 1-6 and Wisdom of Solomon? How will one classify a work when a part of the audience is constituted of uncommitted youths who stood without the circle of the faith and the other part, of the committed who stood in need of further encouragement, counsel and exhortation—as is most probably precisely the case with the Wisdom of Solomon? Stowers' criterion would seem to leave the student in a stalemate in instances of dual audiences. It is questions such as these which we will seek to reckon below in § 2.2.2.

(c)   How much should the student of genres be affected by etymological considerations and how much by modern usage? The underlying Greek meaning of the words *parainein* is "to exhort, recommend, advise" and of *protrepein* "to urge on, impel, persuade." The two are thus very close. Twentieth century usage, however, reveals significantly different applications. Thus in Western study of the Hebrew Bible the terms "paraenetic aim," "paraenesis" and "Paraenetic Literature" have been used in connection with Deuteronomy, the stories of Daniel, Esther, Ruth, Jonah, Tobit, Judith as well as with 2 Maccabees and the Testaments of the Twelve Patriarchs (e.g., Hempel: 140, 153, 154, 187, 188, 192). Even though recent scholarship has not tended to use these terms in connection with Proverbs, Murphy has done so recently of Proverbs 1:8ff. (Murphy: 180) and the term paraenesis enjoys favor when applied to the Pauline letters (1 Thess. 4:1-12; Romans 12-15; 1 Corinthians 5-14) (Koester: 2.55), James (Dibelius, 1976: 3; Perdue, 1981), 1 & 2 Timothy and Titus (Dibelius, 1972: 7; Fiore, passim), and protreptic is used of post biblical, Christian apologetic works (Koester, 2:338-340). Accordingly, the present essay—as indeed the entire volume—is dedicated to exploration and clarification of the nature of the hortatory form and thrust in select biblical and extra biblical works.

1.1.4   A fourth principle underlying this study pertains to the science of genre analysis itself. Any analysis of genre should be informed by an awareness of how the particular genre under study fits into genre analysis overall from the perspective of (a) classical usage, (b) levels of classification, (c) biblical studies and (d) affect on interpretation of individual works. Points (a) and (b) are closely related.

(a)   According to the four main theoreticians of rhetoric in antiquity, there are three main branches of rhetoric. Aristotle called them: forensic, advisory (or political), and display (or epideictic) in accordance with whether the addresses were judges weighing *past* actions, legislators weighing *future* actions or listeners being addressed about the *present* (Aristotle, *Rhetoric* 1.3). The first two types had two main subdivisions. The subdivisions of forensic are accusation or defense (apology) and the subdivisions of the political or deliberative (*eidos symboulēs*) are hortatory *protropē* or dissuasive (*apotropē*) (*Rhetoric* 1.3.3). In view of this distinction, it would seem on the face of it that the major hortatory category should be designated "protreptic" rather than "paraenetic." In the next paragraph, however, it will be shown why this is not so. Similarly for Aristotle display oratory had two main branches in that it was concerned mainly with two main subjects, namely, praise or blame. By the time of Menander (3rd cen. C.E.), however, some twenty-seven kinds of display oratory were distinguished, including the hortatory speech (*protreptikos logos*) which constituted a union of the advisory and display form (Burgess: 109-113).

   Quintilian (c. 35-100 C.E.) makes the important assertion that one must distinguish between genera and species. There are, he averred, only three main *genera*: forensic, deliberative and demonstrative. But *common* to all three genera are to be found the species: to praise or blame, to advise or dissuade, to drive home or refute a charge, as well as conciliation, narration, proof, exaggeration, extenuation, and the molding of the minds of the audience by exciting or allaying their passions (Quintilian, *Institutio Oratoria* 3.4.15). Thus Quintilian as well as Menander alerts us that it would be a mistake to consider hortatory speech either as a sub-division of the deliberative genre alone or as a major genre of as broad a range as forensic, deliberative and display oratory. Accordingly it is submitted here that Paraenetic Literature may be considered as a secondary genre subsidiary to all three main types: the forensic, the advisory (or deliberative) and the epideictic (or display) literature. Focus in this study will fall on the latter two.

(b)   In recent analysis Luis Alonso-Schökel has suggested that we should distinguish between primary literary genre, secondary literary genre and sub-genres (803). This point is well taken and if ignored can lead to undesirable results. In our judgment John J. Collins has made this significant taxonomic error in his study *Apocalypse: The Morphology of a Genre.* Collins has studied apocalypse, a sub-genre, without considering at all the secondary literary genre, Apocalyptic Literature, under which apocalypse might more properly be classified. The error is one wherein a sub-genre has been allowed to usurp the field as if there were no other kind of Apocalyptic Literature save apocalypse—or, as if the two were synonymous. Under Collins' analysis only Daniel 7-12 qualifies as apocalypse, thus his genre analysis fails to foster an examination of the dynamics operative within the book as a whole. If Collins were to acknowledge that he has described a sub-genre and that the larger complex genre, Apocalyptic Literature, cannot be reduced to apocalypse, the chief defect his analysis carries with it would have been remedied. As it stands Collins' error is comparable to acting as if all prophetic speech could comfortably be reduced to its single most important sub-genre, judgment speech (*Gerichtswort*) while speech of salvation (*Heilswort*) would simply be ignored.

In a previous study one of the editors of this volume has presented the case of considering Apocalyptic Literature as a literary category comparable to Prophetic Literature and Wisdom Literature (Gammie, 1976). So it is being suggested here that one may most properly speak of: Wisdom Literature (a major literary genre), Paraenetic Literature (a secondary literary genre), and paraenesis (a sub-genre).

(c)   Prior analysis of the prophetic and wisdom literature further substantiates the appropriateness of the above scheme of classification. In the same way that Claus Westermann demonstrated that prophetic speech is comprised of two major kinds: word of judgment (*Gerichtswort*) and word of salvation (*Heilswort*, Westermann: 37-41), so Rylaarsdam identified two major types of wisdom literature in the following words: "This literature, whether in Egypt, Babylon, or Israel, divides itself into two kinds: *prudential admonitions,* commonly in proverbial form, that may serve the young as directions for a happy and successful life, and *reflective essays* on the meaning and significance of life, often in a pessimistic vein" (italics mine, Rylaarsdam, 4). As we shall see, below, however, admonitions (*Mahnung*) is not a larger, secondary genre, but rather a smaller subgenre. It is accordingly submitted that the first subdivision of the wisdom literature identified by Rylaarsdam as admonitions commonly in proverbial form may more properly be identified as Paraenetic Literature. Admonitions, in turn, may be seen as a sub-genre either to Paraenetic Literature or paraenesis. In any event, Paraenetic Literature constitutes a secondary, and not a major or primary genre. The distinguishing characteristics of this literature and of instructions and paraenesis are set forth below in § 2.

(d)   The importance of the effect of genre analysis on the study of particular works has already been alluded to above in several regards. It has been noted that genre analysis should not simply be taxonomic but productive, heuristic—and that in at least two ways: (i) by enabling the interpreter to observe distinctive variations of the type (see above § 1.1.1) and (ii) by pointing to other works which may profitably be studied together in the same curriculum or course of study (see above § 1.1.2). In classical studies Francis Cairns has convincingly demonstrated what light careful "generic studies," i.e., the study of genera, may throw on speeches typically delivered to or by a traveler about to depart for another country or city (Cairns: 1-69). We have also argued above that genre analysis will ideally contribute to the examination of the dynamics operative in works as a whole rather than arresting analysis at one of the parts. With their statement of these four principles underlying the present study, we now are in a position to proceed to an examination of Paraenetic Literature.

The Main Divisions of Paraenetic Literature

2   Basic distinctions may be made between the composite or complex genre of Paraenetic Literature, its two major composite sub-genres (divisions), and the simple sub-genre of admonitions, warnings, exhortations, biographical examples, precepts, praises (of persons, wisdom and God), *měšalîm*, wisdom sayings, fables, riddles, didactic tales and occasionally diatribes. As Professor Attridge shows below, this list is hardly exhaustive and should include other sub-genres such as sermons or homilies and possibly another hortatory subgenre, *paracleses*. (See also

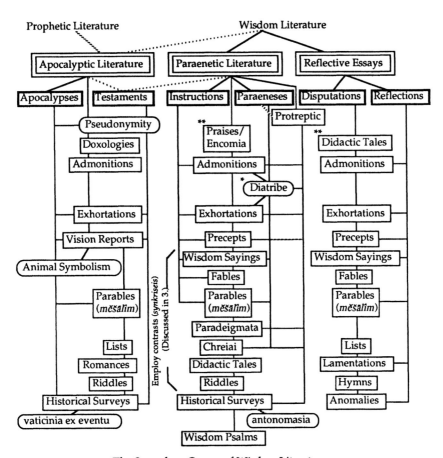

The Secondary Genres of Wisdom Literature

Legend

———————	= usual component
———————	= possible component
⬭	= device rather than sub-genre
▭ (double box)	= Secondary Genres
▭ (bold box)	= Composite Sub-genre (Divisions)
▭	= Sub-genre
*	= May utilize form of the letters
**	= Serve as framing sub-genres

below my "Note on Deuteronomy" in § 2.2.2) Paraenetic Literature, a secondary genre, may be seen as subsidiary either to the major literary genre of the wisdom literature or—to use Aristotle's classification of rhetoric—to the epideictic (or display) literature, symbouletic (advisory, legislative or political), or to the forensic literature.

In the course of our study it became apparent that two main composite sub-genres (divisions) of Paraenetic Literature may be identified, namely, Instructions and Paraeneses (Moral Exhortations). Both, though themselves subsidiary to Paraenetic Literature, are to a certain extent complex genres comprised of component sub-genres. Instructions will be described below in § 2.1 and Paraeneses in § 2.2. Paraenetic Literature may be epitomized as literature of moral exhortation. A regular feature of this literature is its use of comparisons or contrasts. (On this feature, see § 3. below.) Most frequently the aim or goal of Paraenetic Literature will be confirming, that is, to encourage the addressee to continue in the way that he or she has undertaken. Occasionally the style and aim may be protreptic, that is, focused on turning the addressee through a reasoned demonstration to follow the course of action or life styles the author espouses.

2.1   *Instructions*

2.1.1   The complex genre Instruction is one of the major composite sub-genres (divisions) of Paraenetic Literature. This composite sub-genre, Instruction (Egyptian, *sebayit*), flourished in ancient Egypt well over a 2000 year period (Whybray: 54; see also Brunner and Kitchen). It, like Paraenetic Literature, is comprised of the sub-genre admonitions, exhortations, and precepts. In non-Egyptian texts this genre also contained animal fables.

2.1.2   It includes the "Instruction of Vizier Ptah-hotep," "an educational manual for statesmen" from about 2450 B.C.E. (McKane: 55, *ANET*: 234); "The Instruction for King Meri-ka-Re" an old kings' "counsel" for his son "concerned with practical measures for defense of the state, as well as with the qualities of character needed by the holder of …the kingship'" from ca. 2100 B.C.E. (Scott: 27-28); the "Instructions of Amen-em-Opet," "maxims" (Albright: 6) or "teaching" by a tax official from ca. 1100 B.C.E. (Beyerlin: 49) which contains remarkable parallels with Prov 22:17-24:22 in 22 out of the 68 verses in the latter (my count). This list is not inclusive.

2.1.3   From Sumeria the oldest example of this form is "The Instructions of Shuruppak" from ca. 2500 B.C.E., advice and observations reputedly by an antediluvian sage for his son on civic conduct and life in general (West: 3-4, citing B. Alster, *The Instructions of Shuruppak*). The Akkadian text, "Counsels by Wisdom," addressed perhaps by a vizier to his son with advice on a range of topics from selecting friends and companions, honesty, improper speech and the kind of liaisons to avoid, dates from ca. 1350 B.C.E. (Lambert: 96-106). The Aramaic "Words of Ahiqar," ca. 410 B.C.E., (*ANET*, 427-430) which related the story of a falsely accused Assyrian scribe and then goes into "a long series of precepts intermingled with adages and animal fables" (West 13) may also be included in the classification of Instruction.

2.1.4   Biblical passages assigned to this secondary genre are: Proverbs 1-9; 22:17-24:22 and 31:1-9 (see McKane). The syntactic features of the genre have been examined by McKane (51-182) and its form-critical features by Kayatz (15-76). "Such instruction is authoritative; it demands unreserved acceptance and is not offered for critical consideration" (McKane, 51). A basic syntactical element of the Instruction is the use of the imperative and passive with conditional, circumstantial and motive clauses. Kayatz notes several differences between Proverbs 1-9 and the Egyptian Instructions: (1) in the latter the direct address, "my son," is confined to the Prologue; (2) the comprehensive promises connected especially to the admonitions to listen and strive after Wisdom are lacking in the Egyptian texts; and (3) the speech of personified wisdom in the first person singular in Proverbs 8 and 1:20-33 is also without parallel in the Egyptian Instructions (Kayatz: 74-75).

2.1.5   The chief distinguishing feature between Paraenetic Literature and Instructions is that the former may include a miscellaneous and assorted collection of precepts, admonitions whereas the Instructions are typically less assorted, more cohesive and more obviously and closely related to the end of teaching the ruler, noble or scribe addressed.

2.1.6   Praises, similar to what one finds later in the Greek encomia, are a quite regular feature in the instructions. Thus the third and penultimate section of "The Instruction for King Meri-ka-Re" is a hymn in praise of the powers of the sun god (124-138, *ANET*: 417). Self-praise is found in "The Instruction of King Amen-em-het" (ca. 1960 b.c.e.) (ii.1-111.1, *ANET*: 418-19). Scattered praise of the sun god are found in "The Instruction of Ani" (c. 1100 b.c.) (iii 11; vii 15-17; *ANET*: 420). In "Counsels of Wisdom" the sun god, Shamash, although not praised in any sustained fashion is praised nonetheless for rewarding good conduct and punishing the evil (ii 15: Reverse A 30, 41; cf. Reverse B 1-3 *ANET*: 426-27). Praises of the king and of the deity are likewise found in "The Words of Ahiqar" (vii 103-10; x 142-51; *ANET*: 429). Praises appear to be altogether absent, however, from "The Instruction of Vizier Ptah-hotep" and from "The Instructions of Amen-em-Opet."

As will be noted in § 3.5 below, praises in the form of the alphabetic acrostics conclude both the Book of Proverbs (Prov 31:10-31) and Sirach (Sir 51:13-30), are a major feature in Sirach (see esp. Sir 1:11-20; 24; 44-50; 51:1-2) and also occur in the first portion of Proverbs which may be labelled Instruction, (Prov 3:13-18; 8:32-36) but not in Prov 31:1-9 nor in Prov 22:17-24:22 save indirectly in motive clauses (Prov 22:23; 23:11; 24:22).

2.1.7   It should be emphasized that Instruction is a complex or composite sub-genre. Accordingly at least three considerations militate against the advisability of insisting too vigorously or exclusively that the above mentioned works (or portions of works) be called Instructions. (1) The Egyptian *sebayit* ("instruction") may also be properly rendered "teaching" (see Beyerlin: 44-49). (2) Internal clues and self-designation of genre must be given high priority in form-critical classification. Thus in the classification of the "Instruction of Amen-em-Opet," the opening lines suggest that alternative designation of this work are equally arguable: "The beginning of the *teaching* of life, the *instruction* for salvation, all *precepts* for converse with the great, the *rules* for courtiers" (italics mine, Bude transl. in Beyerlin: 49). Similarly, the three "Instructions" in Proverbs are designated by different terms: Proverbs 1-9 ("*mišlê šělōmōh* ["sayings of Solomon"]: Prov 1:1; "admonition of your father....teaching of your mother" [*mûsar ʾăbîkā... tôrâ ʾimmekā*]: Prov 1:8); Proverbs 22:17-24:22 ("*dibrê ḥăkāmîm*" ["words of the wise"]: Prov 22:17); Prov 31:1-9 ("*dibrê lĕmûʾēl*" ["words of Lemuel"]: Prov. 31:1). (3) Because the sub-genre Instruction is *composite*, it would be quite proper to name works in this genre with a title so to indicate, e.g. "The Admonitions *and* Precepts of Meri-ka-Re," "The Story, Adages *and* Fables of Ahiqar," and "The Murder *and* Maxims of Amen-em-Het."

2.1.8   When Instructions occur within larger works such as the Book of Proverbs, it seems permissible to classify the whole as Instructions *and* Sentences, as does McKane, but in the interest of moving beyond taxonomy to exploration of the interaction of the sub-genres within the whole, the classification as Paraenetic Literature is preferable by far.

2.2   *Paraeneses*

Paraeneses (pl., "moral exhortations"; sg. *paraenesis*) are very closely related to Instructions (on which see § 2.1 above). Both may be designated as major sub-divisions of the Paraenetic Literature. Biblical material which follows the pattern of Egyptian Instructions, e.g., Proverbs

1-9 may legitimately be so called. Biblical material such as the Epistle of James which follows the pattern of classical paraeneses such as the Letters of Isocrates (c. 436-338 B.C.E.) to Demonius may legitimately be so called. The extent to which Instructions and Paraeneses overlap is, as shall become apparent, surprising. Utilization of the two terms remains serviceable and should not, in our judgment, be dropped. Much as the designation of a storm accompanied by torrential downpours and high winds either as a hurricane or as a typhoon may serve to alert the reader as to the locale of the storm, so the retention of the terms Instruction and Paraeneses serve to alert the reader of the location of the moral exhortations in question in time and place. The one looks to a model in ancient Egypt, the other to ancient Greece.

2.2.1   *Paraeneses and Precepts.* In the earliest known instance of an ancient Greek author's application of the term *parainesis* ("moral exhortation") to his own work, the term is brought into the closest association with *gnomai* ("principles, precepts, maxims") (*Ad Demonicum* 1, 12). In contrast to those who wrote protreptic discourses (*protreptikoi logoi*) with the narrower end in view of developing persuasive power in speech, Isocrates commends his discourse as one which will perform the greater service of enabling men to be esteemed for sound character (*Ad Demonicum* 4). Accordingly he wishes to give counsel (*symboulein*) on: "(1) the objects to which young men should aspire and (2) from what actions they should abstain; (3) with what sort of men they should associate and (4) how they should regulate their lives" (*Ad Demonicum* 5; 1.7; numbers supplied, LCL). In fairly short order Isocrates not only explains how the soul is developed, "by noble words" (*spoudaiois logois*), he proceeds to enumerate twelve such precepts (*Ad Demonicum* 12-16) which in turn are supplemented by a goodly number of other pieces of advice given chiefly as precepts and exhortations but also, to a lesser extent, as admonitions (17-51).

What is especially interesting about the Letter of Isocrates to Demonicus is that it furnishes us with an important insight with which to differentiate paraenesis. *Paraenesis is a form of address which not only commends, but actually enumerates precepts or maxims which pertain to moral aspiration and the regulation of human conduct.*

Of twentieth century writers who have devoted efforts toward the definition of *paraenesis* (Burgess, 1902, Vetschera, 199-1912, Dibelius, 1920, Malherbe, 1972, Perdue, 1981, Fiore, 1986, and Stowers, 1986) either as a literary sub-genre in its own right or in differentiation of it from other sub-genres such as protreptic, each one without exception has pointed to the presence in paraenesis of "traditional material" or "precepts." Thus Benjamin Fiore translates R. Vetschera's definition of paraenesis as a "literary work which by its structure and aim delineates a collection of precepts which relate unexceptionally to the practical conduct of life, indeed to promote it, as far as it can, and to lead it to virtue" (Fiore: 41, n. 41 citing Vetschera: 7). Dibelius observes that in paraenesis one frequently finds "unconnected sayings which have no real relationship to one another" (Dibelius/Greeven: 3) but then goes on to posit that even though *eclecticism* is a feature of paraenesis, the sayings are frequently arranged on a *catchword* principle (Dibelius/Greeven: 4-5). Dibelius further suggested that paraenesis was not simply a collection of sayings (*gnomologium*) because it was either directed to a specific audience or appeared "in the form of a command or summons" (Dibelius/Greeven: 3). Recently Stanley Stowers similarly maintains that the question of audience, as well as the nature of the material, is of importance in distinguishing *paraenesis* from *protreptic*. The former is hortatory "confirmation literature," pressing its addressees "to continue in a certain way of life" whereas *protreptic* is hortatory "conversion literature that calls the audience to a new and different way of life" (Stowers: 92). Stowers may be correct but the argumentation he gives is not altogether convincing in two regards. (1) Reconstruction of Aristotle's last writing "Protrepticus" hardly exhorts espousal of a "new" way of life for Themiston the king of Cyprus, its addressee, for it commends *phronesis* (lit. prudential wisdom) as the greatest of all goods (Chroust, 15). (2) Because the paraenesis of Isocrates sent to Demonicus king of Cyprus is an epitome of practical and prudential advice, it is hardly likely that Isocrates had in mind the work of Aristotle, as Stowers suggests, when he speaks against the narrower and less noble concerns of "those who wrote protreptic words for their own friends" (Isocrates, *Ad Demonicum* 3). It seems more natural to conclude that Isocrates had in mind the Sophists back to whom "the protreptic speeches can be traced" (Stowers: 113).

2.2.2   *Paraenesis and Protreptic.* (1) *The role of precepts.* In the previous section it has already been argued that paraenesis should be seen in closest connection with precepts. Too hard and fast a line between paraenesis and protreptic, however, should not be drawn. As Stowers points out, Aristotle's "Protrepticus" also contained precepts (Stowers: 92). Protreptic may or may not contain precepts. The presence of precepts and a commending of them as a way of life, however, is not an optional feature for paraenesis. Theodore Burgess put the matter in this way: "Technically the προτρεπτικὸς λόγος is an exhortation to some general course—philosophy, rhetoric, virtue..." In distinction from the προτρεπτικὸς λόγος the παραίνεσις presents a series of precepts which will serve as a guide of conduct under fixed conditions, cf. Seneca, Ep. 95, 7 (Burgess: 230 [a continuation of n. 2., p. 229]).

(2)   *The role of argumentation.* More important than either the audience or content in our judgment is that *protreptic seeks to persuade frequently through a sustained demonstration.* The demonstration in protreptic is more systematic, organized and regular than it is in paraenesis. Thus protreptic employs syllogistic argument such as is found in Aristotle's "Protrepticus." In the Wisdom of Solomon the demonstration is achieved through a forceful and persuasive use of contrasts wherein the superiority of righteous belief in immortality and of the worship of the one true and wise God alone are laid upon the heart of the believer as well as possibly upon potential converts (Wisdom 1:1-6:11, 12:3-19:22). *Diatribe* (the use of popular rhetorical devices) may be found in both paraenesis and protreptic (Malherbe, 1986: 129). The important difference between the two is that in protreptic, the diatribal devices will usually be employed in the context of a larger pattern of demonstration, e.g. Wisdom 13:1-9. Similarly, both paraenesis and protreptic utilize praises or *encomia*, but the former does so in conjunction with a commendation, the latter in conjunction with a more systematically developed urging. Thus the praise of wisdom in the protreptic work Wisdom of Solomon 6:12-12:2 is set within the context of two demonstrative contrasts whereas the praises and one lengthy encomium for the Book of Sirach both frame, and are interspersed in, rather disparate sentences and maxims.

(3)   *Breadth.* Recently Benjamin Fiore has argued that paraenesis is broader in content than a protreptic work (Fiore: 41). He agrees with Vetschera that the paraenesis contains "precepts on how one should live," but suggests that the breadth of area covered by the precepts is broader than the scope of protreptic since paraenesis covers many areas of life such as "culture, friends, enemies, good fortune." In contrast, "Protrepsis, in both rhetoric and philosophy, hopes to lead the addressee to obtain a certain knowledge and the *aretē* [virtue] included in it" (Fiore, 41). Fiore's argument here defends a narrower focus for protreptic but also adverts to point 2 above, namely, protreptic seeks to persuade. Burgess, however, reminds us: "The παραίνεσις as a part of philosophy may have a restricted and personal application, *e.g.,* how to manage servants; or it may be more general, *e.g.,* how to live well. Aristo the Stoic and Cleanthes (Seneca, Ep. 94, 1ff.; 95, 1) favor the more general view" (Burgess: 230 [a continuation of n. 2, p. 229]). Burgess' observations here show that in terms of classification point 1 must take preference over point 3. *In some instances, however, paraenesis may be of quite narrow focus.*

(4)   *Audience.* As indicated above in § 1.1.3, Stanley Stowers has suggested that the primary criterion by which to distinguish between paraenesis and protreptic is that the audience of the former was consti-

tuted largely of the converted and that of the latter of potential converts. This suggestion, however, won't work in instances of a dual audience. Thus James Reese can observe "the whole approach of the Sage [i.e. author of the Wisdom of Solomon] is to encourage his students to pursue their ancestral traditions" (Reese, 1983: 98). The whole he thus sees in large part as confirmation literature—to use Stowers' terminology. Reese argues, however, in favor of a classification of the Book of Wisdom (+ Wisdom of Solomon) as protreptic! Yet in Stowers' view protreptic should be seen largely as conversion literature. Stowers' criterion thus would seem to stand in need of rather radical qualification. Another case in point is the Letter of Aristeas. Ostensibly a work written to King Ptolemy II, to convince this king of the many virtues of Judaism, this piece also clearly has two audiences: both persons in Hellenistic, non-Jewish communities (commending Judaism) *and* the Jewish community (arguing for obedience to the food laws, the prudence of Israelite morality and the superiority of the authorized translation of the Pentateuch) (Gammie, 1986). On the basis of audience alone the student of literature is at a loss as to how to classify this work under Stower's main criterion because its chief goal seems to be to convert the ostensible addressee to sympathy with, and a favorable attitude toward, the Jewish religion. On the other hand, (1) the work is, with one exception (the defense of the food laws), lacking in any sustained or organized argumentation and (2) each of the responding 72 young translators from Judaea utters a maxim. The work thus most naturally may be classified as belonging to the Paraenetic Literature, in accordance with the criteria set forth above in this essay.

Corroboration of the wisdom of the approach to the determination of protreptic argued above in this essay is found in Quintilian in the course of a discussion on "stasis" (Lat. *status*; Gr. *stateis*) for various speeches. A "stasis" is one of three or more of the most basic questions to which any subject of dispute or question may be reduced. Quintilian, following Aristotle, held that there were three "stases": the conjectural, the definitive, and the qualitative in answer to the following questions: whether a thing was done or not, what was done and what kind of thing was done. To these three the rhetorician Athenaeus added a fourth "stasis" (Lat. *status*; Gr. *stasis*): the "protreptic stasis" or "stimulative" (*parometikē*) *id est exhortativum, qui suasoriae est proprius* ("that is, exhortative, which is peculiar to persuasion": *Institutio Oratoria* 3.6.47, my transl.; LCL 1.432). Thus it is suggested on the grounds of historical precedent, clarity and usefulness that the criterion of audience as the decisive determining factor to distinguish between protreptic and paraenesis be dropped in favor of the threefold criteria of: (1) presence or absence of precepts and purpose for which they are adduced; (2) extent of sustained demonstration and organization with a view to persuade; and (3) breadth of topics covered and/or sharpness of focus.

A note on Deuteronomy. Because paraenesis and protreptic are both hortatory, Philo of Alexandria refers to the Book of Deuteronomy as "precepts and exhortations" (*hypothēkai kai paraineseis: De specialibus legibus* I, 299; LCL 7, 272) as well as "protreptic [words]" (*protreptikoi [logoi]: De fuga* 142, 170; LCL 5, 84, 102). In the first reference above *paraineseis* ("exhortations") seems to be used in contradistinction to the precepts. It is in that sense that most modern commentators on Deuteronomy use the word paraenesis, namely, as hortatory and sermonic words which commend the observation of the law. Thus paraenesis is most often used of Deuteronomy 5-11, and often in conjunction with "preaching" in contradistinction to "commandments" (see Mayes: 49; Merendino: 401; Von Rad: 12, 15). (This reading of Philo assumes, of course, that *kai* in the phrase *hypothēkai kai paraineseis* is disjunctive. Modern usage in any event would read the *kai* in the aforementioned phrase disjunctively.) Curiously, scholars of the Hebrew Bible have not sought to exploit the identification among classicists of *paraenesis* as a collection of maxims—where the designation would admirably suit Deuteronomy, the Holiness Code (Leviticus 17-26) and Proverbs as well as Sirach.

2.2.3   *Formal characteristics.* Theodore Burgess argued "The παραίνεσις is practically without formal definition." (Burgess: 230 [a continuation of n. 2., p. 229]). Despite this caveat, Burgess himself asserted that "the essentials of its technical use" may readily be discovered from "the opening portion of Isocrates' 'Letter to Demonicus'" cited above in § 2.2.1, and from Seneca's Letter 95.

(a) As we noted, and sought to establish in § 2.2.1, the presence of *a collection of precepts* is an essential feature in paraenesis.

(b) Paraenesis will also commend the validity of the maxims, precepts, sentences (or statues) which it sets forth through the use especially of *exhortations* (Isocrates, *Ad Demonicum* 17, 18, 19, 20, etc.). The exhortations of paraenesis are frequently accompanied by *motive clauses* (ibid., 19, 21, 24, 46, 47, etc.).

(c) *Admonitions*, though less frequent than exhortations, are a regular feature (Isocrates, *Ad Demonicum,* [*bis*], 16, 23, 29, 32, 27, 39, etc.). These too may be accompanied by motive clauses (ibid., 43).

(d) *Encomia* or praises of righteous persons in paraeneses are not frequently identified as such but rather are found under the rubric of *paradeigmata*, "examples" of noble persons whose conduct, attitudes and life style are held up to be worthy of emulation, or as *chreiai* (Isocrates, "Ad Demonicum," 8, 9, 11, 50; 2 Maccabees 7). In the *chreiai* such positive (and negative) examples are developed "for the purpose of edification" (Fiore: 42). (For a thorough discussion see Fiore: 26-100).

(e) *Addressee*. Paraeneses may be directed to individuals with whom the author stands in a direct, personal relationship (e.g. the letters of Isocrates to Demonicus or Nicocles or those of Seneca to Lucilius) or the paraeneses may be directed to a community in its own name (Deuteronomy), or to a community in the name of a real or fictitious addressee (1 & 2 Timothy, Titus). (For specific examples of the use of direct address, see below under admonitions [§ 3.2.3a] and exhortations [§ 3.3.2].)

2.2.4   *Relation of Paraenesis to Paraenetic Literature*. In §§ 2.2.1-3 we have sought to set forth the nature of Paraenesis as a main division of the Paraenetic Literature. Its similarity to Instructions is obvious in that it holds so many sub-genres in common. Whereas the admonition tended to dominate in instructions, the exhortations do so in paraeneses. Further inquiry also revealed that the place of precepts in paraenesis is more central than the scholarly application of the term paraenesis to Deuteronomy 5-11 would seem to suggest.

One of the chief ways in which sub-division paraenesis differs from Paraenetic Literature is that the latter employs praises or encomia in positions of greater prominence and in greater measure (Proverbs 31:10-31; Sirach 1, 24, 44-51; Wisdom of Solomon 7-9). The praises in paraenesis do not extend to praise of the ideal wife, wisdom personified or God but rather are confined to the *paradeigmata* and *chreiai*.

The mere presence in a work of admonitions and exhortations is not sufficient to warrant its classification as paraenesis. Thus the seven letters to the churches in Revelation 2-3 might well be classified as admonitions and exhortations but not as paraenesis (because of absence of maxims or precepts). On the other hand, passages such as Philippians 4:8-13 and Hebrews 13 certainly qualify because of the assemblage of maxims and precepts.

The Component Sub-Genres of Paraenetic Literature

3.0   *Sygkrisis*. Comparison or contrast between alternative entities, ways or styles is an exceedingly old and yet persistent device in Paraenetic Literature. To cite only a few examples from the ancient Near East, Israel and the New Testament, it is used in the contrast between the "heated man" and the "silent man" (Amen-em-Opet, chs. 2-5, 7, 9-10, *ANET*: 422-32), between the wiseman and the fool (Ptah-hotep 573-84, *ANET* : 414), between the relative merits of trees ("The Dispute between the Date Palm and the Tamarisk," *ANET*:410-11), between the way of the righteous and the way of the ungodly (Psalm 1), the way of life and the way of death (Deut 30:15-20), between the rich and the lowly (Jas 1:9-11), between hearing and doing (Jas 1:22-25), between faith and works (Jas 2:14-26), and between lovers of pleasure and lovers of God (2 Tim 3:2-9). The use of the device of *sygkrisis* in Greek literature has been explored thoroughly by Focke. Though it does not seem to me correct to call "comparison" or "contrast" a form or genre as some have (see, e.g., Reese; 98), the pervasive use of the device among the sub-genres of Paraenetic Literature merits attention. It may be used in any of the sub-genres. Its use, however, in praises, *měšalîm*, wisdom sayings, fables, riddles and didactic tales in particular will be underlined below (in 3.6-3.10).

3.1   *Protreptic*

3.1.1   *Definition.* *Protreptikoi logi* (pl. "moral demonstrations," lit. "hortatory words," sq. *protreptikos logos*) are closely related to paraeneses ("moral exhortations") (on which see §§ 1.1.3, 2.2). Both are hortatory sub-genres and often used interchangeably (as in Philo) but may nonetheless be clearly distinguished (see § 2.2.2). Protreptic works which contain either an interspersing of maxims (as is the case with the Wisdom of Solomon [*passim*]) or a collection of maxims may be designated as a major sub-division of Paraenetic Literature along with Paraeneses and Instructions (see §§ 2.1, 2.2 and the chart above).

3.1.2   In modern, as in classical, usage the term protreptic, rather than *protrepsis* or *protrepseis*, is used whether applied to smaller units or to an entire work (Fiore here is an exception). Thus the Wisdom of Solomon may rightly be classified as "a protreptic" (Reese, 1983: 14) rather than a protrepsis. In the interest of uniformity of designation—and also to call attention to the relatedness of the genres—the designation *protrepsis* would clearly seem to be more appropriate were it not for the fact that the designation *protrepsis* is simply absent from each one of the classical treatises on rhetoric including those by Aristotle and Plato. The latter two employ the term *protropē*, but exceedingly sparingly (e.g., *Rhetoric* A.3.3., *Laws* 11.9208). Thus retention of the term protreptic rather than the introduction of the term *protrepsis* (or an alternative) would seem to be the soundest decision in view of the classical precedent. Modern usage should, in our judgment, seek to show both some correspondence with, as well as awareness of, classical usage.

3.1.3   Formal characteristics of this sub-genre have been listed and discussed in § 2.2.2 above. On whether or not any particular protreptic work should be classified as belonging to Paraenetic Literature, see § 4.5.

3.2   Admonitions

3.2.1   *Differentiation from Exhortation and Precept.* In a recent form-critical study, *The Structure and Ethos of the Wisdom Admonitions in Proverbs,*
Philip J. Nel has stated—too apodictically in our judgment: "There are
only *two* basic forms in the sentence: the wisdom saying (*Aussage*) and the
wisdom admonition (*Mahnwort*): (1982: 17). This pronouncement is defen-
sible on syntactic grounds, but insufficiently differentiated insofar as
content and intention is concerned. Drawing on the studies by Schmidt
and Hermisson on the Sentence, and by Richter and by himself on the
Admonition, Nel has a strong case only if one does not probe too deeply
into content and intention. Thus we submit that the following differentiation is required for more careful study. The *Admonition* must be distinguished from the *exhortation;*[1] and, the *precept* should be distinguished
from the simple *observation*. The first three are recognizable sub-genres of
Paraenetic Literature. The *precept* will usually employ the indicative, but
not all sentences or observations in the indicative are precepts. The *precept*
we may define as a sentence or observation, usually in the indicative,
which instructs and contains an implied or obvious directive for conduct,
e.g., "The plans of the diligent lead surely to abundance, but every one
who is hasty comes only to want" (Prov 21:5). The implied teaching is
evident: seek to avoid hasty actions. An *observation* we may define as a
sentence in the indicative in which attention is drawn to an observable
phenomenon without either implicitly or obviously directing the hearer to
a given course of conduct, e.g. "Hope deferred makes the heart sick, but a
desire fulfilled is a tree of life" (Prov 13:12); "The poor is disliked even by
his neighbors, but the rich has many friends" (Prov 14:20); "Even in
laughter the heart is sad, and the end of joy is grief" (Prov 14:13). In none
of the above examples is any specific action enjoined. The sentence writer
has simply made an observation which he/she has recorded.

　　　Similarly it seems advisable to differentiate between *exhortation*
and *admonition*. The former invites the addressee to a given course of action, whereas the latter warns the addressee against taking a given course
of action or attitude.

　　　The Admonition may employ the same syntactic form as the
exhortation—whether the vetitive (a term which Nel employs for the
imperfect with the negative particle *ʾal*), or the imperfect with the negative
lōʾ—and, like the exhortation, it will usually be followed by a motive-
clause, but the admonition puts the addressee on guard against a given
path of conduct, and admonishes him (or her) with respect to the
potential dangers awaiting: "Let not your heart turn aside to her [the
adventuress's] ways,/do not stray into her paths;//for many a victim has
she laid low;/yea, all her slain are a mighty host" (Prov 7:25-26).

3.2.2   The chief difference between the above understanding of admonition and that of Nel and Richter may be stated as follows. Although Nel is certainly correct in his observation (counter to Richter) that there is no need to posit a separate sub-genre for the prohibitive form (*lōʾ* + imperfect), he includes in the sub-genre instances which would better be classified as exhortations. Thus, most (but not all) usages of the imperatives would best be classified as exhortations. Not discussed above is Richter's certainly correct contention that legal formulations in Israel do favor the prohibitive form (68-146).

3.2.3   *Formal characteristics.* There is a simple and recurring pattern of the admonition which runs through all periods:

(a) Use of the vocative in *direct address*: This feature is confined to the Prologues of the Egyptian Instructions (Kayatz: 74-75). In Proverbs the direct address, "my son" introduces admonitions alone (Prov 1:10, 15; 31:1 [with two other vocatives]) and is also found in exhortations which introduce admonitions (Prov 1:8; 23:19-21, 26-28; 24:21-22). In 1 Timothy a reverse example is found where the direct address ("man of God") is employed in connection with an admonition which introduces exhortations (1 Tim 6:11-12). In the Epistle of James, the direct address is also found in the following admonitions (Jas 1:16; 2:1; 3:1; 4:11; 5:12).

(b) Use of *warnings* with the imperative, jussive, vetitive (jussive + negative particle *ʾal*), prohibitive (imperfect + negative particle *lōʾ*) in Hebrew, and comparable forms in Egyptian, Akkadian, Aramaic, and Greek. This feature is the core of the admonition. Whether or not the vocative case is used in direct address is optional because where the vetitive and imperative are used, the addressee is already being spoken to directly: "Do not enter the path of the wicked,/and do not walk in the way of evil men"//Avoid it; do not go on it;/turn away from it and pass on" (Prov 4:14-15).

As was seen above, admonitions are frequently mingled with exhortations. Several examples will suffice. "Do justice whilst thou endurest upon earth. Quiet the weeper; do not oppress the widow; supplant no man in the property of his father; and impair no officials at their *posts*" (Meri-ka-Re, 47, *ANET*: 415). "Let not your heart envy sinners,/but continue in the fear of the Lord all the day" (Prov 23:17). "[So] shun youthful passions and aim at righteousness, faith, love and peace" (2 Tim 3:22).

(c) *Motive clauses*: A third feature of the admonition is the occurrence of motive clauses. Nel has identified six major kinds of motive clauses for the admonitions in Proverbs (final clauses mostly with *pen* + imperfect; subordinate clauses mostly with the imperfect; result clauses mostly with *kī*; causal clauses mostly with *kī*; predication mostly with *kī*; and, promise with imperfect (and *waw*) (18-74). Some admonitions occur without a motive clause, e.g. 22:28 (but cf. 23:10-11) but the vast majority do. Examples: "Do not slaughter: it is not of advantage to thee" (Meri-ka-Re 48, *ANET*: 415); "Do not talk a lot. Be silent, and thou wilt be happy" (Ani IV, 1, *ANET*: 420); "Do not speak in the hearing of a fool,/for he will despise the wisdom of your words" (Prov 23:9); "Do not rob the poor, because he is poor,/or crush the afflicted in the gate;//for the Lord will plead their cause/and despoil of life those who despoil them" (Prov 22:22-23); "Do not grumble, brethren, against one another, that you may not be judged; behold, the Judge is standing at the doors" (Jas 5:9); "Have nothing to do with stupid, senseless controversies; you know that they breed quarrels" (2 Tim 2:23).

3.3   Exhortations

3.3.1   The exhortation invites, encourages, directs or commands that the addressee pursue a given course of action or adopt a given attitude.

3.3.2   *Formal characteristics.* Use of vocative in *direct address.* As with the admonition, the exhortation will frequently employ the direct address. Thus in Proverbs, "my son" is found with exhortations in the following (Prov 1:8; 2:1; 3:1, 11, 21; 4:10; 6:1, 3, 20; 7:1; 23:15; 24:13). Examples from the New Testament are: "brothers" (Romans 12:1; 1 Thess 4:1; 5:1; Jas 5:7) "Timothy" (1 Tim 1:18; 6:20); "my son" (2 Tim 2:1); "my brothers" (Jas 1:2; 2:1, 14; 5:12, 19), and "my beloved brothers" (Jas 1:19).

    Variety of means of expressing exhortation. The exhortation may be issued through the use of a question: "How long, O simple ones will you love being simple"? (Prov 1:22a), or through a conditional clause: "My son, if you receive my words and treasure up my words....then you will understand the fear of the Lord and find the knowledge of God" (Prov 2:1, 5). Or, the exhortation may employ the jussive with the negative particle ʾal (the so-called vetitive as Nel calls it) or without it: "My son, do not forget my teaching, but let your heart keep my commandments" (Prov 3:1). Or, the exhortation may simply employ the imperative, e.g. "Hear, O sons, a father's instruction, and be attentive, that you may gain insight: (Prov 4:1). Or—to cite an example from the New Testament—an indicative may be used, followed by an infinitive clause: "I appeal (*parakalō*) to you therefore, brethren, by the mercies of God, to present your bodies as a living sacrifice, holy and acceptable to God" (Rom 12:1).

    Motive clauses. As with the admonitions, motive clauses frequently accompany the exhortation. The same motive-clauses listed above in § 3.2.3 for the admonition may also be found for the exhortation. In some instances, of course, the list of motives may be extensive: "(But) the truly silent man holds himself apart./He is like a tree growing in a garden./It flourishes and doubles its yield;/It (stands) before its lord./Its fruit is sweet; its shade is pleasant;/And its end is reached in the garden..." (Amen-em-Opet, Fourth Chapter 6-11, *ANET*: 422). "Keep hold of instruction, do not let her go;/guard her, for she is your life" (Prov 4:13); "Let every person be quick to hear, slow to speak, slow to anger, for (even) the anger of one stalwart (*anēr*) does not work the righteousness of God" (Jas 1:19).

3.4   Precepts

3.4.1   The precept is a "sentence," usually in the indicative, which instructs and contains an implied or obvious directive for conduct.

3.4.2   *Formal characteristics.* Some precepts may be in the imperative (e.g. "Give instruction to a sage, and that one will become wiser still; teach a righteous person, and that one will add to it learning" (Prov 9:9). Some precepts in Hebrew function by juxtaposition which in translation are occasionally rendered as if the first clause were the protasis in a conditional sentence; thus: "If a king judges the poor with equity, his throne will be established forever" (RSV, Prov 29:14). It may be further noted that in the above example as well as in others like it, the second of the two juxtaposed clauses (the apodosis) clearly states a *motive* for acting in accordance with the advice given in the first clause (the protasis) (cf. Prov 17:13; 18:18; 20:20).

The majority of the sentences in Proverbs 10:1-22:16 and Proverbs 25-29 fall into the category of precepts. As suggested above in § 3.4.1., however, some are better understood as observations.

Many precepts contain their own motive as a part of the precept: thus, "The wise will inherit honor,/but fools get disgrace" (Prov 3:35). As a glance at almost any of the sentences in Proverbs 10-15 will show, where predominantly the so-called antithetic parallelism is employed, the precept almost invariably contains both a positive and a negative motive. The aforementioned sentences in Proverbs 10-15 thus employ the device of comparison or contrast which is, as we noted above, a regular feature in the sub-genres of Paraenetic Literature and particularly of those discussed in §§ 3.5-3.10 below.

3.5   *Praises or encomia.*

Praises imply a superiority of the one praised to another one or ones. This is so whether the entity praised is the immortal, a mortal or a virtue such as wisdom or justice. In the treatise "Concerning Epideictic Matters," Menander (3rd century C.E.) distinguishes between "praises *egkomia*) of the gods" (hymns) and "praises of mortals"—of which the majority of praises he analyzed are comprised (Burgess: 109-13). The virtues of piety, prudence, temperance, courage and justice were frequent items in encomia of human beings (Burgess: 130-31) and, of course, in the praises of the gods it was a regular feature to allude to the divine attributes (Burgess: 178).

Praises (poems of praise, hymns of praise) or encomia not only imply or directly state the superiority of the one praised, they are also a recurring and often framing sub-genre of Paraenetic Literature. In the canonical and deutero-canonical literature of the Bible, both Proverbs and Sirach conclude with poetic praises written in styles of an alphabetic acrostic, the former in praise of the ideal wife (Prov 31:10-31) the latter in praise of wisdom personified (Sir 51:13-30). The final chapter in Sirach commences with another type of encomium, a thanksgiving hymn in praise of God (Sir 51:1-12) and the work opens with a praise of wisdom and piety (Sir 1:1-20). Not only is the Book of Sirach framed with texts which approximate the Greek encomia, its most significant division is marked by a hymn in praise of wisdom (Sirach 24) and this work contains the largest encomium in Israelite, sapiential literature which is patterned on Greek models—the so-called "Praise of the Fathers" (Sirach 44-50). Thomas R. Lee (103-256) has shown in a recent study that the latter closely follows the pattern of Hellenistic encomia in its parts: Prooemium (Sir 44:1-15); *Genos* or Enumeration of the *race* or ancestors of the one praised (Sir 44:16-49:16); *Praxeis* or Narration of the *deeds* of the one praised (Sir 50:1-21); Epilogue (Sir 50:22-24). Burton L. Mack (1-137) also demonstrated the Hellenistic indebtedness of the encomia in Sirach 44-50 by uncovering the following slightly more detailed pattern of characterization: 1. Office, 2. Election, 3. Covenant, 4. Piety, 5. Deeds, 6. Setting Context and 7. Rewards.

It is of more than passing interest to note that the Book of Psalms is also framed by a Wisdom Psalm and a hymn which are praises: Psalm 1 is a contrastive praise of one who meditates on the Torah and Psalm 145, which marks the beginning of the concluding of the Psalter as Gerald H. Wilson has recently and convincingly shown, is an alphabetic acrostic in praise of God and the divine kingdom.

Other texts of praise interspersed in Paraenetic Literature in the proto- and deutero-canonical portions of the Old Testament are: (i) of one who finds wisdom (Prov 3:13-18; 8:32-36; Sir 14:20-15:8); (ii) of the scholar-sage (Sir 38:24-34 [in contrast to other, lesser trades], 39:1-11 [in his own right]); (iii) of wisdom (Sir 4:11-19; Wisdom of Solomon 6:12-12:2) (iv) of God (Deut 32; Sir 16:26-17:14; 18:1-14; 39:12-35; 42:15-43:23) and of Israel (Deut 33). The Wisdom of Solomon also concludes with a praise of God for remembrance of God's people (Wis 19:22). In the predominantly epistolary style of the New Testament Paraenetic Literature praise of God are found at the conclusion of a division (1 Tim 3:14) and within the salutation (2 Tim 1:9-10; Tit 1:2-3; Heb 1:1-3). Praises of faith and blessings of endurance are also found in the course of the salutation (2 Tim 1:3-5) and in the body of a work (Jas 1:12).

Since Aristotle, praises, i.e., encomia, have been recognized as constituting the major sub-genre of the epideictic or display oratory (Rhetoric 1.3.3; Burgess: 113). The place of praises and encomia in Sapiential and Paraenetic Literature is evident from the above, but has tended to be overlooked for four obvious and fairly simple reasons. One, most previous studies, including the present anthology and two by one of the editors of this work, have focused on the sub-genre paraenesis rather than on the larger, secondary genre, Paraenetic Literature. Two, the predominance of doxological and encomiastic elements in a given type is often overlooked or ignored in instances where convention has accepted the correctness of alternative classifications (e.g., a number of the poems in praise of Wisdom in Sirach are classified as wisdom poems and hymns; Psalm 1 in praise of the righteous man is classified as a Wisdom Psalm). Three, a justifiable reluctance to label as encomia (a Greek term) any poem which does not have a recognized, precise, and exact correspondent in Greek literature. Four, praise or encomium in *paraenesis* is frequently contained in *paradeigmata* or examples of model conduct and thus the element of praise may remain implicit. It is equally evident, however, that one commends what one praises. Praises—whether expressed in wisdom poems, hymns, or, latterly, encomia—are not peripheral to Paraenetic Literature but integral to it because they invite the reader-hearer to join in the praise of the one commended or that one's way of life.

3.6   *Mĕšālīm*. Since Otto Eissfeldt's important work, *Der Maschal in Alten Testament*, it has been recognized that a central feature in the *māšāl* is the element of comparison. Johannes Schmidt demonstrated that *māšāl* cuts across and includes five different sub-genres (proverb, taunt, oracle, parable and wisdom saying) (2-8). George Lands has recently re-examined the term *māšāl* and re-emphasized the validity of Eissfeldt's insight that all usages of *māšāl* include the notion of *comparison* (Lands, 1978). The demonstration of this fact bears significantly upon the study of the Sapiential Literature, and especially upon those portions which are introduced as *mišlê šĕlōmōh* (Prov 1:1; 10:1). Genre analysis accordingly must be sensitive to ways in which comparisons and contrasts occur in this literature within the several sub-genres. Thus even the so-called single-membered proverb may contain a comparison ("To do righteousness and justice is more acceptable to the Lord than sacrifice": Prov 21:3).

3.7   *Wisdom Sayings.* (1) Contrasts and comparisons predominate, of course, in the two-membered sayings where *antithetic parallelism* is employed. As is widely recognized this form occurs in the vast majority of sayings from Proverbs 10-15 (in 163 out of 183 verses) and in quite a few of the sayings of Proverbs 16:1-22:16 (in 47 out of a total of 190 sayings) (Skladny, as cited by Murphy, 1981: 64). In the above-mentioned verses, the contrast is often drawn between the righteous and the wicked, the wise person and the fool, the simple and the discerning. (2) Even where synonymous parallelism is employed, comparisons are made by the following other means: (a) *juxtaposition*, e.g.,

> The path of the upright—avoidance of misfortune
> (nouns) One who preserves his life—one who
> marks his way (participles)
> (Prov. 16:17 Murphy trans. and notes, 1981: 65).

(b) *similes*, e.g., "Like a bird that is far from its nest,/so is a man who is far from his home (Prov 27:2). (c) *"not-good"*-sayings, e.g., "Without knowledge, even zeal is not good" (Prov 19:2); (d) *"Better" sayings*, e.g., "He who is slow to anger is better than the mighty,/and he who rules his spirit than he who takes a city" (Prov 16:32).

3.8.   *Fables*. Among the oldest of the sub-genres of Paraenetic Literature are the fables or, as W. G. Lambert calls them, Contest Literature. Thus in "The Tamarisk and the Palm" the two trees verbally spar with one another with regard to their respective worthy very much as two college freshmen might vie today with regard to the respective merits of their home towns. A similar contest is found in the other Babylonian fables: "The Fable of the Willow," "Nisaba and the Wheat," "The Ox and the Horse," "The Fable of the Fox" and "The Fable of the Riding Donkey" (Lambert: 150-212).

      In "The Words of Ahiqar" similar contrasts are found pertaining to the ass and the lion, the leopard and the goat, the bear and the lambs, and the brambles and the pomegranate (*ANET*: 428-429).

3.9   *Riddles*. That the riddle in the biblical literature contains a contrastive element is apparent both from the close association between *māšāl* and *ḥîdâ* in Prov 1:6 and from perhaps the best known biblical riddle: "Out of the hunter came something to eat,/Out of the strong came something sweet" (Judg 14:10-18). In "The Words of Ahiqar" the comparative element is apparent: "What is stronger than a braying ass?"—"The load." (*ANET*: 4288). Crenshaw suggests that we may see "disintegrated riddles" in Prov 5:1-6, 15-23; 6:23-24; 16:15; 20:27; 23:27, 29-35; 25:2-3; and 27:20 (Crenshaw: 242). In each one of these citations one or more likenesses is alluded to.

3.10   *Didactic tales.* Though mentioned here last, didactic or paraenetic tales may be considered alongside Instruction and Paraenesis as a major sub-division of Paraenetic Literature. In Johannes Hempel's survey *Die Althebraische Literatur und ihr Hellenistisch-Judisches Nachleben* (140, 153-154, 186), the author identified three types of paraenetic works: (1) those which contain paraenesis (Deuteronomy, 2 Maccabees [in 6:12ff.]); (2) those with a "paraenetic aim" (Daniel 1-6, Esther, Ruth, Jonah) and (3) "paraenetic narrative literature" (Tobit, Judith, and Testaments of the Twelve Patriarchs). In each of the narratives in the second and third categories, and in 2 Maccabees 6-7, the principle of contrast is utilized by the author to underline the virtues of fidelity to Torah, God, one's (or one's adopted) people, compassion or self-control. (In Disputations—a major division of Reflective Essays—such as the Book of Job, the didactic tale is used as a means of framing the entire work just as encomia may be used to frame pieces of Paraenetic Literature.)

4.   *Overall Summation* and summary comments on the productive or heuristic function of the classification Paraenetic Literature.

4.1   The above essay has attempted both to review and to clarify the definition and formal characteristics of several hortatory sub-genres and to suggest the most natural way in which they might be arranged hierarchically. The major unit under examination has been the secondary genre Paraenetic Literature. We have suggested that Paraenetic Literature should be designated as a major sub-division of Israel's Wisdom Literature along with its Reflective Essays (1.1.4) and that it has two major complex or composite genres, Instructions and Paraeneses, and a variety of sub-genres. Works alluded to in this study were not confined to the Hebrew Bible or Old Testament but included the New Testament as well a works from ancient Egypt, ancient Mesopotamia and Hellenistic Egypt. The main divisions of Paraenetic Literature examined were instructions (§ 2.1) and paraeneses (§ 2.2). The component sub-genres of Paraenetic Literature examined were: protreptic (§ 3.1), admonitions (§ 3.2), exhortations (§ 3.3) and precepts (§ 3.4). In sections §§ 3.5-3.10 we also called attention to the remarkable use of comparisons throughout the other sub-genres of Paraenetic Literature (praises or *encomia*, *mĕšālîm*, wisdom sayings, fables, riddles, and didactic tales).

4.2   By pointing to the various elements or components in Paraenetic Literature in the way we have done, we have, it is hoped, identified the most significant elements to be found in Paraenetic Literature. How these various elements interrelate and are interwoven in specific works is, of course, the task of exegesis. Previously such studies have, in our judgment, underplayed the presence and indeed prominence of praises and encomia (which would include macarisms and blessing) in the paraenetic. The use of comparisons in this literature can hardly be missed, but we have sought to give it a formal prominence here in the hope that in the search for a full interpretation of a paraenetic work that this element will be given the place it deserves.

4.3   Another aspect of the above study which merits particular attention is our attempt to demonstrate the clear distinction which obtains between Paraeneses ("Moral Exhortations") and "Protreptic" ("Moral Demonstrations"). Prior to our undertaking this study we had rather assumed, witness the usage of Philo, that paraenesis and protreptic were rather closely related and scarcely distinguishable. Etymology turned out to be misleading (both the Greek *parainein* and *protrepein may* be rendered "to exhort"). Classical usage demonstrated, however, that a key in the classification of paraenesis is the presence of maxims and precepts and a key in the classification of protreptic is the presence of a sustained demonstrative argument with a view to persuade.

4.4   We stand in full agreement with David Tracy that mere taxonomy is not an end in itself. A careful taxonomy, however, of a secondary genre which seeks to identify major component sub-genres may clearly furnish the exegete with a clearer guideline as to which elements and sub-genres to expect so that the exegete in turn may be all the more ready to reflect on how those elements and sub-genres are creatively (or uncreatively!) interrelated in any particular work.

4.5   A second productive value in genre analysis is to be found precisely by the aid of taxonomy. The above study has shown that, because of the importance of collection of maxims or precepts in the classification of paraeneses, the *entirety* of the books of Deuteronomy, Proverbs and Sirach may be assigned without any hesitation to the Paraenetic Literature. Fresh insights into taxonomy suggest which books might fruitfully be studied together *and in comparison one with the other*. Though it is a protreptic work, the Wisdom of Solomon may also be so assigned to the Paraenetic Literature. As in Sirach its maxims are interspersed throughout, but as with each of the paraenetic works examined, the Wisdom of Solomon contains also admonitions, exhortations, praises and (in its case, a most forceful) use of comparisons. By pointing to the hierarchical relationship and holding that a protreptic work may nonetheless qualify as belonging to the Paraenetic Literature, we have thus demonstrated that taxonomic analysis does not necessarily eliminate or argue against the value of comparing works which, though differently classified, in other regards have a number of elements in common. This point may be illustrated by a recent experience of the author. In an exhibit of the paintings and drawings of Paul Klee at the Museum of Modern Art, it became apparent that the painter's message could not be derived solely from pondering one painting. Rather the symbolism the painter employed in earlier (or later) works of seemingly different sorts often furnished this viewer with clues as to the painter's intention. Discovery was made through comparison. It has been my experience in undergraduate teaching over the past two decades that the same is so where there are some significant points of contact between modern literary works and biblical works. Thus in a work such as the Wisdom of Solomon attention not simply to its own classification but to the next higher classification to which it may be placed may lead to the discovery of aspects in the ancient work which other modes of analysis have missed.

NOTES

[1] My colleague agrees with the need for differentiation, but prefers the designations prohibitions (in lieu of my preference for admonitions) and admonitions (in lieu of my preference for exhortations). See Perdue, 1986: 18-19. "Prohibition" I take to be a form or sub-type of admonition. My chief objection to Perdue's understanding of admonition is that the term more readily, in my judgment, carries with it the idea of warning (cf. Ger. *Mahnung* or *Mahnwort*) and thus does not readily suggest the notion of the pursuit of a *positive* course of action.

GLOSSARY

admonitions. (*Mahnungen* or *Mahnwörter*, lit. "warnings" or "words of warning"). Sub-genres or species aimed at dissuasion. (See § 3.2)

apocalyptic literature. A secondary, complex genre which may be considered as subsidiary to both Prophetic and Wisdom Literature. A common device is pseudonymity (*q.v.*). Component sub-genres are: vision reports, historical surveys (which frequently use the devices of *vaticinia ex eventu* [*q.v.*] and animal symbolism), exhortations, doxologies, etc. In the case of Daniel important sub-genres are the romances (*q.v.*) in chaps. 1-6.

apocalypses (Gk. *apokalypseis*, sg. *apokalypsis*, lit. "revelations"). Constitute a major division of apocalyptic literature but subsidiary to it much as paraeneses (*q.v.*) are subsidiary to Paraenetic Literature. These clusters of sub-genres have been form-critically defined most precisely in recent times by John J. Collins (1978).

antonomasia. A device wherein an author avoids the use of proper names but through the use of circumlocutions also manages to make the intended referents fairly plain. Perhaps the best example in the canonical and deutero-canonical literature is found in Wisdom of Solomon 10, e.g., "first father" = Adam; "a wicked man" = Cain; "his brother" = Abel; "a good man" = Noah, or Lot, or Jacob (the context indicates which).

beatitude. A saying which pronounces a person or persons as blessed.

chreiai. Frequently instructive anecdotes of action or speech aptly attributed to a particular person.

complex genres. Larger literary genres which are comprised of lesser, component (*q.v.*) or sub-genres, e.g., the major literary categories (Prophetic literature, Wisdom Literature); secondary literary genres (Apocalyptic Literature, Paraenetic Literature, Reflective Essays); major divisions or clusters of sub-genres within secondary literary genres (apocalypses, instructions, paraeneses, disputations, reflections). In classical rhetoric from Aristotle onwards there were three main categories: forensic (*q.v.*), deliberative (*q.v.*) and epideictic (*q.v.*). Synonym, composite genres.

component genres. Sub-genres. This term is used of sub-genres when the writer or speaker wishes to call attention to the fact that the sub-genres in question are parts of a larger whole (which larger whole may be called by the one using the term, a complex or composite genre).

composite genres. Synonym, complex genres (*q.v.*).

deliberative speech. One of the three main branches of rhetoric in which, according to Aristotle, political orators engaged. Hence this branch of rhetoric is also called "political." The Greek designation of this type, *eidos symboulēs*, also permits the rendering "advisory speech" or "symbouleutic literature" (*q.v.*), of which there were two main types: hortatory (*protropē* and dissuasive (*apotropē*).

diatribe. A device or mode (Malherbe 1986, 129) of popular hortatory speech in which the orator or moral philosopher aimed at moving people to action rather than reflection. The stratagems of the diatribe included rhetorical questions, dialogue with a fictive opponent, satire, irony and paradoxes.

didactic tales. Stories designed to teach (See § 3.10.)

disputations. A division or cluster of sub-genres of Reflective Essays (*q.v.*) in which an argument unfolds between two or more parties of divergent points of view, e.g. the Book of Job.

doxologies. Speech in which praise (Gk. *doxa*) is ascribed to persons or deities; synonym of encomia (*q.v.*).

encomia (Gk. sg. *egkomion*). Praises. An important genre in Paraentic Literature of the Hellenistic period. This genre was held by Aristotle to constitute one of the two major subdivisions of epideictic literature (*q.v.*) and oratory. Mack has recently demonstrated conclusively that the encomia in the section of Sirach entitled "In Praise of the Fathers" (chaps. 44-

50) have been "crafted on the model of this Hellenistic prototype" (128). Encomia in praise of Wisdom are framing sub-genres in the book of Sirach (Sir 1:1-20; 51:13-30). The popularity of encomia or praises in Israelite, paraenetic Literature of the Hellenistic period is undoubtedly due in part to the impact of epideictic literature. Lee supplies an extended survey of the history of this genre (103-206). (See § 3.5.)

epideictic speech. Display oratory; one of the three main branches of rhetoric. For Aristotle there were two main types: praise and blame (such as would be rendered in a funeral oration.) By the time of Menander some 27 sub-types of epideictic speech were distinguished. Quintilian called this branch "demonstrative." Modern day equivalents are, as Reese points out below (§ 4.5), "throw away speeches" such as are given at fundraisers or sports banquets. Attridge suggests we also think of the oratory at wakes, weddings, and national holidays. (§ 1.6)

exhortations. Sub-genres of each of the three main branches of rhetoric, as well as of Paraenetic Rhetoric and Literature, in which the addressee is invited, encouraged, directed or commanded to pursue a given course of action or to adopt a given attitude. The counterpart of exhortations are admonitions (*q.v.*) in which addressees are warned against a given course of action or attitude. (See § 3.3.)

forensic speech. One of the three main branches of rhetoric in which the concern of the orator is to establish the justice or injustice of a past action. In this rhetoric of the law court the speaker will either defend or accuse one of the parties in a law suit. Hence its two chief types are defense (Gk. *apologia*) and accusation (Gk. *katēgoria*). Some rhetoricians call this speech "dicanic" (from the Greek, *dikē*, "[legal] judgment)."

genera. Major classifications, sg. *genus*. According to Quintilian there were only three major genera: the forensic, deliberative and demonstrative.

instructions. A major division of Paraenetic Literature (*q.v.*) which utilize a number of the sub-genres also utilized in paraeneses (*q.v.*). This term is favored for Egyptian works and, among recent commentators, for Proverbs 1-9. (See § 2.1.)

jussive. A "mood" of volition, usually in the third person.

macarisms. Pronouncements of a blessing. All beatitudes (*q.v.*) may be classified as macarisms, but not every macarism is a beatitude. The English word is derived from the Greek, *makarios*; pl. *makarioi* ("blessed").

maxims. Sentences or sayings containing some practical advice.

měšālîm (Heb.; sg. *māšāl*). Usually translated "parables." Johannes Schmidt demonstrated, however, that měšālîm constitute five sub-genres: proverb, taunt, oracle, parable and wisdom saying (*q.v.*) (208) (See § 3.6.)

observations. Sentences or sayings of a more neutral sort than precepts (*q.v.*) in which the reader cannot readily decide whether the phenomenon described is favored or descried. (See § 3.2.1.)

paradeigmata. Models, illustrations, examples (sg. *paradeigma*).

Paraenetic Literature. A complex and secondary literary genre the aim of which is frequently hortatory and instructive. This genre is broader than paraeneses (*q.v.*) and instructions (*q.v.*); the latter two rather constitute its two largest divisions. Some works, e.g., Sirach, which may not justifiably be classified as either instruction or paraenesis, may readily be classified as belonging to this secondary genre.

paraeneses (Gk. *paraineseis;* sg. *parainesis*). Moral exhortations which usually feature an assemblage of precepts (*q.v.*) and comprise a major division of Paraenetic Literature (*q.v.*). Frequently paraenesis is taken to be a synonym for exhortation, or to be aimed at confirming the addressee in a given course of conduct (so Stowers). The latter understanding, however, founders in instances of a dual audience. (See § 2.2.)

political speech. Deliberative speech (*q.v.*).

precepts. Sentences, usually phrased in the indicative mood, which instruct and contain an implied or obvious directive for conduct. (See § 3.4.)

prohibitions. A synonym, form or sub-type of admonitions (*q.v.*).

protreptic. A device or sub-genre of paraenesis (*q.v.*) which seeks to persuade through a sustained demonstration. The distinguishing feature of this device or sub-genre is not to be found in its audience (which does not necessarily consist in the unconverted, as Stowers has affirmed) but in its method of argumentation. Since Aristotle it has been held that protreptic constitutes one of the main divisions of deliberative (i.e., symbouleutic or advisory) speech. Menander (3rd century), however, held that it was one of the 27 sub-types of epideictic oratory and a union of both the symbouleutic and epideictic forms (see Burgess, 109-113 and the discussion in §§ 1.1.4 and 2.2.2 above). The Wisdom of Solomon, a fine example of protreptic, has a dual audience of (primarily) the converted and (secondarily) those who stood at a distance from the faith of Hellenized Judaism. (See § 3.1.)

pseudonymity. A device wherein the actual author conceals his or her identity through the use of an assumed or "false name" (Gk. *pseudon onoma*).

reflections. A main division of Reflective Essays (*q.v.*) and therefore distinct from observations (*q.v.*); loosely structured and often random "thoughts" or considerations of the validity of a stated thesis or theses, e.g., Qoheleth.

Reflective Essays. Comprise a secondary literary genre of Wisdom Literature along with Paraenetic Literature. The term goes back to J. Coert Rylaarsdam (4). The two main divisions or clusters of sub-genres of reflective essays are reflections (*q.v.*) and disputations (*q.v.*).

riddles. Enigmatic sayings which challenge the hearer to determine the referent. (See § 3.9.)

romances. Tales of a faraway land and time in which it often comes to pass that the trials and triumphs of the protagonists miraculously defy the ordinary rules governing life and death.

symbouleutic literature. Advisory or deliberative literature; one of the three main branches of ancient rhetoric. Following Aristotle, ancient and modern analysts posit that there are essentially two divisions of symbouleutic: protreptic (*q.v.*) and apotreptic either urging or arguing against a given course or action or attitude (see Cairns, 1972: 71-72).

syncrisis. (Gk. *sygkrisis*). Contrast or comparison. A favored device of Paraenetic Literature. (See § 3.0)

testaments. Words sworn or uttered, usually upon the approach of death. As a literary form the testaments may be subsidiary either to Apocalyptic or Wisdom Literature or both. It was especially popular in the so-called intertestamental period. In the Testaments of the XII Patriarchs the author shows how each patriarch exemplifies either a virtue or a vice.

vaticinia ex eventu. Prophecies out of the event, i.e., descriptions of events which have already transpired as if they were predictions or prophecies.

vetitive. A grammatical mood favored in Hebrew admonitions; the use of the jussive (*q.v.*) + the negative particle ʾal. This term is used *inter alia* by Nel (1982: 36-39, 65-74).

vision reports (*Gesichtsreden*). A favored sub-genre of both Prophetic and Apocalyptic Literature in which the author relates the contents of a vision of things earthly or heavenly.

wisdom psalms. A group of psalms so classified on form-critical and ideational grounds. In recent times R.E. Murphy (1963) has carefully set forth the criteria for establishing how one may decide whether or not a particular psalm belongs to this category.

wisdom sayings (*Weisheitsprüche*). Didactic sayings based on tradition as well as on experience, e.g., Prov 10:1-22:16.

WORKS CONSULTED

Aristotle   See Freese

Alonso-Schökel, Luis
1967   "Literary Genres, Biblical." Pp. 803–9 in *New Catholic Encyclopedia* 8. Ed. William J. McDonald. New York: McGraw-Hill.

Baumgartner, Walter
1914   "Die Literarischen Gattungen in der Weisheit des Jesus Sirach." *ZAW* 34: 161–98.

Beyerlin, Walter
1978   *Near Eastern Religious Texts Relating to the Old Testament.* Trans. John Bowden. Philadelphia: Westminster.

Brunner, Hellmut
1980   "Lehren," *Lexikon der Ägyptologie* 3:963–991.

Burgess, Theodore L.
1902   *Epideictic Literature.* Pp. 89–261 in *Studies in Classical Philology* 3. Chicago: University of Chicago Press.

Butler, H. E.
1953-66 *Quintilian: Institutio Oratoria.* 4 vols. LCL. Cambridge, MA: Harvard University Press. First published 1921–22.

Cairns, Francis
1972   *Generic Composition in Greek and Roman Poetry.* Edinburgh: University.

Chroust, Anton Hermann
1964   *Aristotle's Protrepticus: A Reconstruction.* South Bend, IN: University of Notre Dame Press.

Cicero   See Rackham and Sutton.

Collins, John J.
1979   *Apocalypse, The Morphology of a Genre. Semeia* 14.

Colson, F. H.
1944-48 *Philo.* 10 vols. LCL. Vols 1–4 with G. H. Whitaker. Cambridge, MA: Harvard University Press.

Conzelmann, Hans
    1972   *The Pastoral Epistles*. Hermeneia. 4th ed. of Martin Dibelius, *Die Pastoralbriefe*. Trans. Philip Buttolph and Adela Collins. Philadelphia: Fortress.

Crenshaw, James L.
    1974   "Wisdom." Pp. 225–64 in *Old Testament Form Criticism*. Ed. John H. Hayes. San Antonio: Trinity University Press.

Dibelius, Martin See Conzelmann and Greeven.

Driver, Samuel Rolles
    1896   *Deuteronomy*. ICC Edinburgh: T. & T. Clark

Eco, Umberto
    1984   *Semiotics and the Philosophy of Language*. Bloomington, IN: Indiana University Press.

Eissfeldt, Otto
    1913   *Der Maschal im Alten Testament*. BZAW 24.

Fiore, Benjamin
    1986   *The Function of Personal Example in the Socratic and Pastoral Epistles*. AB 105. Rome: Biblical Institute Press.

Focke, Friedrich
    1923   "Synkrisis." *Herems: Zeitschrift für Classiche Philologie* 58: 327–68.

Foucault, Michel
    1971   "The Discourse on Language." *Social Science Information*. April: 7–30. Trans. Rupert Swyer.

Freese, John Henry
    1975   *Aristotle: The "Art" of Rhetoric*. LCL 22. Cambridge, MA: Harvard University Press. First printed 1926.

Gammie, John G.
    1976   "The Classification, Stages of Growth and Changing Intentions in the Book of Daniel." *JBL* 95:191–204.
    1986   "The Hellenization of Jewish Wisdom in 'The Letter of Aristeas." *Proceedings of the Ninth World Congress of Jewish Studies*. Division A:207–214.

Gemser, Berend
1963   *Sprüche Salomos*. HAT 16. 2nd ed., Tübingen: J.C.B. Mohr (Paul Siebeck).

Greeven, Heinrich
1976   *James*. 11th. ed. of Martin Dibelius *Der Brief des Jacobus*. Translated by Michael A. Williams. Philadelphia: Fortress.

Hempel, Johannes
1930   *Die Althebräische Literatur und ihr Hellenistisch-Judisches Nachleben*. Wildpark-Potsdam: Athenaion.

Hermisson, Hans-Joachim
1968   *Studien zur israelitischen Spruchweisheit*. WMANT 28. Neukirchen-Vluyn: Neukirchener Verlag.

Hornung, Erik und Othmar Keel, eds.
1979   *Studien zu altägyptischen Lebenslehren*. Göttingen: Vandenhoeck & Ruprecht.

Isocrates.   See Norlin

Kayatz, Christa
1966   *Studien zu Proverbien 1–9*. Neukirchen-Vluyn: Neukirchener Verlag.

Kennedy, George
1963   *The Art of Persuasion in Greece*. Princeton, NJ: Princeton University Press.
1969   *Quintilian*. Twayne World Authors Series. Ed. Sylvia E. Bowman. New York: Twayne.

Kitchen, Kenneth A.
1979   "The Basic Literary Forms and Formulations of Ancient Instructional Writing in Egypt and Western Asia," Pp. 235–82 in *Studien zu Altägyptischen Lebenslehren*. Ed. Erik Hornung and Othmar Keel. Göttingen: Vandenhoeck & Ruprecht.

Koester, Helmut
1982   *Introduction to the New Testament*. 2 vols. Philadelphia: Fortress.

Lambert, W. G.
1960   *Babylonian Wisdom Literature*. Oxford: Clarendon.

Landes, George M.
1978   "Jonah: A Mašal?" Pp. 137–58 in *Israelite Wisdom*. Ed. John G. Gammie *et al*. Missoula, MT: Scholars.

Lee, Thomas R.
1986   *Studies in the Form of Sirach 44–50*. SBLDS 75. Atlanta, GA: Scholars.

Mack, Burton L.
1985   *Wisdom and the Hebrew Epic: Ben Sira's Hymn in Praise of the Fathers*. Chicago Studies in the History of Judaism. Ed. Jacob Neusner. Chicago and London: University of Chicago Press.

McKane, William
1970   *Proverbs*. OTL. Philadelphia: Westminster.

Malherbe, Abraham J.
1972   "1 Thessalonians as a Paraenetic Letter."
1986   *Moral Exhortation, A Greco-Roman Sourcebook*. Library of Early Christianity. Ed. Wayne A. Meeks. Philadelphia: Westminster.
1987   "Hellenistic Moralists and the New Testament." In *Aufstieg und Niedergang der römischen Welt*. Part 2, Vol. 27. Ed. Wolfgang Haase and Hildegard Temporini. Berlin: Walter de Gruyter.

Mayes, A. D. H.
1979   *Deuteronomy*. New Century Bible. London: Oliphants.

Merendino, Rosario Pius
1969   *Das Deuteronomishe Gesetz*. BBB 31. Bonn: Peter Hansen.

Moore, Frank W., editor
1966   *Readings in Cross-Cultural Methodology*. New Haven: HRAF Press.

Murphy, Roland E.
1981   *Wisdom Literature*. FOTL 13. Ed. Rolf Knierim and Gene M. Tucker. Grand Rapids, MI: Eerdmans.

Nel, Philip Johannes
1982   *The Structure and Ethos of the Wisdom Admonitions in Proverbs*. BZAW 158. Berlin/New York: Walter de Gruyter.

Norlin, George
1954-56 *Isocrates*. 3 vols. LCL. Cambridge, MA: Harvard University.

Perdue, Leo G.
1977   *Wisdom and Cult.* SBLDS 30; Missoula, MT: Scholars.
1981   "Paraenesis and the Epistle of James." *ZNW* 241–56.
1986   "The Wisdom Sayings of Jesus," *Forum* 2:1–34.

Philo.   See Colson.

Pritchard, James B.
1955   *Ancient Near Eastern Texts Relating to the Old Testament.* 2nd ed.
        Princeton, NJ: Princeton University Press.

Quintilian See Butler.

Rackham, H. and Sutton, E. W.
1979-82 *Cicero: De Oratore.* LCL. 2 vols. Cambridge, MA: Harvard
        University. First published 1942.

Rad, Gerhard von.
1953   *Studies in Deuteronomy* SBT 9. Trans. David Stalker. London:
        SCM.

Reese, James M.
1970   *Hellenistic Influence on the Book of Wisdom and Its Consequences.*
        AB 41. Rome: Biblical Institute Press.
1983   *The Book of Wisdom, Song of Songs.* Old Testament Message 20.
        Ed. Carroll Stuhlmueller and Martin McNamara. Wilmington,
        DE: Michael Glazier.

Richter, Wolfgang
1966   *Recht und Ethos: Versuch einer Ortung des weisheitlichen Mahn-*
        spruches. Studien zum alten und neuen Testament 15. Munich:
        Kosel.

Rylaarsdam, J. Coert
1946   *Revelation in Jewish Wisdom Literature.* Chicago: University of
        Chicago Press.

Schmidt, Johannes
1936   *Studien zur Stilistik der alttestamentlichen Spruchliteratur.*
        Alttestamentliche Abhandlungen 13/1. Münster: Aschendorff.

Scott, R. B. Y.
1971   *The Way of Wisdom in the Old Testament.* New York: Macmillan.

Stowers, Stanley K.
 1986   *Letter Writing in Greco-Roman Antiquity.* Library of Early
           Christianity. Ed. Wayne A. Meeks. Philadelphia: Westminster.

Terrien, Samuel
 1978   *The Elusive Presence: Toward a New Biblical Theology.* New York:
           Harper & Row.

Tracy, David
 1981   *The Analogical Imagination: Christian Theology and the Culture of
           Pluralism.* New York: Crossroad.

Turner, Victor
 1977   *The Ritual Process: Structure & Antistructure.* Ithaca, NY:
           Cornell University Press.

Vetschera, Rudolph
 1911-12   *Zur griechischer Paraenese.* Smichow/Prague: Rohlicek und
           Sievers.

Weinfeld, Moshe
 1972   *Deuteronomy and the Deuteronomic School.* Oxford: Clarendon.

Wellek, Rene and Warren, Austin
 1956   *Theory of Literature,* 3rd ed. NY: Harcourt, Brace and World,
           Inc.

West, M. L.
 1980   *Hesiod: Works & Days.* With Prolegomenon and Commentary.
           Oxford: Clarendon.

Westermann, Claus
 1964   *Grundformen prophetischer Rede.* Munich: Chr. Kaiser.

Whybray, R. N.
 1965   *Wisdom in Proverbs.* SBT 45. London: SCM.

Wilson, Gerald Henry
 1986   *The Editing of the Hebrew Psalter.* SBLDS 76. Atlanta, GA:
           Scholars.

PART TWO:

MORAL INSTRUCTION IN JUDAISM
AND EARLY CHRISTIANITY

THE DEATH OF THE SAGE AND MORAL EXHORTATION: FROM ANCIENT NEAR EASTERN INSTRUCTIONS TO GRAECO-ROMAN PARAENESIS[1]

Leo G. Perdue

ABSTRACT

The settings for paraenesis often find their unity in the death of the sage. This death is understood in three interrelated ways: historical, ritualistic, and mythic. In the historical setting, the sage prepares for death by issuing to disciples a teaching for life. The personal behavior and the impending "good death" are exemplary. The moment of imminent death is the occasion for the correspondence of teaching and life. In the ritual setting, the disciple is entering a new state of life, social role, or social group. The sage takes leave of the student by providing guidance for the new responsibility. Now the student enters a new level of moral existence that requires a maturity unaided by the guiding presence of the teacher. In the mythic setting, the fiction of the death of the sage constructs a social world in which disciples take up residence and dwell. Teaching and death are incorporated into the collective identity and experience of the group of disciples. In this way, teacher and disciples continue to endure.

0.1.   *Introduction.* In his satire of Peregrinus, a Cynic preacher of the second century C.E., Lucian refers to one of the sage's last acts before his theatrical suicide performed on a funeral pyre:

> The story is that he dispatched missives to almost all the famous cities— testamentary dispositions, so to speak, and exhortations (παραινέσεις) and prescriptions (νόμους)—and he appointed a number of ambassadors for this purpose from among his comrades, styling them 'messengers from the dead' and 'underworld couriers' (*"The Passing of Peregrinus,"* 1).

Lucian noted that in dying Peregrinus wished "to benefit mankind by showing them the way one should despise death." Lucian also lampooned the two efforts by the disciples of Peregrinus to present their teacher in the guise of Socrates: first when he was imprisoned and again shortly after his self-afflicted cremation ("The Passing of Peregrinus," 12, 37).

Despite the satirical nature of Lucian's remarks, they point to the approaching death of the sage as an important occasion for the moral exhortation of disciples who are left behind. Indeed these remarks reflect an ancient rite of passage in the Eastern Mediterranean world, beginning with literature of moral exhortation from the Early Bronze Age and continuing well into the second century C.E.[2] In this paper I shall discuss paraenesis associated with the death of the sage according to the following schedule: 1. Egyptian Instructions; 2. Old Testament Instructions; 3. The Testament Literature; 4. Last Words in Rabbinic Judaism; 5. Graeco-Roman Paraenesis; and 6. Conclusions.

0.2.   Victor Turner focuses on the "threshold (*limen*)" experience, i.e., the stage of liminality, when an individual or group temporarily leaves a prior place in the social structure and prepares for re-entrance at another level. This threshold experience characterizes primarily the initial phase of three spheres of human social life: movement into a new stage (birth, puberty, marriage, parenthood, retirement and death), the assumption of new social roles (occupation, marriage, parenthood, etc.), and entrance into social groups. The recipient is leaving behind an earlier stage, social role, or way or life and stands at the entrance to a new one. Once entered, the past is left behind. Or, to use another common metaphor, one dies to a prior existence and is reborn to a new one. In the order-paradigm of society, paraenesis issued during this liminal experience is both subversive and traditional. Initially it is subversive in destroying the prior social identity of liminals. This destruction is necessary, before rebirth may occur. Paraenesis then takes on a more traditional character in providing the guidance, or nomos, necessary for the new life. In the conflict paradigm, the *communitas* experienced during the liminal period may result in efforts at transformation of the old hierarchical order into an egalitarian one.

        In many instances, the issuance of paraenesis also involves the "death" of the teacher. Indeed subgenres emerged in ancient Near Eastern, biblical, and Graeco-Roman literature which depict the death of famous people, particularly sages or teachers renowned for their wisdom. The nature and function of this death literature may be understood in three ways. The first and most common way is to see the literature representing in some fashion the actual death of the sage and events and sayings thought to be associated with the teacher's final hours. Many paraenetic texts are presented as the culmination of the best and most important wisdom of famous sages who are about to die. This final rite of passage becomes the greatest test of the authenticity of the teacher's way of life. The crisis posed by the teacher's death threatens the stability and integrity of the social world constructed by conversation and presence (21f.). To overcome this threat, the instruction is transmitted to successors and followers and preserved for continued reflection and guidance. The teacher thereby continues to live through the social group formed by his/her instruction and achieves a type of immortality.

A second manner of understanding the death of the teacher centers on the ritual context in which the act of moral exhortation often occurred. In ritual passages, the teacher symbolically "dies" in that (s)he will no longer be present to provide moral guidance for the liminals. Coming into a social group, experiencing status elevation, entering a new social role, and beginning a new stage of life were occasions when new responsibilities called for maturity and possibly even the guidance of other teachers. Included in the ritual death of the past experienced by liminals is the role of their former teacher. While repetition and reflection on the past may continue to be important, this process of remembering is undertaken by those who are expected to act more maturely and responsibly. Thus the narrative account of the teacher's death functioned symbolically during the rituals of passage to a new life.

A third understanding of the "death" of the sage has a mythical character. Groups composed legends of the death of their sages to accompany texts of moral exhortation which became an important element of their social mythos.[3] This mythos preserved and actively shaped their perception of reality. The legend depicting the sage's paradigmatic death combined with paraenesis to aid in the socialization of new members, to legitimate social reality, and to maintain group cohesion. These were accomplished by indicating that the manner in which the teacher faced death authenticated the instruction and the symbolic universe which it helped to shape.[4]

In most of the fully developed narratives which accompany paraenetic texts, these three ways of understanding the meaning of the sage's death are present. Even in paraenetic texts which are not supplemented by narratives, one may on occasion see the early phase of the development of narratives in the sayings or discourse proper. These may involve, for instance, sayings about death attributed to the teacher. From here the steps to the full development of narratives of the death of the sages were taken.[5]

1.1.   *Egyptian Instructions.* John Gammie in the second essay of this volume rightly views Instructions as a complex or composite sub-genre and underlines their prominence within ancient Near Eastern paraenetic literature. Indeed wisdom instructions were the major type of moral exhortation in Egypt (Brunner, 1980: 964–968; Kitchen, 1979: 235–282). The extant instructions (*sb3yt*) in Egypt (as well as in Mesopotamia and Israel) have two formal structures (Kitchen, 1979: 235–282). The first, and earlier form, consists of the

1.   Title—which has three forms: the earliest is "The Instruction of X (titles plus personal name);" the classical formulation is "Beginning of the Instruc-

tion made by X, titles plus personal name)," and the demotic form is "(The) Teaching of X." The address of the "son" is often added to the title.
2.   Main text—the linking together of admonitions and sayings in contiguous sections (Brunner, 1952: 90; and Kitchen, 1979 237f.).[6]

A later type adds either a prologue or more extended narrative between the title and the teaching proper (Brunner, 1952: 90; Kitchen 237f.).[7] The prologue often includes the setting for the instruction, an emphasis placed on the value of the teaching, and a general exhortation to follow its precepts. The narrative is a more extended prologue in which a longer, "biographical" story about the sage and the specific occasion for the instruction is given. The occasion for the issuance of the instruction was normally the impending death of the teacher.

In addition to classical instructions, we have "idealized biographies" found in the tombs of Egyptian nobles, beginning as early as the Old Kingdom and continuing well into the Graeco-Roman period. These are primarily autobiographies in the form of a posthumous speech in which the deceased addresses the visitors to the grave (including the family coming to perform mortuary services) and presents to them his conduct of life in ideal terms (Bergman: 73–104; Edel: 1–90).[8] Indeed two instructions were found on grave stelae: "The Instruction of Sehetepibre" ("The Loyalist Instruction") and "The Instruction of the High Priest Amenemhet." The paraenetic intent is to emphasize to the living the importance of right conduct and to present the idealized life of the deceased as an example for emulation. The rewards for proper behavior include long life, blessings, a good name that continues after death, a proper grave, and life beyond. In these instances, moral exhortation, including the idealized, paradigmatic life of the deceased, is given by the dead to the living.[9]

1.2   "The Instruction for Merikare." Two Egyptian instructions are presented as coming from dying or "deceased" kings who address their successors in proper rule. "The Instruction for Merikare" is a teaching without accompanying narrative, thus surviving in its earlier form (Helck, 1977). However, the Instruction proper does contain information from the life of the king, following at times the idealized biographies of tomb inscriptions. This information points to the three understandings of death found in the fully developed biographies: the preparation of the teacher for his transition to the next world, his ritual death experienced during the ceremonial transfer of rule to his son, and his mythic death which aids in securing and continuing cosmic order. He becomes Osiris, ruler of the underworld, and his son becomes Horus, the son of Osiris, who rules the Kingdom of Ma‘at.

The instruction of King Achtoes (I or III?) is presented to his son and successor, Meri-ka-Re, during the ritual of succession (Frankfort: 101–39). The instruction is either construed as a revelation from the dead (Otto: 114; and Williams: 14–30),[10] or as a teaching issued before the king had actually departed this life (Herrmann: 54). The transfer of rule occurs during the time when society and nature are recreated and their powers refurbished in part by the mythic vitality of the new ruler. The guidance of the father is given for the last time, and the son is to rule responsibly on his own. The father dies both literally and ritually.

The mythic character of kingship is reflected in the ruler's responsibility for the social construction and maintenance of cosmic order, created by Re at the dawn of creation.

> Well directed are men, the cattle of the god. He made heaven and earth according to their desire, and he repelled the water-monster. He made the breath of life (for) their nostrils. They who have issued from his body are his images. He arises in heaven according to their desire. He made for them plants, animals, fowl, and fish to feed them. He slew his enemies and injured (even) his (own) children because they thought of making rebellion. HE MAKES THE LIGHT OF DAY according to their desire, and he *sails by* in order to see them. He has erected a shrine around about them, and when they weep he hears. He made for them rulers (even) in the egg, a supporter to support the back of the disabled (II. 131f., *ANET*: 417).

Kingship was established by the creator to establish and maintain social justice. The admonitions and sayings make this role quite clear. Through cultivating proper speech that circumvents discord and strife, punishment of rebels, beneficent and just treatment of citizens, reward of loyal supporters, and honoring of the gods, order and wellbeing are actualized for Egyptian society.

The content centers on the attainment of wisdom and proper rule: becoming an orator, learning the traditions of the ancestors, respect for nobles, establishing justice, and honoring the gods. While this deceased ruler also passes his glorious accomplishments in review, he also confesses to personal errors which produced social chaos. As a result of his mistakes, the gods punished both the kingdom and him. This unusual admission probably points to the text being a piece of court propaganda which announces publicly Merikare's rejection of his predecessor's harsh measures, an attempt to bring internal political and social strife to an end (Williams, 1964). Other political features of the instruction include the official legitimation of Merikare as successor, the emphasis in the paraenesis on beneficent treatment of nobles, the army, officials, and the population, and the extending of a peaceful overture to Thebes.

In the instruction, the paradigmatic life (successes to emulate and failures to avoid) and the death of the deceased king are designed to provide both a nomos and model for Meri-ka-Re. If the instruction is heeded, he may rest assured that he will join his father in the afterlife:

> (But) as for him who reaches it (eternity) without wrongdoing, he shall exist yonder like a god, stepping out freely like the lords of eternity (*ANET*: 415; see 418).

1.3   *"The Instruction of Amen-em-het."* A similar text is the "Instruction of Amenemhet," attributed to the founder of the Twelfth dynasty (Helck, 1969).[11] While lacking a biographical introduction, this instruction also combines general paraenetic instruction with "biographical" information in the fashion of tomb inscriptions. Amen-em-het's origins are obscure, though he appears to have been a commoner who rose to the high post of vizier under the last king of the 11th dynasty (Tanner: 126f.). The continued contesting of the legitimacy of his rule ultimately eventuated in his assassination.

This instruction is also construed as either a divine revelation from the deceased ruler (Grapow: 97; Posener: 66f.; and Volten: 104f.),[12] or as a teaching composed by the king prior to his death.[13] It was also issued in the same context of ritual succession, when Sesostris came to the throne, either as co-regent or as the sole ruler following his father's death. Thus in the introduction, Amenemhet exhorts his son:

> Thou that hast appeared as a god, hearken to what I have to say to thee, that thou mayest be king of the land and ruler of the regions, that thou mayest achieve an overabundance of good.

The teaching begins with a brief section concerning disloyalty, followed by Amenemhet's recounting of either his assassination or an unsuccessful *coup d'état* by disloyal servants. The text remains unclear as to whether or not this assassination attempt proved successful.[14] In any case, implicit is the king's self-criticism that blind trust and insufficient caution led to his being caught offguard by the assassins. Indeed much of the paraenesis is concerned with this theme of taking precautions against the possible treachery of disloyal servants and the necessity of a king's keeping open a watchful eye for sedition. This confession is followed by the king's laudatory recounting of his many significant exploits in war and peace, serving not only to glorify his own achievements, but also to set forth a model for emulation.

The ending, while textually disturbed, seems to speak of the king's laying aside of his office and making preparations for death, including the installation of a successor to assume the reigns of government (*ANET*: 419). The king faces death, or has already died, in serenity, knowing that the kingship of his son is in place and will continue the mythic order of the Egyptian kingdom.

The historical setting for the rule of Meri-ka-Re is the turbulent First Intermediate Period (2160–2040 B.C.E.) when Herakleopolis and Thebes established rival dynasties competing for control of Upper and Lower Egypt. It is a period when invasion, civil war, and economic disasters undermined the stability of Egypt. Amen-em-het, the founder of the Twelfth Dynasty which begins the Middle Kingdom (2040 B.C.E.), is even assassinated (cf. "The Story of Sinuhe," *ANET*: 18–22). In this time of social chaos, instructions were either written by sages for old kings who wished to choose co-regents to make the transition of government smooth and less disruptive, or attributed to deceased kings whose wise teaching and legitimation of successors were designed to provide order and stability for new rulers. In either case, the lives and deaths of the rulers are both paradigmatic and mythic: wise actions lead to wellbeing for the son and the kingdom, while failures to incorporate the dictates of royal wisdom produce disastrous consequences for successor and people. Thus the king, at the time of death, issues an instruction and provides the model of both things to avoid and actions to pursue. While it may be correct to call these texts political propaganda (Otto: 114f.; Williams: 16–18; Volten: 85), they nevertheless provided a mythos of royal rule for their dynastic successors and attempted to ensure the stability of the Egyptian throne and therefore social order.

These instructions were copied by students in training for scribal professions for many centuries after the original actors were deceased. Helck lists five papyri, one leather roll, three wooden tablets, and fifty-nine ostraca of "The Instruction of Amen-em-het" discovered thus far (1969). The extant copies of "The Instruction of Amen-em-het" come from the 18th to the 20th dynasties (1500–1100 B.C.E.), during the New Kingdom, when the text was a popular one copied by students (ANET: 418). That "The Instruction of Meri-ka-Re" continued to have some important influence is demonstrated by the three extant copies dating some seven centuries after the original composition. Even though royal weaknesses are not covered up, these teachings continued to inculcate loyalty to the Egyptian king and state. Indeed they emphasize the importance of maintaining the social order to scribes in training for royal service in the Egyptian bureaucracy.

1.4   *"The Instruction of Ptah-hotep."* One of the earliest and best known of the classical Egyptian instructions is "The Instruction of Ptah-hotep" (*ANET*: 412–14). While a later development, the narrative attached to the instruction also dates from the Old Kingdom. According to the narrative, the vizier of King Izezi, Ptah-hotep, entreats his lord to allow him to select a "son" to "be a staff in his old age", i.e. to replace him at death.[15] In granting his request, the king instructs his vizier to teach his son how to speak that "he may set an example for the children of officials" (*ANET:* 412). The teaching is a rite of passage in which the sage prepares for his own transition to the future world. In the conclusion, Ptah-hotep exhorts his successor:

> Mayest thou reach me,[16] with thy body sound, and with the king satisfied with all that has taken place. Mayest thou attain (my) years of life. What I have done on earth is not inconsiderable. I attained one hundred and ten years of life which the king gave me, with favor foremost among the ancestors, through doing right for the king up to the point of veneration.[17]

The second meaning of the sage's death is also reflected in this text. The ritual occasion for transmission is status elevation in which the successor to Ptah-hotep's office is given a nomos governing his general decorum. Imitating the tomb biographies, Ptah-hotep praises his own virtues and successes and provides his successor with guidance for service to the king. If this teaching is actualized, the young successor will reap the same benefits which culminate in peaceful transition to the next world.

The instruction of Ptah-hotep also has traces of a posthumous speech, functioning to legitimate the social world of the Old Kingdom to students in training for civil posts in the Egyptian government. By emulating the loyal service of this idealized sage, they too may hope for rewards in this life and perhaps be chosen by the divine king for participation in the next world. And yet the *Tendenz* is not merely individual utilitarianism, for the narrative and instruction provide the social group of sages, normally the royal aristocracy, with a mythos which provides them identity, vitality, and cohesion. The order of Egyptian society, thought to incorporate *Ma'at* in its cosmic dimension, is secured by the socialization of new officials. Indeed, the instruction given to the successor is conventional wisdom, defined as the "ideas of the ancestors" who "hearkened to the gods."[18] This wisdom, as articulated by the successor to Ptah-hotep, is to bring peace and stability to the kingdom and, to develop loyalty and devotion to the king.

The instruction proper provides a series of prohibitions, admonitions, and imperatives sectioned into thematic units dealing with proper behavior for a sage in general and an official in the service of the king. The instruction bears the authority of tradition, the king, the vizier, and the social order characterized by *Ma'at*. *Ma'at* ("truth, order, and justice") is the primeval, divine order of creation which permeates the social order of the Egyptian kingdom. The instruction, grounded in and revitalizing this ongoing order, provides the social knowledge for the roles of the royal officials.[19]

2.1   *Instructions in the Hebrew Bible*. The Hebrew Bible includes several examples of instructions which parallel the exhortatory sections of their Egyptian prototypes (Proverbs 1–9, 22:17–24:22, and 31:1–9). Several are redacted into a narrative context which speaks of the death of the teacher (Gen 47:29–49:33; and 1 Kgs 2:1–12). These instructions, together with the narratives describing the sage's death, are usually identified as "Testament" literature.

2.2.   *The Testament of David*. The Testament of David (1 Kgs 2:1–12), occurring near the end of the Succession Document, shares many of the characteristics found in Egyptian tomb biographies and instructions. These include the three levels of death outlined earlier.

What is especially important is the narrative setting in which the instruction is placed: near death, David instructs his co-regent and successor, Solomon, in matters of state.[20] Now Solomon faces the responsibility of ruling alone, without the presence and support of his father. The instruction would be designed to provide the young ruler with a guide for bringing stability to the empire, torn by civil war and internal struggles for power.

In spite of considerable Deuteronomic redaction, the following royal instruction may be reconstructed from vv. 1–9:

> *Title:* "(The words of King) David (who) charged Solomon his son saying...." (v. 1b).
> *Prologue:* "When it was David's time to die..." (v. 1a). "Be both strong and a man, and keep the charge of the Lord your God, walking in his paths and keeping his commandments, his statutes, his laws, and his testimonies, as it is written in the Law of Moses, in order that you may succeed in all that you do and wherever you may turn, and that you may establish his word which he spoke unto me saying: 'If your sons hearken unto their path, to walk before me in faithfulness with all their heart and with all their soul, there shall not lack to you a man on the throne of Israel.'" (vv. 2–4).
> *Main Text:* (three admonitions/prohibitions)
> a. "Act therefore according to your wisdom and do not allow his (Joab's) gray head to go down in peace to Sheol." (v. 6).
> b. "Act according to loyalty (that there may be those [the sons of Barzillai] who) eat at your table." (v. 7).
> c. "Do not hold innocent (the one who) curses me (the king), for you are a wise man." (v. 9).[21]

The prologue is entirely Deuteronomic, developing this school's understanding of Davidic kings being responsible to the Mosaic law. Indeed, for the D History, the success or failure of individual kings and ultimately the nation, is conditioned by their response to the law of

Moses. After the Deuteronomic exhortation to follow the law of Moses
and the conditional promise that the throne shall continue (vv. 1–4), a
fragment of a royal instruction continues (vv. 5–9), in which David instructs Solomon in the policy of maintaining order in the kingdom: ruth-
less elimination of threats to royal power on one hand, and the reward of
loyal servants on the other (vv. 5–9).[22] While the author of the Succession
Document (2 Samuel 9–20, 1 Kings 1–2) has incorporated narrative details
into the instruction, three major admonitions/prohibitions with motive
clauses attached to the latter two may be reconstructed with some degree
of success.

The content of the original instruction has to do with royal rule,
and, similar to Merikare and Amenemhet, has the common topos of the
beneficent treatment of loyal supporters ("the sons of Barzillai" who are
given a royal pension: "eat at the king's table")[23] as contrasted with the
punishment of revolutionaries (Joab who supported Adonijah for the
throne against Solomon, and Shimei, a Saulide, who participated in the
revolution of Absalom against David). In contrast to two political enemies, Shimei and Joab, whose fates are sealed in the instruction, David
dies the good death: "And David slept with his fathers, and was buried in
the City of David" (v. 10). Like its royal prototypes in Egypt, this text
involves the tendentious legitimation of royal power and its abuse during
a period of political instability, in this case the beginning of Solomon's
reign. Thus the legend of a dying, wise king instructing his successor in
proper rule eventually develops into a fullblown narrative ("The Succession Document"). Yet even in its earlier form the Testament of David
would have provided the social myth necessary to secure stable rule. The
counsel of the dying king to eliminate enemies and reward supporters
becomes a part of Solomon's political rule and may well have served to
legitimate both the dynasty and Solomon's own position when both were
strongly contested (Perdue, 1983: 89–96; cf. Whybray).

Similar to the royal instructions from Egypt, the "Testament of
David" also gives evidence of ritual and mythic features. 1 Kings 1 tells
the story of David's selection of Solomon as his successor and then nar-
rates Solomon's enthronement.[24] The location of the testament in the
Succession Narrative, shortly after the accession of Solomon to the role of
co-regent, suggests a ritual context similar to the two royal Egyptian
instructions discussed above. The enthronement ceremony in Judah may
well have been a part of a larger New Year's festival in which the
kingship of Yahweh over the earth is celebrated.[25] In this larger festival
setting, Yahweh, having defeated the chaos monster, ascends the throne,
judges the nations, and recreates the earth. A variety of texts, including
Psalm 89, secures Davidic kingship in the structures of creation. With the

defeat of the king's enemies and the renewal of the earth during the festive celebration, the monarchy and Israelite society in general are securely established. The ritual passing of rule and the divine selection of the reigning king were part of a social myth constructed by the Davidic dynasty to secure its claim to the throne and to insure the continuance and wellbeing of the kingdom. The Testament of David, reflecting the practice of the dying king and founder of the dynasty instructing his successor in proper rule, would have been an important element of that ritual and mythic tradition.[26]

3.1   *Testament Literature.* Jewish Testament Literature draws heavily from biblical and pagan prototypes (cf. also Gen 49) by placing paraenesis within legendary narratives about the life, and more importantly, the approaching death of sages and especially patriarchs. As indicated by his diagram in the second essay of this volume, Gammie understands the Testament to be a sub-genre of both Paraenetic and Apocalyptic Literature. Nordheim identifies the following features of this genre:

> 1. Beginning frame—the writing of the Testament, the name and age of the composer, the names of the addressees, date and circumstances in which the Testament is given (the imminent death of the father and the gathering of the descendants to hear the last words), and the introduction of the speech.
> 2. Middle section—a look back at the past life of the patriarch, the instruction in which the dying father teaches his descendants about what he has learned from life, and a statement, usually prophetic, about the future.
> 3. Concluding frame—normally a concluding speech formula, specific instructions about burial, and the note that the father died (Nordheim).

3.2   *The Testaments of the Twelve Patriarchs.* While many of these texts have survived, the best known is the *Testaments of the Twelve Patriarchs.* In each segment of the text, one of the sons of Jacob is old and approaching death. He calls together his descendants to leave to them an ethical testament in which he rehearses the key features of his own ethical formation, primarily by referring to incidents from his past. In certain cases he confesses his errors, as does Reuben who laments his propensity for fornication, while in others the patriarch presents himself as a model to emulate (e.g., Joseph). In either case the paraenesis aims to teach the sons how to live, with emphasis placed on two central virtues: the fear of God and love for the neighbor. Death is not an important theme in the testaments. The design is not to aid one through the process of death, but rather to enable one to live wisely and well. Death serves only as the context in which the dying patriarch assembles his most important and best wisdom to transmit to his sons. The teaching is presented as the summation of a famous ancestor, who serves as an example for his sons (Collins and Nickelsburg). The actual instructions to the descendants vary widely in length, some are awkwardly placed in the narrative, and they continue to be the object of later redactions. And it is clear the narrative legends and the instructions had separate histories before being joined. In the redaction, some attempt is made to relate the content of the instruction with the narrative about the patriarch.

Also significant in these testaments is the frequent occurrence of warning: the patriarch foretells Israel's often grim future, but the hope for the listeners is offered in their obedience to the father's teaching. If the paraenesis is followed and the virtuous behavior of the patriarch emulated, then the disaster may be avoided, at least individually. In addition the patriarch experiences the good death of the virtuous sage.

While the later Testament Literature imitates earlier instructions and narrative legends, the mythic quality of the death and the teaching of the patriarch is emphasized. The historical setting for the Testaments of the Twelve Patriarchs, when the legends and teachings are united, is the second century, B.C.E. Our preference is the period immediately prior to the Maccabean revolution in 167 B.C.E., when the Jewish community was attempting to survive in the midst of political and social crisis. The legends of the dying patriarch and his teaching, representing the authentic tradition of the religious and social order from the ancient past, are part of the societal myth of a community threatened by dissolution.[27]

4.1.   *Paraenesis in Rabbinic Judaism.* Post-biblical Jewish literature includes the last words of famous rabbis given during death-bed scenes (Saldarini and Neusner, 1986). These last words, usually quite brief, are introduced by the explanation that the death of the sage is imminent. The more developed type is the deathbed scene in which the rabbi, about to die, is joined by his student(s). A question or action elicits the rabbi's response, and he issues a teaching. The teaching generally includes: burial instructions, exhortations to survivors, a prediction of the disciples' future, the appointment of the master's successor, and a concluding blessing. Finally the rabbi's death is mentioned. Saldarini's (28–45) study of both deathbed scenes and last words leads him to conclude: "The last words and death bed scenes are so constructed as to focus attention on the teaching of the Rabbi." And it is clear that the dying sage is believed to speak in a state of divine inspiration, since in that critical moment he receives the gift of prophesy.

4.2   *The Death of Rabbi Eliezer.* A good example of the above is the death of Rabbi Eliezer (Goldin). According to the narrative, Rabbi Eliezer is mortally ill on a Sabbath eve, and his students gather around him. Hyracanus, his son, enters the room and seeks to remove the tefillin from his sleeping father. Awakening, Eliezer restrains his son's action, and proceeds to chastise his students for not kindling the sabbath lights at the proper hour, the penalty for which can be death. Instead they had busied themselves with removing the tefillin whose use on the Sabbath is only a minor offense. The action then leads to questions about Halakah which the Rabbi answers. This exchange is interrupted by Eliezer's prophecy of Akiba's future martyrdom, to which Akiba responds: "Master, if so, teach me now." Eliezer then proceeds to teach his famous student the three hundred laws of the bright spot (Lev 13:2). The sequence of the questions and answers resumes "until his soul went forth pure." Akiba laments over the death of his master: "Woe unto me, my master, because of thee! Woe unto me, my teacher, because of thee! For thou hast left the whole generation fatherless!" And in the funeral oration he calls Eliezer "my father," makes a comparison of his loss with that experienced by Elisha at the transfiguration of Elijah, and regrets that he has many questions which must remain unanswered.

Saldarini suggests that this genre of Rabbinic story illustrates a form of last words which flourished between 70 C.E. and the end of the second century, when Judaism was struggling to maintain its existence in the Roman empire (28–45). This literature took on the character of a social myth in the efforts to maintain the traditional identity and character of Judaism.[28]

5.1   *Graeco-Roman Paraenesis* (Burgess: 89–261). Many examples of paraenetic texts from Graeco-Roman literature present the death of the sage in its multiple understandings as the occasion for the issuance of the teaching.

5.2.   *Isocrates: "To Demonicus"*. Isocrates, the Greek rhetor whose life encompassed the years 436 to 338 B.C.E., taught in Athens. Three works of a hortatory nature are ascribed to him: "To Demonicus," "To Nicocles," and "Nicocles or the Cyprians."

"To Demonicus" is a paraenetic text, probably written by a member of the school of Isocrates (Malherbe: 119).[29] The fictional occasion is the death of Hipponicus, the father of the youth who is addressed by the teacher. From the discourse we learn that Hipponicus was a friend of Isocrates, had social stature in Athens, and possessed a character of high moral virtue. According to Norlin, the discourse breaks into three major sections: "man in his relation to the gods," "in his relation to men, including society in general, especially parents and friends," and "in relation to himself—the harmonious development of his own character" (*Ad Dem.* 2–3).

The introduction of the discourse begins with an emphasis on the importance of friendship, with Isocrates extending to Demonicus the same friendship he had with his father. And he continues by stressing to the lad that "you are eager for education and I profess to educate; you are ripe for philosophy and I direct students of philosophy" (Ad Dem. 3). This invitation to study indicates the text also has a protreptic function. The text is thus both a moral treatise given to youths (Demonicus is a type of potential convert) to guide them in the development of their moral character and an invitation to study in the school of Isocrates.[30] These youths experience the ritual death of their own fathers as they enter the school of Isocrates and come under the guidance of new teachers.[31]

The recent death of the father is presented as the occasion for the treatise, since Demonicus is now in need of moral guidance in order for him to function in Greek society at the level of a mature and successful adult. Indeed the life of the father, Hipponicus, is to serve as a guide for life: "I have produced a sample of the stature of Hipponicus, after whom you should pattern your life as an ensample, regarding his conduct as your law, and striving to imitate and emulate your father's virtue..." (Ad Dem. 11). The emphasis on models of virtue became the basis for the more developed legends of the lives and deaths of famous sages. As was the case in the ancient Near East, these narrative fictions were attached to paraenetic texts attributed to famous teachers and philosophers. This pseudonymous text from the school of Isocrates is an example of this process in Greek culture, though in this case it is the death of a Greek noble, not the sage himself, that is mentioned.

5.3   *Paraenesis and the Death of Socrates.* Accounts of the death of famous philosophers are well attested in Graeco-Roman literature and developed into a rather substantial literary subgenre.[32] Henry Fischel has listed their common features: the issuing of a testament (usually understood as a will to distribute goods); final admonitions to friends, family, and disciples; and the mention of last sacrificial offerings (90–91, n. 5). The best known classical legend of this type, which also includes paraenesis, is the heroic death of Socrates recounted in Plato's Phaedo.[33]

In this dialogue on the immortality of the soul, intimate disciples and friends have gathered around their imprisoned teacher and, though sorrowing over his impending death, still engage in philosophical discussion. Socrates resorts to paraenesis on two occasions. The first occurs following arguments seeming to undermine Socrates' position that the soul is immortal (Phaedo, 84c f.). Thus the dialogue has come to a standstill, with the disciples overcome by *apistia*, thinking that the master's words have lost their power to convince. To reinstigate dialogue, Socrates issues a paraenetic exhortation that warns against the "hatred of arguments" (misology), i.e., the refusal to continue to seek truth through dialogue, either because of intellectual apathy or excessive skepticism

(Gaiser: 85–86, 155). Unexpectedly, Socrates even accuses himself of perhaps desiring to continue the argument only because of intellectual pride. The moment is dramatic and decisive, since at this point the philosopher's entire teaching and the justification of his life are at stake. This combination of paraenesis and paradigma, Socrates as teacher as well as exemplar and seeker of truth, succeeds in continuing the course of discussion which climaxes in the acceptance of Socrates' position on immortality. Paraenesis receives its power to convict by human example (Gaiser: 155).

Socrates issues a second paraenetic instruction at the conclusion of this dialogue, just before he drinks the hemlock. Crito asks what the disciples could do for him at this critical moment. Socrates responds:

> 'Only what I am always telling you, Crito,' said he, 'and nothing very new: if you take care for yourselves, your actions will be of service to me and mine, and to yourselves too. Whatever they may be, even if you make no promises now; but if you take no care for yourselves and are unwilling to pursue your lives along the tracks, as it were, marked by our present and earlier discussions, then even if you make many firm promises at this time, you'll do no good at all' (115 b).

Once more disciples are exhorted by a sage who dies in serenity and confidence.[34] Indeed, for Socrates true philosophers "are cultivating dying, and for them least of all men does being dead hold any terror" (67E). With the exemplary death of Socrates, there is the conformity of teaching and life, and the threat of disbelief is conquered by the congruence of paraenesis and paradigma.[35]

The response of the disciples to the death of Socrates is one of fear and sadness, "thinking of it as if we were deprived of a father and would lead the rest of our life as orphans" (116A). And yet to the conditional challenge presented by Socrates, Crito gives the expected answer: "Then we'll strive to do as you say" (115B).

Chroust interprets the efforts by Plato and other Socratics to produce a martyr legend within the political background of a newly restored democracy. The attacks against Socrates, understood to be the defender of the oligarchic, aristocratic system of government, were made by the late Sophists who sought to defend the struggling democracy (Chroust: 198, 209–23). Even though there is evidence that Socrates was himself anti-oligarchic, his death was moulded into a social myth that legitimated not only the socratic tradition but also a significant sociopolitical system.

5.4   *The Letters to Lucilius and the Death of Seneca.* The extensive corpus of letters from Seneca to Lucilius provides a *meditatio mortis,* for in them we find the sage not merely reflecting abstractly over the meaning of death, but engaging in preparation for his own demise (Rozelaar: 83–98).[36]

These thoughts were undoubtedly stimulated by the philosopher's old age, poor health, and the efforts of Tigellinus to persuade Nero to rid himself of his former teacher and counsellor.[37]

The last years of Seneca's life were a time of great literary productivity, including the writing of *De Otio, De Providentia, Quaestionis Naturales*, the Letters, and the lost, or perhaps unfinished *Moralis Philosophia*. The Letters appear to have originated during the last three year's of Seneca's life, while he was in retirement in southern Italy.[38] His friend and disciple, Lucilius, was procurator in Sicily, and at the time of correspondence was facing the prospects of his own retirement and approaching death.[39]

These letters exhibit the significant features of the classical letter tradition: *philophrenesis*—a deep friendship between the writer and the addressee, *homilia*—a "common life" between sender and recipient, and *parousia*—the actualizing of the presence of the teacher who is separated from the disciple (Koskenniemi, 1956; Thraede). These factors are enhanced by what Cancik calls *Selbstdarstellung*, the revelation of the private thoughts and emotions of the writer in the intimate context of a letter (Cancik: 46).[40] These letters become the means by which separation is overcome and friendship is sustained and even deepened (cf. 38, I; 40, I; 55, 9, II; 67, 2).[41]

To these common epistolary features is added the paraenetic style, for as teacher Seneca guides the "moral progress" (*otium*) of his friend. Yet this striving towards knowledge and virtue is a lifelong pursuit, one which Seneca is continuing. He is not one who has already arrived at his goal, but rather is on the way to *sapientia* (68,8f., 109,17). Indeed he emphasizes he is engaged in transformation, a kind of "new birth" or transfiguration, which he wishes Lucilius to experience (Letter 6).[42] Seneca attempts to actualize virtue in both his own life and that of his student (cf. Letters 26, 27, 89:23, 115:1). Accordingly, the moral life ever strives to integrate teaching with experience.[43] The philosophical life is a continuation, a journey towards virtue until death becomes that decisive moment when life and teaching have the possibility of achieving unity. Yet the teaching does not die with the teacher. It is to continue to have import for future generations (21:5).[44]

In approaching death, Seneca writes that, while death is unavoidable (Letter 13), its fear needs be conquered so that one may, if necessary, "go forth and meet it" (*Nat. Quaes.* 6, 32,1– 12). To meet death calmly, even to welcome it, requires *praeparatio*, which combines meditation about death with steady progress toward moral perfection, a task that is aided by the hearing and following of precepts. The readiness to die is reached when teaching harmonizes with life. Indeed while writing these letters, Seneca is involved in his own *praeparatio*.

Also important in this readiness is reflection on human models, including those who died an exemplary death (Trillitzsch: 95–112). Seneca describes the noble deaths of several people, including Cato and Socrates, who should stand as models worthy of imitation (71:7).[45] But even more important for Lucilius is the example of Seneca himself.[46] If Lucilius follows the path of his good friend and teacher, he may achieve that same desirable, tranquil death toward which Seneca himself is moving.[47]

Seneca's paradigmatic death is described in poignant fashion by Tacitus (*Ann.* 15:62f.).[48] Arrested and sentenced to death, Seneca's request for his will is rejected by the centurion. He then turns to his friends who have gathered at his side on the day of his death and states that he would leave to them the only remaining and yet most beautiful of all his goods: the image of his life (*imaginem vitae suae*). And if they would remember him, "...they could find in that reputation of virtue the fruit of their unalterable friendship." And as these friends wept, Seneca exhorted them, calling them to steadfastness, to remember and follow the precepts that would enable them also to accept their own fate in serenity and composure. Finally he drinks the poison and dies the death of Socrates. His own death fulfills the proper imitation of the death of which served as the great example for Seneca (71:7). Seneca lived and died according to virtue. Once more paradigmatic death is coupled with paraenesis.[49]

5.5.   *Paraenesis and the Death of Jesus.* Vernon Robbins (171–196) has recently argued that the master-teacher relationship provides the socio-rhetorical structure for the Gospel of Mark. Robbins points to three phases in the relationship: summons and response (1:1–3:6), teaching and learning (3:7–12:44), and farewell and death (13:1–16:8). It is the third phase that points to a convergence and continuation of the stream of tradition about the dying sage from Jewish and Hellenistic sources in the Gospel of Mark. Robbins notes that the third phase, farewell and departure, is divided into two major elements: the discourse about the future (13:1–37) and the acceptance of arrest, trial, and death (14:1–15:47).

Robbins compares Mark with Xenophon's *Memorabilia* 4 and the *Abschiedsrede* ("farewell speech")[50] in biblical and apocryphal literature: Jacob (Gen 47: 29–49:33), Moses (Deut 31: 1–34: 38), Joshua (Josh 23: 1–24: 30), Samuel (1 Sam 12: 1–25) David (1 Kgs 2: 1–9), Tobit (Tob 14: 3–11) and Mattathias (1 Macc. 2: 49–70). In these texts the last phase in the relationship between the teacher and the disciples is separation occasioned by death. The teacher is concerned to transmit the system of thought and way of life to the disciples and to exhort them to continue in the teachings. Thus paraenesis is an important component of Mark 13.

Robbins notes that Mark 13 differs from other farewell speeches and instructions in that Jesus does not recount the past but rather speaks of future events, including the warning to the disciples that they will experience the same trials that Jesus is about to encounter in the final portion of the narrative, but that they will be rewarded if they remain faithful to his teachings. Robbins suggests that what is found in Mark 13 is a "marginal farewell speech" with a "marginal apocalypse" (Robbins: 175).

According to Robbins a third type of discourse, which has important parallels from Graeco-Roman literature, occurs in the opening four verses of Mark 13 along with elements from the farewell speech and the eschatological prophecy. This is the temple dialogue in which Jesus answers a question about the temple with a speech predicting the sanctuary's destruction and detailing the proper course of the disciples. For Jesus the giving of one's life for the Gospel now replaces the giving of one's livelihood to the temple.

These three elements are forged into a new system (Gospel) that calls for suffering and rejection as a part of faithful living (Robbins: 178–79). What Robbins demonstrates, in our opinion, is a movement from the historical understanding of the death of the sage, to the ritual understanding in which present and future disciples enter into a new type of existence based on the teachings of the dying sage which calls for suffering and self-denial, to the mythic understanding in which the suffering, dying sage-king and the promise of the coming of the Son of Man to save the faithful become redemptive events which inaugurate the Kingdom of God. Mark's Gospel takes us through each of these three stages. The construction of this social myth gives cohesion to the Markan community during a period threatening its survival.

6.1   *Paraenesis and the Death of the Sages: Conclusions.* In bringing this discussion to an end, it is clear that a common feature in the issuance of paraenetic literature is the death of the sage understood in three ways: historical, ritual, and mythic.

6.2   *The Dying Teacher and the Issuance of Paraenesis.* Many paraenetic texts are placed within a narrative setting which recounts the approaching death of a sage. Calling together disciples and/or descendants, the sage issues them a teaching for life which serves as a summary of what he/she has learned. The teaching itself does not speculate about the nature of a future life, or what it is like to die. While occasionally admitting mistakes, the teacher more typically praises his/her own virtuous deeds. While other paradigms of moral behavior may be cited, it is clear that the teacher serves as the major model to emulate. Both personal behavior and the impending "good death" are exemplary for disciples who should incorporate the sage's teaching and example within their own lives. Through this process of preparation for death and the issuance of last words, the teacher engages in a rite of passage by which he/she takes leave of this life. The moment of imminent death is that point where there is the possibility of the correspondence of teaching and life. And in one sense the sage has achieved victory over death.

6.3   *Paraenesis and the Ritual Context.* Teaching and legend have their own separate developments before being brought together in their present form. However, even paraenetic texts which have no narrative setting (e.g., The Letters to Lucilius and 2 Timothy) on occasion indicate that the approaching death of the sage is the occasion for the issuance of the teaching.

Paraenesis served as a nomos for future moral behavior, being issued during ritual occasions when the teacher "dies" and the disciples, separated from their teacher, assume a new social identity. While a higher degree of responsibility is taken by disciples, the paraenesis issued during ritual passages continues to provide guidance in the future.

The recipient of the teaching is usually a disciple, at times the offspring, who faces an uncertain future bereft of the guidance of the "dying" teacher. With the teacher's passing, the prospects of anomy and the fear of an uncertain future loom large. The collapse of the world-view constructed by the teacher is an imminent and real possibility. The significant other who has provided the articulation of a meaning structure for existence is leaving. Thus the teaching and the paradigm of the sage's life and ritual death provide a nomos for life and hold out the promise for experiencing a good death, i.e., facing the end without fear and regret and surrounded by disciples and descendants who will preserve what is most valued by the sage: example and teaching.

6.5   *The Mythic Death of the Sage.* In many cases it is clear that a community constructs a fictive world in which a famous figure speaks to them. The teaching and narrative become a social myth designed to shape the group's identity and continue its existence. During a time of threatened collapse these myths take on an even more critical significance, for the preservation of the tradition and the maintenance of the community's existence are the major functions of this literature. On the social level, the paradigmatic death of the teacher is symbolically reexperienced, legitimation is achieved, and the threat of dissolution is overcome. And in the appropriation of the· teaching and its transmission, the community achieves, as it were, its own victory over death.

NOTES

[1] An earlier version of this essay was presented as a public lecture at the Georg-August-Universität Göttingen in the spring of 1983.

[2] Of importance for this study are the related subgenres: instructions, testaments, *Abschiedsreden*, and letters.

[3] See A. D. Nock: 164–86, esp. p. 176. In most cases all we have are these idealized, highly elaborated, often fictive accounts of the sage's death. Even so these accounts do reflect, we contend, one social setting in which paraenesis was issued. Peter Berger notes that death, especially that of significant others as well as the anticipation of one's own extinction, is the most powerful force leading one to question the normative structure in which everyday life functions (23). This is equally true of social groups and even societies as a whole. Thus idealized legends of the death of sages and the paraenesis they give as death approaches provide an important means by which this most serious form of anomy is faced and overcome.

[4] Brunner indicates that Egyptian instructions introduce the students to the social community and its rules of operation (1980: 966).

[5] This process was at work, for example, in the development of the Gospel genre. Beginning with collection of sayings (represented by Q and Thomas), a variety of narratives about the death of Jesus would have eventually developed from ritual occasions in which the sayings were used.

[6] Egyptian instructions belonging to this type include Djedefhor, Merikare, and probably Insinger (cf. Agur and Lemuel in Prov. 30–31).

[7] The instructions having this inserted narrative include Ptahhotep, Khety, Amenemhet, Sehetepibre, "The Instruction of a Man for his Son," "The Instruction of the High Priest Amenemhat," Amennakhte, Ani, and Amenemopet (cf. Brunner, 1980).

[8] For a translation of several of these texts, see Schmid: 202–23.

[9] The book of Qoheleth takes the form of this "autobiographical" narrative.

[10] The precedent for communications from the dead is found in the "letters from the dead" which the deceased sent to and received from the living.

[11] For a detailed discussion of the literary features of this text, see de Buck: 183–200.

[12] In this case, we would have an example of court propaganda, issued to contrast the benign rule of a new king with the harsh reign of his predecessor.

[13] Anthes has suggested that the king, some ten years before his death, instructs Sen-Usert I at the time of his assumption of coregency (176–91).

[14] The "Tale of Sinuhe" makes it clear that Amenemhet was eventually assassinated during the absence of Sesostris I, who was fighting with the army in Libya. The assassination was the result of conspiracy by a court faction supporting the claims to the throne by another royal son.

[15] The terms "father" and "son" are used in wisdom instructions of the ancient Near East for teacher and student and also official and successor.

[16] "Join me in the next world" (*ANET*: 414, n. 32).

[17] "Until death" (*ANET*: 414, n. 34).

[18] A variant of "of them that hearkened to the gods" is "of them that served the forebears," an expression for previous government officials (*ANET*: 412, n. 4).

[19] The fifth or fourth century "Instruction of Onchsheshonq" is a demotic compilation by a priest of Re in Heliopolis (Glanville and Gemser). Composed for peasants, and not for officials and royalty, this instruction is accompanied by a legend of the incarceration of ʿOnsheshonq. Although the instruction has a rural background, the narrative has its literary setting in the city and the royal court, a standard feature of the biographical narrative attached to Egyptian instructions. ʿOnsheshonq is falsely accused of conspiracy and imprisoned. In prison, he undertakes to write an instruction to his son on potsherds from wine jars brought to him each day. This text presents the

motif of the wrongly imprisoned sage who, facing the possibility of execution, issues his "son(s)" moral instruction (cf. Ahikar, *Phaedo* [the death of Socrates], the death of Seneca, and the Pastoral Epistles).

[20] For a discussion of coregency as a political institution in Israel which was borrowed from Egypt, see Ball: 268–79.

[21] For a discussion of the instruction genre in wisdom literature, see Lang.

[22] Viejola (19–20) has attempted to argue that vv. 5–9 are also Deuteronomic. Thus for him the Deuternomic historian (DtrG) is responsible for vv. 1–2, 4aαb, 5–9, while the later, more legalistic D redaction (DtrN), is responsible for vv. 3, 4aβ. I am more convinced by Langlamet's argument that vv. 5–9 are not Deuteronomic (321–79, and 481–528). Instead they belong to a pro-Solomonic stage of the narrative in which David is blamed both for the instability of the empire and Solomon's elimination of political rivals.

[23] See 2 Kgs. 25:27–30.

[24] For a discussion of the ritual of enthronement, see Bentzen, Johnson, Mowinckel,Von Rad: 222–31, and Widengren.

[25] For reconstructions of a possible New Year's festival in Israel, see Perdue, 1974.

[26] We may posit a similar ritual setting for another royal text, "The Words of Lemuel" Prov 31: 1–9), though here we have only the instruction without an accompanying biography. The one who issues the instruction to King Lemuel is the Queen Mother, a role of substantial power and influence in the royal court. While the occasion for the instruction is not specified, an appropriate one would be the ritual enthronement of the new king during the New Year's festival, following the death of the new ruler's father. In Israel the accession of the successor to the throne was immediately after the death of the king, though the ritual enthronement was delayed until the following New Year's. I suggest that this instruction would have been proper during this royal occasion, and is given by the Queen Mother who also has just assumed her official position. With the death of the father, the Queen Mother now assumes the role of one of the major counsellors of the new king, and issues a royal instruction to guide him in his royal affairs.

[27] See the instruction of Tobias by Tobit, who believing he is about to die, instructs his son in how to live his life (Tob 4; cf. 12:6–11, and 14:9f.). Similar to instructions and testaments are the so-called Deuteronomic *Abschiedsreden* (Michel) of famous heroes given shortly before their death (cf. especially Moses in Deuteronomy and Joshua in Josh 24).

[28] One of the clearest examples in the New Testament of the legend of the death of the teacher as the occasion for the issuance of paranesis is Second Timothy. The imprisoned apostle, approaching his death, exhorts Timothy to endure suffering as a good soldier of Jesus Christ, to engage in moral purification, and to beware of false teachers. Here one finds clearly the paradigm of the life of the apostle (3:10–11) for the disciple to imitate:

> Now you have observed my teaching, my conduct, my aim in life, my faith, my patience, my love, my steadfastness, my persecutions, my sufferings, what befell me at Antioch, at Iconium, and at Lystra, what persecutions I endured; yet from them all the Lord rescued me.

Paul also faces his approaching martyrdom with serenity and confidence: "For I am ready on the point of being sacrificed; the time of my departure has come" (4:6–8). Thus Timothy should look to Paul's teaching (cf. 1:13–14), example, and death as the paradigm for his own existence, for he and all those who follow Paul's teaching and example may expect to receive the same reward on the day of victory as he (4:8)

[29] For a detailed examination of the question of authorship, see Emminger: 373–442.

[30] Malherbe notes that protrepsis and paraenesis are often used interchangably. However, he differentiates the two by noting that protrepsis invites people to take up the philosophical path, seeking to convict by contrasting a superior way of life to other less noble ones. Paranaeneis is broader in scope, seeking to provide general rules of conduct in a variety of settings (122–129). For a similar, though not identical, understanding of these two terms, see Gammie's introductory essay.

[31] The death of the father is also the occasion for another text attributed to Isocrates, "To Nicocles." Evagorus, the King of Cyprus, has died and has recently been succeeded by his son, Nicocles. It is at this time that Isocrates presents to the young king instruction in how a ruler should deal with his subjects (Burgess: 38–39).

[32] Nock notes: "Popular story is full of philosophic martyrs who died rather than flatter cruel tyrants, as for instance Theodotus, or the Stoics in Tacitus, and there was a 'death-bed' literature" (1933: 176).

[33] Hackforth notes that in this idealized presentation of the serene death of Socrates the intent was to deepen the impact of Socratic philosophy in human conduct (3).

[34] Gaiser notes: "Die paränetische Besinnung in der Mitte und auch am Schluss des Dialogs erfolgt an dem Punkt, wo der Weg selbst fragwürdig und endlos zu sein scheint" (1959: 185). He emphasizes that paraenesis, enforced by the authority and example of Socrates, allows one to seek once more the truth. Gaiser remarks: "Das paradeigmatische Verhalten des zum Tode gehenden Sokrates beherrscht den ganzen Dialog, kommt aber besonders in der paränetischen Situation in der Mitte und am Schluss des Dialogs zur Geltung. Wie bei der Paranese in der Mitte zu merken ist, dass Sokrates den anderen nicht nur die überwindung der ἀπιστία-Gefahr vormacht, sondern ihnen auch als der zum Tod Bereite voraus ist, so gehören nun auch am Schluss das Vorausgehen in den Tod (115A) und die überwindung der aufkommenden ἀπιστία in der Paränese zusammen" (186).

[35] Gaiser notes: "Vor allem aber liegt das mit der philosophischen Paränese verbundene Paradeigmatische in dem Sokrates-Bild, das in der paränetischen Situation des Gesprächs zu erscheinen pflegt....In der Person des mahnenden Sokrates zeigt auch unmittelbar-wirksam die richtige Einstellung zum λόγος und zu den grössten Dingen und damit die ἀρετή selbst" (185).

[36] Rozelaar notes that 50 of the 124 surviving letters of Seneca speak of death.

[37] This preparation is emphasized in Letters 4, 12, 61, and 70. Of course, being a Stoic, Seneca looked seriously at the possibility of suicide as a door opened by freedom to escape the caprice of fortune.

[38] In defense of his retirement from public affairs, Seneca stressed he was committed, not to leisure time but to hard work. "I have retired not only from men, but from affairs, and especially from my own affairs. It is posterity's business I am doing. For them, I am writing down some things which may be helpful; I am committing to paper salutary admonitions (salutares admonitiones) like prescriptions for useful medicines...." (Letter 8, 1–2).

[39] For the arguments that these letters represent actual correspondence sent by Seneca to Lucilius, see Albertini, 1923: 136f.

[40] She notes: "Der Brief als literarische Form wurde offenbar von Anfang an bei den Griechen als geeignet empfunden, philosophische Paränese verbunden mit autobiographischen Zügen aufzunehmen." For a clear example of Selbstdarstellung, see Plato's Seventh Letter (Edelstein).

[41] Three letters deal in some detail with friendship (amicus) 3, 6, and 9.

[43] Grimal emphasizes: "Die Paränese ist niemals ausschliesslich an den anderen gerichtet. Sie gilt auch für den, der das Amt des Mahners versieht. Damit ist einer der wesentliche Züge der Korrespondenz erschlossen. Entgegen dem Augenscheine ist sie nicht fortlaufende Unterweisung des Schülers durch den Lehrer; sie ist auch ein Voranschreiten des Lehrers zu höheren Stufen der Erkenntnis. Sie ist innere Zwei-

sprache Senecas mit sich selbst ebensosehr wie fortlaufende Aussprache mit Lucilius" (162).

[44] While Letters 91 and 93 are purely paraenetic, 94–95 are theoretical discussions of paraenesis. The role and importance of paraenesis is especially stressed in Letter 94, 44–47.

[45] Another key example are gladiators. For example, reflection and self-control were incorporated in the life of the famous gladiator Canus Julius (*Tranq. an.* XIV 4ff.). What he believed in life, he demonstrated in the manner in which he approached death. Also see the description of Cato's death (*De prov.* II 8f.).

[46] "Das Selbstzeugnis als Exemplum gehört in die Mitte des senecanischen Philosophierens; in ihm wird die Einheit von Leben und Lehre unmittelbar bezeugt" (Cancik: 77).

[47] For Seneca's reflections on death, see especially *Naturales Quaestiones* 6, 32, 1–12. It is especially the conquering of the fear of death that is uppermost in Seneca's exhortation to Lucilius.

[48] The moving description of the death reflects the deep admiration of Tacitus for Seneca. For Tacitus one's values and course of life come expressly into view when death is confronted. In presenting this death scene, Tacitus appears to have been dependent on the subgenre *exitus illustrium virorum*. For a discussion, see Koestermann, 1968.

[49] Cancik emphasizes that Seneca's death is testimony for the congruence of life and teaching, *congruentia vitae et doctrinae* (111–14).

[50] See Michel, 1973.

WORKS CONSULTED

Albertini, Eugene
   1923   *La composition dans les ouvrages philosophiques de Sénèque.* Bibliothèque des Écoles Françaises d'Athenes et de Rome 127. Paris: Thorin et Fontemoin.

Anthes, Rudolf
   1957   "The Legal Aspect of the Instruction of Amenemhet." *JNES* 16: 176–91.

Ball, E.
   1977   "The Co-Regency of David and Solomon." *VT* 27: 268–79.

Bentzen Aage
   1955   *King and Messiah.* London: Lutterworth.

Berger, Peter
   1967   *The Sacred Canopy.* Garden City: Doubleday.

Bergman, Jan
   1979   "Gedanken zum Thema 'Lehre-Testament-Grab-Name." Pp. 73–104 in *Studien zu Altägyptischen Lebenslehren.* ed. E. Hor-

nung und O. Keel. OBO 28. Göttingen: Vandenhoeck & Ruprecht.

Brunner, Hellmut
1952   "Die Weisheitsliteratur." Pp. 90–110 in *Ägyptologie*, HdO 1. Leiden: Brill.
1980   "Lehren." *Lexikon der Ägyptologie* 3: 963–68.

Buck, A. de
1946   "La composition littéraire des Enseignements d'Amenemhet." *Museon* 59: 183–200.

Bütler, Hans-Peter
1974   "Die Epistulae morales im Unterricht." *Seneca im Unterricht.* Ed. Hans-Peter Bütler and Hans Jörg Schweizer. Heidelberg: F. H. Kerle.

Burgess, Theodore C.
1902   "Epideictic Literature." Pp. 89–261 in *Studies in Classical Philology* 3. Chicago: University of Chicago Press.

Cancik, Hildegard
1967   *Untersuchungen zu Senecas epistulae morales.* Spudasmata 18. Hildesheim: Georg Olms.

Chroust, Anton-Hermann
1957   *Socrates. Man and Myth.* London: Routledge & Kegan Paul.

Collins, John J. and George W. E. Nickelsburg, eds.
1980   *Ideal Figures in Ancient Judaism. Profiles and Paradigms.* SBL Septuagint and Cognate Studies 12. Chico: Scholars.

Edel, E.
1944   "Untersuchungen zur Phraseologie der ägyptischen Inschriften des Alten Reiches." *MDAIK* 13: 1–90.

Edelstein, Ludwig
1966   *Plato's Seventh Letter.* Philosophia Antiqua. Leiden: Brill.

Emminger, Kurt
1902   "Ps.-Isokrates πρὸς Δημόνικον." *Jahrbücher für Philologie und Pädagogik.* Suppl. B 27: 373–442.

Fischel, Henry
1973   *Rabbinic Literature and Greco-Roman Philosophy.* Studia Post-Biblica. Leiden: Brill.

Frankfort, Henri
1948   *Kingship and the Gods.* Chicago: University of Chicago.

Gaiser, Konrad
1959   *Protreptik und Päranese bei Platon.* Tübingen Beiträge zur Alter-
        tumswissenschaft 40. Stuttgart: Kohlhammer.

Gallop, David
1975   *Phaedo/Plato.* Oxford: Clarendon.

Gemser, Berend
1960   "The Instructions of 'Onchsheshonqy and Biblical Wisdom
        Literature." *VTSup* 7: 102–45.

Glanville, S. R. K.
1955   *The Instructions of 'Onchsheshonqy.* Catalogue of Demotic
        Papyri in the British Museum. London: British Museum.

Goldin, Judah
1955   *The Fathers According to Rabbi Nathan.* Judaica Series 10. New
        Haven: Yale.

Grapow, H.
1954   "Die Einleitung der Lehre des Königs Amenemhet." *ZÄS* 79:
        97–99.

Grimal, Pierre
1978   *Seneca.* Impulse der Forschung 24. Darmstadt: Wissenschaft-
        liche Buchgesellschaft.

Gummere, Richard M.
1917   *Ad Lucilium epistulae morales.* 3 vols. LCL. Cambridge, Mass:
        Harvard University Press.

Gunn, David
1978   *The Story of King David.* JSOTSup 6. Sheffield: *Journal for the
        Study of the Old Testament.*

Hackforth, R.
1958   *Plato's Phaedo.* Cambridge: University Press.

Harmon, A. M.
1962   *Lucian.* LCL 5. Cambridge: Harvard University Press.

Helck, Wolfgang
1969   Der Text der 'Lehre Amenemhets 1. für seinen Sohn.' Kleine ägypt-
        ische Texte. Wiesbaden: Harrassowitz.
1977   Die Lehre für König Merikare. Kleine ägyptische Texte. Weis-
        baden. Harrassowitz.

Herrmann, Siegfried
1957   Untersuchungen zur Überlieferungsgestalt mittelägyptischen Liter-
        aturwerke. Deutsche Akademie der Wissenschaften zu Berlin
        Institut für Orientforschung 33. Berlin: Akademie-Verlag.

Hook, Larue van
1968   Isocrates. 3 vols. LCL. Cambridge, Ma: Harvard University
        Press.

Isocrates. See Hook.

Jackson, John
1937   Tacitus. The Annals. 2 vols. LCL. Cambridge, MA: Harvard
        University Press. 45.

Johnson, A. R.
1967   Sacral Kingship in Ancient Israel, 2nd ed. Cardiff: University of
        Wales.

Kitchen, Kenneth A.
1979   "The Basic Literary Forms and Formulations of Ancient In-
        structional Writings in Egypt and Western Asia." Pp. 235–82
        in Studien zu Altägyptischen Lebenslehren. Ed. Erik Hornung
        und Othmar Keel. OBO 28. Göttingen: Vandenhoeck &
        Ruprecht.

Koestermann, Erich
1968   Tacitus. Annalen. IV, Bks. 14–16. Heidelberg: Carl Winter.

Koskenniemi, Heikki
1956   Studien zur Idee und Phraseologie des griechischen Briefes bis 400 n.
        chr. Suomalisen Tiedeakatemian Toimituksia Annales
        Academiae Scientiarum Fennicae, Series B, 102,2. Helsinki:
        Suomalaisen Tideakatemia.

Lang, Bernhard
1972   Die Weisheitliche Lehrrede. Stuttgarter Bibelstudien 54. Stuttgart:
        Calwer.

Langlamet, F.
1976   "Pour ou contre Salomon? La rédaction prosalomonienne de I
Rois I-II," *RB* 83: 321–79, 481–528.

Lucian.   See Harmon.

Malherbe, Abraham
1986   *Moral Exhortation, A Greco-Roman Sourcebook*. Library of Early
Christianity. Philadelphia: Westminster.

Michel, Hans-Joachim
1972   *Die Abschiedsrede des Paulus and die Kirche Apg 20, 17–38*. SANT
35. Munich: Kösel, 1973.

Mowinckel, Sigmund
1954   *He That Cometh*. New York: Abingdon.

Neusner, Jacob
1986   "Death-Scenes and Farewell Stories: An Aspect of the Master-
Disciple Relationship in Mark and in Some Talmudic Tales."
Pp. 187–97 in *Christians Among Jews and Gentiles. Essays in
Honor of Krister Stendahl on His Sixty-fifth Birthday*. Ed. George
W. E. Nickelsburg with George W. MacRae. Philadelphia:
Fortress.

Nock, A. D.
1933   *Conversion*. Oxford: Clarendon.

Nordheim, Eckhard von
1980   *Die Lehre der Alten I. Das Testament als Literaturgattung im
Judentum der Hellenistisch-Römischen Zeit*. Arbeiten zum Literatur und Geschichte des Hellenistischen Judentums 13.
Leiden: Brill.

Norlin, George
1961   *Isocrates*. 3 vols. LCL. Cambridge, MA: Harvard University
Press.

Otto, E.
1952   "Weltanschauliche und politische Tendenzschriften." Pp. 111–
19 in *Ägyptologie*. HdO 1. Leiden: Brill.

Perdue, Leo G.
1974   "Yahweh has become King over All the Earth," *RQ* 17: 67–84.
1983   "The Testament of David and Egyptian Royal Instructions."
Pp. 79–96 in *Scripture in Context II*. Ed. William W. Hallo,

James C. Moyer, and Leo G. Perdue. Winona Lake: Eisenbrauns.

1984   "'Is There Anyone Left of the House of Saul...?' Ambiguity and the Characterization of David in the Succession Narrative." *JSOT* 30: 67–84.

Posener, G.
1956   *Littérature et politique dans l'Égypte de la XIIe Dynastie.* Bibliothèque de l'École des Hautes Études 307. Paris: Librairie Ancienne Honoré Champion.

Pritchard, J. B. (ed.).
1968   *Ancient Near Eastern Texts.* 3rd ed. with Supplement. Princeton: Princeton University.

Rad, Gerhard von
1966   "The Royal Ritual in Judah." Pp. 222–31 in *The Problem of the Hexateuch and Other Essays.* New York: McGraw-Hill.

Robbins, Vernon K.
1984   *Jesus the Teacher. A Socio-Rhetorical Interpretation of Mark.* Philadelphia: Fortress.

Rost, Leonhard
1965   "Die Überlieferung von der Thronnachfolge Davids." Pp. 119–252 in *Das Kleine Credo und andere Studien zum Alten Testament.* Heidelberg: Quelle und Meyer.

Rozelaar, Marc
1975   "Das Leben mit dem Tode in der Antike." Pp. 83–98 in *Grenzerfahrung Tod.* Ed. A. Paus. Graz: Styria.

Saldarini, Anthony J.
1977   "Last Words and Deathbed Scenes in Rabbinic Literature." *JQR* 68: 28–45.

Schmid, H. -H.
1966   *Wesen und Geschichte der Weisheit.* BZAW 101. Berlin: Töpelmann.

Tacitus.   See Jackson.

Tanner, Rolf
1974   "Bemerkungen zur Sukzession der Pharaonen in der 12., 17., u. 18. Dynastie." *ZÄS* 101: 121–129.

Thraede, Klaus
1970   *Grundzüge griechisch-römischer Brieftopik*. Munich: C. H. Beck.

Trillitzsch, Winfried
1962   *Senecas Beweisführung*. Deutsche Akademie der Wissenschaften zu Berlin, Schriften der Sektion für Altertumswissenschaft 37. Berlin: Akademie Verlag.

Turner, Victor
1967   *The Ritual Process*. Ithaca: Cornell University Press.

Viejola, Timo
1975   *Die Ewige Dynastie*. Helsinki: Suomalaisen Kirjallisuuden Kirjapaino.

Volten, A.
1945   *Zwei altägyptische politische Schriften*. Analecta Aegyptiaca 4. Kopenhagen: Munksgaard.

Whybray, R. N.
1968   *The Succession Narrative*. SBT 2/9. Naperville, IL: Alec R. Allenson.

Widengren, Geo
1952   *Sakrales Königtum im Alten Testament und im Judentum*. Stuttgart: Kohlhammer.

Williams, R. J.
1964   "Literature as a Medium of Political Propaganda in Ancient Egypt." Pp. 14–30 in *The Seed of Wisdom*. Ed. W. S. McCullough. Toronto: University of Toronto Press.

Würthwein, Ernst
1974   *Die Erzählung von der Thronfolge Davids—theologische oder politische Geschichtsschreibung?* Zurich: Theologischer Verlag.

LIMINALITY AND WORLDVIEW IN PROVERBS 1-9

Raymond C. Van Leeuwen[1]

ABSTRACT

The "root metaphors" or "nuclear symbols" of Proverbs 1-9 are not to be confined to notions of the "way" (Habel) or of "Woman Wisdom" (Camp) but rather the larger metaphoric system and polarity of Wisdom/Folly, Good/Pseudo-Good, Life/Death together with the underlying notion of limits and boundaries created and carved by Yahweh as part of the order of creation. Just as at creation Yahweh set limits to the sea, so has Yahweh set limits within which are to be found wisdom, the good and life. Appeals to transgress the divinely ordained limits appear in Proverbs 1-9 as a negative protrepsis put in the mouth of the pseudo-good. Not only is the keeping of proper boundaries fundamental to justice, transgression of them is the consummate folly which leads to death.

1. *The Metaphoric System of Proverbs 1-9.* Recent study has made clear that metaphors and images do not exist as isolated figures, but that individual metaphors exist in systematic coherence with other metaphors. Generally, human communication employs certain foundational metaphors whose comprehensive character determines the order and coherence of the subsidiary metaphors in a system. Such a basic metaphor is called by McFague (1985) a "root metaphor." Lakoff and Johnson have demonstrated the systematic coherence of metaphors in everyday speech. But such coherence presupposes an even deeper structure of thought which the metaphors in concert express. This structure is the worldview, model, or map of reality which is held by a culture or social group.[2] Thus a social group may employ several root metaphors, each with their metaphoric "system," to express different aspects of a unified worldview. While such metaphors may not perfectly mesh with one another on a surface level, they will nonetheless consistently reflect the same worldview.

The systematic, coherent behavior of images and metaphors in literary works of art is even more remarkable than those of ordinary speech, as countless literary studies have demonstrated. In biblical literature, perhaps the most prominent device for rendering a metaphorical or semantic system explicit is what Sternberg calls "the structure of repetition."

The subunits of Proverbs 1–9 are particularly rich in intratextual cross referencing, repetitions, coordinated contrasts and juxtapositions[3]. Some of these have become commonplaces in scholarly discussion: the two ways, the two women, Folly and Wisdom, Father and Mother as instructors of their Son/s (cf. Habel, 1972; Camp, 1985, Yee, forthcoming). To this list the "houses" of Wisdom and Folly should be added. But a full scale investigation of these phenomena in Proverbs 1–9 remains to be written.[4] In this study only the most salient features and their significance can be pursued.

In 1972 Habel argued that the basic metaphor or "nuclear symbol" of Proverbs 1–9 is *derek* "'the route,' 'the way', 'the road'" (p. 133) or, more precisely, the polarity of "the two ways," one of which leads to life (Murphy, 1966) while the other leads to death. Habel's helpful essay was based largely on the ubiquitous repetition of terms for "road" in our chapters. He argued that

> as a nuclear symbol, "the way" has a system of satellite symbols or images which may be isolated, highlighted, or exalted to a more favorable position in the hierarchy of symbols which develops with a persistent use of and reflection upon the basic symbol and its satellites (p. 133).

In addition to the nuclear symbol (McFague's "root metaphor") of "the two ways," Habel posited two satellite symbols which embodied polar contrasts congruent with "the two ways." These were "the two hearts and the two female companions [or] loves" (135). While Habel's essay suffered slightly from his use of McKane's (1970) developmental scheme based on a dichotomy of sacred and secular (Wilson), his treatment nonetheless laid bare fundamental aspects of the metaphoric system of Proverbs 19.

Recently, Camp (1987) has put forward "Woman Wisdom as Root Metaphor" in Proverbs 1–9,[5] properly pointing to the fundamental significance of personified Wisdom for these chapters. Yet, Camp's work seems to miss dimensions of the text not comprehended by the Woman Wisdom metaphor. Moreover, she seems to misconstrue the nature of the opposition between Wisdom and Folly. This appears evident in certain hermeneutical moves which require, in her own words, "a purposeful misreading of what might be called authorial or editorial intent" (1987: 63). Among these is the attempt to "merge" the two opposed Women into yet another figure, "Woman Language"[6] on the basis of shared vocabulary. This reading draws a wrong conclusion from a correct observation (1987: 71–72, n. 4). Rather, the portrayal of moral indeterminacy, which the ambiguous vocabulary signals, serves to warn the young not to be taken in by superficial resemblances.

In my judgment, neither Habel's "two ways" nor Camp's "Woman Wisdom" are *by themselves* basic or comprehensive enough to be the root metaphor of Proverbs 1–9. Neither alone suffices to give order and coherence to the surface phenomena of Proverbs 1–9. Habel himself is aware that the relationship between "roads" and the two opposed "women" cannot always be explained on the presumption that *drk* is the nuclear symbol.[7] The mutual significance of the roads, the young men, and the two Women cannot be explained by one "root metaphor" or "nuclear symbol." Indeed, the images of road and woman do not at every point perfectly mesh. Rather, both the "roads" and "women" in these chapters are root metaphors which *together* embody different, though related aspects[8] of one underlying worldview. It is our task to elucidate not only this two-fold metaphoric system but to lay bare the "ideological principles [i.e., worldview] upon which it is based" (Geertz: 17). Such an explanation will make explicit the elusive "tacit knowledge" operative in these texts (cf. Sperber: x-xi).

2   *The Protreptic and Paraenetic Functions of Proverbs 1–9.* Most of the book of Proverbs,[9] including chapters 1–9, exemplifies a "paradigm of order" (Perdue, this volume) in which the order of creation regulates and norms socio-moral existence[10] in terms of distinctions and separations of places, times, and functions. In this type of worldview, reality is segmented and order is kept by assigning to all persons, actions, and things their proper limits, time, and place (cf. Prov 27:8).[11] Such thinking typifies many cultures and has been well described by Lévi-Strauss (10). In its present form, I argue, Proverbs 1–9 does not merely embody a worldview (most writings do at least that). Rather, these chapters are primarily concerned to inculcate a particular Yahwistic worldview.

2.1   *Protrepsis.* The social setting of the *instructions*[12] in Proverbs 1–9 is portrayed as parental address to adolescent "sons" about to undertake the journey to full adulthood with its responsibilities and rewards. In this sexually volatile period, a natural topic for instruction is relationships with women, to discourage adultery and to promote marital fidelity (2:16–19; 5:3–20; 6:24–35; 7:5–27). On this literal level, the teaching concerning the "strange woman" may perhaps also function as a warning against Canaanite culture with its sacred prostitution (Böstrom).[13] In addition the instructions generally invite the youths to a just and wise adult life (1:3–4), though these themes are not developed at length (1:10–19; 3:27–35; 6:1–19).[14] Hence, the primary purpose of these chapters is protreptic: to entice the "untutored" (*pty*) to a wisely ordered (8:5–21) and godly life (1:7,29; 2:5; 3:5–12; 8:13; 9:10).

Yet, the specific topics mentioned above are not the heart of these chapters. Marriage and adultery, along with roads and houses, are taken up into an all encompassing symbol system whose basic purpose is to depict the lineaments of a worldview. These instructions ultimately guide "sons" in a quest for cosmic Wisdom. She is portrayed as a desirable, marriageable woman (8:17,34–35; 3:13; cf. 18:22), who invites the naive (*pty*) to her banquet (9:1–6). The major threat to youths is the enticement to a false quest or "way" by the "wicked" (1:10–19; 4:14–19) or, more symbolically, by Woman Folly whose banquet invitation is the negative counterpole to Wisdom's (9:13–18).

The multitude of positive and negative invitations in these chapters are threshold speeches to those on the verge of adulthood. The young are invited (1:10–11) to "enter" (4:14) one of two adult paths just as they are invited to "enter" the house of Folly or Wisdom (9:4,6,16, cf. 7:14–20). Human existence is portrayed as a good or bad road "chosen" (3:31; cf. 1:29) by persons who consequently find themselves enroute either to death or life. The road metaphor has a dual aspect of "already and not yet." The right, the wise road is *already* "life" (2:8–9,20; 3:23; 4:11,18, etc.). Conversely the road of the wicked is *already* dark and pregnant with death (1:15,16,19; 2:19; 4:19) Yet the two paths have a goal, they lead somewhere, they have an "end" (*ʾḥryt*, 5:4,11; cf. 14:12; 16:25) which is either death or life.

It is particularly in connection to these contrary life-goals that the root metaphors of roads and women become congruent. Of the Strange Woman it is said,

> in the end she is bitter as wormwood...
> Her feet go down to death; her steps follow the path to Sheol
> she does not take heed to the path of life; her ways wander... (5:4–6).
>
> Let not your heart turn aside to her ways,
> do not stray into her paths...
> Her house is the way to Sheol,
> going down to the chambers of death (7:25,27).

If youths are warned off the crooked paths of wickedness, they are invited on the way of Wisdom, a quest (2:3–4) that leads to the door of her house (8:34) and ends with a banquet within it (9:1–6), imagery which again reflects the "already and not yet" of human wisdom. The dual metaphorical aspects of road and Woman serve to represent life as goal-oriented and human beings caught in a fundamental eros for either good or evil. Folly and Wisdom both appear as lovable (1:22; 4:6; 7:18; 8:17,21,34–35; cf. 5:19). Good and Evil are both somehow attractive (a matter for later reflection). But Wisdom is the dancing delight of God and humans (8:30–31; cf. Keel, 1974).

2.2   *Paraenesis*. However, these texts also have a profound paraenetic function, to confirm adult sages in their wisdom (1:56). For this audience, male *or* female, the teaching concerning sexual desire strengthens the metaphorical system in which male eros for woman signifies love for Wisdom or infatuation with Folly.

2.3.   *Social Setting and Date*. The texts present their instruction in terms of the universal relation of parent and adolescent, an image that refers ambigiously to literal mothers[15] and fathers and to teachers as metaphorical parents. The authors would seem to belong either to the aristocratic scribal circle or school of the pre-exilic royal court or, more probably, to its post-exilic equivalent in government and temple.[16] The question of the date of Proverbs 1–9 remains a vexed one.[17] But our interest lies rather in the explicit, self-conscious function of these texts as instruction to youth in a situation of passage into adulthood. This function is first of all a *protreptic* one which invites the youth into a life of wisdom. The secondary, *paraenetic* function of Proverbs 1–9 is to remind "sages" of their basic worldview and to confirm them in it.

2.4.   *Human Teaching and Cosmic Wisdom*. After the introduction in 1:1–7, we find two poems: A) the parent's speech in 1:(8–9) 10–19 warning the "son" against joining a murderous gang and B) Woman Wisdom's first speech, in the form of a prophetic judgment against those who have not harkened to Wisdom's voice (Murphy, 1987). The juxtaposition of these two warning speeches effects an identification of the parent's teaching and the voice of Woman Wisdom. In the human voices of parents and teachers, the voice of Wisdom is also heard; humans mediate archetypal Wisdom.

This point is superficially similar to Lang's view that Woman Wisdom symbolizes the traditional teaching of the Israelite school (granting that education has its roots in parental activity). However, Lang's position misconstrues the relation of Woman Wisdom to human teachers. If Woman Wisdom is a goddess, she is a mere fiction, a Durkheimian artifice to symbolize a human social reality, perhaps a somewhat desperate attempt to maintain the authority and sanity of harried teachers beleaguered by inattentive students.[18] But the logic of the text is contrary to this: Wisdom is not merely a deified symbol of human teaching, rather "parental" teaching should and can embody a deeper structure of meaning and normativity which the texts symbolize as Woman Wisdom (6:20–24 reflects the parental mediation of the salvific Wisdom of 2:10–12, 16). To refuse the parental invitation to hear in 1:10–19 puts one on a path (1:19; cf. 4:14–15, 19; 21:16) to death, precisely because it rejects the primal voice of Wisdom who holds life in her hands (1:26–32; 2:10–15; 3:16–26; 4:13; 8:32–36; 9:6).

Though the matter can not be argued here, I presuppose essentially von Rad's (1972) view that in Woman Wisdom we have the "self-revelation" of an archetypal normativity built into the cosmos, a *tertium quid* that mediates between God and the world, a something embedded in the fabric of creation, but which is not simply to be identified with created things. This cosmic Wisdom serves to ground and legitimate human wisdom teaching.

3   *Liminal Thinking in Proverbs 1–9, the Old Testament and the ANE.* It is the thesis of this paper that, underlying the bipolar metaphorical system of positive and negative youths, invitations/calls, "ways," "women," and "houses" in Proverbs 1–9, is a yet more fundamental reality which these images together portray. These chapters depict the world as the arena of human existence. This world possesses two fundamental characteristics. First is its structure of boundaries or limits. Second is the bi-polar human *eros* for the beauty of Wisdom, who prescribes life within limits, or for the seeming beauty of Folly, who offers bogus delights in defiance of created limits. Love of Wisdom means staying within her prescribed cosmic-social boundaries; love of Folly, like love of another's wife, means simply the deadly pursuit of things out of bounds. The other's wife is not *per se* evil. Rather, she is a misplaced good, a good that is not appropriate or proper to one not her spouse. Literal erotic love in these chapters is a symbol, in the proper sense, of cosmic eros for good or evil. For the acceptance or rejection of sexual limits is a particular instance of the general requirement that humans respond to the limits placed on them by creation. Thus, recognition of cosmic structure or limits is inseparable from proper eros or direction.

The images of Proverbs 1–9 thus create a symbolic world of good and evil where good means staying within prescribed religio-moral boundaries and evil means the trespassing of these limits. To stay "in bounds" means life, to go "out of bounds" entails death. Positive human existence is a life within limits, embracing freedom within form. But walking, living, loving beyond the limits ordained by Wisdom leads to death, like a fish out of water. Thus, the roles of the actors in these chapters are wholly concerned with their eros for the opposed liminal images of roads, houses, and women.

3. 1   *The Role of Limina in Proverbs 1–9.* The phenomena of limina in rites of passage have become well known especially through the works of Victor Turner (1967, 1974), and have recently been profitably employed to elucidate biblical texts (Perdue, 1981b, 1983; Cohn). The limen or thresh-

old in a rite of passage must be crossed by an initiate to move from one social status to another. Very often in the liminal period normal rules and social distinctions are suspended and social equality or *communitas* prevails. Such liminal transitions may move an initiate, usually a young person, to a higher social status or may culminate in status reversal.

However, the limina or boundaries which are elaborated in Proverbs 1-9 are not in the first instance markers of social distinctions. Rather, the limina in these chapters are primarily religio-moral, and only in a secondary sense social. Rather, a symbol system is elaborated which defines human existence as constrained by religio-moral boundaries. Crossing these limina means transgressing the limits of the good and entering the realm of death. Thus, the "paths" which the young (and old) walk are good, provided they they remain "in bounds." Contrariwise, evil paths, crooked paths, are "out of bounds." Similarly the "strange woman" is a liminal figure: to enter her "house" is to cross a forbidden boundary into the realm of Sheol.

Like other symbol systems in Old Testament thought, Proverbs depicts the world as segmented by boundaries, by limits that apply to every person, thing, and function (cf. Genesis 1). Limits in the social sphere are grounded in and reflect the segmented order of creation itself. Thus, far from being an isolated theological curiosity[19] within Proverbs 1-9, the famous passage on Wisdom's role in creation (8:22-31; cf. 3:19-20) serves as the cosmological warrant for the paraenesis of the entire collection. The socio-ethical order of Proverbs 1-9 is grounded in the creation order revealed by Wisdom who accompanied God as he set the cosmic boundaries. This was not abstract speculation, but fundamental for the ancient sages' experience of their *Lebenswelt*. In this way they provided a basis for grappling with the indeterminacies of ethico-religious existence. One must distinguish the boundaries that pertain within creation from the fundamental separation that exists between an omnipotent, all-knowing God and humans with their ontic and noetic limits.[20] The concern of Proverbs 1-9 is primarily with intra-cosmic boundaries or norms of transcendent Wisdom. But knowledge and observance of Wisdom's order is inseparable from "fear of Yahweh." Love of Wisdom entails love of Yahweh, and vice versa (von Rad, 1972: 53-73).

Though he does not refer to the instruction genre, Lasine's description of the function of other genres pictures well the socio-religious role of the instruction in Proverbs 1-9 even as it sets a good part of this paper's agenda:

> The idea that liminal myths and symbols, like riddles, can foster recognition of indeterminacy as a means of educating members of a society to make their

models of reality and order both strong and adaptive, has not been exploited to any great extent by biblical scholars (1986: 68).

3.2   *Cosmos and Limina.* Not all cosmologically based ethical systems exhibit a segmented or bounded world order. Instructive in this regard is the contrasting typology of Taoist and Confucian thought offered by Sinologist Norman Girardot. The Taoist and Confucian worldviews entail respectively

> a fundamental opposition between the 'uncarved' and 'carved,' undifferenti-
> ated and discriminatory cultural orders. For both it is the 'creation' of a new
> 'world'—whether primitive or civilizational—that establishes the true princi-
> ples of order and meaning; and for both the issue is one of the emulation of a
> paradigmatic model from the hoary past. The important difference is in terms
> of where that past is located—in myth or history, in an undifferentiated
> cosmogony or a hierarchical cosmology—and how it is interpreted
> (Girardot:78–79).

Taoists see the hierarchical, socially stratified world of the Confucianists as

> unnatural, disharmonic, and ultimately destructive of authentic human na-
> ture and the organismic balance between social and cosmic life. Because the
> hierarchical political and ritual order of civilization attempts to suppress and
> deny once and for all the natural values of spontaneous creativity (*tzu-jan*),
> and the primitive egalitarian/communalistic relativity of cultural existence
> (*ying*), there is a definitive break with the sacred transformational constancy
> of the beginnings (Girardot: 78–79).

Girardot's opposition of myth and history does not apply to Proverbs (or to the Old Testament in general [Knierim, 1981: 73; Roberts; Lang, 1986: 12–13]), but, *mutatis mutandis*, his typology brings into sharp relief the fundamentally "carved" (*ḥq*) worldview of Proverbs. Moreover, Girardot's essay, with others in the volume *Cosmogony and Ethical Order* (Lovin and Reynolds), reminds one not to neglect a fundamental presupposition of the instructions of Proverbs 1–9: that cultural and personal exhortation is grounded in the reality of the created world with its inbuilt normativity. "'Justice and Righteousness'... is imbedded in and in accordance with [God's] creation of the world" (Knierim, 1981: 96–97; cf. 81, 83, 94; Knight: 135, 139–40; Schmid, 1968, 1974).[21] The "good" person is thus one who conforms to the pattern of reality which can be discerned in the world (Von Rad, 1972: 78).

3.3   *Cosmo-Social Limits in Proverbs and Related Texts.* In the *locus classicus,* Proverbs 8:22–31, we encounter a number of stereotypical creation phrases. The phrase in Prov 8:27 is typical, "when he established the heavens" (cf. 3:19; Pss. 89:3; 103:19). This locution belongs to the set of phrases combining the root *kwn* with one or another part of the cosmos.[22]

What is the point of such cosmic references? What use is made of them in the biblical world? A glance at the various contexts, biblical and ancient Near Eastern, in which such imagery appears, suggests that the issues at stake are quite practical and down-to-earth.

An Egyptian cliché serves well to illustrate the point. Othmar Keel describes an Eighteenth Dynasty (1570–1345 B.C.) wall painting from West Thebes:

> In Fig. *124*, a qualified village elder, or perhaps the owner of the field himself, takes the following *oath* while holding the *was*-scepter: 'As surely as the great god endures in the heavens, this boundary stone is properly erected.' From ancient times, the *was*-scepter symbolized the immovability of the pillers of the heavens.... In Fig. *124*, the *was*-scepter held by the person taking the oath may illustrate the stereotyped saying: 'I have set such and such a boundary stone as firmly as the heavens are established.'... The earthly order emulates the heavenly, and like the heavenly, it is guaranteed by the deity" (Keel, 1978: 96).

The same sort of thinking, namely that human boundaries have their warrant in divinely placed cosmic boundaries, underlies Prov 15:25; 22:28; Deut 19:14; 27:17 (cf. Job's complaints in Job 9:24; 24:1–2,12); Hos 5:10; 1 Kgs 21; and Prov 23:10–11:

> Do not remove the ancient boundary[23]
> nor enter the fields of orphans;
> For their Redeemer is strong;
> He will wage their fight for them[24]
> [my translation, cf. 22:22–23].

In Egypt this notion of boundaries was fundamentally rooted in the concept of Maat, an idea combining the notions of world-order, truth, and justice (Frankfort: 63, 64; Gese: 14, n. 4). A key passage is the Old Kingdom text of Ptahhotep:

> IF THOU ART A LEADER commanding the affairs of the multitude, seek out for thyself every beneficial deed until it may be that thy own affairs are without wrong. Justice [Maat] is great, and its appropriateness is lasting; it has not been disturbed since the time of him who made it, (whereas) there is punishment for him who *passes over its laws*. It is the (right) path before him who knows nothing. Wrongdoing has never brought its undertaking into port. (It may be that) it is fraud that gains riches, (but) the strength of justice [Maat] is that it lasts, and a man may say: 'It is the property of my father" (Pritchard, 1969: 412, lines 85–96, my emphasis).

While the last quoted line may refer to Maat as an inheritence (so Wilson in Pritchard), it can also be taken to mean that the just man is saying, in effect, that his plot of ground belongs to him according to Maat, since it was inherited (cf. Lichtheim, 1973: 64). In contrast, the greedy is one who over-steps what Maat has assigned him. In any case, we here encounter, as in Israel, the notion that proper behavior is that which does not "pass over" laws or boundaries set by world order. H. Brunner describes the consequences of the transgression of limits: "Every straying from the path of Order is punished by god, usually without any explicit act of the will; rather the human who consciously or unconsciously errs will automatically stumble" (my translation; cited in Perdue, 1977: 21; cf. Prov 4:19, 27).

3.3.1   *Boundaries and Justice.* The keeping of proper boundaries is fundamental to ancient conceptions of justice. It must be pointed out that boundary thinking has often been misused in human history to rationalize injustice and oppression. Humans often seek to legitimate an unjust human order by identifying it with divine order. This was not the intention of the biblical sages who employed such thinking. Rather, the cosmic order embodies a normativity that judges the status quo as an imperfect realization of the norms of justice. A transcendent cosmic order constantly calls the human order to reformation.[25] Thus the sages would have opposed any attempt to appeal to cosmic order to justify an unjust status quo. Moreover, the various deities of the nations are zealous to protect not only the national boundaries established by them (cf. Jud 12:24 and the preceding diplomatic arguments) but also the boundaries of the poor and needy as symbolized in the persons of the widow and orphan.[26]

In both the Biblical and ancient Near Eastern conceptions, Yahweh or the gods who establish the cosmic order also insure the stability of the social order. It is precisely by virtue of their universal lordship of the cosmos that they have power to do justice in the social realm (cf. Van Leeuwen, 1986: 609). In Egypt, the human task of restoring provincial borders was "compared with that of the creator-god" (Ottosson: 361). In Josh 22:25, it is simply Yahweh who "made the Jordan a boundary between" Israel proper and the trans-Jordanian tribes, Reuben and Gad (cf. Numbers 34 and Josh 14–19).

Although the role of heaven as a stabilizer is not explicit in the Proverbs boundary-marker texts, Israel did employ this image (*kwn* plus *šmym*) in other social contexts (Prov 3:19; Pss 89:3; 103:19). However, we do find similar references to creation, the heavens or heavenly beings, and human limits or justice in several biblical texts. Psalm 146 speaks of

> the LORD... who made heaven and earth,
>   the sea and all that is in them;
> who keeps faith forever;
>   who executes justice for the oppressed;
>   who gives food to the hungry...
> The LORD watches over the sojourners,
>   he upholds (*yʿwdd*) the widow and the fatherless..." (vv. 5b–7,9).

God maintains just boundaries not only in the microworld of the widow and orphan. He also maintains justice and boundaries in the macroworld of international relations. In Ps 74:12–17 we find a cosmological doxology as a basis for a prayer that God may restore his people's place among the nations. In this plea for international justice, the poet declares:

Thou didst divide the sea by thy might;
    thou didst break the heads of the dragons on the waters....
Thine is the day, thine also the night;
    thou hast established (hkynwt) the luminaries and the sun.
Thou hast fixed all the bounds of the earth (hṣbt kl gbwlwt ʾrṣ);
    thou hast made summer and winter.

The argument is that since God has established the cosmic boundaries and order, he ought to do no less for international social order; the enemy has even entered Yahweh's sanctuary on Mount Zion, and order needs to be restored (Petersen: 148–49; cf. Kaiser).

In another context rich with wisdom vocabulary (cf. Deut 32: 28–29), Deuteronomy 32 portrays Yahweh's wise apportioning of the nations. Once again, the passage as a whole deals with the disobedience of God's covenant people and God's judgment and eventual rescue of them. Here God's judgment includes the threat of scattering the people beyond their borders (cf. Deut 4:27) and the obliteration of their memory (32:26) as well as the incursion of enemies into the promised land. God's social work of boundary keeping, if we may call it that, parallels his cosmic creative work, and is dependent upon it, as the language makes clear:

The Rock, his work is perfect;
    for all his ways are justice (cf. Prov 8:22)...
[But t]hey have dealt corruptly with him...
    they are a perverse and crooked[27] generation
Do you thus requite the LORD,
    you foolish (nbl) and senseless (lʾ hkm) people?
Is not he your father, who created[28] you,
    who made (ʿšk) you and established (wyknnk) you?
When the Most High gave to the nations their inheritance,
    when he separated the sons of men,
he fixed the bounds of the peoples (yṣb gblt ʿmym)
    according to the number of the sons of God[29] (Deut 32:4–8).[30]

In Isaiah 10:12, the prophet proclaims that Yahweh "will punish the arrogant boasting of the king of Assyria and his haughty pride." The king has overstepped his limits, even though he was an agent of God's judgment on Israel (cf. 10:5). Significant here is the Assyrian king's claim to *wisdom* in his rearrangement of boundaries:

By the strength of my hand I have done it,
and by my wisdom (ḥkmh), for I have understanding (root byn);
I have removed the boundaries of peoples,
and have plundered their treasuries;
like a bull I have brought down those who sat on thrones...
so I have gathered all the earth... (10:13–14).[31]

In connection with our treatment of Proverbs 1–9, Isaiah's water imagery for the boundary trespass of Assyria is especially illuminating:

the LORD is bringing up against them the waters of the River, mighty and many, the king of Assyria and all his glory; and it will rise over all its channels and go over all its banks; and it will sweep on into Judah, it will overflow and pass on, reaching even to the neck... (Isa 8:7–8)[32]

Contrary to the scholarly commonplace, there are allusions in the Old Testament Wisdom literature to certain of the historical traditions of Israel.[33] While this point cannot be pursued in this context, recall the Proverbs texts mentioned earlier which refer to boundary keeping. In spite of their much heralded employment of Amenemope, these texts (Prov 15:25; 22:28 [cf. Job 9:24; 24:1–2, 12] and Prov 23:10–11) presuppose the historical tradition of the giving of the land. For at that time, Yahweh established boundaries which remained the basis for justice throughout Israel's history. Job similarly acknowledges the *Landgabe*: "what wise men have told, and their fathers have not hidden, to whom alone the land was given, and no stranger trespassed among them (RSV modified, wlʾ ʿbr zr btwkm)" (Job 15:18–19).[34]

In the New Testament book of Acts, this tradition of creation and allotment of boundaries both temporal and spatial is preserved in a speech by Paul:

The God who made the world (ton kosmon) and everything in it, being Lord of heaven and earth... himself gives to all men life and breath and everything. And he made from one every nation of men to live on all the face of the earth, having determined allotted periods and the boundaries of their habitation" (17:24–26).

In the Wisdom of Solomon 7:17–22, such cosmic knowledge of allotted periods and times is a gift of wisdom (cf. Winston).

Thus, in ancient conceptions, including that of Israel, the concomitant human issues of justice and boundaries were predicated upon the existence of a divinely ordained world order.[35] The limits set on human beings have their counterpart and cosmic archetype in the good limits or boundaries, the norms which God has established for creation. We may say that creation order grounds and norms social order.

3.3.2   *Limits in Proverbs 8*. In Proverbs 8:22–31, the cosmic depiction of order by limits occurs in vv. 27–29:

> When he established the heavens, I was there,
>> when he drew (*bhwqw*) a circle on the face of the deep,
> When he made firm the skies above,
>> when he contained[36] the fountains of the deep,
> when he assigned to the sea its limit (hqw),
>> so that its waters might not transgress his command (*l' y'brw pyw*),
> when he marked out (*bhwqw*) the foundations of the earth...

Ḥqq is the key root in this passage. The divine royal activity of establishing cosmic *ḥqwt* is mirrored in the human realm of kings and rulers who "decree (*yḥqqw*) what is just" (8:15). The basic idea of this root has to do with "marking" or "engraving." In the realm of "nature," including the constraints of a mortal lifespan, the divine limits are necessarily observed:

> Since his days are determined (*ḥrwṣym*, "carved"),
>> and the number of his months is with thee,
> and thou has appointed his bounds (*ḥqyw*, Qere)
>> that he cannot pass (*wl' y'bwr*) (Job 14:5, cf v 13).

According to Knierim (1981: 87), the noun *ḥq* "when used in connection with the creation and existence of the world comes close to being the Hebrew word itself for world-order." Though this statement ignores other Hebrew terms for world order (*ḥkmh*, *ṣdq*, H. H. Schmid, 1966), Knierim here correctly emphasizes the essentially "carved" character of the Israelite world.

The words *ḥq* and *ḥqh* also often refer to God's commands to humans. In keeping with the mystery of human freedom, the nouns *ḥq* and *ḥqh* here refer to a "line" or "boundary" which can but ought not to be crossed (Job 26:10; 28:10; 28:26; 14:5; Ps 148:6 ['*br ḥq*]; Jer 5:22, 24; 31:35 [34]; 33:25; Prov 8:29 [cf. 8:27,15]). Here again the terms imply limits within which Israelites are to remain. *Ḥqwt* can be "walked in" as a path to life, but to transgress them leads to death:

> if the wicked...gives back what he has taken by robbery, and walks in the statutes of life (*ḥqwt ḥyym*), committing no iniquity; he shall surely live, he shall not die.... Yet your people say, "The way of the LORD is not just;" when it is their own way that is not just (*l' ytkn drk 'dny whmh drkm l' ytkn*) (Ezek 18:25; cf. Lev 18:4; Ezek 20:16).

As we have seen in Prov 8:15, the root *ḥqq* can also refer to the laws of human rulers which ought to be in conformity with the justice of cosmic Wisdom.

This crossing of limits is also captured in the phrase of Prov 8:29b "so that the waters might not trespass his 'mouth'" i.e., his limiting word of command. The phrase ʿbr py(w) (to trespass [God's] 'mouth' or word] is otherwise only used of humans who trespass limits imposed on them by God. In Numbers 14:41 the limit concerns the geographical boundary of Canaan (ʿbr ʾt hyrdn is elsewhere a frequent expression) which the rebellious Israelites are forbidden to cross. In the Balaam stories, greedy Balaam wrestles with the limits set upon him by Yahweh: "Though Balak were to give me his house full of silver and gold, I could not go beyond the command (ʿbr py) of the LORD... to do less or more" (Num 22:18). Again he says, "'If Balak should give me his house full of silver and gold, I would not be able to go beyond the word (ʿbr py) of the LORD, to do either good or bad (i.e., anything at all) of my own will...'" (Num 24:13). In the only other occurrence of this phrase (1 Sam 15:24), the reference is to the disobedient Saul's confession that he has transgressed the divinely set limits of his kingly office and entered the priestly realm of sacrifice (cf. Uzziah in 2 Chron 26:16–21). The appearance of this phrase in reference to the waters of the chaotic sea in Prov 8:29 establishes the congruity of Wisdom's order with the divine word of command. We might say that to disobey or transgress (ʿbr)[37] the limits set by God via his agent Wisdom is both to act contrary to the nature of reality and to disobey the "word" of God.

While the cosmic limits to the sea are firmly set, except for certain world upside down situations of judgment (Amos 5:8; 9:6 etc.; cf. Van Leeuwen, 1986), in the human realm it is otherwise. Here a perpetual conflict exists between the decreed boundaries and human proclivities for trespassing. This human moral indeterminacy finds its cosmic parallel in the waters which need to be restrained by God's word or ḥq. Water, especially the volatile waters of the sea, is the principle symbol for cosmic indeterminacy or chaos in Israelite thought, as it is with her neighbors. Within the bounds of this paper, only one non-Israelite illustration is possible.

The creation text of *Enuma elish* shows how the civic order of Babylon is founded upon the cosmic order of Marduk who has restrained the destructive waters of Tiamat:

> Then the lord [Marduk] paused to view her dead body,
> That he might divide the monster and do artful works.[38]
> He split her like a shellfish into two parts:
> half of her he set up and ceiled as sky,
> Pulled down the bar and posted guards.
> He bade them to allow not her waters to escape
> He crossed the heavens and surveyed the regions.... (Pritchard, 1969: 67):

Thereupon Marduk apportions to the gods their respective places and prerogatives according to the zodiac and heavenly bodies (cf. Wis. 7:17–

22), "That none might transgress or fall short." Marduk also appoints lesser gods (the Anunnaki) to set the limits of heaven and earth:

As artfully planned...
Marduk the king of the gods divided
All the Anunnaki above and below.
He assigned (them) to Anu to guard his instructions.
Three hundred in the heavens he stationed as a guard.
In like manner the ways of earth he defined.
In heaven and earth six hundred (thus) he settled.
After he had ordered all the instructions,
To the Anunnaki of heaven and earth had allotted their portions
(Pritchard: 68).

Then the Anunnaki respond by building Marduk's earthly abode in Babylon (cf. Deut 32:8–9). Once again, the cosmic order founds the social order and *polis*-building recapitulates cosmogony (cf. the creation language of the Zion Psalms). Important for our understanding of Proverbs 1–9 is the remark that Marduk, in parallel to the heavenly beings, also "defined... the ways of earth." Thus the dynamic or journey-like dimension of life is expressed in the figure of "ways" or "roads" which are "defined," i.e., bounded by limina. In Israel too, cosmic "paths" were bounded, as the parallel of *drk* and *ḥq* in Job 28:26 makes plain:

when he made a decree (*ḥq*) for the rain,
   and a way (*drk*) for the lightning...

The many Old Testament passages concerning the limits of the sea are well-known. But to establish our understanding of the liminal role of the sea in Proverbs 8, it is useful to call attention to the general function of these texts. Their role is to provide an implicit or explicit cosmic basis and norm for discussions and appeals concerning injustice in the human social order. The logic is essentially this: God keeps the chaotic sea within its bounds, thus, where humans have overstepped the bounds of justice, the cosmic Judge is petitioned to restore order to violated boundaries. To put the trespassers, so to speak, "back in their place." The Psalmists pray to God:

who dost still the roaring of the seas,
   the roaring of their waves,
   the tumult of the peoples... (Ps 65:6–7; cf. Rev 18:15).

Yet God my King is from of old,
   working salvation in the midst of the earth.
Thou didst divide the sea by thy might;
   thou didst break the heads of the dragons on the waters.
Thou didst crush the heads of Leviathan...
Thine is the day, thine also the night;
   thou hast established the luminaries and the sun.

Thou hast fixed all the bounds of the earth;
    thou hast made summer and winter... (Ps 74:12–14).

If it had not been the LORD who was on our side...
    when men rose up against us,
then they would have swallowed us up alive,
    when their anger was kindled against us;
then the flood whould have swept us away,
    the torrent would have gone over us;
then over us would have gone the raging waters
    (ʿbr ʿl npšnw hmym hzydwnym)....
Our help is in the name of the LORD,
    who made heaven and earth." (124:1–5,8).

In Job 38, which provides some of the closest conceptual and verbal parallels to Prov 8:22–31, God insists that his cosmic boundaries remain stable, in spite of Job's personal experience of injustice:

Who shut in the sea with doors,
    when it burst forth from the womb...
and prescribed bounds (ḥqy) for it,
    and set bars and doors,
and said, 'Thus far shall you come and no farther,
    and here shall your proud waves be stayed'?
(Job 38: 8–11; cf. 7:12; 9:8, 13; 26:10, 12; Pss 89:10–11; 144:7–8: Jer 31:35–36).

Even the Creation Hymn, Psalm 104, which contains similar language, is not devoid of a concern for justice:

the waters stood above the mountains...
At thy rebuke they fled;
    at the sound of thy thunder they took to flight.
They went up the mountains, they ran down the valleys[39]
    to the place which thou didst appoint for them.
Thou didst set a bound (gbwl)
    which they should not pass (bl yʿbrwn),
So that they might not again cover the earth....
Let sinners be consumed from the earth,
    and let the wicked be no more. (vv. 6b–9, 35).

4   *Liminal Situations in Proverbs 1–9.* Above I referred to Girardot's contrast of "carved" and "uncarved" worldviews. The same opposition may be put in terms of Victor Turner's typology of Structure and Anti-Structure (1967, 1974). Proverbs 1–9 is to be *primarily* (for the crucial exception, see below) characterized as presenting a structured socio-cosmic reality in which disorder, chaos and evil are aberrations which, in due time, prove inherently self-destructive. Such processes of "deed and consequence" or "*habitus* and consequence" (Skladny) function as *relatively* autonomous orders, subject to Yahweh's inscrutable timing. Good behavior consists of staying on prescribed paths, evil actions are trespasses over

forbidden limina. Folly is not staying where you belong, not walking on the path prescribed for you, not being in tune with the order of the cosmos.

4.1   *Negative Rites of Passage.* Significantly, the fullest portrayals of *rites de passage* in Proverbs 1–9 occur within dissuasive parental speeches. The liminal processes depicted by the parent are negative in character and constitute religio-moral status reversals. The teacher, either mother or father (1:8; 6:20; 23:22, 24–25; 31:1–2;40 most of the parental speeches in Proverbs 1–9 are not specified as to gender), warns her youthful "son" by encapsulating in her own speech the subversive paraenesis of the wicked. Thus the paraenesis has a "mythic function" which serves its "pedagogical purpose through increasing awareness of indeterminacy [i.e., liminality] in special 'safe' conditions" (Lasine: 49). The speeches of the "sinners" and, later, of the Woman Stranger, are rendered safe and harmless by being bounded within the teaching of the parent and the social setting of Instruction. And, ultimately, the invitations of the wicked are set within a larger framework of cosmic justice which shatters their promises of worldly success.

The young son addressed in Proverbs 1–9 reflects the common biblical view of human nature:

> every person is created by an all-seeing God but abandoned to his own unfathomable freedom, made in God's likeness as a matter of cosmogonic principle but almost never as a matter of accomplished ethical fact.... [Human's are caught in] a double dialectic between design and disorder, providence and freedom (Alter, 1981: 115, 33 in Lasine, 1986: 49–50).

The speech of sinners reported by a parent to a son in Prov 1:11–14 is the best example of subversive protrepsis reflecting a negative *rite de passage*. Here, in Turner's terms, the three ritual stages of "separation, margin (limen, 'threshold'), and aggregation (reincorporation)" (cf. Perdue's introduction) are represented *in nuce*.

The inexperienced son (psychosocially a prime candidate for a *rite de passage*) is warned by his parent, "My son, if sinners entice you, do not consent... (1:10). The parent incorporates the subversive protrepsis of the wicked into his own speech. In it, the sinners invite the youth to join them in a murderous roadside ambush (1:11, 16; cf. 4:14–17). This path constitutes a separation from law-abiding society, and the violent acts of bloodshed and robbery, as if in an ancient Mafia, mark the threshold which the young man must cross to join the gang. Thus would he be "incorporated" into a society from which there is no return. And, in contrast to the segmented society of Proverbs, the company of sinners represents itself as a perpetual Turnerian *communitas* making egalitarian and utopian claims:

> we shall find all precious goods;
>   we shall fill our houses with spoil;
>   throw in your lot among us,
>   we shall all have one purse... (1:13–14).

A significant liminal symbol occurs in the sinner's speech:

> like Sheol let us swallow them alive and whole
>   like those who go down to the pit (1:12).

The mouth-of-Sheol figure captures the limitless appetite of greed (cf. Plöger: 16), but also condemns the sinners out of their own mouth: their activity places them on the limen not only of legitimate society, but at the very maw of death. We should note also that the image of swallowing-the-living occurs in Ps 124:2–5 coupled with water, Israel's basic metaphor for the indeterminacy of limina:

> if it had not been the LORD who was on our side,
>   when people rose up against us,
> then they would have swallowed us up alive,
>   when their anger was kindled against us;
> then the flood would have swept us away
>   the torrent would have gone over us;
> then over us would have gone the raging waters.

The society of brigands in Prov 1:1–19 offers the illusion of perpetual marginality with the egalitarian prosperity of *communitas*. The parent, however, warns the son of the inherent instability of such anti-structure. For the limits set by Yahweh/Wisdom are the boundaries of life. The end of sinners is death, and thus the parent sounds a theme that rings throughout 1–9 and the entire book:

> these people lie in wait for their own blood,
>   they set an ambush for their own lives.
> Such are the ways of all who get gain by violence;
>   it takes away the life of its possessors (1:18–19).

Plöger (15, 17, 20; cf. Lang, 1986: 15) thrice suggests that the parent's example of greed and murder is "an extreme case" which "admits no generalization." This seems a puzzling suggestion in a century that has known two World Wars, countless small ones, and an infinity of terrorist acts both political and personal. It is true the parent's vignette portrays radical evil, which some scholars locate in the Persian or Greek era, but such violence is universal (Ringgren 1981: 15). It is also an American reality, as M. Scott Peck's analysis of the stateside social background of the

Mylai massacre in Vietnam reminds us. The parent is brutally realistic and lays out the issues in line with the Prologue to 1–9: "receive instruction in wise dealing, righteousness, justice, and equity (ṣdq, wmšpt, wmyšrym)" (1:3; cf. 2:9; 8:8, 9, 15–16, 20). It is necessary to attend again to the literal sense of such a passage in order to dispel scholarly myths of Proverbs as a book of bourgeois complacency (cf. Knierim, 1984: 43–44). The dissuasive protrepsis of Prov 1:10–19 would be as suitable on the lips of a mother in Chicago's South Side, or of a father to a potential KGB or CIA recruit, as it would be to the mother of an Israelite lad considering joining one of the bloody rival gangs in the days of Abimelech (Judg 9:4, 25, 29).

These issues of justice and righteousness, of keeping proper boundaries, are of unceasing relevance to the basic problems of the modern world. Most of the world is concerned about territoriality, both international and intranational, both political and private. One need only point to Russia and Afghanistan, India and Sri Lanka, Israel and the West Bank-Gaza Strip, Ireland and England, Cyprus and Greece and Turkey, South Africa and the so-called homelands, the USA and Central America. In these places, justice does not merely concern national sovereignties. Rather it concerns the division of land between rich and poor, catholic and protestant, Tamil and Indian, peasant and landowner. On the level of peasant existence, the issue is adequate ground to feed one's family.

The account of a young man's invitation into a community of death in Prov 1:10–19 has its parallel in the deadly invitations of the Strange Woman or Woman Folly (7:10–27; 9:13–18) to cross her threshold. Moreover, Prov 1:10–19 is echoed by Prov 2:12–15 and 4:14–16, 19. In Chapter 2, the son is urged to pursue wisdom which will keep him both from wicked men and the Woman Stranger. First, Wisdom will

> deliver... you from the way of evil (drk rʿ)
>   from people of perverted speech,
> who forsake the paths of uprightness (ʾrḥwt yšr)
>   to walk in the ways of darkness (drky ḥsk).
> who rejoice in doing evil
>   and delight in the perverseness of evil (thpkwt rʿ);
> those whose paths are crooked (ʾrḥtyhm ʿqšym),
>   and who are devious in their ways (nlwzym bmʿglwtm) (2:12–15).

Second, and parallel to the deliverance from "people of perverted speech," wisdom rescues the young from the Strange Woman (ʾšh zrh 2:16–19). The language and images of 2:12–15 (re the wicked) and of 2:16–19 (re "strange woman") are deliberately parallel and belong to the same semantic field. In particular, the striking repetition of the opening words in lines one and two of each section (v. 12 lhṣylk... mʾyš...// v. 16, lhṣlyk mʾšh zrh; vv. 13, 17 hʿzbym//hʿzbt) establishes the wicked man and the strange woman as parallel entities from whose seductive speech (Aletti, 1977) and deadly paths Wisdom alone can rescue.

This point needs to be made, for it is an important clue regarding the symbolism of evil as feminine in Proverbs 1–9. It is true that adultery is considered a great evil in Proverbs and the Old Testament. However, in Proverbs 1–9, evil is not inherently feminine any more than Good or Wisdom is inherently feminine (*pace* Camp), nor is literal seduction and adultery *per se* the primary concern of these chapters (*pace* Crenshaw, 1981: 86–89). Rather, literal adultery and seduction are incorporated into a symbolic system of good and evil, life and death. If the short poems are isolated, they serve as warnings against marital infidelity. But in the larger context of Proverbs 1–9, they serve as powerful metaphors to reinforce the primary message of the collection. *In this world there are two contrary loves: for Wisdom, Good, and Life or for Folly, Pseudo-good, and Death.*

Woman Folly is a powerful literary figure. She shows that invitations to cross proscribed limina are as seductive as a beautiful woman to an adolescent boy suffering from testosterone poisoning. Conversely, Lady Wisdom offers humans the delights of love within limits, of *communitas* within the bounds of monogamy. In a quite different cultural sphere, Plato's *Symposium* builds a similar dual symbolic edifice on the basis of paedophilia.

Yee (forthcoming) lays a convincing foundation for the position that, throughout Proverbs 1–9, Woman Stranger/Folly is an antithetical counterpart to woman Wisdom. The various depictions of negative women are simply alternate formulations of essentially one figure just as *bynh, tbwnh, d't,* and a cluster of related concepts serve to round out the picture of Woman Wisdom (*Hkmh*) in these chapters.

4.2   *Positive Rites of Passage: Water and Women in Proverbs 1–9.* Like honey (Prov 5:3; 24:13–14; 25:16,27; 27:7), water is a fluid entity that can symbolize the difficulty of marking and keeping limits. Too much honey is not good (25:16, 27; 27:7), but the honey proper to a man is very sweet indeed (24:13–14, referring to wisdom). The strange woman's lips drip honey in invitation to enter forbidden orifices (5:3,[41] 9:16), to cross illicit limina (9:14 *pth byth,* 16a), to drink "stolen waters." "Stolen waters," she says, "are sweet" (9:17a) combining honey and water in what is surely one of the loveliest images ever to flow from the mouth of death. There is a metaphorical resonance between the deadly openings of the strange woman's body and the opening to her house, the crossing of whose limen or threshold puts one in the realm of death (Alter, 1985: 181–82):[42] "do not go near the door of her house (*pth byth*)" (5:8b) for "her house is the way to Sheol, going down to the chambers of death" (7:27; cf. 2:18–19; 5:5; 9:18; Job 30:23).

All this is in contrast to Woman Wisdom who pronounces a blessing just before the famous passage where she builds her house and invites the simple to come inside (9:1–6):

> Happy is the man who listens to me,
>   watching daily at my gates,
>   waiting beside my doors (*pthy*)
> For he who finds me finds life
>   and obtains favor from the LORD.

Significantly, the last verse has its precise counterpart in the acquiring of a wife:

> He who finds a wife finds good
>   and obtains favor from the LORD (18:22).

Thus the passage into a wholesome and healthy adulthood, which entailed for the Israelite male a faithful marriage, has its deeper source in a love for Wisdom. The young are invited, and the old reminded, to enter Wisdom's house where life is served as food and drink. As noted above, in the cosmic realm God has set wise limits to the fluid sea which else might overwhelm the earth. In the same way humans must set limits to the flow of their sexual fluids:

> Drink water from your own cistern,
>   flowing water from your own well.
> Should your springs be scattered abroad,
>   streams of water in the streets?
> Let them be for yourself alone,
>   and not for strangers (*zrym*) with you (cf. 5:10).
> Let your fountain be blessed,
>   and rejoice in the wife of your youth…
> Let her affection/breasts "water you" (*yrwk*, cf. 7;18)
>   at all times with delight,
>   be infatuated always with her love.
> Why should you be infatuated, my son,
>   with a strange woman (*'šh zrh*)
>   and embrace the bosom of an adventuress?
> For a man's ways are before the eyes of the LORD,
>   and he watches all his paths (Prov 5:15–21).[43]

In terms of the symbol system of Proverbs 1–9, the water images of this passage[44] are a crucial anchor for the line which connects the human world of boundaries to the cosmic limina which God by Wisdom set to the waters at creation (Prov 8:24,27,29).

It also gives us an important clue as to the nature of legitimate *communitas* in the worldview of Proverbs 1–9. Turner has pointed out that every healthy society requires both structure and anti-structure: any given society needs a healthy interaction of structure and *communitas* (Turner, 1974: 238, 268; cf. 1969: 130 and Lasine's discussion, 1986:60).

> The varied expressions of *communitas* such as monasteries, convents, socialist bastions, semireligious communities and brotherhoods, nudist colonies, communes in the modern counterculture, initiation camps, have often found it necessary to surround themselves with real as well as symbolic walls—a species of what structural sociologists would call 'boundary maintaining mechanisms.'... Thus to keep out structure, structure has to be constantly maintained and reinforced.... What seems to be needed...is... to discover what is the right relationship between structure and *communitas* at a given time and place in history and geography, to give to each its due.... What seems to be the case is that the social has a free or unbound as well as bonded or bound dimension, the dimension of *communitas* in which men confront one another not as role players but as 'human totals,' integral beings who recognizantly [sic] share the same humanity" (Turner, 1974: 269).

Where then in the bounded world of Proverbs 1–9 does this necessary dimension of healthy *communitas* take place? It seems to me that the proper place of true *communitas*, of legitimate equality and comradeship in love, is *symbolized* by the liquid abandonment of married love in chapter 5. Here the two sexes are one flesh, a *communitas* where fellowship exists without the rules and clothing markers of structured society (Gen 2:23–25; Song of Songs). This reality has its parallel at Sinai. As Cohn (18–19) has shown,

> for the covenant brotherhood forged at Sinai, "structure is not opposed to *communitas*... but rather completes and guarantees it." In fact, "the law makes *communitas* possible" (Lasine, 1986: 60).

In Proverbs 1–9, Wisdom offers love within limits, freedom within form, life within law. It is within the bounds of cosmic order that human freedom and fellowship are nurtured.

In contrast to Wisdom, Woman Stranger and sinners promise a *communitas* of wealth and unbridled passion. Their invitations, however, conceal only a *communitas* of death (1:32; 2:18; 5:5; 7:26,27; 9:18).[45]

NOTES

[1] An earlier version of this paper was read at the 1987 Annual Meeting of the Society of Biblical Literature in Boston.

[2] This anthropological point is, not uncritically, described by Geertz: "Culture is most effectively treated, the argument goes, purely as a symbolic system... by isolating its elements, specifying the internal relationships among those elements, and then characterizing the whole system in some general way—according to the core symbols around which it is organized, the underlying structures of which it is the surface expression, or the ideological principles upon which it is based" (Geertz: 17). Geertz rejects the "purely" of the above description and insists on "thick description" of "the informal logic of actual life," of behavior as "symbolic action."

3 These important phenomena are often dismissed by commentators. Lang (1986: 15–16) is typical: Proverbs 1-9 is "not... a consciously contructed [sic] literary work, but just a collection of didactic poetry, a collection of brief discourses and poems for use in teaching, a reading text that serves as a source book for teachers.... *No passage presupposes another.* Some parts are almost identical in content and may be exchanged readily" (my emphasis). If it were true that "no passage presupposes another," then the task of interpretation would be impossible. Such assumptions concerning the text allow a reader's "imagination" free rein (Lang, 1986: 6), but miss precisely those literary devices which create "foolproof compositions"—texts difficult to counterread. Of course, "no text can withstand the kind of methodological license indulged in by the rabbis in contexts other than legal, or by critics who mix up their quest for the source with the need to fabricate a new discourse.... Short of such extremes, biblical narrative is virtually impossible to counterread. The essentials are made transparent to all comers: the story line, the world order, the value system" (Sternberg: 50).

4 Dennis Pardee's detailed study of Proverbs 2 should be forthcoming shortly in VTSup. However, Pardee does not treat chapter 2's relation to other subunits in 1-9 (written communication).

5 In her 1985 book, Camp had noted the lack of evidence for an Israelite "goddess" Wisdom (cf. Albright, Lang, 1986) and that Boström's "interpretation of personified wisdom as a substitute for Ishtar presents theological problems as well. What is the relationship of a female figure, presented as a goddess, to Yahweh?" (1985: 28). In her most recent work on Woman Wisdom, however, Camp entertains the idea of Wisdom as a "Goddess," not so much on the basis of historical and exegetical argument as on the desiderata of feminist theology (1987: 61).

6 "Together, Woman Wisdom and the Strange Woman help constitute another metaphor, Woman Language, or, in biblical terms, 'Lady Tongue.'... Bonded in her humanity to the Strange Woman whom she opposes, Woman Wisdom enters into the fray of human existence.... Woman Language offers two fruits, death and life, and those who become her lovers can expect to taste of both" (1987: 52). This "allegoresis" literally confuses good and evil, which Proverbs everywhere insists on keeping radically separate. The ambiguity of the tongue in Prov 18:21 regarding life and death, like the opposition of the two Women in Proverbs 1-9, reveals the dangerous moral indeterminacy of things which are superficially the same. It is not necessary to follow Buhlmann's translation and exegesis to reach this conclusion: "Tod und Leben sind in der Gewalt der Zunge, und das, was man liebt, dessen Frucht isst man" (Bühlmann: 318–21)

7 "Wisdom is exalted... in such a way that the nuclear symbol of the way seems to be relegated to the background" (1972: 141).

8 On the "aspectual" character of ancient Near Eastern depictions of reality, see Keel (1978:9–11). The same reality or object can be portrayed through a "multiplicity of approaches" which modern, Western thought might find contradictory or inconsistent.

9 The Agur speech in Prov 30:1–4 may be an exception.

10 Such "paradigms" of cosmic order, with variations, are found throughout the ancient Near East. J. Halbe's extensive critique of H. H. Schmid's emphasis (1968, 1974) on "altorientalisches Weltordnungsdenken" in OT thought does not adequately recognize the extent to which the ancient oriental cultures shared common presuppositions about reality, in spite of their specific cultural differences.

11 Among the important agenda for Old Testament and ancient Near Eastern studies is the systematic comparison of symbol systems, both with regard to their commonalities and their differences (cf. Knierim, Schmid 1968). While it cannot be pursued here, near the top of such an agenda must be the comparison of creation thought in wisdom writings and, for example, the priestly writings or Jeremiah, particularly with regard to the liminal systems involved. The typology of different

types of creation thought offered by Knight focuses on distinctions among them and not on their underlying commonalities. In any case, the task is barely begun. For the priestly writings, much work has already been done on the organization of social space and morality in terms of holy/clean/unclean as cosmic categories. Cf. Douglas (1966); Alter (1979); Soler (1979 = 1973); Wenham; Cohn (a suggestive but preliminary study); and essays by Douglas, Carroll, Leach, and Davies in Lang (1985).

12 Lang's (1972) distinction between *weisheitliche Lehrrede* (instruction) and *Weisheitsrede* (speech of Wisdom; 1:20–33; 8:136; 9:1–6) is not crucial for our purposes. It should be noted that the speeches of Wisdom, like those of Folly, always appear as quotations set in a narrative framework by a human teacher.

13 The wide semantic applicability of *zr//nkry* to things "strange," "forbidden," and sometimes merely "(an)other" (Prov 27:2; 20:16//27:13) prohibits one seeing in the *'šh zrh* an exclusive preoccupation with Canaanite culture. Moreover, the profounder role of the "strange woman" is to elaborate Woman Folly in contrast to Woman Wisdom.

14 As Ploger (xxi, xxiii) has pointed out, Proverbs 1–9 is not rich in themes. In my judgment, this paucity of topics stems from the *literary* purpose of these chapters. As a written composition they provide a hermeneutic, worldview introduction to the saying collections which follow in chapters 10–29. The sayings fill out the thematic detail lacking in the Prologue of the book. Cf. Camp (1985).

15 Cf. Prov 31:1–9 and Andreasen.

16 Cf. Gordis, McKane (1965/1983), Kovacs, Camp (1985).

17 See Kayatz and Lang (1986) for representative pre-exilic arguments, Gese (1984: 206) and Camp (1985) for post-exilic.

18 Wisdom's "presentation is aimed primarily at classroom behavior and not at behavior outside of school.... Thus the topic of the lesson is learning and the obstinate student..." (Lang, 1986: 20).

19 Lang's (1986: 3–4) misreading of von Rad should be noted: "The book [of Proverbs] includes... three poems [in chs. 1, 8, 9] that are 'completely isolated: They seem to stand like erratic blocks on their own, unconnected with their surroundings'" [quoting von Rad, 1972, 144]. Von Rad, however, is referring to the poems in Proverbs 8, Job 28, and Sirach 24. Lang further misrepresents von Rad by ignoring the latter's crucial qualifications: "*At first sight* these texts appear to be completely isolated.... But one should also ask whether this range of ideas is not, nevertheless, to be understood against a wider contextual background" (my emphasis). Moreover, the speeches of Wisdom in Proverbs 1, 8, and 9 to which Lang refers display many connections with their textual surroundings as a mere study of verbal repetitions makes plain.

20 Von Rad (1962: 439–440; 1972: 97–110). Cf. David Tracy's claim, cited by Collins (1977: 47), that all common human experience "will bear at least the 'family resemblance' of articulating or implying a limit-experience, a limit-language, or a limit-dimension."

21 It is a commonplace of modern historicism that the variety of symbolizations of cosmic order discovered by historical and anthropological studies entails the unknowability or nonexistence of cosmic *cum* ethical norms. For a basic arguments against this historicistic prejudice, see Strauss (1953).

22 See Forrest on the root *kwn* in collocation with aspects of creation other than "the heavens."

23 No need to emend, cf. 22:28.

24 This passage has its famous parallel in the Ramesside "Instruction of Amenemope," Chapter 6 (Lichtheim, 1976: 151–52).

25 "For the recognition of universal principles forces man to judge the established order, or what is actual here and now, in the light of the natural or rational order; and what is actual here and now is more likely than not to fall short of the universal and unchangeable norm. The recognition of universal principles thus tends to prevent men

from wholeheartedly identifying themselves with, or accepting, the social order that fate has allotted to them" (Strauss: 13–14).

26 As random examples of Mesopotamian boundary thinking, one may compare the restoration of the boundary between Lagash and Umma (Albrektson: 17–18, 55; cf. 63), the Middle Assyrian laws on encroaching bounded property and moving boundary stones (Pritchard: 186), and the Kudurru inscriptions with their curses (Keel, 1978: 97). H. H. Schmid (1968) and Perdue (1977: 85–94) provide convenient summaries of the underlying world-order concepts (*me, parṣu, mešaru, kettu*) operative in Sumer, Babylon and Assyria.

27 *'qs.* (Brueggemann).

28 *Qnk,* cf. Prov 8:22.

29 So RSV with Qumran and LXX.

30 Cf., in the context of cosmic ordering and delimitation of the sea, Job 38:7, "Where were you... when the morning stars sang together, and all the sons of God shouted for joy?" (cf. Ps 148:2–3).

31 The end of this poem, Isa 10:18–19, is illuminated by the parable in 2 Esdr 4:13–21. The forest and the sea each seek to steal territory at the other's expense. But their contrary plans were in vain because God had set to each its limit (vv. 16–17, 19, 21). The parable has a double application. First, that human understanding is limited to earthly matters (v 21). Second, the parable serves as a literary anticipation of the seer's main concern. He seeks to understand the *human* problem of why God does not keep boundaries: "things which we daily experience: why Israel has been given over to the Gentiles as a reproach..." (v 23). This theme, employing the imagery of forest and sea, is taken up in 5:23–30.

32 The ascription and dating of these Isaianic passages is quite irrelevant to our purpose of establishing the symbolic configuration of the worldview in Proverbs 1–9. Each author works with a shared set of traditional metaphors, symbolic givens, and fundamental presuppositions and elaborates them, like Lévi-Strauss's *bricoleur* (1966: 16–22), according to the needs of his semantic project.

33 See, e.g., Fishbane's suggestive note (1985: 347, n. 80) on the "clustered terminology" of Prov 16:4–7; 19:9, 11, 16–17 in relation to the tradition of Exod 34:6–7.

34 "The author takes a strictly Israelite point of view. Doctrine could be preserved intact, so long as the nation lived without admixture with foreign peoples. At that far-off time, 'no stranger passed among them'" (Dhorme, 1984: 215) cf. Joel 4:17b.

35 Crenshaw (1976: 34) believes that "creation belongs under the rubric of justice." I would reverse the key terms: "justice belongs under the rubric of creation." Cf. Knierim (1981) and Schmidt (1968, 1974). Otherwise Crenshaw's remarks on the mutuality of justice and creation are very much to the point.

36 So McKane (1970: 223, 355).

37 There are several other uses of *'br* to indicate trespass of cosmic or commanded limina. *'br bryt* is common; sometimes *'br twrh* occurs. The cosmic context of Isa 24:5 is noteworthy: "The earth mourns and withers; the heavens languish together with the earth. The earth lies polluted under its inhabitants; for they have transgressed the laws, violated the statues (*'brw twrt ḥlpw ḥq*), broken the everlasting covenant." See also Prov 22:3 "the simple transgress and are punished" = 27:12.

38 This phrase strikes one as a notion befitting the aesthesis of wisdom thought. But at the time of writing, I do not have access to the Akkadian text and pertinent scholarly resources.

39 Contrast RSV.

40 Cf. Andreasen (1983) on the role of the queen mother in ancient Israel.

41 Significantly, what first strikes the reader of Prov 5:3–11 as a warning against literal seduction is explicated as the rejection of Woman Wisdom who speaks through

the mouth of human instructors (5:13): "How I hated discipline, and my heart despised reproof!" (5:12–13 with verbal echos of 1:23, 29, 30).

[42] "The structure of living organisms is better able to reflect complex social forms than door posts and lintels.... The body is a model which can stand for any bounded system. Its boundaries can represent any boundaries which are threatened or precarious. The body is a complex structure. The functions of its different parts and their relation afford a source of symbols for other complex structures.... [We must] be prepared to see in the body a symbol of society, and to see the powers and dangers credited to social structure reproduced in small on the human body" (Douglas, 1966: 115; cf. 1975:47–59). But in Proverbs 1–9, what is at issue is not, in the first instance, mere social limits re sexuality. Rather, sexual relations and limits, are employed in a figurative "meta-language" on the divinely bounded nature of reality itself.

[43] Job accepts the ethical norms of Proverbs 1–9 and uses similar imagery:

"if my step has turned aside from the way... if my heart has been enticed (npth) to a woman, and I have lain in wait at my neighbor's door... For I was in terror of calamity from God (ky phd ʾly ʾyd ʾl; Job 31:7, 9, 23; cf. Prov 1:26 etc.).

[44] Goldingay's belief that this passage is disordered and that vv. 15–19 better suit the Song of Songs than their present literary surround does not commend itself. I am indebted to the insightful analysis of my colleague, Arie Leder, in an as yet unpublished paper.

[45] Job 3:17–19 describes the undifferentiated *communitas* of death.

WORKS CONSULTED

Albrektson, Bertil
   1967   *History and the Gods: An Essay on the Idea of Historical Events as Divine Manifestations in the Ancient Near East and in Israel.* Coniectanea Biblica, OT Series 1. Lund: Gleerup.

Albright, W. F.
   1919/20   "The Goddess of Life and Wisdom." *AJSL* 36:258–294.

Aletti, Jean-Noël.
   1976   "Proverbes 8,22–31. Étude de structure." *Bib* 57: 25–37.
   1977   "Seduction et Parole en Proverbes I-IX." *VT* 27: 129–44.

Alter, Robert.
   1979   "A New Theory of Kashrut." *Commentary* 68:46–52.
   1981   *The Art of Biblical Narrative.* New York: Basic Books.
   1985   *The Art of Biblical Poetry.* New York: Basic Books.

Amsler, Samuel
   1981   "La sagesse de la femme." Pp. 112–16 in Gilbert, *La Sagesse de l'Ancien Testament.* Ed. M. Gilbert. Gembloux: Ducolot.

Andreasen, N. A.
1983   "The Role of the Queen Mother in Israelite Society." *CBQ* 45:
        179–194.

Boström. Gustav.
1935   *Proverbiastudien: Die Weisheit und das Fremde Weib in Spr. 1–9.*
        Lunds Universitets Årsskrift. N.F. Avd. 1. BD 30. Nr. 3. Lund:
        Gleerup.

Brueggemann, Walter.
1977   "A Neglected Sapiential Word Pair." *ZAW* 89: 234–58.

Bühlmann, Walter.
1976   *Vom Rechten Reden und Schweigen.* OBO 12. Freiburg, Schweiz:
        Universitätsverlag.

Camp, Claudia V.
1985   *Wisdom and the Feminine in the Book of Proverbs.* Bible and Liter-
        ature Series 14. Sheffield: Almond.
1987   "Woman Wisdom as Root Metaphor: A Theological Consider-
        ation." Pp. 45–76 in *The Listening Heart.* Ed. Kenneth G.
        Hoglund *et al.* JSOTSup 58. Sheffield: JSOT.

Clines, David J. A.
1978   *The Theme of the Pentateuch.* Sheffield: JSOT.

Cohn, R. L.
1981   *The Shape of Sacred Space: Four Biblical Studies.* AAR Studies in
        Religion 23. Chico, CA: Scholars.

Collins, J.J.
1977   "The Biblical Precedent for Natural Theology." *JAAR* 45,
        Supplement B, 35–67.

Crenshaw, James L.
1976   "Prolegomenon." Pp. 1–60 in *Studies in Ancient Israelite Wis-
        dom.* Ed. James L. Crenshaw. New York: Ktav
1981   *Old Testament Wisdom: an Introduction.* Atlanta: John Knox.

Dahood, Mitchel.
1968   "Proverbs 8, 22–31: Translation and Commentary." *CBQ* 30:
        512–21.

Dhorme, Édouard.
1984   *A Commentary on the Book of Job.* Nashville: Thomas Nelson.

Douglas, Mary
  1966   *Purity and Danger: An Analysis of the Concepts of Pollution and Taboo*. London: Routledge and Kegan Paul.
  1975   *Implicit Meanings: Essays in Anthropology*. London: Routledge and Kegan Paul.

Dürr, Lorenz
  1938   *Die Wertung des Göttlichen Wortes im alten Testament und im antiken Orient: Zugleich ein Beitrag zur Vorgeschichte des Neutestamentlichen Logosbegriffes*. Leipzig: J. C. Hinrichs.

Fishbane, Michael.
  1985   *Biblical Interpretation in Ancient Israel*. Oxford: Clarendon.

Forrest, R. W. E.
  1979   "An Inquiry into Yahweh's Commendation of Job." *SR* 8: 159–68.

Geertz, Clifford.
  1973   *The Interpretation of Cultures*. New York: Basic Books

Gese, Hartmut.
  1958   *Lehre und Wirklichkeit in der alten Weisheit. Studien zu den Sprüche Salomos und zu dem Buch Hiob*. Tübingen: Mohr (Paul Siebeck).
  1984   "Wisdom Literature." Pp. 189–218 in *The Cambridge History of Judaism. Vol. One, Introduction; The Persian Period*. Ed. W. D. Davies and Louis Finkelstein. Cambridge: Cambridge University

Gilbert. M., ed.
  1981a   *La Sagesse de l'Ancien Testament*. BETL 51; Gembloux: Duculot.
  1981b   "Le discours de la Sagesse en Proverbes, 8." Pp. 202–18 in *La Sagesse de l'Ancien Testament*. Ed. M. Gilbert. Gembloux: Duculot.

Girardot, Norman J.
  1985   "Behaving Cosmogonically in Early Taoism." Pp.67–97 in *Cosmogony and Ethical Order*. W. Lovin and Frank E. Reynolds. Chicago: University of Chicago Press.

Goldingay, John E.
  1977   "Proverbs V and IX." *RB* 84:80–93.

Gordis, R.
1944   "The Social Background of Wisdom Literature." HUCA 18: 77–118.

Greenfield, Jonas C.
1985   "The Seven Pillars of Wisdom (Prov. 9:1)—A Mistranslation." *JQR* 76:13–20.

Halbe, Jörn.
1979   "'Altorientalisches Weltordnungsdenken' und altestamentliche Theologie: Zur Kritik eines Ideologems am Beispiel des israelitischen Rechts. *ZThK* 76: 381–418.

Habel, Norman C.
1972   "The Symbolism of Wisdom in Proverbs 19." *Int* 26: 131–157.
1985   *The Book of Job.* OTL. Philadelphia: Westminster.

Harris, Scott L.
1983   "Wisdom or Creation? A New Interpretation of Job XXVIII 27." *VT* 33: 419–427.

Hermisson, Hans-Jürgen.
1968   *Studien zur israelitischen Spruchweisheit.* WMANT 82. NeukirchenVluyn: Neukirchener.

Hoglund, Kenneth G. *et al.* eds.
1987   *The Listening Heart: Essays in Wisdom and the Psalms in Honor of Roland E. Murphy, O. Carm.* JSOTSup 58. Sheffield: JSOT.

Kaiser, Otto.
1962   *Die Mythische Bedeutung des Meeres in Ägypten, Ugarit und Israel.* BZAW 78. Berlin: Töpelmann.

Kayatz, Christa
1966   *Studien zu Proverbien 1–9. Eine form- und motiv-geschichtliche Untersuchung unter Einbeziehung ägyptischen Vergleichsmaterials.* WMANT 22. Neukirchen Verlag.

Keel, Othmar
1974   *Die Weisheit Spielt vor Gott: ein ikonographischer Beitrag zur Deutung des mesaḥäqät in Spr 8,30f.* Freiburg, Schweiz: Universitätsverlag/Göttingen: Vandenhoeck & Ruprecht.
1978   *The Symbolism of the Biblical World: Ancient Near Eastern Iconography and the Book of Psalms.* New York: Seabury.

Knierim, Rolf P.
1981   "Cosmos and History in Israel's Theology." *HBT* 3:59–123.
1984   "The Task of Old Testament Theology." *HBT* 6: 25–57.

Knight, Douglas A.
1985   "Cosmogony and Order in the Hebrew Tradition." Pp. 133–57
        in *Cosmogony and Ethical Order*. Ed. Robin W. Lovin and Frank
        E. Reynolds. Chicago: University of Chicago Press.

Koch, Klaus.
1983   "Is There a Doctrine of Retribution in the Old Testament." Pp.
        57–87 in *Theodicy in the Old Testament*. Ed. James L. Crenshaw.
        Philadelphia: Fortress.

Koch, Klaus, ed.
1972   *Um das Prinzip der Vergeltung in Religion und Recht des Alten
        Testaments*. WDF 125. Darmstadt: Wissenschaftlich Buchgesell-
        schaft.

Kovacs, B.
1974   "Is There a Class-Ethic in Proverbs?" Pp. 171–90 in *Essays in
        Old Testament Ethics*. Ed. James L. Crenshaw and John Willis.
        New York: Ktav.

Lakoff, George and Mark Johnson
1980   *Metaphors we Live by*. Chicago: University of Chicago.

Lang, Bernhard.
1972   *Die weisheitliche Lehrrede: Eine Untersuchung von Sprüche 1–7*.
        Stuttgarter Bibelstudien 54. Stuttgart: Katholisches Bibelwerk.
1975   *Frau Weisheit: Deutung einer biblischen Gestalt*. Düsseldorf:
        Patmos.
1979   "Schule und Unterricht im alten Israel." Pp. 186–201 in *La
        Sagesse de l'Ancien Testament*. Ed. M. Gilbert. Gembloux:
        Duculot.
1983a   "The Yahweh-Alone Movement and the Making of Jewish
        Monotheism." Pp. 13–59 in *Monotheism and the Prophetic
        Minority*. Ed. Bernhard Lang. Sheffield: Almond.
1983b   "Die Sieben Säulen der Weisheit (Sprüche IX 1) im Licht
        Israelitischer Architektur." *VT* 33:488–91.
1986   *Wisdom and the Book of Proverbs: An Israelite Goddess Redefined*.
        New York: Pilgrim.

Lang, Bernhard, ed.
1985   *Anthropological Approaches to the Old Testament*. Ed. Bernhard Lang. IRT 8. Philadelphia: Fortress.

Lasine, Stuart.
1986   "Indeterminacy and the Bible: A Review of Literary and Anthropological Theories and Their Application to Biblical Texts." *Hebrew Studies* 27:48–80.

Leder, Arie.
unpub.   "Proverbs 5:2,3 and Repetition."

Lemaire, André.
1981   *Les Écoles et la Formation de la Bible dans l'Ancien Israël*. OBO 39; Fribourg: Éditions Universitaires.

Lévi-Strauss, Claude.
1966   *The Savage Mind*. London: Weidenfeld and Nicolson.

Lichtheim, Miriam
1973   *Ancient Egyptian Literature, Volume I: The Old and Middle Kingdoms*. Berkeley: University of California Press.
1976   *Ancient Egyptian Literature, Volume II: The New Kingdom*. Berkeley: University of California Press.

Lotman, Jurij.
1977   *The Structure of the Artistic Text*. Trans. G. Lenhoff and R. Vroon. Michigan Slavic Contributions 7. Ann Arbor: University of Michigan.

Lovin, Robin W. and Frank E. Reynolds (eds.)
1985   *Cosmogony and Ethical Order: New Studies in Comparative Ethics*. Chicago: University of Chicago.

Luyster, Robert.
1981   "Wind and Water: Cosmogonic Symbolism in the Old Testament." *ZAW* 93:1–10.

McFague, Sallie
1985   *Metaphorical Theology: Models of God in Religious Language*. 2nd ed. Philadelphia: Fortress

McKane, William
1965/83   *Prophets and Wise Men*. London: SCM.

1970   *Proverbs: A New Approach*. OTL. Philadelphia: Westminster.

Murphy, Roland E.
  1966   "The Kerygma of the Book of Proverbs." *Int* 20: 3–14.
  1985   "Wisdom and Creation." *JBL* 104: 3–11.
  1987   "Wisdom's Song: Proverbs 1:20–33." *CBQ* 49: 456–60.

Ottosson, Magnus.
  1975   "g^{e}bhul." Pp. 361–366 in *Theological Dictionary of the Old Testament*. Vol. 2. Ed. G. J. Botterweck and H. Ringgren. Grand Rapids: Eerdmans.

Peck, M. Scott
  1983   "Mylai: An Examination of Group Evil." Pp. 212–253 in *People of the Lie: The Hope for Healing Human Evil*. New York: Simon and Schuster.

Perdue, Leo G.
  1977   *Wisdom and Cult: A Critical Analysis of the Views of Cult in the Wisdom Literatures of Israel and the Ancient Near East*. SBLD 30. Missoula: Scholars.
  1981a   "Paraenesis and the Epistle of James." *ZNW* 72: 241–56.
  1981b   "Liminality as a Social Setting for Wisdom Instructions." *ZAW* 93: 114–26.
  1983   "The Testament of David and Egyptian Royal Instructions." Pp. 79–96 in *Scripture in Context II: More Essays on the Comparative Method*. Ed. William W. Hallo *et al*. Winona Lake, Indiana: Eisenbrauns.

Petersen, Claus
  1982   *Mythos im Alten Testament: Bestimmung des Mythosbegriffs und Untersuchung der mythischen Elemente in den Psalmen*. BZAW 157. Berlin: de Gruyter.

Plöger. Otto.
  1984   *Sprüche Salomos: Proverbia*. BK 17. Neukirchener Verlag.

Pritchard, James B, ed.
  1969   *Ancient Near Eastern Texts Relating to the Old Testament*. 3rd ed. with Supplement. Princeton: Princeton University Press.

Rad, Gerhard von
  1962   *Old Testament Theology*. Vol. 1. New York: Harper and Row.
  1970   *Weisheit in Israel*. Neukirchen-Vluyn: Neukirchener.
  1972   *Wisdom in Israel*. Nashville: Abingdon.

Ringgren, Helmer.
1947   *Word and Wisdom: Studies in the Hypostatization of Divine Qualities and Functions in the Ancient Near East.* Lund: H. Ohlssons.
1981   *Sprüche.* ATD 16 (3rd ed.). Göttingen: Vandenhoeck &
Ruprecht.

Roberts, J. J. M.
1976   "Myth *Versus* History: Relaying the Comparative Foundations." *CBQ* 38: 1–13.

Rylaarsdam, J. Coert.
1946   *Revelation in Jewish Wisdom Literature.* Chicago: University of
Chicago Press.

Schmid, Hans Heinrich.
1968   *Gerechtigkeit als Weltordnung.* BHT 40; Tübingen: J. C. B. Mohr
(Paul Siebeck).
1974   *Altorientalische Welt in der alttestamentlichen Theologie.* Zürich:
Theologischer Verlag.

Sklandy, Udo.
1962   *Die älttesten Spruchsammlungen in Israel.* Göttingen: Vandenhoeck und Ruprecht.

Soler, Jean.
1973   "Sémiotique de la nourriture dans la Bible." *Annales, E.S.C.* 28:
943–55.
1979   "The Semiotics of Food in the Bible." Pp. 126–138 in *Food and
Drink in History: Selections from the Annales Economies, Sociétés,
Civilisations.* Vol. 5. Ed. Robert Forster and Orest Ranum.
Baltimore: Johns Hopkins University Press.

Sperber, Dan.
ND   *Rethinking Symbolism.* Cambridge Studies and Papers in Social
Anthropology. Cambridge: Cambridge University.

Sternberg, Meir
1985   *The Poetics of Biblical Narrative: Ideological Literature and the
Drama of Reading.* Bloomington: Indiana University.

Strauss, Leo.
1953   *Natural Right and History.* Chicago: University of Chicago.

Turner, Victor
1967   *The Ritual Process.* Ithaca: Cornell University.
1974   *Dramas, Fields, and Metaphors.* Ithaca: Cornell University.

1974   *Dramas, Fields, and Metaphors.* Ithaca: Cornell University.

Van Leeuwen, Raymond C.
1986   "Proverbs 30:21–23 and the Biblical World Upside Down." *JBL*
          105: 599–610.
1988   *The Problem of Literary Context in Proverbs 25–27: Structures,
          Poetics, and Semantics.* SBLDS. Atlanta: Scholars.

Wenham, Gordon J.
1979   *The Book of Leviticus.* Grand Rapids: Eerdmans.

Wildiers, N. Max.
1982   *The Theologian and His Universe: Theology and Cosmology from
          the Middle Ages to the Present.* New York: Seabury.

Wilson, Frederick M.
1987   "Sacred and Profane? The Yahwistic Redaction of Proverbs
          Reconsidered." Pp. 313–334 in *The Listening Heart.* Ed. Kenneth
          G. Hoglund *et al.* JSOTSup 58. Sheffield: JSOT.

Winston, David.
1979   *The Wisdom of Solomon.* AB 42. Garden City: Doubleday.

Yee, Gale A.
1982   "An Analysis of Prov. 8:22–31 According to Style and Struc-
          ture." *ZAW* 94: 58–66.
Forthcoming "'I Have Perfumed my Bed with Myrrh': The Foreign
          Woman (*ʾiššâ zārâ*) in Proverbs 1–9." *JBL.*

WHO'S CATERING THE Q AFFAIR?
FEMINIST OBSERVATIONS ON Q PARAENESIS

Amy-Jill Levine

ABSTRACT

While both men and women were incorporated in the community that produced Q, the earliest stratum of Q instruction recognizes men as liminal and women as providing the support for the preservation of this unconventional lifestyle. The later recognition of women's roles is occasioned not only by the increasing importance of the support networks—particularly as churches began to form—but also by the community's taking stock of its own composition in light of its rejection by the dominant structure.

Introduction

1.1   Any study of Paraenetic Literature must move beyond the questions of genre to address issues of function. Determination of a particular form should lead to suggestions concerning such matters as the audience to which the material was addressed or which it would most likely influence, the effect the rhetoric had on that audience, and the potential for the discourse to be appropriated by different communities over time. In some cases, form and function are well-matched. Thus, Ancient Near Eastern Wisdom Literature—as Leo Perdue demonstrates—fits various of John Gammie's classifications, and its societal function can be mapped according to Victor Turner's categories with relative ease. Similarly, Christian documents like the Epistle of James (Perdue, 1981b) and the Epistle to the Hebrews can be analyzed according to the same categories.

1.2   But the application of formal and functional categories to subversive paraenesis, such as the Q material from the early Jesus movement,[1] is more problematic. The transfer of formal criteria primarily derived from courts and philosophical schools to pronouncements made in the byways of the Galilee is uneasy. Further, the implicitly male and elitist orientations of Turner's paradigms (Bynum) complicate the hypothesis of egalitarianism frequently applied to Q. Indeed, given the present lack of any sustained inquiry into the lifestyles of Jewish women in Palestine for the period under question, discussion in general of the egalitarian nature of the Q1 community remains doubly speculative: not only do we lack clear information on the results of the transformation occasioned by subversive paraenesis, we also lack a well-constructed model of the women's prior circumstances. We know neither where they came from nor where they went.[2] These difficulties are not, however, insurmountable. Form-critical analysis of the two principal strata of Q paraenesis combined with a critical application of Turner's categories of liminality and antistructure offers both confirmation of and qualifications to the popular hypothesis that Q represents a discipleship of equals.

The Form of Q

2.1   John Kloppenborg's claim (1986a,1987) that the two principal levels of Q, marked by substantial use of imperatives, rhetorical questions, programmatic statements, and aphoristic conclusions, conform to sapiential models is the starting point for this study. He classifies the earlier layer—Q1 (e.g., Q=Lk 6:20b–49; 9:57–62; 10:2–16, 21–24; 11:2–4, 9–13; 12:2–12, 22–34; 13:24–30, 34–35; 14:16–24, 26–27, 4–35; 17:33)—which persuades through appeal to observation of nature and of ordinary human relationships, as sapiential "instruction" aimed at a sectarian group.[3] Q2, marked by apocalyptic motifs and greater antipathy to nonreceptive Judaism, contains paraenetic forms best compared to Hellenistic gnomologia and chreiai collections. It is in this material (e.g., 3:7–9; 16b–17; 7:1–10, 18–23, 24–26; 31–35; 11:14–15, 17–18a, 24–26; 27–28, 39b–44, 46–52;12:42b–46; 17:34) that the gentile presence in the community is acknowledged and that specific references to women members of the group appear. Because instruction is more closely associated with Ancient Near Eastern and Jewish traditions (e.g., Merikare, Proverbs, Ben Sira), Kloppenborg's discussion of form complements his observations of the thematic divisions between Q1 and Q2. The materials he assigned to the earlier stratum conform to what a Jewish, whether Aramaic or Greek speaking, audience would regard as familiar. The later material represents the second stage of Christian development, in which the missionary focus of the community has turned toward the gentiles.

2.2   Taking its cue from Elisabeth Fiorenza (1983), Perdue's introductory essay argues that Q might be "best understood as a wisdom instruction seeking to subvert the prevailing social order of Roman Palestine and to construct a new social reality." Consequently it should be classified as subversive rather than legitimating wisdom. Subversive paraenesis does not project a timeless and harmonious world in which change is viewed as disruptive and in which social inequality is regarded as divinely and/or naturally sanctioned. Rather, by serving as a critique of the prevailing social institutions and calling into question normative attitudes, subversive instruction reflects what Perdue calls the "conflict model of the world." For example, Q1 employs observation of nature to undercut Deuteronomic views of social divisions and to argue for the equality of all, pious and sinner alike, in the eyes of the deity (e.g., 12:22–31). Similarly, using the rhetoric of the structure for anti-structural purposes, the polemical stratum of Q employs Sophia language to suggest that its own wisdom is what existed at creation and what has been compromised by the prevailing status quo (cf. 11:49–50). Put in feminist terms, the conflict model espoused by Q does not perceive "patriarchy" ("hierarchy" as opposed to "*communitas*", in Turner's terms) to be inherent in the universe or in the divine mind.

2.3   Q's subversive tendencies also follow J. G. Williams's distinction between "the 'aphoristic wisdom of order' which rests on the collective voice of 'the fathers' and the 'wisdom of counter-order' characterized by individual insight and criticism of tradition" (27, cited by Kloppenborg, 1987: 274–75; cf. Perdue's introductory essay, following Crossan). While Kloppenborg notes that this formulation does not explain the consistent ascription of instruction to named sages—who, presumably, would be part of the establishment—the formulation does in fact fit the Q hypothesis well. The device of anonymity, like that of assigning wisdom to royal figures, reinforces traditional values and so would be inappropriate for de-legitimating rhetoric. In addition, making a rhetorical break from Egyptian and Ancient Near Eastern legitimating instructional literature, Q1 is not presented as parental advice. The shift in rhetoric from parent to the less conservative "teacher" (κύριος, 6:46) moves the form closer to that of gnomologium, which, appropriately, is better suited to a small group than to the society at large.

Liminal vs. Marginal

3.1   Kloppenborg has also profitably applied Turner's social categories to Q. For example, he observes that the posture disciples who follow Q instruction (e.g., 6:27–35; 10:2–10) are to take with respect to the world is "best described as permanently liminoid" (1986b: 51 and n. 69). Q's "ethic of radical discipleship...reverses many of the conventions which allow a society to operate, such as the principles of retaliation, the orderly borrowing and lending of capital, appropriate treatment of the dead, responsible self-provision, selfdefense and honor of parents" (Kloppenborg, 1987: 318). The rhetoric of Q is, moreover, replete with Turner's symbols of liminality: nakedness (cf. 12:28), status reversal

(14:11/18:14b), poverty (6:20–21), etc. (Turner, 1967b: 95, cf. Perdue, 1981: 116). And Q2 reveals a community's reaction to the expected pressure the dominant structure places on those who invert or negate its ideals. That Q encourages liminality, a breaking away from the status quo, is not in doubt.

3.2   Yet what would motivate an individual to make such a break is less clearly suggested by the Q strata. Traditionally, early Christian discourse has been viewed as addressing Palestinian social and cultural marginals; the stories and sayings ascribed to Jesus are seen as having a particular interest in those who live in the "interstices in the fabric of pious society and everyday life" and those who are "rejected by pious society," such as sinners and tax collectors (Kloppenborg, 1986b: 53). Indeed, the first three beatitudes do have a direct appeal to the disadvantaged. However, such a construct of the Q1 audience and community requires clarification. Marginal status should be assessed in terms of both volition and degree: the Q1 community is on the margins by choice, and it is not primarily comprised of individuals at the bottom of the social system. While the Q1 appeal is made to the poor and while its proponents may even have adopted "the poor" as their self-designation (Gal 2:10; Rom 15:26; and the "Ebionites"), the community itself should not be viewed as comprised of those on the lowest or even necessarily lower economic rungs. The principal address of Q1 practical wisdom is to those who are able to give up their accoutrements of the status quo—home, money, family—not those who lack them in the first place.[4]

3.3   The Q1 community is, in modern terms, a counter-cultural social experiment, but it has not yet either adopted an apocalyptic stance that looks forward to the end of the present order nor has it solidified its own position vis-à-vis the dominant structure. Polemics against the unreceptive dominant order appear in the second stage of Q, at the time when the original message had been rejected and the peaceful optimism of the early communities had, consequently, been eliminated. And only at the Q2 stage, when those who have chosen the path of liminality are rejected by the status quo, do the liminals become marginal. In other words, it is less that the marginals of society comprise the Q community than that the Q community creates marginals.

3.4   This distinction is supported by a comparison of Q's countercultural ethic to Cynic rhetoric and lifestyle. For example, the remarks ascribed to Jesus, like those of the Cynics, contain social critique, direct appeals to individuals, argument based on common sense and natural law rather than received tradition, and disavowal of conventional authority. Cynic chreiai also lack appeals to parental authority (See Mack; Kloppenborg, 1987).[5] More intriguing, the Cynic ethic cautions against the interpretation of Q1 material as eschatological in orientation.[6] On the one hand, following H. D. Betz, Kloppenborg (1987: 189) suggests that "in Q the criticism of wealth is based not on philosophic teaching [as it is for the Cynics] but upon an apprehension that the imminent kingdom will bring about a radical transformation of human life." On the other, the earlier Q material less suggests entry into the new world, be it eschatological or earthly, than it does a dropping out of the old. Perhaps Q1 should best be described as advocating the surety of the eschaton, and Q2 then shifts the focus to its imminence.

3.5   The noneschatological thrust of Q1 comports with Perdue's introductory observations concerning the twin functions of subversive instruction. Like Job, it could through its cooptation of traditional forms encourage a destabilizing attitude or behavior, or like apocalyptic it could posit a new social order with its own code of behavior. Q1 is closer to the first category: norms are called into question on the authority of an individual. And unlike either Q2 or apocalyptic, Q1 does not offer much detail concerning either reentry into society or conduct in the new order. The poor are blessed, the mourners comforted, and the community told to be merciful, to turn the other cheek, and not to be "anxious about your life, what you shall eat, nor about your body, what you shall wear" (12:22). The individual is removed from social anchors, but is not fully reincorporated. This "permanent liminal"—particularly when seen in the context of Perdue's conflict model—embodies virtues which subvert the present order and which reveal only implicitly the expectation of the new reality to come. Consistent with these lacks of specifics, the early tradition does not incorporate "conventional subjects of moral exhortation:" the state, civil concord and responsibility, sexual conduct, anger, slavery and freedom, etc. (Malherbe, 1986:144–61; cf. Mack: 64). For the liminal, questions of civic responsibility are irrelevant, and the behavior to be encouraged is "normally passive or humble" (Turner, 1967b: 95). Yet for the marginal of Q2, response to authority becomes an issue (e.g., 11:39–52) and the community turns from humble invitation to vituperative attack.

Limits of Liminality

4.1   Those who subscribe fully to Q1 instruction—the missionaries who carry neither purse, nor knapsack, nor sandals (10:2–12)—remain in a perpetually liminal status. Since they therefore lack basic needs such as food and shelter, they require support from others who have not relinquished ties to the dominant social structure. While such mendicants are defined and define themselves in opposition to the general system and the conventional wisdom, like the Cynics, they depend on that very system to provide negative selfdefinition (cf. Malherbe, 1982: 54) if not positive physical support. For the Q1 mendicants, this need for support was exacerbated by the effect of their instructional stance. Those who transgress or undermine social norms, be they hippies or Jesus people or members of nudist colonies, will likely find themselves reviled by the dominant group. And that rejection by the prevailing culture is indicated by the polemics of Q2.

4.2   The existence of two categories—the mendicant and the supporter—incorporated into the Q community challenges the notion of a "discipleship of equals." Q1 presents some material that all can receive, and other material addressed to specific sub-groups. Comparing Q6:39–45 to Rom 14:2–23 and Jas 4:11–12, Kloppenborg (1987: 185) observes that the Q material is aimed at teachers who do not follow the ethical and behavioral model set by Jesus; thus there are divisions within the community. But these divisions cannot be viewed along the lines of Paul's metaphor of the body of Christ; all the parts are not equal. In terms of Q instruction, the exhortations given in 10:2–12 cannot be received by all sympathetic to the general message. Rather, some—those closest to the paradigm of Jesus—take to the road; others, the ones to be harvested (10:2) and the children of peace (10:6), provide them support. While the early Jesus movement may have been discipleship of equals, that equality should be qualified: the mendicants are all equal on one level, and those who comprise the supporting network are equal on another.[7]

4.3   This division within the Jesus movement indicates that questions of women's roles must address not only two strata of material, Q1 and Q2, but also two modes of participation, mendicant and supportive. Material external to Q indicates that women such as Peter's mother-in-law and Martha and Mary of Bethany were part of the supporting network. Even the one Q parabolic image of a woman connects her with food preparation (13:20), and so implicitly with the support network of the wandering missionaries.[8] These women qua women are marginal in relation to the cultic status quo since they are never fully integrated into all structures of patriarchal power (e.g., they cannot serve as priests in the Temple or even enter the inner court). And their marginality is increased through their association with the Jesus people, as Q2 demonstrates. Because they are marginal (although in terms of status and power it is unclear *how* marginal they were), the message of Q1 would have appealed to them. But it is by no means evident that the instruction of Q1 is addressed to them, and it is equally unclear that they comported themselves according to the requirements of the missionary instruction. Only in Q2 are women explicitly viewed as on the same level with the men in the community; the son faces the same problems as the daughter-in-law.

4.4   Although remarks in Q1 are applicable to women and men alike—both sexes mourn and are anxious about food and clothes—and so demonstrate egalitarian *potential*, they do not do more. The rhetoric remains masculine: exhortations such as the discussion of the tunic and of walking the extra mile in 6:29-30 refer to the power of the Roman army to conscript Jewish men; in 6:35c the desired goal is to become "sons" (υἱοί) of the Most High, not "children" (τέκνα); in 6:40 the model is master and disciple (both in masculine singular); 6:46-49 offers the model of the construction worker, an occupation associated with men, etc. While the sayings ascribed to Jesus in both Q1 and Q2 have a specific focus on groups marginal to the Palestinian social structure, women *qua* women are not specifically mentioned. And indeed, there is little demonstrable evidence that instruction in general was directed at women. Van Leeuwen's contribution in this collection argues that the adult sages to whom Proverbs is addressed are "male or female," but the protrepsis there is directed primarily to the male. That is, while "woman wisdom" is for everyone, "woman folly" appears applicable only to men. The distinction between universal potential and limited application are suggested as well by Q's ethnic concerns. While gentiles too feel hunger and thirst, the comforting paraenesis of Q1 was probably not directed to them; the gentile component of the movement is noted only in the Q2 material.

4.5   That the community itself recognized the egalitarian potential of its rhetoric or indeed that the potential was brought to fruition receives ambiguous support from external sources. Other Christian texts offer several rhetorical models for the elimination of sexual distinction, but the practical implications of the language remain debatable. The pre-Pauline formulation in Galatians 3:28, fully in line with Turner's theory, eliminates distinctions of race (Jew and Greek), class (slave and free), and sex (male and female [οὐκ ἔνι ἄρσεν καὶ θῆλυ]). the applicability of this saying to the Palestinian community is complicated by its diaspora context, its unclear role in praxis (does it indicate social roles or ontological-soteriological status?), etc. The heavenly model presented in Mark 12:24-27 contains both an elimination of sexual difference and a reversal of the conventional views of life and death. Here the language is consistent with Turner's categories, but the otherworldly setting removes the material from an earthly practicality. The final logion of the Gospel of Thomas also seeks to eliminate sexual difference in the new realm, but here the elimination is not only done in an eschatological context, it is accomplished at the subsumption of the female into the male. Finally, such apocryphal writings as the Acts of Paul and Thecla present women in liminal positions: celibate, transvestite, homeless, and characterized by renunciation. Yet these represent later traditions removed from the context of Jewish Palestine.

4.6   Within the gospel material, although absent from Q, are several references to the women from Galilee who like the disciples chose to leave their homes to follow Jesus. An association of their lifestyle with that of the women addressed by Q1 is complicated both by the difficulties of Lucan redaction and the model provided by some Cynic rhetoric. Luke has coopted the potentially egalitarian rhetoric of Q to support a more patriarchal agenda. The third gospel mentions one "wife" (θυνή), Joanna, among the women from the Galilee; she is depicted as apparently separated from her husband Chuza the steward (8:3, cf. her addition to the list of women at the tomb in 24:10). But Luke does not represent Joanna or the other women as equivalent to the disciples: rather, 8:13 establishes them as the model for the support network. Consistently, Luke 14:26–27 states: "If any one comes to me and does not hate his own father and mother *and wife* and children and brothers and sisters and indeed even his own life, he cannot be my disciple." For Luke, but perhaps not for Q, the wandering missionaries are all men (see Fiorenza: 145–47). The reference to the "wife" is redactional: not only is it absent in Matt 10:37, and not only does the later Q 12:53 lack a reference to spouses, but Luke 18:29b adds the same reference to Mark 10:29b.[9]

4.7   From Q's silence, we cannot determine whether the Q1 group fully incorporated women as either mendicant or supporter, or as both, or as neither. Yet this silence should not be weighted too heavily. First, that women were part of Q2 is indicated by 12:51–53, this polemical material could, with caution, be retrojected back to the formation of the original group. Second, Q is also surprisingly silent on other salient matters, including ethnic stereotypes, politics, human nature in general, friendship, and the admonition to seek wisdom itself (Carlston).[10] Such absence from the text does not necessarily indicate lack of presence in the community in which the text was formed: those responsible for the composition of Q, living in Roman Palestine, surely formed some opinion of the local political situation; living in towns rather than in a monastery like their fellow sectarians at Qumran, they surely had some notion of everyday life.

4.8   Feminist revisionism has also tackled the question of silence. One often helpful suggestion is that the silence of the sources may be due not to lack of information on women's diverse powers but to suppression of them. For example, because Luke-Acts tends to portray women not in leadership roles but as facilitators for the men (cf. 8:1–3) and, especially, because the later church limited women's roles (cf. 1 Cor 14; 1 Tim 2, and cf. Quinn's essay in this collection), one could claim that such limitations were motivated by an excess of women's powers. Citing Fiorenza (109), Perdue argues that "as a rule, prescriptive injunctions for appropriate 'feminine' behavior and submission increase whenever women's actual social and religious status and power within patriarchy increase." However, it is dangerous to apply this argument indiscriminately to the silence of the Q material. First, the argument itself does not stand the test of universal applicability: negative rhetoric about as well as laws against Jews increased in the late antique period at precisely the time that their social status was not on the rise. And second, any equation between laws against women and silence concerning them must be made with caution. Silence may not indicate absence, but the evidence to this point does not allow an argument for presence either.

From Text to Theory

5.1   Caroline Bynum's correctives of Turner's system make, with some modification, at least three points applicable to the Q material.[11] First, she suggests that "liminality itself—as fully elaborated by Turner—may be less a universal moment of meaning needed by human beings...than an escape for those who bear the burdens and reap the benefits of a high place in the social structure." Following liberation theologians like Gutierrez, Bynum observes that it is the powerful who stress activities of *imitatio Christi* like "(voluntary) poverty, (voluntary) nudity, and (voluntary) weakness." Those truly marginal to the status quo usually express their concern not as weakness but as struggle (109). Second, men employ feminine images, nudity, weakness, etc. as a means of expressing the liminal state at conversion (110, cf. Turner, 1967b: 95).[12] Finally, men profess an antistructural ideal by seeking social contact with women *qua* women-as-marginal. Association with a woman—particularly one in a state of "radical apartness" punctuated by illness, low social status, etc.—allowed men a "means of escape from and reintegration into status and power" (p. 110).

5.2   Bynum's application of liberation theology models to studies of the rhetoric of liminality supports the hypothesis that Q1 was not addressed to those on the margins of the Palestinian socioeconomic system. Q1 does not suggest that the members of the community were "truly marginal": not only is there no struggle, the members of the *communitas* are enjoined to rejoice in their marginality, to become "more marginal" rather than to change the system.

5.3   A rhetoric of weakness rather than gender is characteristic of Q1's subversive instruction: Jesus exhorts his followers to rejoice rather than to despair in their poverty, hunger, and homelessness (6:20; 9:58). Moreover, these images are not specifically associated with women. Rather, the dominant symbol of weakness with whom the members of the community are identified is that of the child. For example, 10:21 speaks of the reception of the instruction by the "babies" (νηπίοι); and 11:11–13 depicts the hearers as children given good gifts by their heavenly father. Not unlike the Hebrew prophets, the Q1 material does not recognize women as paradigmatically poor or weak. Consequently, the imagery is not "feminized." This omission may be explained in one of two ways. Either women of the culture were not characteristically poor and weak, in which case their presence in the rhetoric would be inappropriate. Or, the women were so marginalized, but were not recognized as being such within the cultural imagination.

5.4   The language of status reversal is present in Q, but its sexual component is not. Liminal individuals become associated with babies both metaphorically and literally (e.g., their lack of a means of livelihood); as Turner states, in rites of passage the order of birth and death are reversed and one dies to "become a little child" (1974: 64). Further, the analogy between disciple and child supports his suggestion that the elite within a specific social group undergo humiliation, penance, etc. in order to achieve *communitas* (1967: 201–3). The subordinated, on the other hand, seek some sort of status elevation. These observations highlight the economic and political status of Turner's liminal individuals as opposed to their gender. If women were fully to undergo the Turnerian process of liminality, then either they need originally to have some elevated role in the society against which their liminality should be defined or some sign of gendered status reversal would be expected: that is, just as liminal men are described in feminine terms, liminal women should be described in masculine ones. Yet the paraenesis of the early Jesus movement puts women in a double bind. Since there is no language of gender reversal, the woman made inferior through patriarchal sexism does not achieve status elevation through association with men. Moreover, the "structurally superior" man is not reminded that woman is the inferior category in the binary opposition of man/woman. From this silence, one might again conclude that women were not viewed as (overly) subordinate to men. And if in fact the women were in a subordinated position, then their acceptance of Q's instruction would have exacerbated their inferior status vis-à-vis the majority. They may have found comfort, but their inner peace was eventually placed in conflict with adverse external pressure.

5.5   Bynum's third point, that men professing the subversive instruction have recourse to liminality through their association with women, has some applicability to the non-Q traditions. Jesus heals women, associates with women who are identified as sinners, is accompanied by women from Galilee, etc. But even in these cases, while the evidence indicates that women formed the support network for (male) mendicants from the Jesus movement as well as most likely for Jesus himself, there is surprisingly no indication that Jesus sought out the company of women in particular. Rather, the focus is on those more traditionally viewed as marginal: "sinners"; the sick; tax collectors; the poor. For the Q1 community, regeneration through liminality does not need to be obtained through contact with women. They have the memory of Jesus himself.

5.6   And it is this contact which brings about the major utilization of feminine imagery in Q: the association of Jesus with Sophia. The first major supplementation of the sapiential instruction of Q1 by Q2 polemic concerns the functional unity of Jesus with Sophia: 7:35; 11:49–51a/b; and 13:34–35 (Kloppenborg, 1987: 319–20). The Sophia figure is fully supernatural and fully conventional. She sends envoys to call her people to repentance (cf. Wis 7:27; Prov 1:20–33, 8:1–21), and her envoys, according to the Deuteronomic pattern (11:49; 13:34–35), are killed. While 7:31–35 does not mention the death of the messengers, the content of the saying does indicate that the messages of Sophia's children (τέκνα), who are most likely to be identified with John and Jesus, have been rejected. Although Q2 applies feminine imagery to Jesus, this imagery cannot be construed as representing liminality through its attendant feminized metaphors of weakness, humiliation, etc. That the community connected Sophia imagery to Jesus may indicate that it felt comfortable using feminine images. While this comfort may have been occasioned by the increasing recognition of the role of women by Q2, it is just as easily explained by the wisdom background of the Q1 instruction and by a nativistic attempt to reclaim the tropes of the dominant tradition. Sophia would be an expected representative of the divine in Jewish instruction. Indeed, the connection of Jesus and Sophia may indicate less an appreciation for the role of women in the Q community than a slight discomfort with feminine images. That is, since Sophia is a conventional motif in wisdom literature, her direct association with Jesus may be less a "feminizing" of the teacher than a "masculinizing" of the mythical source of that teaching.

Implications and Conclusions

6.1   The flip side of the call to liminality and structural disengage-
ment is the negative effect antistructure can have particularly on women
(although, as the apocryphal acts indicate, women are not the only ones
distressed by the dissolution of marriage and the minimization of gender
roles occasioned by celibacy). The diaspora churches to some extent
solved this problem by having couples (Priscilla and Aquila, Junia and
Andronicus) jointly engage in missionary work. But the Palestinian traditions do not record such joint endeavors except through the silence of the
reconstruction of Q: wives and husbands are not among those left behind
by new disciples. Yet the men described by the gospels as following Jesus
are not explicitly accompanied by wives, nor are the women from the
Galilee explicitly accompanied by husbands. Nor should one with full
confidence read the accounts of the women from Galilee as prefiguring
the mendicant missionaries of Q1.

6.2   That women were members of the Q community is clear. But
that they were deliberately addressed by Q1 paraenesis and fully incorporated into the mendicant lifestyle Q1 commends is less so. Perhaps they
were able to experience liminality through their association with the
mendicants (an ironic reversal of Bynum's observation concerning the
association of men in search of liminality with women in Medieval
Catholicism); perhaps their participation in certain rituals such as baptism
and fellowship meals afforded them the experience.[13] Unfortunately, Q
neither supports nor undermines these hypotheses. The instruction of Q
appears to have attracted women as it did men, and places them both at
least in the supporting network. Yet the full presence of women within
the community is not acknowledged until the second stage of Q. Here,
when the rhetoric shifts from benign instruction to harsh gnomologia,
when the tone shifts from invitation to polemic, the community
recognizes its own composition. The language incorporates not only sons
and fathers, but makes explicit mention of mothers, daughters, mother-in-
laws and daughter-in-laws (12:53); here are included the two women
grinding together (17:35), here even the Queen of the South appears
(11:31). The women are present, but they are not present as ontologically
liminal or as socioeconomically marginal. They are rhetorically
incorporated as attached to their families, as engaged in the work of
support, and as implicitly in possession of wealth and status.

6.3   Only when the movement experienced pressure from and finally
rejection by the dominant society did it seek its own self-definition. Such
concern became necessary at the moment when a chosen liminal ethos
becomes less a voluntary act than a constraint imposed by the majority. In

that hour, the movement was forced to look inward as well as outward beyond the world of Jewish Palestine. Diachronically, the community drew from the wisdom tradition and recovered the image of Sophia to enhance the paraenetic message of their teacher. In that hour as well, the social experiment became an eschatologically oriented cult. Synchronically, the members took stock of who they were and found within a strong presence of women. And with their representation of these women defined by familial and domestic roles, the Q2 *communitas* began as well the movement from sect to church, from social experiment to institution.

NOTES

[1] On the "early Jesus movement," see *inter alia*, Mack, Kloppenborg (1987), Gager, Fiorenza, Theissen (1978), Borg.

[2] Brooten (1985, 1986) offers programmatic suggestions concerning the development of the model. See also Luise Schottroff and Fiorenza.

[3] For formal analysis, see Kloppenborg, 239, 306–16. On wisdom forms in Q (e.g., beatitudes, admonitions, instructions, wisdom psalms, proverbs, aphorisms) see the listing in Perdue (1986).

[4] Turner (1967b: 125) compares his neophytes in the liminal phase to good Samaritans, Kerouac's Dharma Bums, and court jesters. They are all "persons or principles that (1) fall in the interstices of social structure, (2) are on its margins, or (3) occupy its lowest rungs." Full weight must be given to that "or." For further methodological considerations on "poor" as a symbolic rather than purely economic term, see Theissen (1983) and the references there.

[5] Mack has demonstrated that the pronouncement stories in Mark are constructed on the model of Cynic chreiai and frequently contain Cynic themes (184). The classification suggests why few remarks on politics and institutional reform have been received in the early Jesus tradition: the Cynic concentrated on human interaction and not institutional structure (64, cf. Malherbe, 1982). For cautionary notes on Mack's conclusions concerning the historical Jesus and the adaptation of Cynic models by the evangelists, see Horsley, and Scott: "There is no doubt that the Jesus tradition was amenable to Cynic revision and it clearly happened in the early process of writing (composing) the tradition in the Greek language."

[6] Kennedy (66) observes, for example, that "nowhere does the sermon [6:20b–49] present the great promise of the Kingdom of God as an incentive to action." See also Scott.

[7] Similarly, Turner points to the need for the exercise of extreme authority by elders over juniors within the liminal state (1974: 64; 1967a: 99–100). Because of the dangers of liminality, those in the realm of the utmost behavioral freedom must be controlled. While the neophytes within the movement may be fully equal, hierarchy still exists. For further discussion of the "graduated series of norms" from the mendicants to the supporters, see Theissen (1978,1983).

[8] Luke 15:8–10 may also be from Q, although it lacks a Matthean parallel. Here too the description fits the support mode: the woman is in the home rather than on the road, and she has not given away all her economic assets. The connection of women with leavening is complicated by the dominant metaphorical connotations of leaven. As Scott (forthcoming) observes, "The physical characteristics of leaven abet the metaphor for corruption. Leaven is made by taking a piece of bread, storing it in a

damp, dark place until mold forms. The bread rots and decays, until it ferments, unlike modern yeast which is domesticated" (cf. also Exod 12; Gal 5:9; 1 Cor 5:7; Mark 8:15; Matt 16:12; Luke 12:1). While Scott argues that the parable of the leaven reverses the convention and so reveals a "voice at odds with common wisdom," one must wonder both why this subversive reinterpretation is connected with women and how the parable was received by its early audience. Positively viewed, the parable revalues both women and leaven: neither is symbolic of corruption. Jesus has thereby inverted traditional wisdom images as he inverted traditional paraenesis. Negatively seen, Jesus has implicitly reinforced not only woman's domestic, supporting role but also her negative cultural associations.

[9] Nevertheless, mention of the wife would not be surprising given analogies to Paul (1 Cor 7:29), and those Cynic and Stoic teachings which advise separation from the family. On the Cynic side, cf. references to Hipparchia, the wife of Crates (Fiorenza: 89). Lucian (*The Runaways*, 18–19) claims that "Cynics carry off wives on the pretext of making philosophers out of them" (Stambaugh and Balch: 114). Theissen (1983) discusses the relation between Luke 14:26 and 1 Cor 9:4–5 in the context of "inferences from norms."

[10] Carlston suggests that the "total absence of conventional 'wisdom' about women" is occasioned by Jesus' view that sexual equality was a "self-evident fact." However, three counter-arguments still exist: references to women do not appear because the material is not addressed to women; the men to whom the material is addressed have no personal dealings with women; or women's subordinate position was "self-evident."

[11] While acknowledging the contributions his categories of analysis make to the study of history and religion, she observes that "his theory of religion is inadequate because it is based implicitly on the Christianity of a particular class, gender, and historical period" (105). Unfortunately, all of Bynum's points cannot be tested for Q because of the gaps in the evidence. For example, she observes that "when women recount their own lives, the themes are less climax, conversion, reintegration and triumph, the liminality of reversal or elevation, than continuity" (108).

[12] Symbols of liminality include images of birth like nakedness, of death like illness and the tomb, of darkness, eclipses, invisibility, poverty, wilderness, etc. They also include particularly female-identified motifs such as menstruation and the womb. For an interpretation of the outreach program ascribed to Jesus according to the metaphor of "wombishness," see Borg (133).

[13] My thanks to Leo G. Perdue for his helpful comments on the function of ritual in the Q community.

WORKS CITED

Betz, Hans-Dieter
    1985   *Essays on the Sermon on the Mount*. Philadelphia: Fortress.

Borg, Marcus J.
    1984   *Conflict, Holiness and Politics in the Teachings of Jesus. Studies in the Bible and Early Christianity*. New York and Toronto: Edwin Mellen.

Brooten, Bernadette J.
    1985   "Early Christian Women and Their Cultural Context: Issues of Method in Historical Reconstruction." Pp. 65–91 in *Feminist*

Perspectives on Biblical Scholarship. Ed. Adela Yarbro Collins. Society of Biblical Literature Centennial Publications 10. Chico, CA: Scholars.

1986   "Jewish Women's History in the Roman Period: A Task for Christian Theology." Pp. 22–30 in *Christians Among Jews and Gentiles*. Ed. George W. E. Nickelsburg with George W. MacRae. Philadelphia: Fortress.

Bynum, Caroline Walker
1984   "Women's Stories, Women's Symbols: A Critique of Victor Turner's Theory of Liminality." Pp. 105–25 in *Anthropology and the Study of Religion*. Ed. Robert L. Moore and Frank E. Reynolds. Chicago: Center for the Scientific Study of Religion.

Carlston, C. E.
1980   "Proverbs, Maxims, and the Historical Jesus." *JBL* 99: 87–105.

Crossan, John Dominic
1983   *In Fragments: The Aphorisms of Jesus*. San Francisco: Harper and Row.

Fiorenza, Elisabeth Schussler
1983   *In Memory of Her. A Feminist Theological Reconstruction of Christian Origins*. New York: Crossroad.

Gager, John
1975   *Kingdom and Community*. Englewood Cliffs, NJ: Prentice-Hall.

Horsley, Richard A.
1987   *Jesus and the Spiral of Violence. Popular Jewish Resistance in Roman Palestine*. San Francisco: Harper and Row.

Kennedy, George A.
1984   *New Testament Interpretation through Rhetorical Criticism*. Chapel Hill and London: University of North Carolina Press.

Kloppenborg, John S.
1986a   "The Formation of Q and Antique Instructional Genres." *JBL* 105: 443–62.
1986b   "Blessing and Marginality. The 'Persecution Beatitude' in Q, Thomas, and Early Christianity." *Forum* 2:36–56.
1987   *The Formation of Q. Trajectories in Ancient Wisdom Collections*. Philadelphia: Fortress.

Mack, Burton L.
    1988   *A Myth of Innocence. Mark and Christian Origins.* Philadelphia:
            Fortress.

Malherbe, Abraham
    1982   "Self-Definition Among Epicureans and Cynics." *Jewish and
            Christian Self-Definition.* Vol. 3. Ed. Ben F. Meyer and E. P.
            Sanders. Philadelphia: Fortress.
    1986   Moral Exhortation. A Greco-Roman Sourcebook. Library of
            Early Christianity 4. Philadelphia: Westminster.

Perdue, Leo G
    1981a   "Liminality as a Social Setting for Wisdom. *ZAW* 93: 114–26.
    1981b   "Paraenesis and the Epistle of James." *ZNW* 72: 241–56.
    1986   "The Wisdom Sayings of Jesus." *Forum* 2: 1–35.

Schottroff, Luise
    1983   "Women as Followers of Jesus in New Testament Times: An
            Exercise in Socio-Historical Exegesis of the Bible." Pp. 418–27
            in *The Bible and Liberation. Political and Social Hermeneutics.* Ed.
            Norman K. Gottwald. Maryknoll, NY: Orbis Books.

Scott, Bernard Brandon
    1990   "Jesus as Sage—An Innovating Voice in Common Wisdom.
            Forthcoming in *The Sage in Israel and the Ancient Near East.* Ed.
            John G. Gammie and Leo G. Perdue. Winona Lake, IN: Eisen-
            brauns.

Stambaugh, John E., and David L. Balch
    1986   *The New Testament in Its Social Environment.* Library of Early
            Christianity 2. Philadelphia: Fortress.

Theissen, Gerd.
    1978   *Sociology of Early Palestinian Christianity.* Philadelphia: Fortress.
    1983   "The Sociological Interpretation of Religious Traditions: Its
            Methodological Problems as Exemplified in Early Christian-
            ity." Pp. 38–58 in *The Bible and Liberation. Political and Social
            Hermeneutics.* Ed. Norman K. Gottwald. Maryknoll, NY: Orbis
            Books.

Turner, Victor
    1967a   *The Forest of Symbols: Aspects of Ndembu Ritual.* Ithaca, NY:
            Cornell University Press.
    1967b   *The Ritual Process. Structure and Anti-Structure.* Ithaca, NY:
            Cornell University Press.

1974   "Metaphors of Anti-Structure in Religious Culture." Pp. 63–84 in *Changing Perspectives in the Scientific Study of Religion*. Ed. Allan W. Eister. New York: John Wiley and Sons.

Williams, J. G.
1981   *Those Who Ponder Proverbs: Aphoristic Thinking and Biblical Literature*. Sheffield: Almond.

Paraenesis, Excess, and Ethics: Matthew's Rhetoric in the Sermon on the Mount

James G. Williams

ABSTRACT

This essay employs both anthropological and literary models to explicate the SM, which is parenetic in form and content. These models, by helping to open windows into what the SM shares with its heritage and environment, enable us simultaneously to see what is unique about it. The Matthean rites of passage or initiation introduce the disciples to a vision in which the passion of the Christ and eschatological reward are translated into a new ethical mode that encourages concrete acts of love and nonviolence as the reenactment of redemption. The general and typical elements of parenesis are subsumed by this transformational process into a rhetorical mode of "excess" (Kermode). The collection of the sage's teachings, which by its very character allows considerable flexibility for development, is thus changed into a passionate discourse that could be read or heard as the teacher's farewell even before he and his followers embark on their mission!

0.1   The Sermon on the Mount (hereafter (SM) is paraenetic. It is informed by the intention to give moral and spiritual instruction expressed in imperatives taking an aphoristic or gnomic form (McDonald: 138, n. 67; Perdue, 1981b: 241). More specifically in terms of the morphology presented by John Gammie in this issue, the SM is replete with that form of address

> *which not only commends, but actually enumerates precepts or maxims which pertain to moral aspiration and the regulation of human conduct* (§2.2.1.).

As such it belongs to a broad category of literature that Gammie describes as a "secondary genre" under "wisdom literature." It is, in Gammie's terms, a "subgenre" which is closely related to and may employ other subgenres such as encomium, admonition, exhortation, paradeigma, chreia, etc. I shall return to Gammie's analysis in part I of this essay.

0.2   The SM has an obviously Jewish character, as is evident when one sets it against biblical and rabbinic traditions. To what extent is it derived from Q material? Can it be clarified in light of Hellenistic literature and rhetoric, with special reference to the forms and function of paraenesis in Hellenistic culture? I shall attempt a response to these questions, but above all I wish to set out what I view as the uniqueness of the SM.

0.3   In order to clarify the uniqueness of the SM, it is necessary to say something about the religious, social, and literary contexts in terms of which it may be construed. Both the form and content of the SM point to a group of committed disciples who go apart with their teacher and are instructed by him concerning the meaning of the separated or sacred community that gathers around him. This is not to say that the SM is a reliable expression of any particular historical situation or event. However, the literary form and style and the theological content suggest a process that must have been operative in actual community life, namely "rites of passage" (Turner). The followers of the master are separated from their familiar social networks, given new and startling instructions that call conventional wisdom into question (e.g., Matt 5:38–48), and incorporated into a new order (e.g., Matt 5:3–12).

0.4   I mentioned in the opening paragraph that the SM is paraenetic. This means that for the audience—certainly for the internal narrative audience of the SM—the precepts of the teacher offer models of thought and conduct in typical situations. Moreover, this paraenesis is the dominant literary form in a collection of teachings. The collection of "words of the wise" was a common Near Eastern and biblical wisdom genre. James Robinson and John Kloppenborg have argued that the "words of the wise" was a form adapted to the needs of the early wisdom tradition as seen in Q and the Gospel of Thomas. I have found their studies helpful and stimulating, although I have disputed this thesis in the case of Q (Williams, 1988).

0.5   In sum, I shall employ both anthropological and literary models to explicate the SM. These models, by helping to open windows into what the SM shares with its heritage and environment, enable us simultaneously to see what is unique about it. The Matthean rites of passage or initiation introduce the disciples to a vision in which the passion of the Christ and eschatological reward are translated into a new ethical mode. The general and typical elements of paraenesis are subsumed by this transformational process into a rhetorical mode of "excess" (see III.A.). And the collection of the sage's teachings, which by its very character allows considerable flexibility for development, is changed into a passionate discourse that could be read or heard as the teacher's farewell even before he and his followers embark on their mission!

1.1   *Notes on the Comparative Study of Genre*

Although I have learned much from the form criticism of yesteryear and the more recent studies in comparative literature and rhetoric, I think that two essential matters are frequently neglected, if not ignored completely: (1) the specificity of certain texts in their concrete contexts, and (2) the character of genre as reader practice as well as classification of forms.

1.2   I shall lead off these observations by noting Betz' argument that the literary genre of the SM is the Greek *epitomē*. He holds that in keeping with the Hellenistic tradition of the epitome, the SM presents "the theology of Jesus in a systematic fashion....Its function is to provide the disciple of Jesus with the necessary tool for becoming a Jesus theologian...," that is, "to theologize creatively along the lines of the theology of the master" (15). I have found Betz' essay useful, particularly his explication of the motif of the "two ways" in the SM. I shall discuss this motif later. Here I would register two problems that I have with his thesis. One is that an internal reading of the SM and the Gospel of Matthew should tell the reader that the SM is not a condensation or summary of a larger system of the master's philosophy, as in the epitome (see Betz: 13). It may be deceptively like such a summary from the standpoint of an external literary comparison (e.g., if one looks from the vantage of certain instances of the epitome and tries to find similarities in other works). The SM, however, follows the design of a larger mosaic, and thus it presupposes and alludes to the whole rather than summarizing it. I hope this will become clear from parts II and III of this study.

1.3   The second problem could be taken as a sub-category of the first one: Betz' instances do not offer real support of his argument. Epictetus' *Enchiridion*, one of his primary examples, seems as far removed from the SM as the proverbial distance of Athens from Jerusalem. To show what I mean I shall quote a relatively short "canon" or "rule" from the *Enchiridion*:

> Upon every accident, remember to turn towards yourself and inquire what faculty you have for its use. If you encounter a handsome person, you will find continence the faculty needed; if pain, then fortitude; if reviling, then patience. And when thus habituated, the phenomena of existence will not overwhelm (X: 379).

Here the elder or teacher instructs the learner and the style is sententious. It fits what Gammie calls paraenesis as a subgenre of a secondary genre. But in terms of the rhetorical style (to be discussed in III.A.), the subject matter taken up, and the relation of the teacher to the disciple (and concomitantly, the sort of community in which they are bound to each other), they are as different as night from day. (See further the discussion in endnote 1.)

1.4   On the other hand, my intention is not to say that the epitome and other Hellenistic forms are unrelated to the SM. To my mind, the best view of the matter is that new genres were created out of pre-existing genres, on the analogy of the metaphoric process in which two previously separate understandings in different fields of meaning are brought together in a new configuration (Gerhart and Russell). Indeed, perhaps part of our problem is that of thinking rigidly in terms of a genre into which a work either does or does not fit. Suppose, however, we followed the suggestion of Fredric Jameson that readers have inherited a "generic system," which is a set of forms determining audience expectations within "a constellation of ideal relationships"? By contrast, the work itself would be viewed as "a concrete verbal composition."

> We must then understand the former as constituting something like an environment for the latter, which emerges into a world in which the genres form a given determinate relationship among themselves, and which then seeks to define itself in terms of that relationship (153).

He says there are two alternatives: a work may be viewed in terms of a given genre or it may, "by proposing a new synthesis, make an implicit commentary on the [generic] system itself" (*ibid.*). He says, furthermore, that "the relationship between the genres may itself play a signifying and functional role within the individual work itself" (154).

      "Proposing a new synthesis" may amount to the beginning of a new genre if the work is received and imitated in the formation of a new tradition. I think, for example, of a work which was certainly the prototype of many modern and contemporary authors and critics, namely, Samuel Taylor Coleridge's *Biographia Literaria*. In it Coleridge takes his own life as the backdrop and the lives and works of other poets as the immediate subjects of what he really wants to write about. His real subject is the imagination as a power linking sensibility and mind, literature and philosophy.

1.6   To return to Jameson's two alternatives, my working hypothesis is that the process resulting in the formation of the narrative gospel was an implicit critique of the system of genres that prevailed in the Graeco-Roman world (see Williams, 1985: 201–14 and 1988: 87–109). To focus on one literary element in the gospel genre, paraenesis, it has been assumed from the work of pioneering critics like Dibelius that paraenetic sayings are general and unoriginal (Dibelius, 1975: 5). Leo Perdue objects, in considering the issue of social settings, that it is rather odd to suggest that an author who compiles a paraenetic text, even if he uses a good deal of unoriginal material, would not choose admonitions and other traditional materials to address real issues in the life of the community itself (1981b: 247).

In other words, from a social-critical standpoint, the student can get some idea of real issues in the life of a community even when traditional material is used. I would go farther than Perdue in holding that new communities may and do use unoriginal materials, but see it and shape it in new ways. I propose that in light of his social setting and theology of salvation, Matthew formed paraenetic material into the SM. The SM is an original work as Matthew made it over from Q, and its teachings were to be perceived by the teacher's students as new.

1.7   The SM can be read and understood in a dialectical relation to other genres and subgenres. Studying this dialectical relation aids the reader to get a sense of its historicity—its manner of representing the human situation of remembrance and care as addressed by Jesus and the early Christian tradition. Mary Gerhart has pointed out that genre is a matter of the reader's or hearer's *performance*, the production of a new reading, as well as of classifying frames of reference according to forms predetermined in a given culture or tradition (Gerhart). My primary problem with Gammie's otherwise very helpful morphology of paraenetic literature is that he only touches on this productive, performancial aspect of genre. Even in his section on the productive or heuristic function of paraenetic literature, his concerns remain chiefly taxonomic. He thinks in terms of the *relation* of elements and subgenres in a particular work (4.4.) and mentions *comparison* of works, but I am concerned with the dynamics of tradition whereby new experiences lead to new readings and new works. (And vice-versa, of course: new readings and works may be the occasion of fundamental life-changes.)

As indicated in my introductory comments, I think the most helpful models for clarifying this dialectical relationship of genres are to be drawn from studies of the initiation process, the dominant literary features of paraenesis, and the distinctive literary and theological themes of the Gospel of Matthew. Finally, the SM must be read on its own terms within the Gospel of Matthew.

2.1   *The Two Ways*

First to set the scene of the SM. It is the first of five long discourses in Matthew. All of them except parts of ch. 13 are directed to the "disciples" or intimate followers (chs. 5–7; 13; 18; 24–25; the Twelve in ch. 10). Whether the number is limited to the Twelve in 5:1 is not clear. The discourse in chs. 5–7 is given on a mountain, as is the final, apocalyptic speech (24:3). It is informed by eschatological assumptions and is addressed to the blessed ones who make up the messianic community centered in the teachings of Jesus Messiah. The sententious form and paraenetic purpose of much of the material in the SM has been recognized since Dibelius (1935) and Bultmann. This material generally fits Gammie's description of paraenesis (Gammie, 1 and 2.2.2.).

2.2   However, to get better literary critical bearings on paraenesis in the Hellenistic Jewish context I shall focus first on the motif of the *two ways*, which was deeply imbedded in the Jewish tradition (LaPorte: 109–114; McDonald, 77; cf. Betz: 286–90). It is articulated in a kind of recapitulatory exhortation in Matt. 7:13–14 (see Gammie, 2:5, on paraenesis and exhortation):

> Enter through the narrow gate, for the gate is wide and the way is easy that leads to destruction, and those that enter by it are many. For the gate is narrow and the way is hard that leads to life, and those that find it are few.

In the Torah, the exhortations so characteristic of Deuteronomy reach a high point in the command to choose between life and death (Deut 30:15–20), and many of the proverbs in the Book of Proverbs circle around the alternative paths of life and death (Prov 10:2; 12:28; passim). The image of the two ways is important in the ethical reflections of Philo (LaPorte: 110), and it was well known to the rabbis (Abot 2:1; Berakot 28b; Sifré Deut. as quoted in Montefiore and Loewe: 549). I do not, however, presently know of another instance where it is expressed in exactly the form of Matt 7:13–14. Matthew 7:13 falls within the ancient Jewish form of the instruction proverb with a motive clause (see Gammie, loc. cit.). The instruction proverb expressed an imperative or prohibition, followed by a reason supporting the instruction. For example:

> Speak not into the ears of a fool, for he will despise the wisdom of your words (Prov 23:9).

In the SM the contrast of the two ways takes place in two stages and from two points of view: (1) The contrast between the way of the Jesus Messiah community and the way of the ancient tradition that it both presupposes and transcends. In this stage, ch. 5, the messianic teacher appeals to his own authority as over against the scriptural tradition (5:17–48). The authority of the messianic teacher is then presupposed in the second stage. (2) The second stage involves the juxtaposition of faith and righteousness to unfaith and unrighteousness (chs. 6–7). Chapter 5 contains fewer examples of the subgenre of paraenesis than the other section, chs. 6–7, which is more conventional and easier to compare to paraenesis as known from the Jewish tradition and Greek sources.

I shall first focus on chs. 6–7. Chapter 5 articulates a unique Christian principle which Matthew expresses in his distinctive manner. This principle will be explicated in section 3 of the paper.

2.3   Chapters 6 and 7 exhibit four of the five features of Hellenistic paraenesis that Perdue, in his study of paraenesis in the Letter of James, derives from Malherbe and finds applicable to James. These four are traditional and unoriginal material, general applicability of precepts, admonitions already known or heard, and a close, even intensely intimate relation of teacher to student (Perdue, 1981b: 242–46). Even the Our Father, 6:9–13, is not original in the general sense that all the elements, from the invocation "Our Father in heaven" to the petition for speedy fulfillment of the divine rule, are known from Jewish sources (Moore: 208, 212–13). Perhaps the Lord's Prayer has a certain eschatological sharpness which its analogues might not have in the Jewish texts and which it certainly does not display in Luke's form of the prayer in Q (Lk. 11:2–4). But the deduction of this eschatological urgency comes in great part from its proximity to the distinctively Matthean material in chapter 5 and its overall context in Matthew.

The most unusual passage in chs. 6–7 is 7:21–23. Its instructional content is not exceptional, a kind of eschatological variation on the "faith without works" theme found also in James (Jas 2:26). However, the claim of the messianic teacher to be the eschatological judge is quite striking. Moreover, in the context of Matthew, specifically in relation to the teaching on love of enemies (5:44–48) and the parabolic pronouncement on the sheep and the goats (25:31–46), it takes on the character of what I would call an "ethical mysticism" (to be discussed below).

2.4   The one feature cited by Perdue that is not present in chs. 6 and 7 is the use of the *paradeigma* (pl. *paradeigmata*). Paradeigmata are "human examples of virtue who embody the type of behavior the teacher admonishes his audience to emulate" (1981b: 245). Jesus speaks of no great and famous worthies like heroes, generals, kings, or philosophers, as in Greek and Roman sources. Nor does he mention, as in the Letter of James, important figures from the scriptural tradition such as Abraham, Rahab, Job, and the prophets (Jas 2:14–26; 5:7–11, 13–20). There are exemplars indeed, mainly negative models, which the messianic teacher presents in some of his admonitions (Gammie: 2.4.) and in two metaphorical sayings:

And whenever you pray, you shall not be like the hypocrites.... (6:5).

> Therefore do not be like [the gentiles who heap up empty phrases in prayer] (6:8).

> And whenever you fast, do not look dismal, like the the hypocrites.... (6:16).

> Whoever therefore hears these words of mine and does them will be like a wise man who builds his house upon the rock.... (7:24).

> And whoever hears these words of mine and does not do them will be like a foolish man who built his house upon the sand.... (7:26).

These models are of the stuff of traditional wisdom. Unlike the paradeigma most of them are negative and they do not name a specific person known for his deeds or misdeeds. In fact, it is striking that in the four canonical gospels there are, arguably, no paradeigmata in the strict sense. The believers are charged and invited to be *like* certain figures in the parables, and by implication in the context of the gospel narratives they are to be like Jesus. In other words, Jesus himself is the main paradeigma or paradigm. I would surmise two reasons for this. One is that paradeigmata were originally a Hellenistic form and thus not a literary convention in Jewish wisdom literature (see Mack on the encomium: 128–137). There was, of course, a growing Hellenistic influence, even in the early Jesus movement, but this factor could have been outweighed by the other, which was the role of Jesus in the gospels as the enactor and interpreter of his own teachings. The latter reason touches on the larger context of the gospels and their distinctiveness as genre.[1]

2.5   The most likely candidate for direct borrowing from Hellenistic forms that I find in the SM is the paraenetic topic (McDonald: 70–83). The Hellenistic topos was made up of instructional sentences that both urged a certain type of conduct or attitude and gave brief reasons for the instruction; sometimes they included rhetorical questions. The mode of presenting topics in Matthew 6 and 7 may have been influenced by this Hellenistic form and style of paraenesis. The quotation from the Enchiridion of Epictetus in part I of this paper is a good example of Greek paraenesis. Another appropriate instance is found in parts of Epicurus' letter to Menoeceus as quoted by Diogenes Laertius. The letter deals with "conduct of life" (*biōtikōn*, X.117).

> Those things which without ceasing I have declared unto thee, those do, and exercise thyself therein, holding them to be elements of the good life. First believe that God is a living being immortal and blessed.... (X.123, trans. slightly modified).

> Exercise thyself in these and kindred precepts day and night, both by thyself and with the one who is like thee.... (X.135, trans. slightly modified).

Most of Matthew 6 and much of Matthew 7 is paraenetic. Many of the topoi are peculiar to Matthew in the synoptic tradition (6:1–4, 5–8, 16–18; 7:6, 15), but Q had already gathered some paraenetic material that Matthew and Luke used (Matt. 6:19–21/Lk. 12:33–34; 6:25–33/Lk. 12:22–31; 7:1–2/Lk. 6:37–38, 42; 7:7–8/Lk. 11:9–10; 7:13–14/Lk. 13:23–24; Matt. 5:39–42, 44, 48 will be mentioned below).

2.6   If paraenesis is taken in the very specific sense of a subgenre of a secondary genre of wisdom literature, then it does not seem that the synoptic gospels make extensive use of it. Most of the specific paraenetic forms in Matthew and Luke are from Q.[2] Why does paraenesis not have a greater part in the gospels as a whole? It may be that the parable was so associated with Jesus and the chreia was so useful in the tradition's tendency in telling the Jesus story, that paraenesis was effectively ignored or displaced (see Williams, 1988).

The paraenetic sayings unique to Matthew encompass three of the negative models already mentioned (two in the unit on prayer, 6:5–8, one in the topos on fasting, 6:16–18); they also include the teaching on almsgiving (6:1–4), not being anxious about tomorrow (6:34), not throwing pearls before swine (7:6), and warning about false prophets (7:15). He expands a Q saying in 7:13–14 (Luke 13:23–24). In addition, we find other Q sayings in ch. 6, as listed in the previous paragraph. Why did Matthew not only concentrate Q material in chapters 6 and 7, but compose his own paraenetic strings? The question becomes even more complex and intriguing when we observe the paraenesis in chapter 5, which is where the evangelist has put his own signature most clearly on the discourse. The saying on light, 5:16, may be understood as paraenetic, particularly within the context of 5:13–16, and so too may the forbidding of oaths, 5:34–37. Part of the teaching on adultery is paraenetic, 5:29–30 (cf. 18:8–9), but it may be based on Mark 9:43–48. There are three paraenetic Q passages in chapter 5: 5:39–42, on retaliation; 5:24–25, on reconciliation; and 5:44, 48, on love of enemies. The latter verse, "You must therefore be perfect (*teleioi*) as your heavenly Father is perfect (*teleios*)," illustrates the distinctive character of Matthew's moral theology. It brings to a climax the exhortations to lead a life of moral perfection (=transformation). The parallel in Luke 6:36, "Be compassionate (*oiktirmonēs*), just as your Father is compassionate (*oiktirmōn*)," does not have the same climactic function and in content must be closer to Q.

     Why does the writer otherwise make little use of paraenesis in his gospel, yet turn to it as the dominant mode of communication in the SM, especially in 6:1–7:15? There must be something here not apparent to a reader removed from Matthew's life-setting. In § 3.4 of this paper I will propose that this something has to do with the passion and death of the messianic revealer.

2.8   With the penultimate topic of the SM, 7:21–23, the discourse moves away from paraenetic wisdom and back toward the distinctively Matthean message of ch. 5. This topic thus offers a good transition from the discussion of the second stage of the discourse to a consideration of the first stage. Matthew 7:21–23 has its parallel in Luke 6:46 and 13:26–27. If Luke's use of the material is closer to Q, then we can mark out sharply the Matthean themes of the authority of the messianic teacher and an ethical mysticism that is rooted in a transformation of the principle of sacrifice. The exclusiveness of the Matthean Jesus and the break with the Judaic tradition is seen in Jesus' audacious claim to authority over the "way" or "gate" into the kingdom of God. At the same time this claim recognizes that names and institutions count for little in an eschatological perspective.

> Not everyone who says to me, "Lord, Lord," shall enter into the kingdom of heaven, but the one who does the will of my Father in heaven (7:21).

Luke's version, Lk. 6:46, could simply be construed as the words of an authoritative teacher who wants to know why followers do not actualize his counsel. The topic continues:

> Many will say to me on that day, "Lord, Lord, did we not prophesy in your name, and in your name cast out demons, and in your name do many mighty works?" And then I will declare to them, "I never knew you; depart from me, O workers of iniquity." (7:22–23).

The Lucan parallel, Lk. 13:26–27, belongs to a parable of judgment. In Matthew Jesus enters into the parable, so to say: he speaks as the final judge. His saying reads as a summation of the parable-like pronouncement on the sheep and the goats in Matt 25:31–46. The participants in the reign of God do not necessarily call the name of the Messiah-Teacher, but they serve him whenever they help another in distress. Although the messianic communalists are exhorted to surrender themselves and see themselves totally in light of the reign of God, they cannot know, short of the eschaton, who God's true servants are. Meanwhile, they are to love their enemies and understand that the Father "makes his sun rise on the evil and on the good and sends rain on the just and on the unjust" (5:45). Even the apparent workers for the Kingdom who cast out demons may turn out to be evildoers! Those who serve God do not necessarily have the inside names or "catchwords" for the works they are doing.

        This point of view expressed at the end (the actual climax) of the SM is what I would call "ethical mysticism": the reality of the Lord is not simply locatable in name and doctrine, but is encountered in the sphere of moral intentions and acts. The Gospel of Matthew places a radical demand on the disciples, yet it affirms that all morality, and certainly any kind of moralism, is not only inadequate before God—but the moralizing labels that are assigned on the human level are invariably wrong! The key to this ethical mysticism lies in chapter 5 of Matthew and its relation to the passion of the Messiah.

3.1   Matthew 5: Excess, Fulfillment, and Sacrifice

In an interesting discussion of the social settings of paraenesis, Perdue has drawn upon the studies of Victor Turner in order to describe the social setting of wisdom instructions (Perdue, 1981a and in this issue, "Social Character"). Conceiving a dialectical model of structure and anti-structure for clarifying social roles, customs, and rituals, Turner employs van Gennep's analysis of rites of passage in delineating three phases of these rites: separation from the dominant social structure; liminality, in which the initiate is not supported by the social and cultural elements of the community; and incorporation, the initiate's assumption of a new role in the social structure. Perdue argues that the phase of liminality is the characteristic setting of wisdom instructions. The liminal situation may be the occasion of a "subversive paraenesis" that seeks to undermine the prevailing social order (this issue, "Social Character": § 2.2.) This model derived from Turner and van Gennep certainly illuminates the SM.

The presupposition of the SM is that the self-understanding of the addressees is marginal in relation both to the dominant Judaic tradition and the Roman governmental structure. The disciples are to be "radicals" in the sense that they are called upon to live out in thought, word, and deed the very *root* of what God intends. The site of the discourse, a mountain where the disciples are drawn aside to receive the revelatory teachings of Jesus, represents a geographical symbolism that belongs to the language of ritual process and provides a narrative backdrop for the ethical expression of the themes of fulfillment and transformation. Having been separated from their previous circumstances, the disciples are now in a liminal setting as they are in the process of being incorporated into the new community of the messiah-teacher.

3.2   A Rhetoric of Excess

The authority of the messianic teacher is that of fulfillment. He comes not to abolish the law and the prophets but to fulfill them. Not a dot or iota of the law will perish until the fulfillment of God's designs, and likewise even the *least* of the commandments is to be obeyed. "For I tell you, unless your righteousness be more than that of the scribes and Pharisees, you will never enter the kingdom of heaven" (5:20). The demand for radical obedience is expressed in an hyperbolic rhetoric which Frank Kermode has perceptively called a *rhetoric of excess*. Not even the smallest mark of the (written) Torah is to be considered null. Even the least of the commandments is to be observed. The members of the elect community must be *more* righteous than the acknowledged teachers of the Torah, whose opponents called them "separatists," *pĕrûšîm* ("Pharisees"). The disciples of Jesus are even more "separated," so to say, than the Pharisees; their righteousness is to be radical, otherwise they will *never* (*ou mē*) enter the Kingdom (5:20).

This rhetoric of excess is structured in 5:21–48 by a series of contrasts between the old Torah and the new commandments of the messianic teacher. Each contrast is introduced with the formula, "You have heard that it was said," which was a formulaic way of citing Scripture. The rabbinic formula was *šene ʾĕmar*, "as it is said" (e.g., Abot 1:17, *inter alia*). After stating what was said (written in Scripture), Jesus then follows with the antithetical "But I say to you." The pairs of contrasts:

> You shall not kill/to be angry with or insult your brother is to be liable to judgment
>
> You shall not commit adultery/looking lustfully at a woman is already adultery
>
> To divorce one's wife it is necessary to give her a divorce certificate/divorce prohibited except for adultery
>
> You shall not swear (oaths) falsely/do no swear at all
>
> *Lex talionis* ("eye for an eye," etc.)/do not resist the evildoer
>
> You shall love your neighbor and hate your enemy[3]/love your enemies

Parallels of some sort have been found in rabbinic and Essene sources for most of these exhortations in the antitheses. But we do not find elsewhere this rhetoric of excess or assumption of authority by the individual teacher. The Pharisaic-rabbinic tradition claimed to be the "tradition of the fathers," which is to say that however innovative the rabbis might be— and some of them were quite innovative—the authority with which they spoke, the *voice* to which they gave utterance, was always in principle the voice of the elders, the sages of the past who had transmitted the oral revelation given at Sinai (Abot 1:1; on voice see Williams, 1981: 78–80). Jesus, by stark contrast, is depicted as the messianic teacher, the one embodying the new order of God. In other words, his voice represents the voice of God for the messianic community that the Gospel of Matthew addresses. The consequence is that some of the features of Hellenistic paraenesis discussed in section 2 will not apply in Matthew 5. No matter whether some of the teachings are traditional and unoriginal: they are to be received and acted on as completely new. They present themselves as *not* having been heard before—even if they actually have been in some form. The only really valuable paradeigma in history is the Teacher himself.

To bring the rhetoric of excess and the call to radical obedience into better focus, let us look at a topic in Matthew 5, the teaching on retaliation.

> You have heard that it was said, "An eye for an eye and a tooth for a tooth," But I say to you, Do not resist the one who is evil; but whoever strikes you on the right cheek, turn to him also the other one; and if anyone would sue you and take your coat, let him have your cloak as well; and whoever forces you to go one mile, go with him two miles. Give to the one begging from you, and do not refuse the one wanting to borrow from you (5:38–42).

To take this style of rhetoric literally would be just as foolish as trying to obey the teaching on adultery by engaging in self-mutilation (5:27–30). If someone hits me am I to say, "Now hit me again"? If I were to lose $1,000 in a lawsuit, should I offer the winning party another one thousand on Christian principles?

The best way of making sense of the teaching on retaliation is to recognize both the rhetorical style and the serious nature of the summons. One interpreter who has done just that with great insight is Robert Tannehill. He points out that the antitheses in Matthew 5 are not legal rules, which involve quite another genre. The legal prescription should be manageable in an easily understood literal sense (that is, there should be a clear consensus on definition). It deals with behavior, and if it deals with intention it still has to have provable action as its base. And finally, it must permit deduction as to the range of its application or how it might be amended if it turns out to be unclear. Tannehill points out that the language of the antitheses is not legal, but of a rhetorical type that would be employed for persuasion and instruction: the "focal instance." By this he means a case from a larger field of reference which is intensified in order to achieve clarity. The case as stated must be both specific and extreme. Its extremeness—part of Matthew's rhetoric of excess—is for the purpose of contrasting the advocated teaching with ordinary human behavior, so inducing a new way of looking at the whole field of behavior. In this case the field of behavior covers responses to violations of one's person or excessive demands placed upon the person.

To discuss specifics, verses 39–42 have the same core of meaning as Luke's version of Q in Lk. 6:29–30. Yet a comparison of the two shows that Matthew extends the pronouncement: "Do not resist one who is evil....and if anyone forces you to go one mile, go with him two miles." A similar teaching elsewhere in Matthew also has a Lucan parallel, but again, Matthew's form of it exaggerates to an extent that would be senseless if taken literally:

> Then Peter came up and said to him, "Lord, how often shall my brother sin against me, and I forgive him? As many as seven times?" Jesus said to him,"I do not say to you seven times, but seventy times seven!" (Matt 18:21–22; see Luke 17:4).

The Greek of the last phrase could be read "seventy-seven times." Either way, it is clearly hyperbole. Would one keep a record of having forgiven someone and feel cleared of the obligation after the 77th time? Rather than defining forgiveness as behavior, which any genre of law would do, this saying requires a way of seeing the other person that always keeps the possibility of forgiveness open.

The teaching on retaliation in Matthew 5 is a focal instance in the same field of reference as the teaching on forgiveness in Matt 18:21–22. The way of seeing things that it urges is not understood at all if one were to go around turning the other cheek if it were slapped, etc. What the messianic teaching entails is to find concrete modes of behavior which stem from the will to encompass the offender and the enemy in one's own community of being.

The exhortation to nonretaliation is brought to a head in Matt 5:43–48, on loving one's enemies. The messianic communalists are to be "perfect" as the heavenly Father is perfect. In other words, they are to imitate the Father. In the narrative context of Matthew the concrete paradeigma is the Messiah-Son (see § 3.4). The Teacher teaches that the ones separated out for mission in the eschatological community must see everything in a new way. This includes the knowledge that even the seemingly evil and unjust ones are given the benefit of divine providence—God's sun shines on them too and his rain falls also on them.

3.3   The Principle of Sacrifice

Why should believers love their enemies? My response to this point has been that the SM is centered in an ethical mysticism whose focal point is the affirmation that both the acting subject who is inside the messianic community and the other—even the hostile other—are encompassed by God's loving care. And if one were to approach the question from a sociological or sociopsychological standpoint, then undoubtedly the mutual support of the messianic community, with the messianic teacher at the center of its authority structure, would loom large as a motivating factor. But cutting through these other theological and socio-logical factors is the the deepest and most important source of motivation: *the principle of sacrifice*, which was transformed into a new religious mode in Matthew's depiction of the messianic community.

Kermode has put his finger on this principle in pointing out the structure of fulfillment and its relation to transformation in Matthew. Referring to the theme of fulfillment in Matthew 5, Kermode comments, "Fulfillment requires transformation, and transformation entails a certain excess" (388). Matthew 5 demands exceeding the requirements of the Law of Moses.

> The letter of the Law is complete in the minutest detail; one must believe that, exactly as a devout Jew believes it, yet still believe that the Law must be transformed, that it must unexpectedly bear the weight of Jesus' gnomic excess, must though already full be fulfilled (389).

Jesus' "gnomic excess" is the rhetorical side of the transformation both presupposed and advocated.

By definition "transformation" means exceeding some previous form as something is reshaped and reconstituted. Most of our uses of the verb predicate a fundamental change in which something is broken down and converted into something else.

In a religious context excess and transformation are realities that originally and typically revolve around the principle of sacrifice, which involves a breaking down of the sacrificial victim in order to reconstitute symbolically the human community for which it is sacrificed (Girard, 1977). Here I must limit myself to a summary statement about how the principle of sacrifice is realized literarily in the Hebrew Bible and the New Testament.[4]

In the narratives of the Hebrew Bible all the key founding figures undergo a trial of some sort, and in fact their very lives are endangered in many instances. We find this in the stories of Cain and Abel, Abraham and Isaac, Jacob and Esau, Joseph and his brothers, Moses and Aaron, and David and his brothers. (This pattern also applies to Job, but he is not so obviously a founding figure as these personages who appear in the Law and the Prophets.) The pattern is properly termed "sacrificial." The favored one of God is the younger son. The older son loses out to the younger, who supplants him. The younger is always a shepherd, whereas the older is a farmer or hunter. The one exception to the younger brother's success is the tale of Cain and Abel. In this tale nothing is concealed about the sacrificial atmosphere of the deed. The blood of the murdered brother "cries out" to God from the ground, and God banishes Cain from the arable soil, putting a sign on him that is simultaneously a mark to protect him and a reminder of the curse upon him. Cain leaves the Lord's presence and goes to live in the land of Wandering (Hebrew *nôd*). In other words, the exception to the pattern of the younger brother superseding the elder proves the rule, for the murder of Abel tells how the origins of mankind are out of kilter.

There is a relationship between biblical narrative patterns and the most fundamental divine command concerning the offering of sacrificial victims. This command is the demand to offer the first-fruits and the first-born to God, as in this statute:

> You shall not delay to offer from the fulness of your harvest and from the outflow of your presses. The firstborn of your sons you shall give to me. You shall do likewise with your sheep and your oxen.... (Exod 22:29–30, RSV).

The firstborn is to be offered to God. In the historical period, and probably before, the command was doubtlessly usually fulfilled by a symbolic substitution of some sort. But the point is that we find here the theological principle that life belongs to God; the forms of life can be used and violence averted only if these forms of life are redeemed. Since this principle validates a form of violence committed on a human or animal victim, it may be viewed as a rationalization that conceals a deep religious and cultural problem (so Girard). In any event, the required redemption of life for human use is achieved through sacrifice of first fruits and firstborn sons (see also Exod 34:19–22). Likewise in the tales of origins the firstborn is "sacrificed," so to speak, for the benefit of the younger son, who is the chosen of God and whom the Israelite audience knows to be its link with the promises of the God of Israel. But the younger son becomes, in his turn, a kind of victim who is threatened both by human beings and by God (Gen 22:1–19; 32:23–33; 37:19–30; 39:7–20; Exod 4:24–26).

The same generative religious pattern is realized in the New Testament. Paul states it expressly in Romans 8:18–30. The Son of God is "the firstborn of many brothers" (Rom 8:29). They, like the Son, suffer in the present age, but these sufferings are to be succeeded by "adoption as sons, the redemption of our bodies" (Rom 8:23). Once one knows the biblical background out of which this language comes, one could read that to mean: "Believers in Christ are 'younger sons' and, like their Elder Brother, victims in the present age, but they, like him and through him, will be delivered from this victimage."

In all four gospels the passion narratives form the largest bloc of coherent narrative material. The language of sacrifice is most noticeable in Mark, where the Son of man "came not to be served but to serve, and to give his life as a ransom for many" (Mark 10:45). In Mark the disciples are to imitate Jesus as a kind of sacrifice in that they are to engage in a ministry of self-giving in the name of the Son of man.

But mention of this ministry touches on a crucial point: however ambiguous the gospels may be at points concerning sacrifice, particularly the death of Jesus construed as sacrifice, still the gospel writers do not understand this death as the same thing as Temple sacrifices that are merely transferred to the one chosen, the victim-son. The crucified one is not so much an involuntary victim as one who gives his life voluntarily (Mark 10:45; 14:22–25, 36; John 15:13; cf. the hymn quoted by Paul in Phil. 2:6–11 and, in the Hebrew Bible, Isa. 52:13–53:12). The gospel accounts of Jesus' death point to the end of the sacrificial cult as a new era dawns (Matt 26:51–54; Mark 15:37–39; Luke 23:45; John 2:18–22; 4:16–23).

The Gospel of Matthew, for its part, is distinguished by a rhetoric of excess that expresses the themes of fulfillment and transformation. The redemptive salvation event becomes in the Matthean view a constituting reality *that is represented in the moral acts and intentions of the disciples, the ideal members of the messianic community.* To love one's enemy and not to resist the evil doer is the transformation of sacrificial offerings into renewal of the self and deeds of self-giving. These deeds are the "more" that Jesus exhorts his listeners to do in Matthew. "If you salute only your brothers, what more (*perisson*) are you doing than others?" (5:47). "Unless your righteousness be more (*perisseusē*) than that of the Pharisees, you will never enter the kingdom of heaven" (5:20).

The Jesus of Matthew teaches in parables "what has been hidden since the foundation of the world" (Matt 13:35, citing Ps 78:2). What is hidden is revealed in another passage as the divine order prepared for the servants of God "from the foundation of the world" (25:34). This speech in Matthew 25:31–46 reads like a parable in which Jesus as Son of man becomes both speaker and subject.

It is significant that this parabolic speech, or allegory if one prefers, is placed just before the account of the Last Supper on the first day of Passover (Matt 26). The juxtaposition implies a relation of Jesus' passion and this speech, in which the servants of God are those to whom the Ruler of the new age appears in the guise of "the least of these my brothers." It is to them that the Ruler says,

...I was hungry and you gave me food, I was thirsty and you gave me drink, I was a stranger and you welcomed me, I was naked and you clothed me, I was sick and you visited me (25:35–36).

3.4   *Paraenesis and Sacrifice Transformed*

Matthew's transformation of the principle of sacrifice into a christologically based moral way may explain why the SM is replete with paraenetic instruction, especially in chapters 6 and 7. It was pointed out that the paraenetic style in that section is peculiar. For one thing, Matthew had to collect a number of sayings that were evidently scattered about in Q. Of course, a model for the discourse was probably already present in Q (Luke 6:20–49), and this Q speech already included some paraenesis (Luke 6:27–30, 31, 36, 37–38, 42). Nonetheless, Matthew added considerably to the paraenetic material with sayings unique to him in the Synoptics (5:16, 34–37; 6:1–4, 5–8, 16–18; 7:6, 15; for occasional similarities and parallels in extracanonical texts, see Funk). Yet the paraenetic passages in the rest of Matthew are few, particularly if one looks for concrete instances of the subgenre itself. Of these others, just three are found only in Matthew (10:17; 11:28–29; 23:9–10). Why, then, is the SM "paraenetic"?

I propose that the answer lies in what the author of the Gospel of Matthew does in forming his version of the Christian ethos out of the primitive sayings tradition, Hellenistic modes of moral instruction, a developing Christian Passion tradition, and the ancient tradition of the death of the sage. It is in the death of the sage, I think, that we find the key to the paraenesis of the SM. Leo Perdue has shown that paraenesis is often connected with the paradigmatic death of the ideal sage in ancient Near Eastern, Jewish, and Greek sources. He summarizes:

> Calling together his disciples(s) and/or descendants, the sage issues them a teaching for life which serves as a summary of what he has learned. The teaching itself does not speculate about the nature of a future life, or what it is like to die....While other paradigms of moral behavior may be cited, it is clear that the teacher himself serves as the major model to emulate....The moment of imminent death is that point where there is the correspondence of teaching, life, and paradeigma. And in one sense the sage has achieved victory over death (this issue, "Death of Sage").

Perdue comments concerning the social function of the dying sage's paraenesis:

> In many cases it is clear that a community constructs a fictive world in which a famous figure speaks to it. The teaching and narrative become a social myth designed to shape the group's identity and continue its existence. During a time of threatening collapse these myths take on critical significance, for the preservation of the tradition and the maintenance of the community's existence are the major functions of this literature (ibid.).

As Perdue points out, the most well known legend of the paradigmatic death of a sage was that of Socrates, which served as a model not only to Greek and Roman philosophers but also to Christian thinkers (see Döring).

When we examine the SM, we see that in many respects it fits the main features of Perdue's description. Clearly it is paraenetic and "a teaching for life" as no other Matthean discourse is. I would hesitate to describe it as a "summary," just as I think the word "condensation" is misleading (see discussion of Betz' thesis in section 1). However, I did describe it as a speech that "presupposes and alludes to the whole." And I have commented that one reason there are no paradeigmata in the SM is that Jesus himself is the main paradigm.

Lambrecht offers support of the last point in his study of the SM. He concludes that in the beatitudes, Matt 5:3–12, "the Matthean Jesus paints..., as it were unintentionally, a full-length portrait of himself. He is the paradigm, the great model...." (66). To bolster his argument Lambrecht cites other texts in Matthew (8:17; 11:28–30; 12:18–21; 21:5; note *praus*, "meek" or "humble," in 11:29 and 21:5). He refers also to the parabolic judgment speech, 25:31–46, in which the Son of man is present in the anonymous needy person. To Lambrecht's list I would add two passages which are of a different sort from his, but which also reflect the Matthean picture of the messianic teacher as moral model:

> [Pilates' wife sends a message to him:]
> "Have nothing to do with that righteous man (*dikaio*), for I have suffered much over him today in a dream" (27:19).

> [Jesus says to his disciples:]
> "It is enough for the disciple to be like his teacher, and the servant like his master" (10:25; see Luke 6:40).

Finally, the true conclusion of the SM, 7:21–23, reads like a kind of warning before the teacher departs. As already pointed out, it is a miniature form of the speech in 25:31–46. It is a statement that alludes to a period of separation before the Lord is seen again "in that day." The wisdom parable of 7:24–27 functions as an epilogue that reinforces and caps off the teacher's "last words."

In other words, the SM must surely have reminded anyone in a Jewish or Graeco-Roman setting of the final testament of the ideal sage. The paraenetic style and the clear implication that the teacher himself is the model to emulate were features of a pervasive picture of the ideal teacher's death. And if these features were not enough to suggest that connection, the warning in 7:21–23 could be construed as a kind of anticipatory farewell warning. Yet this "final testament" is not chronologically final in the story Matthew tells. Why not?

I propose that Matthew either understood or intuited that the passion, death, and resurrection of Jesus were related at their deepest level to the ethical demands of the SM. That insight, together with the tendency to cherish the teachings of the master (Q), led Matthew to shift the final teaching to the beginning of the master's instruction of his disciples. Or to put it another way, for Matthew the redemptive paradigm of the suffering that saves is *already present*, the "end" is already actual in the "beginning." Sacrifice becomes moral transformation.[5] In other words, the author of Matthew engages in a new reading of the tradition in which a metaphoric process is at work: two different fields of understanding (wisdom and sacrifice), in which the key models are perceived as disparate if not incongruous (sage and victim), are brought together by means of displacing the dying sage's farewell speech to the beginning of his ministry and associating his paraenetic precepts with the passion of the Teacher whose death reveals God's intention to aid all victims and end their plight. I know, of course, that I have produced a new reading of Matthew's new reading; the two are inseparable, even if necessarily distinguishable. However, I think the connection of genre to performance and creation of new texts in the process of interpretation cannot be denied.

4.   Conclusion

The disciples who go apart and come to their master at the mountain are initiated by instruction into the redemptive community. This community is a manifestation of the kingdom of God. The Kingdom is not simply an object or "place" to be attained in the eschaton; it is also and much more an actual occurrence when the Son of man is served in the guise of the needy neighbor. This is the central ethical-religious impulse of the Matthean gospel; it expresses itself in a rhetoric of excess that converts paraenetic wisdom into the Teacher's passionate discourse in which the Cross and Resurrection are moved into the middle of the learners' lives.

NOTES

[1] Sirach or Ecclesiasticus, c. 180 B.C.E., concludes his work with paradeigmata, chs. 44–50. It should be noted, however, that the Wisdom of Solomon, otherwise so permeated with Hellenistic thought, does not call by name a single figure in its account of Israelite salvation history, chs. 10–19. The ancestors and the prophets are kept completely in the realm of the typical and the exemplary. Also pertinent to this discussion of genre, Leo Perdue, in a letter to me, has suggested that the sage-teacher may be the implied model for the son-learner in the biblical and ancient Near Eastern wisdom texts that are attributed to the persona of a sage that is named. This suggestion should be taken into account in exegesis of Matthew. Perdue develops one aspect of his argument in a paper on paraenesis and the death of the sage (in this issue), which I cite in the section 3.4 of this essay. On another genre matter, Vernon Robbins has dealt with the Graeco-Roman tradition of the suffering teacher-king, making special reference to the parallels between Dio Chrysostom's description of the Persian practice of taking a prisoner as a mock king and Mark's portrayal of the passion of Jesus (Robbins). Imitating the suffering teacher-king would thus not be unique to the gospels. Now genre is clearly much more than literary classification; it enables the reader to approach and understand a text, and as such is always related to praxis, as

Gerhart has emphasized. If the gospel form as we find it in the New Testament had been utterly new it would \not have been understood by anyone in the Hellenistic context. The same point applies to the specific way of viewing the roles of Jesus in any of the gospels. We need to find good ways of determining how literary works may be similar in some respects and different in others. Jameson has made a contribution to that project (see section 1). Would it also be of use to articulate genre concepts analogous to Hjelmslev's theory of the sign, with its distinction between the form and substance of "expression" and the form and substance of "content"? It is conceivable that Mark could have formally utilized a ritual motif such as the mock king to fill out his theme of the suffering servant of YHWH from Isa 52:13–53:12. Yet he must have understood it differently from the perception in a sociocultural setting where the king is either an actual ruler or one who is forced to assume the role as a victim for a brief period in order to fulfill a ritual function (so Robbins' examples). This is a traditional mythical theme in which the narrative sides with the social order against the victim, whereas the gospel story sides with a "king" who voluntarily takes the part of victims (see Girard, 1977, 1978, 1985, and 1986, and Williams, forthcoming in *RSR*). The difference is crucial. Part of the problem is that Robbins "saturates the text" (La Capra) with external literary and historical contexts, but he does not do justice to internal literary and historical contexts (the biblical and primitive Christian traditions).--On the question of the genre of the narrative gospel, see my book (1985) and forthcoming essay in *Semeia*.

2 Q paraenesis: Luke 6:27–30, 31, 35, 36, 37–38, 42; 9:60; 11:9–10, 35; 12:4, 22–31, 33, 58; 13:24 (part of a chreia in Luke—see Matt 7:13–14); 17:3. Paraenetic material peculiar to Matthew in the Synoptics: 5:16, 34–37; 6:1–4, 5–8, 16–18; 7:6, 15; 10:17; 11:28–30; 23:9–10. Unique to Luke: 10:20, 37; 12:35; 14:8, 12. Commands given in a situation like the announcement of the Son of man's coming in Luke 17:22–37 are not instruction but prophetic warning. However, one could conceivably include such forms and examine the interaction of wisdom and prophetic or apocalyptic modes.

3 Nowhere in the Hebrew Scriptures or in the rabbinic texts is hatred of enemies commanded. Some of the Psalms and prophetic writings appeal to the God of Israel to condemn or destroy the enemies of the individual or of Israel, but the other five antitheses clearly intend to cite commandments (prohibitions) and statutes stated in the Torah. At this point the evangelist forces the Torah to fit his pattern, with unfortunate results.

4 Williams (1985/86) and "Celui qui vient après: un modèle littéraire-structurale de l'interprétation de la Bible," unpublished lecture give April 10, 1985 at the University of Strasbourg.

5 Leo Perdue has commented by letter on this paragraph:

> If the SM had its own separate transmission history before being redacted into the Gospel of Matthew, it could be seen as the teaching of the Jesus who has already died (and then risen). Also, if Eugene Boring is right, Q certainly understood its sayings as those of the "risen" (or perhaps better stated, "exalted") Lord. Certainly, Matthew's audience (Jewish Christians?) knew the story of the dying/rising Jesus. The teaching is that of the risen Christ who has departed, left his teachings, but is coming again.

Although I do not accept Boring's description of Q as a prophetic document (see Boring, and Williams, 1988), I consider it likely that Q presupposes the risen, vindicated Lord. I would thus surmise that Matthew's rhetoric in the SM is his own way of mediating between Q's teachings of this risen, vindicated Lord and Mark's anchoring of Jesus' teachings in the period of his earthly ministry.

WORKS CONSULTED

Betz, Hans Dieter
  1985   "The Sermon on the Mount (Matt 5:3–7:27): Its Literary Genre and Function." Pp. 1–16 in *Essays on the Sermon on the Mount*. Ed. Hans Dieter Betz. Philadelphia: Fortress.

Boring, M. Eugene
  1982   *Sayings of the Risen Jesus: Christian Prophecy in the Synoptic Tradition*. SNTSMS 46. Cambridge: Cambridge University Press.

Bultmann, Rudolf
  1963   *The History of the Synoptic Tradition*. Rev. ed. Trans. J. Marsh. New York: Harper and Row.

Coleridge, Samuel Taylor
  1975   *Biographia Literaria*. London: J. M. Dent.

Dibelius, Martin
  1935   *From Tradition to Gospel*. Trans. B. L. Woolf. New York: Scribner's Sons.
  1975   *James: A Commentary on the Epistle of James*. Trans. M. A. Williams. Philadelphia: Fortress.

Döring, Klaus
  1979   *Exemplum Socratis: Studien zur Sokratesnachwirkung in der kynisch-stoischen Popularphilosophie der frühen Kaiserzeit und im frühen Christentum*. Wiesbaden: Steiner.

Epictetus   See Higgenson.

Funk, Robert W.
  1985   *New Gospel Parallels*, Vols. 1 and 2. Philadelphia: Fortress.

Gerhart, Mary
  1988   "Genric Competence in Biblical Hermeneutics," *Semeia* 43: 29–44

Gerhart, Mary and Russell, Allan
  1984   *Metaphoric Process*. Fort Worth: Texas Christian University Press.

Girard, René
  1977   *Violence and the Sacred*. Trans. P. Gregory. Baltimore: Johns Hopkins.

1978   *Des Choses Cachées depuis la Fondation du Monde.* Paris: Grasset.

1985   *La Route Antique des Hommes Pervers: Essais sur Job.* Paris: Grasset.

1986   *The Scapegoat.* Trans. Y. Feccerro. Baltimore: Johns Hopkins.

Hicks, R. D.
1958   *Diogenes Laertius. Lives of Eminent Philosophers.* 2 vols. LCL. Cambridge, MA: Harvard University Press.

Higgenson, T.W.
1866   *Enchiridion,* in *The Works of Epictetus.* Boston: Little, Brown, and Co.

Hjelmslev, Louis
1961   *Prolegomena to a Theory of Language.* Madison: University of Wisconsin.

Jameson, Fredric
1975   "Magical Narratives: Romance As Genre." *New Literary History* 12: 135–63.

Kermode, Frank
1987   "Matthew," *The Literary Guide to the Bible.* Eds. Robert Alter and Frank Kermode. Cambridge: Harvard University: 387–401.

Kloppenborg, John
1987   *The Formation of Q.* Philadelphia: Fortress.

LaCapra, Dominick
1983   *Rethinking Intellectual History: Texts, Contexts, and Language.* Ithaca, NY: Cornell University Press.

LaPorte, Jean
1975   "Philo in the Tradition of Biblical Wisdom Literature." Pp. 103–41 in *Aspects of Wisdom in Judaism and Early Christianity.* Ed. R.L. Wilken. South Bend, IN: Notre Dame University.

Laertius, Diogenes   See Hicks.

Lambrecht, Jan, S.J.
1985   *The Sermon on the Mount.* Good New Studies 14. Wilmington, DE: Glazier.

Mack, Burton L.
1985 *Wisdom and the Hebrew Epic: Ben Sira's Hymn in Praise of the Fathers.* Chicago: University of Chicago Press.

McDonald, James I.H.
1980 *Kerygma and Didache: The Articulation and Structure of the Earliest Christian Message.* SNTSMS 37. Cambridge, MA: Cambridge University Press.

Montefiore, C.G. and Loewe, R.
1974 *A Rabbinic Anthology.* New York: Schocken.

Moore, George Foote
1962 *Judaism in the First Centuries of the Christian Era.* Vol. 2. Cambridge, MA: Harvard University Press.

Perdue, Leo G.
1981a "Liminality As A Social Setting for Wisdom." *ZAW* 93: 114–26.
1981b "Paraenesis and the Epistle of James." *ZNW* 72: 241–56.

Robinson, James M.
1971 "LOGOI SOPHON: On the Gattung of Q." Pp. 71–113 in *Trajectories through Early Christianity.* Ed. H. Koester and J.M. Robinson. Philadelphia: Fortress.

Robbins, Vernon K.
1984 *Jesus the Teacher.* Philadelphia: Fortress.

Tannehill, Robert C.
1975 "The Focal Instance," *The Sword of His Mouth.* Philadelphia and Missoula, MT: Fortress and Scholars: 67–77.

Turner, Victor
1969 *The Ritual Process.* Ithaca, NY: Cornell University Press.

Williams, James G.
1981 *Those Who Ponder Proverbs: Aphoristic Thinking in Biblical Literature.* Sheffield: Almond.
1985 Gospel Against Parable: Mark's Language of Mystery. Decatur and Sheffield: Almond.
1985/86 "The Sermon on the Mount As A Christian Basis of Altruism," *Humboldt Journal of Social Relations* 13: 89–112.
Forthcoming "The Innocent Victim: René Girard on Violence, Sacrifice, and the Sacred." *Religious Studies Review.*

1988   "Parable and Chreia: From Q to Narrative Gospel," *Semeia* 43: 85–114.

PARAENESIS AND THE PASTORAL EPISTLES: LEXICAL OBSERVATIONS BEARING ON THE NATURE OF THE SUB-GENRE AND SOUNDINGS ON ITS ROLE IN SOCIALIZATION AND LITURGIES*

Jerome D. Quinn

ABSTRACT

The Collection of Pastoral Epistles (PE) exhibits the major features of the paraenetic epistolary style as described by pseudo-Libanius. As letters they reflect the features of *philophrenesis, parousia,* and *homilia*. As paraeneseis they represent the instruction of a community by an apostle entrusted with their care. This moral exhortation, like paraenesis in general, is irrefutable and incontestable. The social functions of paraenesis included socialization, legitimation of a new world, and the reinforcement of identity. Liturgical and ritual settings of paraenesis included baptism (primary social role), ordination and marriage (secondary socialization). Yet Christian paraeneseis in these settings were subversive, for it came into conflict with both the Jewish and Graeco-Roman Cultures and their supporting world-views.

1.1   The oldest Christian writings that have survived intact are in the epistolary genre,[1] and twenty-one compositions within the larger collection that we call the New Testament have been grouped formally as an epistolary. The gathering of Christian letters into collections was already occurring in the second century and several of these collections included letters under the name of Paul.[2] The second-century titles for each of these compositions distinguish between letters to churches and those to individuals, a distinction already presumed in the Muratorian Fragment. There were codices in circulation in the second century that contained only the letters to churches.[3] One infers that there were separate codices containing the letters that purported to address individuals.

1.2   The old seam is still visible in the present order of the Pauline epistolary where First and Second Timothy, Titus, and Philemon close a collection which has begun with nine letters to churches. Among the oldest witnesses to the order in which the letters to individuals were read, the Muratorian Fragment and Ambrosiaster presuppose that Titus was followed by First and Second Timothy. In that order they would be read as a collection which would thus have its own story to tell and its own teaching to transmit.[4] The vocabulary, syntax, and style that are peculiar to these letters as well as their special subject matter (scarcely found in the ten other Paulines) have prompted their modern sobriquet, the Pastoral Epistles (hereafter, PE). The title itself implies that they are to be understood not simply as separate epistles but collectively with a perspective and coherence proper to an epistolary collection. In the Hellenistic and Roman worlds such collections were common enough. They were ordinarily in prose but those of Horace are in hexameters, of Ovid *Ex Ponto* in elegiacs. The epistolaries of a Cicero, a Horace, a Pliny, were actually written by the persons named; most of their content had had a preexistence in separate compositions that we would call an actual correspondence between persons, though doubtless written with an eye to eventual collection and publication. Other epistolary collections are literary constructs whose author need not necessarily be the person under whose name the letter is penned. Such is the case with the five collections of Cynic epistles,[5] the group of seven letters to as many churches that open the Book of Revelation (1:4–5; 2:1–3,22), and the third century correspondence between Paul and Seneca.[6]

1.3   But what, one asks, does the epistolary collection as such add to the epistolary genre? The individual letter in the Hellenistic world was received as a gift expressing a friendly relationship (*philophronesis*), as a sign of the writer's presence (*parousia*), and as conversational speech with the recipient (*homilia*).[7] When an ancient reader encountered a collection of letters, what did that development of the epistolary genre suggest over and above the *philophronesis, parousia,* and *homilia* of the individual composition? Even in a file or in an archive a collection of letters implies that the communication which they record and transmit was considered for some reason to be of more than ephemeral importance. When a collection of letters is actually published, the reader assumes that the author and/or collector was convinced that the matters written about were of lasting importance to a wider public, but precisely as letters. Thus the reader was to understand that the person under whose name the correspondence appeared had his good at heart and cared about him, that the letters indeed brought him personally into the life and presence of his reader. A collection of letters said simultaneously that not only the matter communicated was important to the public for whom the collection was published, but that the person in whose name it came was himself important and considered his reader important too.[8]

1.4   The PE may well have originally appeared as an epistolary collection (rather than as individual letters) in the last quarter of the first Christian century.[9] In any case they were certainly being read by second-century Christians as a collection of letters, and thus they brought Paul as a person of importance, "a herald and apostle, ...the gentiles' teacher in faith and truth" (1 Tim 2: 7) into their lives. In this correspondence they still encountered an apostle who cared for those who believed in Christ Jesus and a teaching that still had significance for them.[10] The epistolary collection enabled Paul to converse with a new generation as he had once used individual letters to span the geographical distance between himself and his widely scattered congregations of believers.[11]

2.1   *Linguistic Soundings.* The apostolic conversation in the PE takes the literary form of paraenesis which is developed through the materials in the church orders of Titus and First Timothy and finally in the paraenetic testament of Paul in Second Timothy. The characteristics of the paraenetic form, its traditional ethical exhortations of a universally applicable character, addressed to an audience that is paradigmatic or typical rather than concretely historical, have been systematically analyzed since the beginning of this century. The recent renascence of studies in the ancient theory of epistolary rhetoric can still more sharply focus the significance of the paraenetic form in general and specifically the form of epistolary paraenesis. The PE never describe their discourse as paraenesis any more than they designate themselves as letters. Yet the ancient Christian world certainly received them as epistolary compositions. Did they also read them as paraenesis? And if so, what did that form mean to them?

2.2   Between 300–600 A.D., the pseudo-Libanius on epistolary styles classified forty-odd types of letters. Leading his list was the paraenetic style, *parainetikē,* which he defined thus:

> The paraenetic style is that in which we give someone paraenesis (*parainoumen*), persuading (*protrepontes*) him to pursue something or to avoid something. Paraenesis (*hē parainesis*) is divided into two parts, i.e., persuasion and dissuasion. Some also call it the advisory style (*symboleutikēn*), but incorrectly, for paraenesis differs from advice (*symboulēs*). Paraenesis is paraenetic speech (*logos parainetikos*) that does not admit a counter-statement (*antirrhesin ouk epidechomenos*) . Thus, if someone should say, "We must honor the divine," no one contradicts (*enantioutai*) this paraenesis, unless he is insane in the first place. But advice (*symboulē*) is advisory speech that does allow a counter-statement. Thus, if someone should say, "We must wage war, for we stand to profit a great deal by it," another might counter, "We must not wage war for war has many results, including defeat, captivity, wounds, and often enough a city's utter destruction."[14]

The rhetorician's description of paraenesis as an exhortation to pursue or to avoid a given course of action certainly coincides with the results of modern analysis of the form. Is his confident distinction of the paraenetic form from the advisory actually borne out by what the Greek before his day had designated as paraenesis?

2.3   The Greek terms in the *ain- cluster are generally used in connection with uttering words that are charged with meaning or importance,[15] and the first extant use of *parainesis* in Aeschylus, *Eumenides* 707, denotes the great closing charge that Athena has delivered to the people of Athens to establish thereafter a judicial system. The goddess did not deliver her speech for it to be discussed or refuted. It offered the only alternative to the unspeakable Furies which one would indeed have to be mad to entertain. The cognate *parainein* occurs in the preceding play of the trilogy when, in reply to Pylades' urging to count all men enemies rather than gods, Orestes replies, "In my judgment you have won the point and you charge me well (*paraineis moi kalos*)." That paraenesis could be ignored; there was no refuting it.[16] This sense surfaces regularly not only in the later dramatists[17] and poets[18] but also in the historians[19] and philosophers.[20]

2.4   The rare occurrences of the *parain- cluster in the papyri witness negatively to the solemn, literary character of the terminology. The somewhat more frequent use in the inscriptions indicates that these words belonged to the vocabulary of public charges and recommendations.[21]

2.5   In Hellenistic Jewish literature, in the latest strata of the Septuagint, Wisd. 8:9 has Wisdom giving *parainesis* to the grief-stricken, evidently an encouragement that no sane man spurns. The verb appears in 2 Macc 7:25–26; 3 Macc 5:17; 7:12 (*s.v.l.*), referring in the first two instances to a king's charge which is practically indistinguishable from a command. In the first example, the refusal to obey it is rhetorically enhanced by the solemnity with which it is given and the seriousness with which it is expected to be received. In Symmachus Eccl. 8: 2, Qoheleth says, *ego parainō* (no verb in Hebrew) *rhēsin basileōs phylassein*, and in his version of Ps 119:56,100, *paraineseis sou* translated *piqqudeyka*, i.e. the precepts of God which the psalmist has been and is keeping.

In Philo regularly God's commandments are *paraineseis*, a term which serves also as his alternate title for Deuteronomy.[22] The first command in Eden gives Philo an occasion to explain at length why this is *parainesis* and how it differs from injunction and prohibition which are aimed at those who are wrongdoers. *Parainesis* is rather akin to the act of teaching those who are beginning to learn how to do right and avoid wrong. In this case the teaching is explicitly that of the one Lord and God directed to every single human person.[23] In another treatise God's words are to the human soul like those of physicians, "giving holy *paraineseis* precisely as irreversible laws (*hosper nomous akinetous*)".[24] The last words of Moses and the succession of Joshua call for the *parain- language when Philo writes *On Virtue*.[25] In his *Embassy to Gaius*, as he distinguishes a ruler's order (*prostaxis*) from a counselor's paraenesis, the reader remembers that, whereas a counselor could not issue an order, a ruler could also give paraenesis.[26]

In Josephus,[27] as well as in the Testament of Abraham,[28] paraenesis can be ignored but it is irrefutable. The case is the same in the Testaments of the Twelve Patriarchs when Gad says, "And now, my children, I charge (*parainō*) you, love each one of you his neighbor and root out hatred from your hearts. Love one another in deed and word and the soul's thought.[29]

2.6   Terms from the *parain- cluster do not appear in the first generation Christian letters. The verb appears later only in Acts 27:9, 22, but with the sense already documented in profane and Jewish Greek.[30] Paul's paraenesis about the ill-fated voyage can only be proved by the event. It cannot be argued and obviously can be ignored. In second-century Christianity the verb reappears in Ignatius with similar force,[31] as well as in Irenaeus.[32] Clement of Alexandria declares that the formation given by the Logos-Educator can take a paraenetic form that is intended to be obeyed.[33]

In the eucharistic prayer of the *Apostolic Constitutions*,[34] the stages of salvation history proceed from the period when humanity was subject to the natural law (*meta physikon nomon*), through the time of legal paraenesis (*meta nomikēn parainesin*) by Moses, to the prophetic corrections (*meta prophetikous elegchous*) and the angelic administrations (*kai tas aggelōn epistasias*) of later ages. Here, as in Philo or Symmachus, the Mosaic legislation is termed paraenesis not because it was optional advice but because it was an unarguable charge to do good and to avoid evil. Thus the specific force of the *parain- cluster, argued for by pseudo-Libanius, appears in fact regularly in ancient Greek composition, pagan, Jewish, and Christian. That the distinction between advice and paraenesis was not always observed in the living language is not astonishing. The rhetorician's schoolmasterly correction would not have occurred had there not been literate men who took *parainesis* as completely synonymous with *symboulē*.[35]

3.1   *Conclusions.* The PE as a collection slip like a hand into the glove of pseudo-Libanius' description of the paraenetic epistolary style. As letters they communicate the *philophronesis, parousia,* and *homilia* of an important person. As paraenesis to do good and avoid evil (see 1 Tim 1:5; 2:1–4; 6:17–19, etc.) they take the form of a heartening and wholesome[36] charge (1 Tim 6:1–5; 2 Tim 1:13–14; 2:8–14; 4:1–5) from the one who has been divinely entrusted with the apostolic care of the public to whom the letters speak (see 1 Tim 1:8–16; 2:1–7; 2 Tim 1:8–11). This paraenesis is ultimately intended for a community[37] and it looks to the future members of that community and their welfare (1 Tim 4:1–5; 2 Tim 3:1–9). The various prophetic elements used in this form[38] as well as the divine authentication behind the figure who delivers its content (see Titus 1:1–4) combine to make this public charge incontestable.

3.2   The paraenetic form also sheds light on the development of the materials within the collection of the PE. The church orders that constitute Titus and First Timothy contain liturgical, creedal, and catechetical elements. They culminate in the apostle's last will and testament which occupies most of Second Timothy (2:1–4:8). In the history of the *parain- terminology traced above, a concern for provision for the future through a process of transmission and succession already appeared in Philo. Here in the PE that concern lies behind the testamentary form of Second Timothy. The irrefutable, incontestable character of paraenesis reaches its highest pitch when it takes the form of a will. The last words of the apostle to his legitimate child (1 Tim. 1:2; see 1:18; 2 Tim. 1:2; 2:1) admit of no refutation. The heir cannot argue with the patriarchal will. He may indeed ignore or reject his inheritance, but there is no escaping the terms on which it comes to the one who does accept it, the responsibilities he assumes, the goods for which he must answer.[39]

3.3   There is accordingly every reason to infer from the content and epistolary genre of the PE that they were written in the form of paraenesis as the Hellenistic world understood that term. The modern literary criticism which has classified the PE as paraenetic is not inaccurate but incomplete, missing one note which the ancient Greek heard often in paraenetic discourse, *antirrhesin ouk epidechomenos* ("not admitting refuta- tion). As Perdue (introductory essay, §2) has noted, the ancient perception of what constituted paraenesis had its limitations. All that an ancient author considered irrefutable first principles were not beyond the reach of criticism. Hidden and even unconscious agenda, personal as well as so- cial, sometimes dictated their ethical programs. In this problematic it is worth asking why the New Testament authors never called their teaching paraenesis and scarcely used the related terminology.[40] Is this departure from the linguistic usage of the society which they addressed a hint of another approach to the validity and authority of Christian moral forma- tion?

4.1   *Social Settings for Certain Paraeneses in the Pastoral Epistles:*
Sacramental Liturgies

The lexical analysis of paraenesis in the previous part of this essay (§§1.1–3.3) stopped short at the question of sources for paraeneses which the PE marshaled in epistolary form. That question could be framed with another heuristic device, by sorting out some of the social settings and functions of paraenesis (as in Perdue: 246–56; and in his introductory essay for this volume). Functionally paraenesis is a potent instrument of socialization, i. e. a verbal means in bringing about "the comprehensive and consistent induction of an individual into the objective world of a society or sector of it" (Berger and Luckmann: 130). Paraenesis implies a setting in which an older and experienced person helps a younger, inexperienced recipient of his or her knowledge to enter a new group or to shoulder new duties. "The liminal period" (Turner, 1967: 94–111; using Van Gennep, 1909 and 1960) unfolds in a ritual process of leaving the old order, then a state of suspension or "liminality, " and finally entering a new order or social group (Turner, 1969: 94–130). Ritual generally is "a public cognitive system" (Price: 9) in which "sacred symbols function to synthesize a people's ethos—the tone, character, and quality of their life, its moral and aesthetic style and mood—and their worldview—the picture they have of the way things in sheer actuality are, their most comprehensive ideas of order" (Geertz, 1966: 3; see 1957: 421–22, 426–27). Christian ritual or liturgy is no exception. I contend that the PE for some of their paraeneses exploited already traditional (though not necessarily stereotyped) liturgical materials.

4.2   In terms of a Christian community, paraenesis is particularly appropriate for the public recommendations and charges that accompany entrance into the community as such (the primary socialization) or entry into special social roles within the community (secondary socialization). The baptismal sacrament (in its widest sense, including the catechumenate and the readings, hymns, prayers, homilies, and the like which surround the public profession of Christian belief and immersion in water) would be regarded by the sociologist as belonging to the primary socialization of the person becoming a Christian. The Christian celebrations of marriage and of the dedication of persons to ecclesial ministries (ordinations) are examples of secondary socialization within the Christian social order.

The process of socialization aims at palpable change in the individual as he or she crosses the threshold into a new mode of existence (Turner, 1967: 101–2). This change becomes evident in the conduct and then the character of the person whose life is being "re-created" by entering this group or assuming a new role within it. Paraeneses, positive and negative (see Pseudo-Libanius in §2.2 above), are among the means used to urge this transformation, particularly of conduct. It is regularly given, not to be argued with, but to be acted upon (see J. Gammie's introductory essay,

§1.2; §2.2.1, 2). Thus Titus 2:11–14 cites a baptismal confession urging parenaetically an ethical transformation of life as the neophyte crosses the threshold into the new order of Christian believers. Titus 3:4–7 ("the message meant to be believed") is from a didactic baptismal oration, whose paraenetic force has been increased by its enclosure in a "before (verse 3)/after" schema. See the charge given in the course of the ritual of making a new chief among the Ndembu, which Victor Turner (1969: 101) calls a "harangue" but which is nothing less than ethical paraenesis that is conceived of as irrefutable.

The society or world which the one undergoing socialization is in some sense leaving has become inadequate and unsatisfactory; but leaving it is traumatic, for the former order too had its meaning, its directives, its values, its unquestioned presuppositions (see P. Berger: 19–24). The baptismal initiation and the paraenetic discourse within it offer another *nomos*, another worldview and concept of order by which a person can structure out life, meaning, and goals (recall Philo's name for Deuteronomy was precisely *paraineseis, De agricultura* 84 etc.). In this problematic one would *a priori* anticipate that a paraenesis that occurred within Christian socialization, and specifically within the liturgical expressions of that socialization, would accent strongly the visible, ethical changes expected of the candidate for baptism (not to mention marriage or ordination). *De facto*, that is precisely what one encounters in Titus 2:12 as the paraenesis describes the grace that "disciplines us to disown godlessness and worldly lusts, and to live in a sensible, honest, godly way in this present age."

The justification or legitimation of the new world or order into which the neophyte is being inducted is particularly important when the old order still advertizes attractive alternatives and the limitations of the new order are coming to light (Berger: 29–30). Paraenesis makes its case by appeal to non-theoretical processes that are of an intellectual character as well as volitional (Berger: 21). In general the intellectual grounds which legitimate the new social order involve traditional data, interpretative schemata, and received wisdom (Berger and Luckmann: 94 cite sapiential and ethical maxims and proverbs; also see J. Gammie's introductory essay, §2. 2.1, 2). Specifically the paraenetic legitimation of the Christian world or roles within it appeals to the OT scriptures, to the sayings of Jesus, to the texts of public worship—synagogal as well as Christian—and, probably from the first Christian generation onwards, to the heroic figures of that generation (Jervell, 1972: 19–39 and 1984: 54–56 on first-century traditions rather than tradition; cf. 2 Tim 3:10–17 with Perdue's introductory essay here, §2.5).

The volitional grounds for paraenesis embrace the norms for conduct in the new order as proposed by an authoritative teacher, as well as the sanctions for breaking the rules and the rewards for keeping them. In this connection it is helpful to recall the function of the "significant other, " i. e. the person who introduces the aspirant into the new group and with whom a strong affective bond is established (Berger and Luckman: 130–31). Such a person's life, example, teaching, and directives facilitate the initiate's entrance into the new order or role which he seeks. The "Paul" of the PE is such a figure for Titus and Timothy, and the Pauline ministers of these letters appear at times to function thus for others (so Titus 1:5–9; 2: 7; 1 Tim. 4:6–16 etc.; see also Fiore). With the frequent use of the first person plural, the PE identify Paul and his coworkers with the community into which the one baptized is being initiated. In this perspective, the faith, the worship, and the practice enjoined by the paraenesis of the PE are not simply abstract doctrine, empty rituals, and jejune rules; they are the faith as Paul and his generation preached it, the worship they participated in, the conduct that they demanded. "You can...hear and see justification [by faith] in the worship of the church" (Jervell 1984: 63).

Finally, paraenesis aims at reinforcing a sense of identity with a group and a sense of separation from those who do not believe or do not conduct themselves as the group does. Paraenetic exhortation sketches in black and white, with clear lines between those inside and those outside. Thus the hearer is forewarned and forearmed for conflict. In a Christian setting paraenesis looks to the parousia with its definitive revelation of who is "in" and who is "out" of the new world. Again, as Titus 2:13 puts it, "as we wait for the blessed hope revealed in the glory of Jesus Christ, our great God and savior."

5.1   There is an embarrassment of riches in the PE of materials that have some link with Christian liturgy and some of those materials have their precedents in the practices of Jewish prayer (see Charlesworth: 2.671–697 on Hellenistic synagogal prayers, citing parallels to the prayer in 1 Tim 1:17 etc.; also Fiensy). Several passages have been or will be encountered whose liturgical origin is argued on stylistic as well as more material criteria (without necessarily repeating all the arguments) and which exemplify situations for secondary socialization. The charge cited from an ordination liturgy in 1 Tim 6:11–16 and traces of similar charges in Titus 1:6–9; 2:7–8; 1 Tim 3:1b–6 etc. will be surveyed first. Then, it will be suggested that some of the teaching on marriage in the PE cites the formulas as well the liturgical charge given in a first-century, Christian marriage ceremony.

5.2   Over 30 years ago in the Bultmann *Festschrift* (Käsemann: 261–
68), Ernst Käsemann argued that 1 Tim 6:11–16 is probably a citation from
a liturgical charge at ordination. The text develops in three stages: first the
precept in an imperatival address to the "man of God" to pursue a sestet
of ethical qualities (*tauta pheuge...de* belongs to the redaction and not to
the source), which shades off into an appeal to the baptismal initiation by
which the man of God had publicly entered the society of believers (v.
12b). Then the speaker, in the first person singular (*in persona Pauli* in the
redaction), with an appeal to God as bestower of all life and to the Christ
who was crucified as king (the reference is to the trial as narrated in Luke
23:2–3), urges this "man of God" to keep the Pauline charge unblemished
until the parousia (v. 13–14). Finally, the mention of the parousia becomes
an occasion for a solemn doxology that occupies the closing two verses
(15–16). The final "Amen" as well as several phrases within this final
doxology (the most frequently cited passage of the PE in the second
century) may ultimately have come from Hellenistic synagogal liturgy
(Charlesworth: 2.682, 695). The allusions to synagogal liturgical usage as
well as the Septuagintal expressions of the doxology serve to legitimate
the worship which it urges in the new order of Christian believers. Just as
the PE authenticate their epistolary paraenesis by citing this traditional
text from Christian liturgy, so the liturgical paraenesis authenticates itself
by an appeal to the previous usage of the OT and the liturgy of the
Temple or of the synagogue.

The central paraenetic block in this charge includes verses 13–14.
At this point, as the PE conceive it, the one who presides over the ordination and who delivers the liturgical charge is the Apostle himself. That
heroic figure from the previous generation is heard recalling the example
of Jesus in his passion and commanding an integral Pauline teaching for
which the ordinand must undergo judgment at the parousia. Paul, at least
for the PE, has become the "significant other" for the one receiving a new
role in the church by ordination and the apostle effectively eclipses the
original deliverer of the charge, placing it beyond a believing hearer's
refutation.

The opening imperatival address of this charge urges good
conduct upon the "man of God" with a catalogue of six virtues. This
paraenesis, at the threshold of a new way of life, aims at an evident
change in conduct (or a conversion) that ought to characterize the new
mode of existence in the Christian community. Warrant for and legitimation of such a charge are grounded in the public baptismal confession of
the "man of God" (v. 12b). Nor should one underestimate the theological
density of such lists which precisely as sapiential directives of an
"intensely concentrated nature" may strike the casual reader as "trite"

(von Rad: 247; see J. Gammie's introductory essay, §1.1.4b–c for a discussion of Paraenetic Literature and paraenesis as a secondary literary genre and sub-genre of the major literary genre of wisdom literature).

The appearance of the virtue list at the opening of this archaic Christian ordination paraenesis suggests a further inference. Certain other lists or catalogues of virtues in the PE may be from similar sources. Thus, the author of Titus 1:6–9 could be citing his list or lists from the ordination liturgies for presbyter-bishops in other congregations. First Timothy 3:1b–7 then could be based on the charge in an ordination for a bishop and 1 Tim 3:8–10, 12–13, on the charge for the ordination of deacons. First Timothy 3:11 might be from a liturgical charge addressed to single women who had a diaconal role.

5.3   There is no particular reason for confining the question to the ordained ministries. If the Christian liturgies for ordinations had paraenetic charges to pursue good acts and avoid bad ones, then it is antecedently possible that another area of secondary socialization, that is, Christian marriage, had similar liturgical paraeneses. An example may be found in Titus 2:4–5 where the septet of family virtues (which the older Christian women in the household teach the young women preparing for marriage) may come from the traditional liturgical charge that the older women had learned in the Christian celebration of marriage.

A final and most controversial example of liturgical paraenesis in the PE also occurs in a citation from the liturgy of marriage. The text of the charge coincides substantially with 1 Tim 2:11–15; 3:1a. The best editions of the NT now read "the message meant to be believed" (3:1a) with the preceding verse 2:15 (or verses). "The message" in this instance (as in certain others) is a citation from a liturgical celebration in a particular church (probably that in which the PE themselves took their origin). It probably ought to be classified as an example of a non-traditional, subversive teaching which confronts the norms that the contemporary society does not question (see Perdue's introductory essay in this volume, §2.2).[41]

The pre-Christian history of marriage liturgy in Judaism is scanty (Tobit; 4Q 502; Friedman; Hruby: 15–28); the early Christian sources are just as sparse (Studer: 51–85; Stevenson: 3–32; 1986: 138–51; Nautin; Crouzel). The scene in a Roman church can be visualized if we recall the lunette of the *Velatio* in the Cemetery of Priscilla (about 250 C.E.; see Bourget 1965: 38, plates 69–70; Fasola and Manicelli: 28–29, plate 53; Carletti: 17–18, plate 2). There a young man, holding an unfolded, red-edged veil, stands somewhat behind a young woman who holds a partially unrolled scroll. Both turn slightly to their right toward an elevated, high-backed chair, with low armrests, upon which is seated a bearded, bareheaded elderly man, wearing a long tunic and hooded cloak. He is extending his right hand toward the young woman. The chair, his posture, the gesture all suggest a teaching situation (Dagens: 124, 126) in a Christian marriage liturgy in which this venerable figure (a bishop or a presbyter? see Ign. *Pol.* 5.2) addresses a bride holding the official Roman document listing her duties (as well as her husband's). The young man holds the *flammeum*, the Roman bridal veil, which he will place on his bride's head.

"The message meant to be believed" at the end of 1 Timothy 2 is in fact a citation from an already traditional paraenetic charge given to the Christian bride as she married before a bishop or presbyter (perhaps in a Roman congregation). Formally, 2:11–15 appear almost as abruptly in their context as does the ordination charge of 1 Timothy 6; whereas 2:8–10 have liturgical directions for Christian men and then women generally, verses 11–15 use *gynē* only in the singular and always with the meaning "married woman, wife" (which the singular has everywhere in the PE). The "wife" here has the position of the "man of God" in the ordination charge though he is addressed with singular imperatives. The ritual for marriage as well as that for ordination is a "public, cognitive system" and within it the bride learns about the new role which Christian marriage gives her. The presiding celebrant (who speaks in the person of Paul in the PE) urges the bride in polite third person forms to learn quietly and compliantly; in *his* church and its liturgy (perhaps the preexistent document alluded to in 1 Cor 14:34–35, 2 Cor 11:2–3; see de la Potterie; Ellis: 214–15) a wife is not permitted to teach her husband and exercise authority over him. The paraenesis is legitimated by an explicit appeal to the data of the Genesis narrative of the creation and the fall of Adam and of his wife, Eve (see Perdue's introductory essay to this volume, §2.5; Geertz 1957: 422, 424, 426–27,[42] 435–436). Note the depiction of their marriage on the Velletri sarcophagus of around 300 C.E. (Dacquino: 195; Van der Meer/ Mohrmann: 54, plate 104; Gough: 34, plate 29; Snyder: 40, plate 17). Commentators have suffered acute, chronic theological dyspepsia about the demonstrative force of this citation. The citation does not and was never intended to prove anything, but the facts narrated illustrate a point that the first-century presider-homilist considered irrefutable because of the practice of his Jewish Christian church and its interpretation of the Jewish Scriptures.

The marriage charge reaches its apogee in its promise that a husband and wife will find salvation in parenthood (*teknogonia*[43]), provided "they continue in faith and love and holiness, with self-control. The PE have no time for Christians who "forbid marrying" (1 Tim 4:3). The Christian liturgy of marriage refutes them in advance. This bride has chosen to marry and she is no less a Christian for that; "a person will be saved by the rearing of children" (note the impersonal passive, *sōthēsetai*, is not necessarily confined to a feminine subject; contrast 1 Tim 5:14). The closing list of virtues reminds one of the opening of the ordination charge (not to mention the citation of the Community Rule in the marriage ritual in 4Q 502, *Groupe* 2, frag. 16; *DJD* 7.87). The proviso lays bare the ultimate and Christian basis for the final judgment upon the role that this bride is assuming, with her husband, the goodness of their life in Christ.

To return to the *Velatio* lunette in the Cemetery of Priscilla, it is provocative, in the light of the preceding observations, to notice that opposite the scene of the Christian marriage there is at the right corner of the lunette a painting of the same young woman, seated and holding a baby. In the center of the lunette there is standing an *orante* figure (Snyder 1985: 19–20), simply dressed, with head veiled and hands stretched out, flat, with fingers extended, the oldest illustration of the directives about women in 1 Timothy 2. This was the way a well-to-do Christian, Roman matron in the latter part of the third century had her tomb decorated, to show that she had married, prayed, and lived according to the Scriptures and the Pauline practice of her church. Her veil may suggest the Jewish Christian antecedents of the worship in her church and family.[44]

6.1   *Summary*. In summary then the subgenre of paraenesis constitutes part of the verbal membrane through which a later age receives some perspectives on the ancient Semitic, Hellenistic, and Roman worlds. Those ancient societies were by and large, from our point of view, conservative, resisting change, reluctant to experiment, suspicious of innovation.

The Christian movement was, from one aspect, old, insofar as its normative literature, its ethos and world-view, even its founders and original members were Jewish. Yet, from another aspect, the Christian movement was a new one, a liberating and liberal social phenomenon, provoking change, occasioning experiment, welcoming new ways of doing old things.

6.2   Paraenesis had an inherent tension in such a setting, for it represented the traditional, the formal conventions, that which had been received, particularly from Judaism. Yet it was in the service of an essentially new social phenomenon, the Christian churches, which used paraenesis as an instrument of a socialization which the contemporary world, religious as well as secular, could only regard as subversive, if not revolutionary.

6.3   The public worship of the Christian communities, their liturgy, was an intellectual as well as a volitional system. This worship involved more than words; it demanded time and space for performance as well as the physical presence and participation of the worshippers and on occasion it employed material things (water, bread, wine) in its celebrations. In such a setting Christian believers kept finding their specific identity as well as that which separated them from an ambient society. Liturgical worship confronted the individual who participated with the inadequacies of the prevailing values and presuppositions about human existence, and it presented a new world-view and ethos which simply demanded moral change. In a word, liturgy issued in paraenesis.

6.4   Both primary (baptismal) and secondary (ministerial or nuptial) socializations of the Christian occur within liturgical settings (as just described). The emphasis upon ethos in each stage, the good acts to be pursued and the evil ones to be avoided, rather than upon the essential nature of the socialization in question and its specific functions, coheres with the paraenetic bent of the liturgical rites of passage.

NOTES

*A corrected and lightly supplemented and revised form of Quinn 1981, republished here as 1.1–3.3 with the kind permission of the original editors.

[1] Vielhauer: 58–64; for his treatment of paraenesis, 49–57; for the PE 215–37; further background materials are cited in note 7 below.

[2] Second Peter 3:15–16; Polycarp, *Phil.* 13.2; Musurillo: 88, §12; and see Quinn, 1974: 379–85 for the details of what is sketched here, adding Sparks: 180–81, as well as Dahl 1978: 233–77.

[3] Thus P46 which includes Hebrews, apparently in virtue of its being directed to a congregation rather than its coming under the name of Paul. In this connection note that the collection of seven letters later called catholic epistles followed another principle for their titles which always use the name of the person from whom the letter professed (or was thought) to originate, James, Peter, John (!), Jude. See C. H. Roberts: 60–62.

[4] See Quinn, 1978a: 63–64 and 1980: 3.289–99. In the latter essay a case is proposed for the Pastorals as an epistolary that corresponds to that interest in the sender's life, personality, and character which is documented in the ancient theory of epistolary rhetoric (see W. R. Roberts: 440, §227 and Malherbe 1977b: 62–63, 70–71). On ancient letter collections in general see G. Constable.

[5] Malherbe 1977a.

[6] Hennecke and Schneemelcher: 2.133–141. In all of these instances the letters are actually before us as a collection. Their preexistence as separate compositions is a matter for historical criticism, as is the relation of their texts to the audience whom they profess to address as well as to the author from whom they profess to come. Identification of the genre does not *ipso facto* settle the historical questions.

[7] The fundamental analyses of Hellenistic rhetorical theory on letters are by Koskenniemi and Thraede; see also Doty: 11–12; Dahl, 1976: 538–41; White.

[8] Dodds: 137–38, on the benefits of belonging to a community within which "there was human warmth: someone was interested in them, both here and hereafter."

[9] See Quinn, 1978: 74–75.

[10] See 2 Tim 1:2; the apostolic parousia figures in 1 Tim 3:14–15; 4:13; in the Muratorian Fragment (lines 60–61) Philemon and the PE are *pro affecto /sic/ et dilectione*.

[11] Note the patterns in the use of the second person singular in the PE, and see Dahl 1972: 261–71.

[12] See Schroeder: 303–04, 643, with literature cited there; Perdue; Johnson.

[13] Foerster: 9.28–29,36 (§§ 4–5, 52). Both text and an English translation are available in Malherbe, 1977b: 62–63, 70–71; see pp. 10–11 for an introduction to the literature concerning this work.

[14] Libanius later appends a sample letter in the paraenetic style (see references in note 13). It reads:

> Dear Sir, Always be an enthusiastic follower of virtuous men. For it is better to be well spoken of when following good men than to be reproached by everyone for being in bad company.

[15] Chantraine: 35–36.

[16] *Choëphori*, 903; see Aeschylus' other uses of the verb in *Persae* 224, and *Prometheus* 266, 309, and perhaps in *Oxyrhynchus Papyri* 2249.17.

[17] Sophocles uses only the verb; see especially *Philoctetes* 1434; *Oedipus Coloneus* 464. Euripides uses the noun in *Helena* 316 and in Fragment 1079.2, *ouk esti lypēs allo pharmakon...hos andros esthlou kai philou parainesis*. Among the comedians, see the verb in Aristophanes, *Frogs* 1132, 1420, and Menander, *Aspis* 184, where the counseling of friends is exactly what the law (*nomos*) prescribes; *Phasma* 49; Koerte fragments 59.3; 209.6; 532.

[18] The content of the charge which teachers give their students in Pindar, *Pythian* 6,23 and *Isthmian* 6,68, is irrefutable.

[19] Thus Herodotus 5,51; 9,44; Thucydides 2,45.88; and especially 4, 59; for further references see LSJ 1968: *s. v.*

[20] Thus Plato, *Laws* 773A; 811B (cf. 933B and Plutarch, *Moralia* 14C for synonyms which practically coincide in meaning); *Gorgias* 521D-E; *Ion* 537A; 540D; cf. Xenophon, *Cyropaedia* 3,3,50 and Sextus Empiricus, *Adversus Mathematicos* 1,271.278 (where *anagkaia* appear to be *parainetika*); 2,12.36; 6,8–9; 6,12; 9,128.130 (where Sextus refutes what is proposed as beyond contradiction). In the Cynic epistles (see Malherbe 1977a: 60, 62, 186), see Crates 9 (*parainoumenon*); 10 (*parainō* twice); and King Darius to Heraclitus 1 (*parainesesin*). Seneca in *Epistulae morales* 95 poses the question "whether this part of philosophy that the Greeks call *paraeneticen* and we Latins call *praeceptivam* (see *Epistula* 94) suffices to perfect wisdom."

[21] *Inscriptiones Graecae* 1²136.2; W. Dittenberger, Sylloge³89.40; 557.30–35; see Thucydides 1.139; 2.13.

[22] See Philo, *De Agricultura* 84; *Quis Rerum Divinarum Heres Sit* 114; *De Decalogo* 39, 82, 100; *De Specialibus Legibus* 131; *De Praemiis et Poenis* 83, 156.

[23] *Legum Allegoriarum* 93–97, 101.

[24] *De Somniis* 69; see 101 for his distinction between *he parainesis* and *to diatagma* (an explanatory statement). Aristotle, *Politics* 1269A 9, has not much good to say about human *nomoi akinetoi*.

[25] *De Virtute* 68–71.

[26] *De Legatione ad Gaium* 69–70.

[27] *B.J.* 5.87–88; *A.J.* 1.201.

[28] *Testament of Abraham (A)* 9.

[29] *Testament of Gad* 6.1 *s.v.l.*

[30] The reading of D in Luke 3,18 is notable, for after citing a series of the Baptist's prophetic injunctions, the summary statement reads, *polla...hetera parainon* (for *parakalon*).

[31] *Magnesians* 6.1; *Smyrnaeans* 4.1.

[32] Irenaeus, *Adversus Haereses* 1.1,2; 4.60,1 (Harvey, I, 5,2 and II,287,5, where the Latin version, *praecipias/ hortabantur*, is notable).

[33] *To men eis hypakouen to parainteikon eidos, Paedagogus* 1,1 (Stählin 90,28); see John Chrysostom, *On Titus 4,1* (PG 62.683).

[34] *Constitutiones Apostolicae* 8.12.30.

[35] Theodoret of Cyrrhus (*ob.* 458) in his *Graecarum Affectionum Curatio* 9,63 (ed. J. Raeder, *Theodoreti...*, Leipzig 1904, p. 238, line 18), in explaining the apostle's teaching in First Corinthians 7 on the unmarried, notes that Paul is giving paraeneses not laws (*ou nomous alla paraineseis eisengkon*).

[36] The Philonic use of medicinal imagery in connection with paraenesis has been observed (footnote 24). See Malherbe 1979: 19–35, where he contends (against M. Dibelius and H. Conzelmann) that the health/disease imagery in the PE designates considerably more than that which is correct and reasonable teaching.

[37] It is more than a coincidence that each of the PE concludes with a blessing in the second person plural.

[38] See Quinn 1979: 345–368.

[39] On Second Timothy as a testament, see Vielhauer: 236, as well as Berger: 190–231.

[40] An answer to this query may take one into the area of rhetorical criticism, as explained and practiced by Kennedy: 3–38; 145–46, 154.

[41] The rest of the passages that constitute "the Christian teaching that ought to be believed" have this controversial, "subversive" character more or less near their surface. Thus Titus 3: 4–8a offers a Pauline teaching about justification, ignoring that of the judaizers (see Reumann: 234–35); 1 Tim 1:15 accents one of the most controversial aspects of Jesus' ministry in singling out his mission to sinners; 1 Tim 4: 7–8 takes on the cult of physical fitness and athletics in Hellenism; 2 Tim 2:11–13 is an *apologia* wrung from a congregation under persecution.

The paraenesis of the marriage charge of 1 Tim 2:11–14, particularly that of 2:15–3:1a, bucks the current structures of both Judaism and Roman society on several counts. The directives for the wife in 2:11–14 scarcely conform to the social standing of Roman wives in their homes, where they enjoyed more than a little wealth and independence *vis à vis* their spouses. From the beginning Jesus and his disciples were in conflict with provisions of the Torah and the religious practice of their Jewish contemporaries as they appealed to Genesis and the original divine institution of marriage to justify their own rejection of divorce and remarriage. Their charismatic self-assurance was no less in conflict with the marriage practice of the Hellenistic and Roman world which not only countenanced divorce and remarriage but also infanticide and a certain contempt for marriage and procreation. Some Christians did not leave these views behind upon conversion and/or marriage (see 1 Tim 4:2–3; 5:14).

Augustus' revival of Roman legislation (see Ovid, *Fasti* 2.139) that aimed at regaining social control of the liminal experiences of marriage and birth remained a dead letter (thus Tacitus, *Annales* 3.25). "The Christian message meant to be believed" at 1 Tim 2:15 and the end of marriage charge flies in the face of current Roman *mores*, accenting the importance of children in the marriage of Christians, the salvific obligation of both husband and wife to rear the offspring they bear (thus excluding the exposure of unwanted children), and the overarching importance for both parents of faithfulness, love of God and neighbor, and "a sensible holiness."

Notable about this paraenesis is that it was not conceived of as law or ethical philosophy as such but as worship. Its locus is the liturgy of marriage, the worship generated by the faith of the Christian community, which provides the passage through this potentially most disruptive moment (see Perdue's introductory essay, §5; Donelson: 183–187, 193, 198). *Lex orandi lex agendi*, "the way one prays ought to dictate the way one acts," to paraphrase an old theological maxim.

[42] This observation is important enough to have before one's eyes. Geertz writes: "The need for...a metaphysical grounding for values seems to vary quite widely in

intensity from culture to culture and from individual to individual, but the tendency to desire some sort of factual basis for one's commitment seems practically universal; mere conventionalism satisfies few people in any culture. However its role may differ at various times, for various individuals, and in various cultures, religion, by fusing ethos and world-view, gives to a set of social values what they perhaps most need to be coercive: an appearance of objectivity. In sacred rituals and myths values are portrayed not as subjective human preferences but as the imposed conditions for life implicit in a world with a particular structure."

[43] The Greek term refers to both parents here as elsewhere in the Greek Fathers (the case is otherwise in secular Greek); see Clement of Alexandria, Diognetus, Methodius of Olympus, Theodoret of Cyrrhus, *et al.* as well as the commentaries of Cajetan and Lock on this passage. The citations can be verified and examined in a print-out of *teknogonia* from the *Thesaurus Linguae Graecae* of the University of California, Irvine, CA 92717. The use here of such a print-out is gratefully acknowledged.

[44] Contrast the plate in the *New Catholic Encyclopedia* 11.674 with that in 10.712 where the head is uncovered.

WORKS CONSULTED

Berger, K.
  1974   "Apostelbrief und apostolische Rede/Zum Formular früchristlicher Briefe." *ZNW* 65: 190–231.

Berger, P. and Luckmann, T.
  1967   *The Social Construction of Reality*. Garden City, NY: Doubleday.

Berger, P.
  1967   *The Sacred Canopy*. Garden City, NY: Doubleday.

Bourguet, Pierre du
  1965   Early Christian Painting. Trans. S. W. Taylor. New York: Viking.

Carletti, S.
  1982   *Guide to the Catacombs of Priscilla*. Trans. A. Mulhern. Vatican City: Pontifical Commission for Sacred Archaeology.

Chantraine, P.
  1968   *Dictionnaire étymologique de la langue grecque*. Paris: Klincksieck.

Charlesworth, J. H., ed.
  1985   *The Old Testament Pseudepigrapha*. Vol. 2. Garden City, NY: Doubleday.

Constable, G.
  1976   *Letters and Letter Collections*. Typologie des sources du Moyen Age occidental 17. Turnhout: Brepols.

Crouzel, H.
1983   "Liturgie du mariage chrétien au Vᵉ siècle selon l'Epithalame
        de saint Paulin de Nole." Pp. 619–26 in *Mens Concordet Voci:
        pour Mgr. A. G. Martimort*. Paris: Desclée.

Dacquino, P.
1984   *Storia del Matrimonio cristiano alla luce della Bibbia*. Torino: Elle
        di ci.

Dagens, C.
1971   "A propos du cubiculum de la 'Velatio'. "*Rivista di Archeologia
        cristiana* 47: 119–29.

Dahl, N. A.
1962   "The Particularity of the Pauline Epistles as a Problem in the
        Ancient Church."Pp. 261–71 in *Neotestamentica et Patristica:
        Freundesgabe O. Cullmann*. Ed. W. C. van Unnik *et al.* Leiden:
        Brill.
1976   "Letter," Pp. 538–41 in *IDB Sup*. Nashville: Abingdon.
1978   "The Origin of the Earliest Prologues of the Pauline Letters."
        Semeia 12: 233–77.

Dodds, E. R.
1965   *Pagan and Christian in an Age of Anxiety*. Cambridge: Cam-
        bridge University Press.

Donelson, L. R.
1986   *Pseudepigraphy and Ethical Argument in the Pastoral Epistles*.
        Tübingen: Mohr.

Doty, W.G.
1979   *Letters in Primitive Christianity*. Philadelphia: Fortress.

Ellis, E. E.
1981   "The Silenced Wives of Corinth (1 Cor. 14:34–5)." Pp. 213–20
        in *New Testament Textual Criticism: Its Significance for Exegesis;
        Essays in Honour of Bruce Metzger*. Ed. E. J. Epp and G. D. Fee.
        Oxford: Clarendon.

Fasola, U. M. and Mancinelli, F.
1981   *Catacombs and Basilicas: The Early Christians in Rome*. Trans. C.
        Wasserman. NY: Scala Books distributed by Harper and Row.

Fiensy, D. A.
  1985   *Prayers Alleged to Jewish: An Examination of the Constitutiones Apostolorum.* Brown Judaic Studies 65. Chico, CA: Scholars.

Fiore, B.
  1986   *The Function of Personal Example in the Socratic and Pastoral Epistles.* Analecta Biblica 105. Rome: Pontifical Biblical Institute.

Foerster, R.
  1963   *Libanii Opera.* Leipzig: Teubner, 1927.

Friedman, M. A.
  1980/81   *Jewish Marriage in Palestine: A Cairo Geniza Study.* Vols. 1 & 2. NY: Jewish Theological Seminary of America.

Geertz, C.
  1957   "Ethos, World-view and the Analysis of Sacred Symbols." *Antioch Review* 17: 421–37.
  1966   "Religion as a Cultural System." Pp. 1–46 in *Anthropological Approaches to the Study of Religion.* Ed. Michael Bainton. London: Tavistock.

Gough, M.
  1974   *The Origins of Christian Art.* New York: Praeger.

Hennecke, E., and Schneemelcher, W.
  1964   *New Testament Apocrypha.* 2 Vols. Philadelphia: Westminster.

Hruby, K.
  1986   "Symboles et textes de la célébration du mariage judaïque." Pp. 15–28 in *La Celebrazione cristiana del Matrimonio: Simboli e Testi.* Atti del II Congresso internazionale de Liturgia, Roma, 27–31 Maggio 1985. Studia Anselmiana 93. Analecta liturgica 11. Ed. G. Farnedi. Rome: Pontificio Ateneo S. Anselmo.

Jervell, J.
  1972   *Luke and the People of God: A New Look at Luke-Acts.* Minneapolis, MN: Augsburg.
  1984   *The Unknown Paul: Essays on Luke-Acts and Early Christian History.* Minneapolis: Augsburg.

Johnson, L. T.
  1978/79   "II Timothy and the Polemic Against False Teachers: A Re-examination." *Ohio Journal of Religious Studies* 6/7: 1–26.

Käsemann, E.
1954   "Das Formular einer neutestamentlichen Ordinationparä-
        nese." Pp. 261–68 in *Neutestamentliche Studien für Rudolph
        Bultmann*. Ed. W. Eltester. Berlin: Töpelmann.

Kennedy, G.
1984   *New Testament Interpretation through Rhetorical Criticism*.
        Chapel Hill and London: University of North Carolina Press.

Koskenniemi, H.
1956   *Studien zur Idee und Phraseologie des griechischen Briefes bis 400 n.
        Chr*. Helsinki: Academia Scientiarum Fennica.

Lowrie, W.
1947   *Art in the Early Church*. 2nd ed. Harper Torchback. NY: Harper
        and Row.

Malherbe, A. J.
1977a   *The Cynic Epistles: A Study Edition*. SBL Sources for Biblical
        Study 12. Missoula, MT: Scholars.
1977b   "Ancient Epistolary Theorists." *Ohio Journal of Religious Studies*
        5: 62–63, 70–71.
1979   "Medical Imagery in the PE." *Texts and Testaments: Critical
        Studies in Honor of Stuart D. Currie*. Ed. W. E. March. San
        Antonio, TX: Trinity University Press.

Musurillo, H.
1972   *The Acts of the Christian Martyrs*. Oxford: Clarendon.

Nautin, P.
1984   "Le rituel de mariage et la formations des Sacramentaires
        'Léonien' et 'Gélasien'." *Ephemerides Liturgicae* 98: 425–457.

Perdue, L. G.
1981   "Parenaesis and the Epistle of James." *ZNW* 72: 241–56.

Potterie, I. de la
1979   "'Mari d'une seule femme': le sens theologique d'une formule
        paulinienne." Pp. 619–38 in *Paul de Tarse Apôtre du notre Temps*.
        Ed. L. de Lorenzi. Rome: Abbey of St. Paul outside the Wall.

Price, S. R. F.
1984   *Rituals and Power: the Roman Imperial Cult in Asia Minor*.
        Cambridge. Cambridge University Press.

Quinn, J.
1974   "P46—The Pauline Canon?" *CBQ* 36: 379–385.
1978a   "The Last Volume of Luke: the Relation of Luke-Acts and the Pastoral Epistles." Pp. 62–75 in *Perspectives on Luke-Acts*. Ed. C. H. Talbert. Macon, GA: Mercer.
1979   "The Holy Spirit in the Pastoral Epistles. " PP. 345–68 in *Sin, Salvation, and the Spirit; Commemorating the Fiftieth Year of the Liturgical Press*. Ed. D. Durken. Collegeville, MN: Liturgical.
1980   "Paul's Last Captivity." Pp. 289–99 in *Studia Biblica III*. Ed. E. A. Livingstone. Sheffield: JSOT.
1981   "Parenesis and the Pastoral Epistles." Pp. 495–501 in *De* la Torah au Messie: Melanges Henri Cazelles. Ed. J. Dore, P. Grelot, M. Carrez. Paris: Desclée.

Rad, G. von
1965   *The Problem of the Hexateuch and other Essays*. Edinburgh: Oliver and Boyd.

Reumann, J.
1982   *Righteousness in the New Testament: with responses by Joseph A. Fitzmyer and Jerome D. Quinn*. Philadelphia/ NY: Fortress/ Paulist.

Roberts, C. H.
1979   *Manuscript, Society and Belief in Early Christian Egypt: the Schweich Lectures of the British Academy 1977*. London: Oxford University.

Roberts, W. R.
1932   *Demetrius on Style*. LCL. Cambridge, MA: Harvard University Press.

Schroeder, D.
1976   "Exhortation." Pp. 303–4 in *IDB Sup*. Nashville: Abingdon. "Parenesis." P. 643 in *IDB Sup*. Nashville: Abingdon.

Snyder, G.
1985   *Ante Pacem: Archaeological Evidence of Church Life Before Constantine*. Macon, GA: Mercer University Press.

Sparks, H. F. D.
1941   "The Order of the Epistles in P46." *JTS* 42: 180–181.

Stevenson, K.
1982   Nuptial Blessing: A Study of Christian Marriage Rites. Alcuin
        Collections 64. London: S.P.C.K.
1986   "Van Gennep and Marriage—Strange Bedfellows? A Fresh
        Look at the Rites of Marriage." *Ephemerides Liturgicae* 100: 138–
        51.

Stowers, S.
1986   *Letter Writing in Greco-Roman Antiquity.* Library of Early
        Christianity. Ed. W. A. Meeks. Philadelphia: Westminster.

Studer, B.
1986   "Zur Hochzeitsfeier der Christen in den westlichen Kirchen
        der ersten Jahrhunderte." Pp. 51–85 in *La Celebrazione cristiana
        del Matrimonio: Simboli e Testi.* Atti del II Congresso inter-
        nazionale de Liturgia, Roma, 27–31 Maggio 1985. Studia
        Anselmiana 93. Analecta liturgica 11. Ed. G. Farnedi. Rome:
        Pontificio Ateneo S. Anselmo.

Thraede, K.
1970   *Grundzüge griechisch-römischer Brieftopik.* Munich: Beck.

Turner, V.
1967   *The Forest of Symbols.* Ithaca, NY: Cornell University.
1969   *The Ritual Process.* Chicago: Aldine.

Van der Meer, F. and Mohrmann, C.
1958   *Atlas of the Early Christian World.* Trans. and ed. Mary Hedlund
        and H. H. Rowley. New York: Thomas Nelson.

van Gennep, A.
1909   *Les rites de passage.* Paris: Libraire Critique, E. Nourry.
1960   *The Rites of Passage.* Trans. M. Vizedom and G. Caffee.
        Chicago: University of Chicago Press.

Vielhauer, P.
1975   *Geschichte der urchristlichen Literatur.* Berlin: de Gruyter.

White, J. L.
1984   "New Testament Epistolary Literature in the Framework of
        Ancient Epistolography." Pp. 1730–1756 in *Aufstieg und
        Niedergang der römischen Welt.* Vol. 2. Ed. Wolfgang Haase and
        Hildegard Temporini. Berlin: de Gruyter.

PARAENESIS IN A HOMILY (λόγος παρακλήσεως): THE POSSIBLE LOCATION OF, AND SOCIALIZATION IN, THE 'EPISTLE TO THE HEBREWS'

Harold W. Attridge

ABSTRACT

Section 1 of this essay reviews the analyses proposed by Profs. Gammie and Perdue in an attempt to locate the "Epistle to the Hebrews." In the process it detects an element of tension between the two primary treatments. Section 2 of the essay offers an analysis of the formal features of Hebrews and suggests the definition of another sub-genre, the "homily" or λόγος παρακλήσεως, within the generic taxonomy proposed by Gammie. Section 3 of the essay analyzes the social function which Hebrews might be designed to serve. It is seen to aim not to socialize new members of a group, to legitimate a structure of authority, or to polemicize against an external social unit and its symbol system, but to reinforce the identity of a social sub-group in such a way as not to isolate it from its environment.

1.1   The text known as the Epistle to the Hebrews presents an interesting test case for the theoretical descriptions of a genre of paraenetic literature developed in the introductory essays by Professors Gammie and Perdue. Both the ways in which it supports those definitions and the ways in which it suggests refinements of them are illuminating.[1]

1.2   That the editors thought it worthwhile to treat Hebrews in this study is no doubt based upon the fact that there are numerous hortatory[2] elements in the text. Hebrews urges its addressees to take the word of God seriously (2:1-4); to hold fast to a traditional confession (3:6, 14; 4:14; 10:23); to strive to enter the rest promised by God (4:11); to approach boldly God's gracious throne (4:16); to follow in Christ's footsteps "into the sanctuary" (10:19-21); to live a life of faith, hope, and love (10:22-25); to endure (10:34-36; 12:4, 12-13); to imitate Jesus (12:3); to pursue peace and sanctity (12:14); to love one another (13:1); to show hospitality (13:2); to remember imprisoned fellow believers (13:3); to keep marriage holy (13:4); to remember and obey leaders (13:7, 17); to follow Jesus in his acceptance of public reproach (13:13); to offer sacrifices consisting of praise and deeds of loving kindness (13:16); and, finally, to pray for the unknown author of the work (13:18). The whole of Hebrews, therefore, seems to be a likely candidate for the "secondary genre" of "Paraenetic

Literature." Moreover, at least a portion of the text, chapter 13, or at least 13:1-6, conforms to Gammie's criteria for the sub-genre of paraenesis, defined as (§ 2.2) "a form of address which not only commends, but actually enumerates precepts or maxims which pertain to moral aspiration and the regulation of human conduct."

1.3   In addition to the explicit exhortations, there are other formal elements within Hebrews which Gammie has included as characteristics of "Paraenetic Literature" generally. At least one major portion of Hebrews, chapter 11, can be readily characterized as a collection of what Gammie (§§ 2.2.3d and 2.7) calls *paradeigmata* or *encomia*. The precise way in which the examples of the chapter function might be debated, and the results of that debate might support a classification of Hebrews in the sub-genre of protreptic rather than paraenesis.[3] At present, I simply want to note features identified as elements of the whole "secondary genre." Some formal features associated with admonitions, a constituent of both instructions and paraeneses, are present, including warnings to avoid the danger of apostasy (3:12; 4:1; 6:4-12; 12:25), greed (13:5), or strange teachings (13:9). Characteristic of both warnings and exhortations, as defined by Gammie (§§ 2.4.3b and 2.5.2), are the use of vocatives in direct address (3:1, 12; 10:19) and the presence of motive clauses (e.g., 2:2-4; 4:15; 10:19b, 26; 12:17; 13:2b, 5b). A characteristic attributed to exhortations (Gammie, § 2.5.2) is variety in the means of expressing hortatory remarks. Hebrews exemplifies the trait in its frequent alteration between imperatives[4] and hortatory subjunctives.[5]

Prima facie, at least, there would seem to be enough material here to justify including Hebrews in a collection of hortatory literature or, to be more precise, within the "secondary genre" defined by Gammie as "Paraenetic Literature."

1.4   But where within that secondary genre should Hebrews be located? A part of the problem with pursuing further the relationship of Hebrews to the proposed taxonomy is that the boundaries between sub-genres are rather fluid, and many of the components of the sub-genres (e.g., chreiai or riddles) most appropriately define forms, or relatively small units of discourse, which can on occasion be used as the exclusive components of a collection. More often, however, such units are combined into complex compositions, the generic characteristics of which involve more than the sum of their parts. Hebrews, in any case, is not a collection of any one or two of the component elements of the Paraenetic Literature defined by Gammie.

It is equally, if not more, difficult to fit Hebrews as a whole into one of the defined sub-genres, "instructions" and "paraeneses." Gammie himself, as noted above, only goes so far as to include Hebrews 13 into the latter genre. The rest of the work, which he does not discuss, does not fit very well in that category, since it is obviously much more than a collection of enumerated precepts, maxims or the like.

The essays of Gammie and Perdue discuss another sub-genre, loosely related to paraenesis, namely protreptic, in which it might be possible to classify Hebrews. Yet precisely what this sub-genre is supposed to be remains unclear. For Gammie (§ 2.2.2) protreptic is discourse which "seeks to persuade, frequently through a sustained demonstration." He arrives at this rather encompassing definition, which seems general enough to apply to all kinds of oratory, in critical dialogue with other scholars who have wrestled with a definition of protreptic. It is interesting that one of the definitions rejected by Gammie, that of Stowers, is adopted, with minor qualifications, by Perdue.[6] The latter notes Gammie's critique of Stowers, but still defines protreptic (Perdue, § 4.1) in terms of conversion or as discourse concerned "with entrance into the path of life," over against paraenesis, which is literature aiming at confirmation or "continuance in the course undertaken." Although a few scholars such as Kosmala have claimed otherwise, Hebrews is clearly addressed to people who share a Christian confession which they are bidden to maintain (Heb 4:14; 10:23). Thus, Hebrews would have to be protreptic on Gammie's formal definition, which attempts to differentiate collections of hortatory sayings, etc., from discursive texts using such materials. On Perdue's functional definition, however, Hebrews cannot be protreptic, but must be classed within the sub-genre of paraenesis.[7]

It is interesting, by the way, that at one point Perdue prefers (§ 2.6) to give the label "sayings collection" to the sub-genre which Gammie styles paraenesis. Here Perdue seems to slip into a formal, not functional analytical mode. Yet if his "sayings collection" is the same as Gammie's "paraenesis," this is no more suitable a home for Hebrews than is protreptic, even with the qualification that the sub-genre is supplemented by letters in the Graeco-Roman world. Hebrews is certainly more than a collection of sayings, whether its function is paraenetic, protreptic, or something in between.

There is one further definition of protreptic mentioned in Gammie's essay, that of Fiore, who distinguishes it from paraenesis by virtue of its narrowness of focus. That restricted notion of protreptic is problematic for Hebrews. While there is a focus on faith or fidelity throughout the work, and especially in chapters 11 and 12, there is much else, both generic virtue[8] and specific precepts, especially in chapter 13.

We come to the conclusion that, while it seems intuitively obvious that Hebrews should belong to the "secondary genre" of "Paraenetic

Literature," it does not fit well into any of the sub-genres which are said to comprise or be substantially related to that secondary genre.[9] Its sub-genre might be defined as protreptic, on the broad formal definition of Gammie, or paraenesis, if one accepts the functional definition of Perdue and abstracts it from his equation of this sub-genre with "sayings collections."

1.5   One reason for the lack of fit, apart from the conceptual tension between the definitions of Gammie and Perdue, has to do with the data base on which the inductive definition of the whole secondary genre and the two (or three) major sub-genres is based. That data base consists primarily of one part of the Wisdom literature of the ancient Near East, including, but by no means confined to, the sapiential literature of the Israelite tradition. Hebrews is certainly related genetically to that tradition, since it uses motifs from it and on occasion (12:5-6) explicitly cites it. Nonetheless, as a whole literary work, it simply does not look much like a distant cousin of Amen-em-opet, Qoheleth, or Ben Sira, but like a member of quite another tribe.

1.6   One might also consider where Hebrews might fit in the classical rhetorical trichotomy, which stands in a loose relationship to the literary genres of various levels defined by Gammie. His observations (§ 1.1.4) on the overlap among the rhetorical categories are sound, and the trichotomy is descriptive rather than analytical. That is, it is not composed of distinct and airtight compartments. Hebrews is a good case in point. If it has to be given only one of the three labels, it should probably be, by process of elimination, epideictic. The work is clearly not forensic, attempting to adjudicate the propriety of some past actions. Neither is it primarily symbouleutic, despite the fact that it does give advice, both generic and specific. In the most general terms, it celebrates the ongoing significance of a person and certain events connected with him. The celebration functions to reinforce values and commitments associated with that person and those events. Yet in reinforcing those values and commitments, it issues admonitions and specific recommendations. Thus, the discourse is generically similar to the kind of oratory that one could hear in antiquity, and can hear even today, at wakes, weddings, funerals, national holidays, and, in some churches at least, on major holy days. In short, Hebrews is an epideictic oration, with a few, appropriate symbouleutic elements.

2.1   So far we have been testing the "fit" between Hebrews and Gammie's formalist and Perdue's functionalist definitions of Paraenetic Literature. We have found, in addition to severe tension between the two definitions where they might be relevant to Hebrews, some points of contact. At this juncture I would like to take a different tack in attempting to relate Hebrews to a secondary genre of "Paraenetic Literature" and work more inductively from the formal patterns detectable within the text itself.

2.2   There is, of course, a great deal in Hebrews besides its exhortations, admonitions, and the like. One of the perennial challenges to interpreters has been to understand the relationship between its exhortations and its doctrinal or expositional[10] material. Is the piece really a dogmatic treatise with a bit of hortatory window dressing or is it fundamentally a pastorally oriented, hortatory work, with some loosely connected scriptural exegesis and argumentation? Although most critics eschew both horns of the dilemma and say that Hebrews is a combination of exhortation and doctrinal development, the relationship between exhortation and the rest of the work has seldom been adequately analyzed. Yet, I would suggest that understanding that relationship is essential to making sense of either element. The scriptural exposition and doctrinal development ultimately have a hortatory aim and an important part of the exhortation derives its force from the doctrinal or expository development.

The connection between exposition and exhortation is not simply a feature of the work as a whole but is connected to a formal pattern readily detectable in important portions of Hebrews. This formal pattern is most clearly present in the block of material extending from 3:1 to 4:14.[11] The section begins with a preface (3:1-6) which, in good epideictic fashion, involves a *synkrisis* or comparison of Christ and Moses. That comparison serves to introduce the theme of fidelity. A citation from Psalm 95 (Heb. 3:7-11) provides a scriptural foundation for a summons to a faithful response to God's word. Expository comments, focused on specific verses of the Psalm, explain the significance of the events of the Exodus generation and their relevance to the present situation of the addressees (3:12-4:10). All this exposition leads to the exhortation (4:11) to "strive to enter the rest" mentioned in the Psalm. The section concludes with a bit of festive prose (4:12-13) celebrating the penetrating power of God's word, a power which has just been felt in the way in which the ancient text, with its call to hear God's word "today," was made to address the "today" of the addressees. The pericope continues with a bit of transitional exhortation (4:14-16).

The same pattern is found elsewhere in the text. Scholars have often noted the similarity to 4:14-16 in the phrasing of the exhortation at 10:19-21. The significance of that parallel consists in the fact that both sections serve as transitions linking a well-defined unit with its context. In the case of the later transition, the block of material which it follows has the same formal pattern obvious in the case of chapters 3 and 4. An intro-

ductory paragraph (8:1-6) introduces themes that are to be exploited in the
body of the exposition. A scriptural text, Jer 31:31-33, serves as the basis
for further development (8:7-13). The themes and motifs of the introduction and the scriptural citation are interwoven in a complex fashion in five
discrete and concentrically arranged blocks of exposition extending from
9:1 through 10:10.[12] There is no explicit exhortation issued at this point,
but the moves made in this exposition will bear significant paraenetic fruit
later in the text. Immediately after the expository arguments of 9:1-10:10
there is a summary paragraph which functions much as does the florid
passage on God's word at 4:14-15. It concludes the whole pericope begun
at 8:1 by summarizing its fundamental thrust and repeating key verses
from the scriptural citation of Jeremiah 31, which had served as the text
for the expository development.

The pattern of introduction, citation, expository development,
and conclusion most fully exemplified in these two sections is partially
replicated in other portions of Hebrews. Chapter 7 lacks the proem and
begins directly with a complex paraphrase of scripture (7:1-3). This is
followed by a sometimes playful, but also quite serious, exposition of the
text in three discrete segments (7:4-10, 11-19, 20-25), followed by a bit of
highly ornate prose about the heavenly High Priest who is really the
object of the whole discourse (7:26-28). There is no hortatory application,
because this expository sections serves, along with the more complex
material of the following chapters, as the basis for the final hortatory
chapters. Yet another example of the pattern can be found in 12:1-13. An
introductory paragraph (12:1-3), with vivid athletic imagery serves as a
transition from the preceding chapter and its paradigmatic encomium on
faith and the faithful. The summons to imitate the endurance exemplified
by the ultimate model of faith is then developed through the citation
(12:4-6) and exposition (12:7-11) of Prov 3:11-12. A hortatory conclusion
(12:12-13) summarizes the summons to follow Jesus by recalling the
athletic imagery of the opening verses.

2.3   I suggest that in all of these sections of Hebrews the analogous
formal pattern is not accidental, and in fact is a constitutive feature of
what should be defined as another major sub-genre within the "secondary
genre" of paraenetic literature. This sub-genre, though alluded to by
Perdue (§ 3.2, end) as "instruction and *homilies*," does not play a part in
either the formal or the functional discussion of paraenetic literature of
the introductory essays because of the previously mentioned limitation of
the data base.[13] For texts that evidence the pattern of formal introduction,
scriptural citation, exposition or thematic elaboration, and application,
one might use the modern terms "homily" or "sermon." There is also an
ancient term which is particularly apt. At the conclusion of Hebrews, in

the epistolary postscript (13:22), the body of the work is described as a λόγος παρακλήσεως or "word of exhortation." The same collocation appears at Acts 13:15, when in a synagogue service, after the reading of the Torah and the prophetic haftarah, Paul and Barnabas are asked if they have a λόγος παρακλήσεως for the congregation.[14] One does not need to presume the historicity of the account in Acts in order to recognize that the term is probably a technical literary designation for a certain kind of oratorical performance. I suggest, then, that we label this sub-genre of Paraenetic Literature as homiletic or, if a Greek term be preferable in order to avoid anachronistic connotations, I suggest "paraclesis."[15]

2.4   It may be worth reflecting for a moment on the relationship between this proposed oratorical type and the three canonical categories of classical rhetoric. We have already noted that there are some difficulties in fitting Hebrews within that descriptive scheme of classification, although the difficulties are by no means as severe as those affecting its inclusion in the sub-genres of Paraenetic Literature proposed by Gammie. One reason for the difficulty arises from the paradigmatic cases out of which the three highly general categories of classical rhetorical analysis emerged. Forensic oratory was suited to the law courts, or more properly to the people assembled as jury; deliberative was that suited to the legislative assembly, or the people assembled to legislate; epideictic was that suited to the people assembled for occasions of solemn festivity or mourning. It is not unexpected that new forms of rhetoric emerged in social situations and institutional settings not found in classical Athens. The Hellenistic synagogue would have been one such setting. There the weekly confrontation with a revered text set the stage for a new rhetorical occasion, defined by the necessity of actualizing the significance of that sacred but often strange piece of literature for a community in, but not entirely of, the social world of the Hellenistic polis. Paraclesis, I suggest, is the newly minted rhetorical form that actualizes traditional scripture for a community in a non-traditional environment. It certainly has affinities with the classical forms of oratory, and those who regularly practised it probably had some training in rhetorical art, but paraclesis is in fact a mutant on the evolutionary trail of ancient rhetoric.

3.1   Thus far I have been probing, on the basis of the test case of Hebrews, the formal elements of the definition of Paraenetic Literature proposed in the introductory essays. I would like to conclude by exploring briefly the functional proposal made primarily by Perdue, that there are four possible functions of hortatory literature: protreptic, socialization, legitimation, and conflict. The sub-genre which I have defined tentatively as paraclesis could, I suspect, serve all these functions, although it is less suited for protreptic than for the others. This is a suspicion or very provisional working hypothesis rather than firm conclusion, since the subgenre is hardly well delimited or widely recognized. What we have on the table at present is a paradigm case of paraclesis, Hebrews.

3.2   Unfortunately none of the four functions as defined by Perdue fits Hebrews very well. As already indicated, it is clearly not a work with a protreptic function, since it appeals to people who already share common values and religious symbols.

Neither does Hebrews socialize by providing a "comprehensive and consistent induction of an individual into the objective world of a society or a segment of it" to use Berger and Luckmann's definition of the function of socialization, cited by Perdue (§ 4.2). Interestingly enough, Hebrews uses the language of instructing children (5:11-14), but this is a common metaphorical use of widespread categories of Hellenistic educational theory.[16] It functions as an ironic *captatio benevolentiae* before Hebrews launches into its elaborate expositions of the figure of Melchizedek (chapter 7) and of the nature of Christ's high-priestly action (chapters 8-10). The appeal is ironic because it says to the addressees that they are like children who can only take the pablum of elementary doctrine. The anticipated response is, "No, we are ready to take on the difficult stuff." To that, Hebrews responds, "Then let's pass over the basics and go on" (6:1), a move which has often caused commentators consternation. Neither here nor anywhere else does Hebrews give instruction about social roles or states, the sort of socializing envisioned in the definition. It may be that another form of socializing is involved, as we shall see.

There are some indications of what might be taken to be "legitimation" or "socially objectivated knowledge that serves to explain and justify the social order," to cite once again Perdue's (§ 4.3) citation of Berger. There is at least the reference to the community's leaders whom the addressees are urged to remember and imitate (13:7). These leaders are probably departed founders of the community, and the addressees can contemplate the "outcome of their behavior" (τὴν ἔκβασιν τῆς ἀναστροφῆς). In addition, the addressees are urged to obey current leaders, who must anxiously anticipate giving an account of their charges (13:17). These two verses of the final exhortation (or paraenesis in Gammie's sense) certainly seem to have an obvious legitimating function, since they support an authority structure and suggest a motivation for adhering to it. It might be possible to construe the rest of Hebrews as a preparation for this appeal. The call to adhere to the "confession" (3:6, 14; 4:14; 10:23) could be construed as an attempt to reinforce the ideological basis on which those in a position of leadership exercise their authority. If such an analysis were to be pursued, it would be operating at the level of a latent social function of this particular discourse. It is certainly not the case that the whole of this discourse, as contrasted with 1 *Clement*, 1 Peter, or the Pastoral Epistles, is manifestly concerned with problems of community organization or structures of authority.

There are elements of Hebrews that clearly reflect a situation of conflict. The addressees, or at least the implied addressees, had undergone some sort of persecution involving public humiliation, confiscations, and imprisonment (10:32-34). If the language of 12:4, "you have not yet resisted to the point of shedding blood," is not simply part of the pugilistic imagery appropriate to the athletic metaphor of the context, it may indicate that the persecution involved nothing more serious than what is described in chapter 10. One of the clear aims of the exhortations is to prepare the addressees for more of the same. The motif of caring for prisoners explicitly recurs at 13:3, but there are more interesting and significant elements relevant to a situation of conflict.

Several of the examples of faith in chapter 11 are portrayed with particular attention to the situation of the addressees. The image of the sojourning strangers, Abraham, Sarah, Isaac, Jacob, and Joseph (11:8-22), buoyed by their hopes for a true heavenly homeland, is neither a description of the technical legal situation of the addressees,[17] nor is it purely metaphorical, describing the state of the soul lost in the world of matter, as interpretations of Hebrews against a Gnostic background, advanced, for instance, by Käsemann, Schierse, and Grässer, tend to maintain. It is, rather, an appropriate image for a community that has suffered the social ostracism and obloquy described in chapter 10. Similarly, Moses is described in a way that focuses on his social alienation. Most intriguing is the remark that he "bore the reproach of Christ" (11:26). The precise meaning of that remark within the confines of the story of Moses are debated, and it is unclear whether Moses is depicted as functioning as a salvific figure who met opposition analogous to that which Jesus experienced, whether he exercised his difficult leadership of the people of God in view of a visionary experience of the future Messiah, or whether he received the "reproach of Christ" in some other sense.[18] The function of the remark is, however, clear. Moses is portrayed as one more in a long line of faithful people of God who suffered for that fidelity. Moreover, his suffering, the endurance of shame, is precisely the sort to which the addresses had been exposed.

The ultimate example of faith is, of course, Jesus, the "inaugurator and perfecter" (12:2) of the virtue. In the description of his suffering which follows that compound epithet, what is given prominence is not the physical agony, but the "shame" of the cross. Jesus is then proposed as the model "athlete" of faith to be watched and imitated by those who run the race in his footsteps. The most relevant quality for this mimetic activity is the way Jesus endured verbal abuse (ἀντιλογία) from sinners. Christians experiencing the loss of social standing envisioned in 10:32-34 are thus called upon to accept the same sort of abuse.

Part of the background to Hebrews is certainly a situation of some sort of social conflict, and it might be possible to construe the doctrinal and expository sections of the text as laying the foundations for a response to that situation. The elaborate imagery of the Heavenly High Priest, in the eternal "order of Melchizedek," who performs a definitive sacrifice for the removal of sins and the establishment of a lasting covenant, could be construed as a way of creating or sustaining an alternative symbolic world that enables the addressees to make sense of and to endure the opposition which they receive from society as a whole. The case is certainly as plausible, if not more so, than the "legitimation" model. Yet, just as that model seemed inadequate to the whole of Hebrews, so too the conflictual model fails to account for the whole of the text.

Although Perdue's category of conflict is rather abstract, and may, if fully developed, be flexible enough to accomodate a variety of persuasive strategies, it may be inappropriate as a description of the function of Hebrews. The term itself seems to suggest something of a polemical stance and Perdue's description (§ 4.4) of the conflict function as one that "undermines the legitimacy of the prevailing order of the society and competing communities by calling into question the social knowledge undergirding their symbolic universe" surely reinforces that perception. Whether Hebrews conforms to that definition has been a major problem in the history of its interpretation.

There are certainly what might be construed as blatantly anti-traditional elements in the text, such as the denigration of the Law (7:11-19) and the cult (9:1-10; 10:1-4), and the warning against strange teachings, which seems to have something to do with Jewish or Jewish-Christian practices (13:9). Such elements provide the basic evidence for the common construals of Hebrews as a text designed to prevent a relapse to the ancestral religion or some contemporary offshoot of traditional Judaism that is competing with the author's community. If it is the work's aim to wean the addressees from Judaism, it is remarkable how small a role an appeal to keep free from the Israel of the flesh plays in the explicit hortatory segments of the text. Only in the warning of 13:9 does the author seem to draw an explicit practical consequence from his anti-traditionalist language. Yet that verse is shrouded in ambiguities revolving around the image of the "altar" which it deploys. A clear warning against conversion or relapse it is not.

Focus on the anti-traditional elements of the text can lead to a classification of the work's paraenetic function as conflictive in too narrow a sense. Such a focus fails to appreciate how the overtly polemical remarks function within the work as a whole. Rather than the cutting edge of Hebrews' hortatory program, they seem to be rather traditional or vestigial elements, now used as components of the comparative or "syncritic" strategy of the epideictic oration. The oration as a whole appeals for continued and renewed commitment to the Jesus tradition in a situation uncomfortable for that tradition and by people who, for various reasons, may have lost their initial enthusiasm for that commitment. The importance of the tradition is displayed by comparing its chief elements with other individuals and institutions of recognized worth, emphasizing the absolute superiority of the subject of the oration over the object of comparison.

3.3   This rather abstract analysis of the hortatory program of Hebrews can be made more specific. In the process, the hortatory function of the text and its unity as an example of "paraclesis" can be suggested. The hortatory program of Hebrews can, with only minor oversimplification, be thematically summarized with the hortatory subjunctives of the transitional remarks at 4:14-16. On the one hand, the addressees are urged to "hold fast" (κρατῶμεν), specifically to the "confession" of faith which they have professed. On the other, they are urged to "approach" (προσερχώμεθα), specifically to God's gracious throne as a source of aid. The fidelity (πίστις) which is of so much concern to Hebrews[19] can readily be understood as a combination of both the "static" and "dynamic" qualities suggested by these two exhortations.

Among what might be termed the more static elements, the addressees are urged to pay special attention to the message of scripture and not slip away (2:1); to hold on, especially to their confession (10:23), but also to other hallmarks of their initial Christian experience, their "boldness" (παρρησία, 3:6; 10:19, 35), and the "hope" (ἐλπίς, 3:6; 6:11) which is intimately connected with it. The exhortation to "endurance" (ὑπομονή, 10:36; 12:2, 7), a virtue evident in their past response to harassment and persecution (10:32-34), is also a thematically "static" element.

At the same time, the addressees are called to more "dynamic" virtue, imaged by movement in various directions. They are summoned, in terminology probably derived from the cultic sphere, to "approach" (προσερχώμεθα) the throne of God to find mercy and aid (4:16; 10:22) and to strive to "enter" (σπουδάσωμεν...εἰσελθεῖν) God's rest (4:11); to "carry on" (φερώμεθα) to maturity (6:1).

The call to a more dynamic virtue, to movement, takes a different twist in the final, primarily hortatory chapters. In the paradigmatic encomium on faith in chapter 11, fidelity, which involves the more "static" virtues of endurance exemplified particularly in Israel's martyrs (11:35-38) and in some aspects of the story of Moses (11:25, 27), also prominently features the "dynamic" virtue of movement. This movement is not, however, defined in terms of entry, to a temple or throne room, but in terms of exit, from Mesopotamia to an unknown promised land (11:8); from a land of oppression (11:27, 29); or, in the most general terms, from an earthly to a heavenly homeland (11:13-16).

The summons to follow Jesus in chapter 12, which describes the "approach" which has already taken place (12:18, 22), also calls the addressees to movement, not to entry or to a cultic approach, but first "to run the race" (τρέχωμεν τὸν...ἀγῶνα), a dynamic way of encouraging endurance (12:1).

An even more drastic reversal of the imagery of movement occurs in the exhortation of the final chapter to "go forth" (ἐξερχώμεθα) to a realm of suffering and prayerful service (13:13). The reversal in the direction of the movement imagery parallels and is grounded upon a key reversal in the christological exposition.

In the descriptions of Christ's salvific activity, the dominant image is one of movement out of the world in its present state into the transcendent sphere of God's presence. Thus the Son is one who has "taken his seat on high" (1:3), who has entered into a glorious condition above the angels, a state to which he leads God's other children (2:10). He has passed through the heavens (4:14), or through the heavenly tabernacle (9:11),[20] and entered into the heavenly sanctuary (9:12, 24). All of this imagery of movement into the transcendent or eschatological realm of the presence of God seems designed to assure the faithful that they do have access to God (10:19-21) and to undergird the summons to them to approach God (4:14) in true worship (9:14).

Yet the movement through the heavens into the heavenly paradigm of the earthly tabernacle stands in tension with another image of movement dramatically deployed at the climax of the central expository chapters. There, at 10:5-10, Christ's decisive sacrificial act, by which effective expiation is achieved and a lasting covenant inaugurated, is seen to be something achieved not in a transcendent sphere but in Christ's "body" (10:10), after he has "entered the world" (10:5).

The shift in the imagery of the exhortations, which after chapter 10 focus ever more strongly on movement out into the world, parallels and is grounded upon the reversal in the expository imagery. That is hardly surprising, given the role in the exhortations of the theme of imitating the fidelity ultimately exemplified by Jesus (12:1-3).

3.4   The function of the hortatory program of Hebrews then is not primarily to engage in polemic. Neither is it involved in the *construction* of a conceptual or symbolic universe that will serve as an alternative to those of the dominant society or of competing sub-groups. Such a symbolic universe has already been constructed.[21] Hebrews cleverly plays with inherited symbols and images. It juxtaposes and develops them in its expository sections in interesting new ways. The function of such expository play is confirmatory. It reinforces the validity of the symbolic universe to which the addressees are supposed to adhere. This confirmation stands in service of a hortatory program to accept willingly and to use creatively a marginalized social status. This piece of paraclesis serves primarily not to socialize new members of a group, to legitimate a structure of authority, or to polemicize against an external social unit and its symbol system, but to reinforce the identity of a social sub-group in such a way as not to isolate it from its environment.

4.   *Conclusion.* Although portions of Hebrews conform rather precisely to the generic classification of paraenesis offered by Gammie, the work as a whole can be integrated into that sub-genre only with difficulty. Neither does the functional analysis of traditional hortatory literature offered by Perdue quite apply to Hebrews. The work as a whole might exemplify a sub-genre of Paraenetic Literature not considered in the introductory essays, in large part because of the ancient near eastern data base on which those essays are primarily constructed. Certain formal patterns which serve as structuring devices in many parts of Hebrews suggest that the work is a homily or a bit of "paraclesis." In such a work exhortation is grounded in exposition and application of traditional materials, here scripture and christological imagery. The exhortation of Hebrews functions to confirm the values and commitments of a community suffering social ostracism, while it insists that those values require engagement in, not separation from, the opposing society.

NOTES

[1] This essay reflects the work on Hebrews more fully contained in my commentary on the book in the Hermeneia series published by Fortress Press (1989).

[2] I am using the term in a very general and non-technical sense, much in the way that Gammie does in his remark that "Paraenetic Literature may be epitomized as literature of moral exhortation" (§ 2).

[3] The generic classification of Hebrews 11 is a complicated matter which I do not propose to resolve here. I would want to argue that Hebrews 11 is in fact a review of sacred history presented as an encomium, but on the virtue of faith, exemplified in the

lives of the faithful, who are thus paradigms of the virtue praised. The closest formal parallel is the encomium on Wisdom in Wisdom of Solomon. Philo *Virt.* 198-205 is somewhat similar. For a straightforward list of *exempla virtutis*, cf. 1 Macc 2:49-64; 4 *Macc.* 16.16-23; 18.11-13.

[4] Cf. 3:12, 13; 10:32, 35; 12:3, 7, 1 2, 14, 25; 13:1, 2, 3, 7, 9, 16, 17, 18, 24.

[5] Cf. 4:1, 11, 14, 16; 6:1; 10:22-24; 12:1, 28; 13:13, 15.

[6] Their divergent assessments of what "protreptic" means is a major difference between the two introductory essays.

[7] Correspondence on the point after the essays for this volume were written indicates that Gammie and Perdue consider themselves to be using terminology in a consistent fashion. I remain skeptical about whether their respective taxonomic schemes are entirely compatible. Hebrews is protreptic if protreptic is discourse which "seeks to persuade, frequently through a sustained demonstration" (Gammie). But little persuasive prose is excluded! Hebrews is not protreptic if the latter deals with "entrance into the path of life," over against paraenesis which is literature aiming at confirmation or "continuance in the course undertaken" (Perdue).

[8] Note the faith hope and love triad at 6:10-12 or 10:21-25.

[9] The note on Gammie's chart of the secondary genres of wisdom literature indicating that paraeneses "may utilize the form of letters" is of some interest in view of the "epistolary" character of Hebrews. Although it has traditionally been grouped with canonical epistolary literature and has at least the concluding elements of an epistle (13:19-25), Hebrews lacks a formal epistolary protocol and is, therefore, at best a marginal member of the genre. Even if the epistolary character of the concluding frame element is taken seriously, that says little about the generic character of the bulk of the work. Much could be set in an epistolary frame, including the Book of Revelation.

[10] I am again employing the most generic and, I hope, non-technical way of referring to the non-hortatory portions of Hebrews.

[11] This formal classification is hardly new. See Clemen and, on this pericope in general, Hofius.

[12] On the formal analysis of this section, see Attridge (1989).

[13] Had material such as later Yelammedenu and proem homilies been included in the overall collection of Paraenetic Literature, the delineation of a sub-genre such as I have described might have been facilitated. As Aune (202) notes, it is anachronistic to make too facile an identification of New Testament materials with either later Jewish homiletic pattern. Nonetheless, a comprehensive study of the formal patterns of actual or possible homilies in both early Jewish and Christian traditions remains a desideratum.

[14] Cf. also 2 Macc 15:11, where the term is used to describe a speech of Judas Maccabaeus.

[15] In modern critical literature Hebrews has often been labeled a homily. See most recently Aune, 212-14. That label can, however, be based on a more precise analysis of formal and contentual patterns of the text.

[16] For examples of similar imagery, cf. Philo *Agr.* 9: ἐπεὶ δὲ νηπίοις μέν ἐστι γάλα τροφή, τελείοις δὲ τὰ ἐκ πυρῶν πέμματα, καὶ ψυχῆς γαλακτώδεις μὲν ἂν εἶεν τροφαὶ κατὰ τὴν παιδικὴν ἡλικίαν τὰ τῆς ἐγκυκλίου μουσικῆς προπαιδεύματα, τέλειαι δὲ καὶ ἀνδράσιν ἐμπρεπεῖς αἱ διὰ φρονήσεως καὶ σωφροσύνης καὶ ἁπάσης ἀρετῆς ὑφηγήσεις. "But seeing that for babes milk is food, but for grown men wheaten bread, there must also be soul-nourishment, such as is milk-like, suited to the time of childhood, in the shape of the preliminary stages of school learning and, such as is adapted to grown men, in the shape of instructions leading the way through wisdom and temperance and all virtue," or Epictetus *Diss.* 2.16.39: οὐ θέλεις ἤδη ὡς τὰ παιδία ἀπογαλακτισθῆναι καὶ ἅπτεσθαι τροφῆς στερεωτέρας, "Are you not willing, at this late date, like children, to be

weaned and to partake of more solid food." Cf. also Philo *Congr.* 19; *Migr. Abr.* 29; *Som.* 2.9; *Om. prob. lib.* 160, and Epictetus *Diss.* 2.16.39; 3.24.9. See Schlier and Thüsing.

[17] This interpretation of similar language at 1 Pet 1:1; 2:11 has, of course, been defended by Elliott who recognizes (55 n. 75) that the terminology for resident aliens are metaphorical in Hebrews. How the metaphor works is not clear.

[18] In general, see D'Angelo.

[19] The topic has been treated frequently, see especially Grässer, and, subsequently, Rusche, Dautzenberg, Schoonhoven, and Thompson (53–80).

[20] The interpretation of the image of 9:11 and its relationship to that of 4:14 is highly controverted. To resolve the problems of the verse is impossible in the context of this essay.

[21] For a thorough discussion of the traditions underlying Hebrews, see Loader.

WORKS CONSULTED

Attridge, Harold W.
1986   "The Uses of Antithesis in Hebrews 8–10." in *HTR* 79:1–9.
1989   *Hebrews.* Hermeneia. Philadelphia: Fortress.

Aune, David E.
1978   *The New Testament in Its Literary Environment.* Philadelphia: Westminster.

Clemen, C.
1896   "The Oldest Christian Sermon," *Expositor* 5: 392–400.

D'Angelo, Mary Rose
1979   *Moses in the Letter to the Hebrews.* SBLDS 42; Missoula: Scholars.

Dautzenberg, Gerhard
1973   "Der Glaube im Hebräerbrief." *BZ* 17:161–77

Elliott, John H.
1981   *A Home for the Homeless: A Sociological Exegesis of 1 Peter, Its Situation and Strategy.* Philadelphia: Fortress.

Grässer, Erich
1965   *Der Glaube im Hebräerbrief.* Marburg: Elwert.

Hofius, Otfried
1970   *Katapausis: Die Vorstellung vom endzeitlichen Ruheort im Hebräerbrief.* WUNT 1. Tübingen: J.C.B. Mohr (Paul Siebeck).

Käsemann, Ernst
1984   *The Wandering People of God: An Investigation of the Letter to the
        Hebrews.* Trans. Roy A. Harrisville and Irving L. Sandberg.
        Minneapolis: Augsburg.

Kosmala, Hans
1959   *Hebräer—Essener—Christen.* SPB 1. Leiden: Brill.

Loader, William R. G.
1981   *Sohn und Hoherpriester: Eine traditionsgeschichtliche Unter-
        suchung zur Christologie des Hebräerbriefes.* WMANT 53.
        Neukirchen: Neukirchener Verlag.

Rusche, Helga
1971   "Glauben und Leben nach dem Hebräerbrief: Einführende
        Bemerkungen." *BibLeb* 12: 94–104.

Schierse, Franz-Josef
1955   *Verheißung und Heilsvollendung: Zur theologischen Grundfrage
        des Hebräerbriefes.* Munich: Zink.

Schlier, Heinrich
1964   "γάλα," *TDNT* 1:645–47.

Schoonhoven, Calvin R.
1978   "The 'Analogy of Faith' and the Intent of Hebrews," Pp. 92–
        110 in *Scripture, Tradition and Interpretation: Essays presented to
        Everett F. Harrison by his Students and Colleagues in Honor of his
        Seventy-fifth Birthday.* Ed. W. Ward Gasque and William S.
        LaSor. Grand Rapids: Eerdmans.

Thompson, James W.
1982   *The Beginnings of Christian Philosophy: The Epistle to the Hebrews.*
        CBQMS 13. Washington: Catholic Biblical Association.

Thüsing, Wilhelm
1967   "'Milch' und 'Feste Speise' (1 Kor 3,1f und Hebr 5,11–6,3).
        Elementarkatachese und theologische Vertiefung in neutesta-
        mentlicher Sicht." *TThZ* 76: 233–46, 261–80.

PART THREE:

RESPONSES

A Semiotic Critique: With Emphasis on the Place of the Wisdom of Solomon in the Literature of Persuasion

James M. Reese

ABSTRACT

This paper examines both the influence of Aristotle's *Protreptic* and his division of rhetoric. As an alternative to the sociological and taxonomic methodologies of Perdue and Gammie, I think a semiotic approach, based on the inference model of encyclopedia better illustrates how various literary streams came together in the philosophical tradition to produce a vast literature of persuasion in the Hellenistic era. More specifically one may demonstrate by the semiotic approach that even though the Wisdom of Solomon bears closest affinity with what has been identified as protreptic rather than with paraenesis, one should refrain from too earnest an endeavor to pour it into the molds of classical rhetoric which did not remain fixed.

1.1   If Perdue's opening essay in this volume places faith in the analysis of the social setting of paraenesis as act and Gammie's essay on taxonomy places hope in the analysis of paraenesis as form, I seek to show in this essay that there is "yet still a more excellent way" to analyze texts of moral exhortation, namely, the way of semiotics and the inference model of encyclopedia (see especially §§ 3.1, 3.2, 4.3 and 8.1 below). Perdue focuses on the occasions for paraenesis; Gammie focuses on classification and definitions, whereas the semiotic approach focuses not on fixed genres but on the signs of a literary text and the motives and intentions of the discourse under scrutiny. In this essay I utilize the encyclopedic model of Umberto Eco by examining the classical understanding of protreptic in Aristotle (§ 2) and the usefulness of semiotics in approaching classical categories such as epideictic literature (§§ 3 and 4). I then point to the modifications and blending of the classical categories in Hellenistic rhetoric (§ 5). Next I examine a recent application of the dictionary approach by Bizetti, and show where and how it is deficient (§ 6). Next but last I examine the various ways "diatribe" was understood in antiquity and is understood now—thus again showing the superiority of the semiotic way. To serve as a case in point and to give this essay further coherence, I have throughout concentrated on those rhetorical categories which have had particular applicability to the Wisdom of Solomon. In the final portion of this response I question whether the Wisdom of Solomon contains the kind of socialization Perdue and others see as usually reflected in the Paraenetic Literature and paraenesis. The "signs" and the encyclopedic approach suggest that the Wisdom of Solomon should be located elsewhere (§ 8) and not so confined or limited (§ 9).

1.2   When I first read the Greek text of the Wisdom of Solomon after reading through the Greek translation of the Hebrew Scriptures, I was struck by the difference in style and literary sophistication. The shift in vocabulary and tone pointed to an author familiar with Hellenistic culture. My efforts in interpreting this work led me to ask what role such a learned creation played in the cultural situation of Jews living among educated Greeks. Why, for example, should an anonymous author, using vocabulary that pointed to Alexandria a generation before the birth of Jesus, adopt the persona of the model sage of Jewish tradition, King Solomon, to organize this sustained appeal to seek "justice," that is, integrity of life?

2   *Role of Aristotle's Protreptic*

2.1   In many ways the Wisdom of Solomon recalls the literature of spiritual direction that is associated with the Platonic tradition (Kustas: 35) as well as the goal of numerous protreptics or exhortations to philosophy that are recorded in catalogues of Greek literature (Burgess: 254). In this paper I want to suggest that research in semiotics provides methodological tools to help explain the role that the Wisdom of Solomon could have played in maintaining the identity of a metropolitan community of Hellenistic Jews.

2.2   A. J. Festugière discusses themes that continually surfaced in the "moral diatribe" of Hellenistic philosophy. He treats them under five headings: the vanity of human things, the uncertainties of life, the inconstancy of Fortune, journeys, solitude (Festugière, 1949: 519-28). The roots of these themes already appeared in the lost *Protreptic* of Aristotle, written before the death of Plato in 348 B.C.E. So many fragments of it are preserved in Iamblichus that several attempts have been undertaken for its reconstruction. A look at two recent attempts will help orient this survey of a rhetorical tradition with which the author of the Wisdom of Solomon was evidently familiar.

2.3   Ingemar Düring gives little historical background but points out many related texts and provides a thorough commentary. He relies chiefly on the *Protreptic* of Iamblichus, the neo-Platonist who died about 330 C.E. Düring accepts chapters 5-12, a discourse of over 6,000 words (about the length of the Wisdom of Solomon) as practically a continuous excerpt from Aristotle's work, with a few additions and some editing by Iamblichus. Aristotle was following "the earliest example of a typical protreptic preserved to us," namely, Plato, *Euthydemus* 278e-282d (Düring: 19).

During's judgment on Plato's *Euthydemus* as a protreptic needs qualification on two counts. 1) Even though Socrates in this dialogue commends the pursuit of wisdom by means other than those advocated by the sophists, this dialogue is both heavily satirical and dramatic in form—neither of which constitutes an essential aspect of protreptic. 2) In defense of his designation of the *Euthydemus* as protreptic, Düring is telescoping history because Plato had experimented with protreptic themes throughout his life. In fact, "the whole philosophy of Plato can be called an 'exhortation to wisdom,' that is, to the determination and the practice of that science called virtue" (Festugière, 1973: 11). The origin of this type of discourse is usually attributed to the Attic orator Isocrates in his Cyprian discourses addressed to prince Themison. Aristotle transformed the method of demonstration by combining "demonstrative reasoning with dialectical and rhetorical arguments, adding a dash of philosophical poetry" (Düring: 32). The kind of reasoning practiced in Aristotle's *Protreptic* was not abstract; he insisted that wisdom could not be separated from doing good. The life devoted to philosophy not only leads to reform of the state but alone brings pleasure and happiness (Düring: 15-16).

2.4   Anton Chroust, the other recent reconstructor of Aristotle's work, is not as optimistic about the fidelity of the editing of Iamblichus to the original text and sequence of the *Protreptic*. Yet he is confident that it is possible to recover Aristotle's method of "successive approximation," that is, of gradually drawing a series of tentative conclusions until he achieved the final goal of his argument (Chroust: xii). It is clear that the aim of the *Protreptic* was to urge readers to pursue philosophy, which was identified with the practice of prudential wisdom (*phronēsis*). Continuity with Aristotle's insistence on the practical role of wisdom in guiding citizens to a moral life permeates the Wisdom of Solomon. Lady Wisdom is the giver of all those qualities that make life a worthwhile journey, including the four basic virtues of the Platonic tradition: prudential wisdom (*phronēsis*), justice, courage, self-control (Wisdom 8:7).

2.5   It is well to add here that the great difference in form and content between Aristotle's *Protreptic* and the Wisdom of Solomon does not prevent their possessing a literary continuity. As will be explained below, semiotics proposes a dynamic continuity in definitions that provides for organic growth and creativity. The period between 200-50 B.C.E. was a time of leveling of diversity between segments within

Hellenistic culture. After that, from the time of Cicero, arose an age of religious dogmatism and philosophical eclecticism. Hellenistic culture had become widespread but its strength was also dissipated, as is evident from the multiplication of manuals or "Introductions." These displayed a syncretism that reduced the distinctive classical philosophies to a culture in which earlier demarcations had become blended and blurred (Festugière, 1949: 341-50). Cultured Jews did not escape this influence, as can be seen from the writings of the prolific and eclectic Philo. He bears witness to the widespread influence of Hellenism in the many allusions to philosophical exhortations found in the commonplaces that fill his writings (Festugière, 1949: 519-54).

2.6   In view of the large number of tracts entitled *Protreptic*, and especially the enormous influence of that of Aristotle, one may wonder why so few of these survived. The reason is no doubt the superficiality of their content. This also accounts for the fact that the protreptic was never studied at length as a literary genre by any ancient grammarian. Protreptics covered hortatory aspects of edifying literature that were too closely linked to specific situations to be of much interest later (Fiore: 39). Modern scholarship "has not always avoided the danger of giving too static an idea to something that was essentially fluid in form" (Marrou: 410). To come to a better understanding of this dimension of Hellenistic literature, then, it is necessary to turn to epideictic literature, which is one of Aristotle's three divisions of rhetoric.

3   *Value of a Semiotic Approach*

3.1   Before making a few observations on epideictic literature, I want to explain the value of approaching this question from a semiotic perspective. George A. Kennedy speaks of rhetoric as "that quality of discourse by which a speaker or writer seeks to accomplish his purposes" (Kennedy, 1984: 3). We can take that statement as a definition and deal with it from a semiotic point of view. In a careful analysis of the traditional approach to definition through the Porphyrian tree, Umberto Eco demonstrates that this method "blows up in a dust of differentiae." For there is "no bidimensional tree able to represent the global semantic competence of a given culture" (Eco: 68). This insight makes clear why the majority of critics, whether ancient or modern, failed to come to agreement with respect to definitions and divisions of literary genres. John Gammie's chart and Glossary in this volume illustrates difficulties in treating the morphology of literary genres. The criterion of sign cannot be based on the equivalence model of definition but demands the inference model of encyclopedia.

3.3   A semiotic approach to definition can help readers come to terms with the variety in terminology and classifications used in describing forms of Greek epideictic literature. The long survey of Theodore C. Burgess illustrates the diversity. Not only were rival philosophical schools competing against one another to establish a terminology, but members of the same school often adopted idiosyncratic terms of expression within the same tradition. These orators were frequently occupied with producing expositions for special civic or family occasions that served only the particular moment. They had no permanent impact or appeal to insure their preservation (Burgess: 97). Some of the literary techniques they employed were valuable and reappeared in various rhetorical displays so that they became features of several literary genres. It is not surprising that some of these techniques (like diatribe, discussed below in § 7) are often called genres.

4   *Understanding Aristotle's Contribution and Influence in the Light of Semiotics*

4.1   George Kennedy helps us to put the vast enterprise of Greek rhetoric into perspective when he writes, "Aristotle's objective in writing his *Rhetoric* was not to describe Greek rhetoric but to describe this universal facet of human communication," namely, that rhetoric is "a universal phenomenon which is conditioned by basic workings of the human mind and heart and by the nature of all human society" (Kennedy, 1984: 10). The ultimate goal of rhetorical analysis was "the discovery of the author's intent and of how that is transmitted through a text to an audience" (Kennedy, 1984: 12). Many attempts on a variety of levels, starting with the-Bible-as-literature movement, have applied principles of classical rhetoric to biblical writings. Even today, critics differ widely as to the best way to deal with biblical books as literary productions. Kennedy suggests two reasons for a lack of consensus: l) failure of critics to take into account "traditions of Jewish speech" (Kennedy, 1984: 12); 2) an inability to integrate "distinctive religious rhetoric" into the Greek and Roman approach. For theirs was a "legal and political rhetoric that is largely described in classical handbooks on the subject" (Kennedy, 1984: 6).

4.2   Following the lead of Charles S. Peirce, students of semiotics can ascribe this second failure to a change of "interpretant" in religious writing. The shift in the goal of communication necessarily affects the working of language as a system of signs and the operation of its speech acts. Peirce repeated the importance of this concept of interpretant again and again without ever developing a systematic presentation of the way it operates. It is "either a sign or an expression or a sequence of expressions which translate previous expressions" and which, "besides translating the Immediate Object or the context of the sign, also increases our understanding of it" (Eco: 43). By showing how texts open up new avenues of understanding, the interpretant involves readers in an ongoing process of interpreting them on more than one level. The full content of text as a network of speech acts is actualized only in a series of interpretation events.

4.3   The decisive role of the interpretant explains why Eco sees a "disguised encyclopedia" behind every dictionary definition. The implications of this insight are that commentators cannot be content with creating a set of fixed categories to place each piece of writing into a neat pidgeon hole or unchanging genre. The dynamic approach of semiotics calls upon modern readers to embrace historical tension as a condition for fruitful dialogue with ancient spiritual classics. In this way semiotics offers new possibilities for determining the place of the Wisdom of Solomon in its complex transcultural environment.

4.4   Writing out of his legal and political situation, Aristotle divided rhetoric into three parts, determined by the three types of audiences to be instructed. These three types were: 1) juridical or forensic—to enlighten judges about some past conduct that needed to be approved as legitimate or punished as illegal; 2) political—to foster deliberation within a competent group about supporting or rejecting some mode of future action over which it had authority; 3) epideictic or display or ceremonial—to mark some special occasion or to celebrate an event or to praise or blame some person at this moment (Aristotle: 1358b1-28).

It is clear that this very specific division of rhetoric grew out of Aristotle's historical and cultural situation. If he had lived in another civilization, the division would have been different. In no way does this division provide a substantial theoretical basis for developing a universal theory of literary genres. In fact, these divisions are not mutually exclusive (Kennedy, 1980: 73-75). As the political situation changed, it was not in the public arena that theories of rhetoric grew. Rather, development took place in the systems of education, especially in philosophical schools.

4.5   *Understanding Epideictic Literature in Aristotle's and Modern Terms.* The general survey of epideictic rhetoric made by Burgess in 1902 still contains valuable information about various philosophical schools. He warns that the term epideictic covered a variety of meanings not only at different times but even at the same time among different groups. That is, rival schools used the term epideictic to describe a wide range of speeches that sought to give pleasure and to appeal to the emotions (Burgess: 93-94). In many ways the field of epideictic rhetoric corresponds to the "throw away" speeches that are obligatory in our society at fund raisers, sports banquets and the like. Some of the subtypes listed by ancient grammarians are: birthday speech, farewell speech, praise of a city, a general's speech before battle. From the four kinds listed by Aristotle— funeral oration, panegyric, encomium, and paradoxical encomium (to make the worse appear the better)—orators added a number of other kinds. Some of them were, as Nida points out, "transitional." Menander gives rules for 23 varieties in the third century B.C.E. (Burgess: 105-112). Their use multiplied so much that Burgess states that over 150 writers of epideictic are recorded from Ion (450 B.C.E.) to Ioannes Argyropulus (1450 C.E.) (Burgess: 254).

Burgess describes epideictic as "a style of prose in which ornateness is introduced in a conscious effort to please" (215). Among its most frequent themes are virtue, justice, friendship, piety, pleasure, wealth, and the soul (Burgess 247). The first major treatise devoted to epideictic was evidently the one attributed to Dionysius of Halicarnassus in the first century B.C.E. No doubt it was treated elsewhere, but those treatises failed to survive because they were part of insignificant exercise manuals for students (Burgess 106-9).

The work of Burgess was influential in encouraging Robert Jewett to locate Paul's Letter to the Romans in the subtype of "ambassadorial letter" and to analyze it as a rhetorical composition (Jewett: 10-12). Such extrapolation is dangerous because it conceives of the ancients as following rigid categories of fixed literary genres. Moderns who impose prescriptive roles on the categories found in Greek and Roman grammars to describe extant compositions of famous orators and philosophers lose sight of their creative flexibility and of the variety prevailing among Hellenistic writers (Kee: 133). Knowing the origin of a given form is not equivalent to knowing its enduring nature and use, even by members of the same tradition. Jewett gives too much authority to the study that Burgess himself calls a "general survey within limits" when he treats it as "the definitive study of epideictic literature and oratory," and relies on it for authority to fix the nature of a Pauline letter (Jewett: 7). Likewise, because forms of expression associated with epideictic existed in a variety of literary genres, the existence of literary comparison (syncrisis) in the Wisdom of Solomon is not of sufficient significance to conclude that it belongs to the area of epideictic (see Burgess: 125). Syncrisis was one of the commonplaces (topoi) that appeared in many forms of rhetorical and philosophical writings available to any knowledgeable writer during the last half of the first century B.C.E. (Burgess: 211). Its appearance in a work is not decisive for fixing the literary genre.

5   *Modifications of the Classical Categories in Hellenistic
        Rhetoric and the Location of the Wisdom of Solomon*

5.1   What was happening between Aristotle's *Rhetoric* and the writing of the Wisdom of Solomon was the expansion of topics treated originally under philosophy into the domain of epideictic. As philosophy
interacted with the rhetorical tradition, a mingling took place that was
"first noticeable in a union of the paraenetic and epideictic elements"
(Burgess: 277). The resulting syncretistic compositions were called both
paraenetic and protreptic. Here again terminology was flexible, because
the two types were distinguished by Seneca but identified by Iamblichus
(Burgess: 229). Obviously the quality of these oratorical works varied;
many were simply reproductions of creations by original thinkers. Several
popular forms impacted on the Wisdom of Solomon: kingship tracts,
encomium, diatribe, paraenesis and protreptic. Of the kingship tracts only
fragments survive. Without their necessarily pointing to any direct borrowing, the titles used by the Wisdom to describe its audience suggest
cultural links and a similar interest in anthropology (Reese: 72-87). These
designations include: "you who judge the earth" (1:1), "kings" (6-1), and
"tyrants of peoples" (6:21).

5.2   In the rest of this paper I shall examine how I judge the Wisdom
of Solomon relates to the encomium, diatribe, paraenesis and protreptic.
Its second part, often called "the book of Wisdom proper" (Wisdom 6:12-
16; 6:22-10:21), celebrates personified Wisdom as God's throne partner
and benefactress of humanity. As such, it raises the question whether this
section should be classified as an encomium, a genre that would fix it in
the realm of epideictic literature.

6   *The Limits of the Dictionary Approach: A Recent Example.*

6.1   Paul Bizzeti's recent lengthy study of the Wisdom of Solomon, in
which he uses structure as the principal key for designating the book's
literary genre, classifies the entire work as an encomium of personified
Wisdom. Structure, he rightly argues, is an integral part of discourse, not
an extra. His masterful analyses of the text of the entire book uncovered
examples of literary artistry never previously noted by commentators.
These instances offer additional witness that the Wisdom of Solomon was
a carefully composed literary production carried out in a scholastic environment rather than a popular appeal in a political struggle (Reese: 117-
21). In his efforts to explain why the author placed so much emphasis on
formal elements, Bizzeti surveyed epideictic literature and studied its
rhetoric of display. He divides works with an epideictic goal into three
general uses: 1) to develop an argument; 2) to play with a theme; 3) to

operate within the large area that lies between these two uses (Bizzeti: 115-24). Since one of the common subjects of epideictic was to praise a particular individual and praise of Lady Wisdom figures prominently in the Wisdom of Solomon, Bizzeti investigated the history and features of the encomium. This form had its origin in lyric poetry, but it figured prominently in rhetoric from Aristotle to Cicero. One striking conclusion reached by Bizzeti was that he could apply a schema characteristic of the encomium to the structure of the Wisdom of Solomon as a whole, namely: preamble, praise, syncresis, and epilogue (Bizzeti: 117). While recognizing that certain features of this schema do not fit this schema, Bizzeti nevertheless argues that the work as a whole was designed as an encomium of Lady Wisdom (141-80). He freely admits that objections may be made to this choice of genre. For example, Wisdom 10:20-19:9 is addressed directly to God, in the style of a hymn. And the book exhibits a strong eschatological thrust foreign to the Hellenistic encomium. In fact, the detailed analyses he himself undertook show that the book often breaks out of the tone of an encomium to invite its readers to see the God of salvation revealed in Jewish Scriptures.

6.2   Why then does Bizzeti push for the genre of encomium in spite of all the difficulties involved? His choice flows from his expressed wish to show that the Wisdom of Solomon is a unity, written in a well-known genre, rather than a collection of disparate pieces. Certainly his careful literary analyses of the individual parts and their connections provide a forceful argument for the book's unity. However, to adopt a static, dictionary approach to genre puts unnecessary restraints upon the creative genius of the work's author (Bizzeti: 181). By locking himself into Hellenistic rhetorical categories, Bizzeti neglects other traditions and influences and refuses to credit the author with an ability to adapt to a specific set of social conditions. For example, I have shown that the method of presenting Lady Wisdom has striking parallels with the popular Isis aretalogies of that era (Wisdom 7:22-10:21). Their threefold structure consists of: 1) a description of the nature of Isis; 2) an explanation of the powers that Isis displayed on behalf of her worshipers; 3) a listing of her works throughout history in favor of humanity (Reese: 43). The author of the Wisdom of Solomon follows this schema but incorporates it into a wider concern for the special care that Lady Wisdom exercised toward the Jewish community, which, he illustrates with a lyric description of his own personal religious experience with her. The form of this section of the book is original but comes closer to the scholastic sub-genre of "problem" than to encomium. The author opens with questions: what is Wisdom? How does she come about? Then he proceeds to answer them (Reese: 105-109).

6.3   A semiotic method provides an alternate approach to the classification of discourse—such as is practiced by Bizetti and, to an extent by Gammie—one that is not absolute and unchanging, but informed by a variety of motives. Semiotics offers ways to develop "a systematic way of talking about 'motives' and 'intentions' of discourse" (Beale: 55). This approach shifts the focus of attention from fixed genres to the actual experience of the appeal and impact of the rhetoric, which aims to change hearts and minds and symbolic universe (Beale: 76).

7   *A Note on the Meaning and Various Roles of Diatribe: The Encylopedic Approach Illustrated*

7.1   The nature and role of diatribe in Hellenistic literature has evoked a variety of studies among students of Hellenistic rhetoric. Authur Darby Nock gives a helpful description of this elusive feature as "a species of popular sermon or causerie, commonly written in a pointed style and rich in vivid similies and metaphors" (Nock: 1.26). I argued that both the opening section of the Wisdom of Solomon dealing with the series of striking contrasts between the upright and the impious (Wisdom 1:1-6:11; 6:17-20) and the profound philosophical reflections contrasting divine justice and human folly in part three (11:15-15:19) are best identified as belonging to this sub-genre (Reese: 109-16). In making that choice I rely both on their formal elements and on indications that reflect the author's concern to prepare mature Jewish students for challenges facing their faith in a cosmopolitan Hellenistic culture. Recent studies of Stanley Kent Stowers on diatribe point out many links between diatribe and "the situation of the philosophical school" (Stowers 48, 68, 75-76). The tone of the Wisdom of Solomon points to an author familiar with that milieu (Reese: 154-59).

The twenty-second colloquy of the Center for Hermeneutical Studies of the Graduate Theological Union and the University of California at Berkeley on April 25, 1976 was devoted to shedding light on diatribe within the Greek rhetorical tradition. The published protocol contains the presentation of George L. Kustas on diatribe and reactions by various participants, plus discussion. He repeats a point stated often, namely, that the ancients frequently spoke about diatribe but never as a literary genre. "There is no place in the ancient world where you could go to study it as such and no one to instruct you in it" (Kustas: 3). The term had specific and general, technical and popular, positive and pejorative connotations. The argument about whether it can be called a genre is a modern one, based on "a tendency to describe diatribe exclusively in terms of origin" (Kustas: 4). That tendency has trapped some commentators and limits the value of their criticism of the Hellenistic writings, which were more diverse than compositions of the Classical period, because the interpenetration of rhetoric and philosophy blurred distinctions between literary productions. At the same time, "There is a point at which diatribe moves from being a tactic to acquiring formal status, when, that is to say, the tactics are in such supply that they inform the overall pattern of discourse" (Kustas: 5).

Comments by participants in the colloquy illustrate how widely the term diatribe was used. Their remarks illustrate the "disguised encyclopedia" at work in ancient definitions of diatribe. Especially enlightening is the additional intervention appended to the protocol after the colloquy by Dr. Barbara P. Wallach, who wrote a dissertation on the history of diatribe. She explains the need to study this "hybrid or mixed genre" in the various social contexts in which it emerged and was modified, as well as its antecedents among classical orators and philosophers. Only after the first century C.E. did the tendency to systematize rhetorical forms become extreme. Grammarians at that time started to impose their desire for order upon earlier writings. In reality, the term started out as a specific figure of speech and appears as such in Aristotle. Only later did it approach the nature of compositions we now associate with "a diatribe" (Kustas: 27-32). In epideictic oratory diatribe was an adornment; in forensic, a tactic; in the philosophical essay, it was an appeal; in modern criticism, it is often a genre.

7.2   The tensions relating to diatribe uncovered in that interdisciplinary colloquy provide a striking illustration of the principle developed by Eco that the semiotic form of a definition is encyclopedic. As each participant enriched the discussion with interdisciplinary comments, the picture of diatribe became more complex and complete. By their interchange these scholars showed how the various elements and motives operative in diatribe provided the context in which orators and philosophers were able to experiment with and enrich their various traditions and create new forms of Hellenistic wisdom (Kustas 12). Polemic parts of the Wisdom of Solomon belong within the technique of diatribe. Especially brilliant examples are the scorn heaped upon the just sufferer by his ungodly opponents (Wisdom 2:1-20) and the carefully constructed argument against honoring Eon as divine (Wisdom 13:1-9; Reese: 51, 111).

8   *Paraenesis and/or Protreptic*

8.1   In the opening essay of this volume Leo Perdue remarks that protreptic and paraenesis refer to "two distinct, but connected stages along the way to virtue: entrance to the path of life and continuance in the course undertaken." Both forms are appropriate for liminal situations in which recipients are challenged to make a decisive choice. Both the artistry and contents of the Wisdom of Solomon point to such a social setting. But the sustained address to God and the lack of specific precepts point the work toward protreptic. The contrast with the use of precepts in the Pastoral Letters, recently studied by Benjamin Fiore, offers a striking illustration of different motives. He demonstrates how the Pastorals borrow paraenetic forms and devices from the philosophical tradition. Orations devoted to praising a hero or a virtue were vehicles used by traveling philosophers to exhort their audiences to "do likewise." Such orations contributed to the marriage of epideictic and paraenesis. They created the environment both for the blending of forms and for attempts to define literary genres more rigidly (Fiore: 39). Fiore concludes that paraenesis "covers many areas of life, e.g., culture, friends, enemies, good fortune, all of them under the aspect of their usefulness for obtaining a happy and virtuous life" (Fiore: 41). This attention to examples of application is an element lacking in the Wisdom of Solomon.

8.2   The absence of attempts at socialization, which Perdue's opening essay sees "reflected in most traditional Paraenetic Literature," is decisive in locating the Wisdom of Solomon at a different stage from paraenesis to specific modes of conduct. For example, the book concludes with a set of involved comparisons, a carefully crafted syncrisis to justify a choice of trust in God who cares for the faithful in all circumstances (Wisdom 16:2-19:21). These contrasts incorporate "a defense of God's justice and warnings that are characteristic of the protreptic genre" (Reese: 102).

8.3   Although the title "protreptic" was a common one for the writings of ancient philosophers, there is "no extant rhetorical treatment (of protreptic) as a distinct form of epideictic oratory" in Hellenistic Greek (Burgess: 230). Why? Possibly because authors preferred the flexibility of a form that put less restraint on their mode of expression while grammarians preferred to explain more fixed genres. The freedom associated with protreptic characterizes the Wisdom of Solomon. As John Gammie writes in his programmatic essay above, "In the Wisdom of Solomon the demonstration is achieved through a forceful and persuasive use of contrasts wherein the superiority of righteous belief in immortality and the worship of the one true and wise God alone are laid upon the heart...." I continue to find the designation of protreptic best for a work which draws upon both rhetorical and philosophical traits that are often found in Hellenistic culture and which synthesizes these for religious motives (Reese: 117-21). Compositions of this nature continued among ancient Christian philosophers like Clement of Alexandria and survived into the Middle Ages.

9   *Conclusion*

A semiotic approach starts with literary works as signs, rather than with definitions of grammarians. This approach will not always attempt to assign a fixed place to an ancient text according to the more rigid limits of classical categories. A case in point is the Wisdom of Solomon. Our study has shown that one should avoid putting the Wisdom of Solomon into a defined category within the literature of persuasion. As with any masterpiece, it continually reveals itself in creating its audience. Its author used both Israel's religious traditions and contemporary culture as the interpretant that produced a unique work. Further application of semiotics will no doubt uncover more about this celebration of Lady Wisdom, prudential wisdom and the God of both. In this complex work two great cultures collude but never fuse.

WORKS CONSULTED

Aristotle   See Roberts.

Bizzeti, Paulo
    1984   *Il Libro della Sapienza: Struttura e genere letterario.* Brescia: Paideia Editrice.

Burgess, Theodore
    1902   *Epideictic Literature.* Pp. 89–261 in *Studies in Classical Philology* 3. Chicago: University of Chicago Press.

Chroust, Anton Hermann
    1964   *Aristotle: Protrepticus. A Reconstruction.* South Bend, IN: University of Notre Dame Press.

Düring, Ingeman
    1961   *Aristotle's Protrepticus: An Attempt at Reconstruction.* Göteborg: Acta Universitatis Gothoburgensis.

Eco, Umberto
    1984   *Semiotics and the Philosophy of Language.* Bloomington, IN: Indiana University Press.

Festugière, A. J.
    1949   *La Revelation d'Hermes Trismégiste. II Le Dieu Cosmique.* Paris: J. Gabalda.
    1973   *Les trois "Protreptiques" de Platon: Euthydème, Phédon, Epinomis.* Paris: J. Vrin.

Fiore, Benjamin
  1986   *The Function of Personal Example in the Socratic and Pastoral Epistles*. AB105. Rome: Biblical Institute Press.

Jewett, Robert
  1982   "Romans as an Ambassadorial Letter." *Int* 36: 5–20.

Kee, Howard Clark
  1983   *Miracle in the Early Christian World*. New Haven, CT: Yale University Press.

Kennedy, George A.
  1980   *Classical Rhetoric and Its Christian and Secular Tradition from Ancient to Modern Times*. Chapel Hill, NC: University of North Carolina Press.
  1984   *New Testament Interpretation through Rhetorical Criticism*. Chapel Hill and London: University of North Carolina Press.

Kustas, George L., et al.
  1976   *Diatribe in Ancient Rhetorical Theory*. Protocol of the Twenty-second Colloquy. Berkeley: Center for Hermeneutical Studies.

Marrou, H. I.
  1932   A History of Education in Antiquity. Trans. George Lamb. Madison, WI: University of Wisconsin Press.

Nock, Authur Darby
  1972   *Essays on Religion and the Ancient World*. 2 vols. Ed. Zeph Stewart. Cambridge, MA: Harvard University Press.

Reese, James M.
  1970   *Hellenistic Influence on the Book of Wisdom and its Consequences*. AB 41. Rome: Biblical Institute Press.

Roberts, W. Rhys
  1954   *Aristotle. Rhetoric*. New York: Modern Library.

PARAENESIS: A FEMINIST RESPONSE

Claudia V. Camp

The majority of the essays in this collection use traditional form-criticism and Victor Turner's social-anthropological method of liminality to define and delineate the major literary and social features of paraenesis and paraenetic literature. Concentrating on especially the essays treating the Hebrew Bible, this response offers a feminist critique of both the methodologies employed to analyze Paraenetic Literature and the texts themselves. A feminist methodology reveals the patriarchal elements of texts, methods, and interpretations, and raises new and important questions about the role and place of women in the cultures which produced paraenesis and Paraenetic Literature.

0.1   The preceding essays in this volume cover a wide range of literature while employing an interesting cross-section of methodologies, some very traditional (e.g., Gammie's morphological study) and others less well-known in biblical studies (e.g., Perdue's and Van Leeuwen's Turnerian anthropology and Reese's semiotics). Although this juxtaposition of methodological continuity with the old and openness to the new is valuable in itself, it seems to me that biblical studies has reached a stage of critical self-consciousness with respect to its methods that is not fully in evidence in these essays. While acknowledging at the outset the sheer informational value provided by this collection, I shall seek to present a constructive critique focused on the methods used. I shall discuss those essays dealing with Hebrew Bible and/or intertestamental material.

0.2   I take it as a given, after more than a decade of liberationist (generally) and feminist (specifically) criticism, that scholars understand the ideologically formed nature of our methods and the ideologically shaped nature of our sources. Although some texts yield fruitful results with the application of purely literary methods, it would seem that acute and rigorous sociological analysis would be a crucial perspective to take on ancient texts whose purported purpose is "the providing of guidance for the moral life" (so Perdue). Moreover, given the immediacy in the scholarly guild of questions as to the relationship of text and society, and of literary as opposed to historical modes of criticism, a collection of studies on such a self-consciously social-formative genre as paraenesis would seem to be an excellent opportunity to advance the state of the art at what might be considered a "meta-critical" level. The collection as a whole is uneven on these accounts, although some important contributions have certainly been made. My evaluation will cover the following issues: (1) the types of social analysis done (or not done) in these essays; (2) what has been learned (and not learned) about the relationship of "the act and form" of paraenesis to society; (3) the analyses done of the relationship of moral exhortation to religious symbolism, especially as it relates to the question of authority.

Types of Social Analysis

1.0   Interestingly, what seems to be the favored mode of social analysis among these students of paraenesis is Victor Turner's model of liminality (Perdue, Van Leeuwen, Levine, Williams, Quinn). While this model has provided valuable insights, the reliance of six essays on it may render the analytical perspective of the volume as a whole somewhat narrow, unless we are to assume that the bulk of paraenetic activity took place in the context of *rites de passage*, which I doubt. The model works best when it is tempered with other perspectives.

1.1.1   Analysis based on the liminality metaphor works particularly well in Perdue's essay on "Ritual Passage, the Death of the Sage, and Paraenesis," where the content of the material studied—the sage's deathbed teachings—is patently suited to the method. One of strengths of Turner's work is its capacity to allow the analyst to do what Clifford Geertz (borrowing from Gilbert Ryle) calls "thick description," that is, the analysis of the interaction of cultural forms at multiple levels: religious, commonsensical, aesthetic, ideological, etc. (3–30). As I shall elaborate in § 3, Perdue uses the liminality framework to advantage to explicate the interaction of myth, ritual and social reality.

1.1.2   Even here, however, the generalizing movement of this cross-cultural model obscures some interesting differences among cultures that one more attentive to particularities (Geertz comes especially to mind) might have surfaced. For example, granted the important liminal phase that death always and everywhere invokes, what might the differences be between a culture such as Egypt, where the sages assumed a life after death, and Israel, where the death of the body meant the death of the personality as well? I shall return to this example in § 3.

1.2.0   Raymond Van Leeuwen's thesis also depends heavily on the liminality model, again offering some worthwhile insights, but suffering more from its limitations than did Perdue's piece. His basic agenda, adapted from Lasine (68), is sound, viz., to show that the instruction genre "can foster recognition of indeterminacy as a means of educating members of a society to make their models of reality and order both strong and adaptive...." This is particularly well demonstrated in his discussion of the incorporation of the speeches of the wicked men and the strange woman into the parents' teaching, thereby "increasing awareness of indeterminacy in special 'safe' conditions" (quotation from Lasine, 49).

1.2.1   There are, however, two flaws that I see in Van Leeuwen's use of Turner's liminality model. One is his tendency to idealize it and abstract it from a concrete social setting. The other is his failure to subject his application of it to Proverbs to any sort of feminist critique. (The latter problem is also acute in Quinn's otherwise informative study of paraenesis and ritual, especially when he describes the marriage paraenesis in 1 Timothy 2 as "subversive").

1.2.2   The idealization shows up first in an adaptation Van Leeuwen makes on Turner's method, namely, the distinction between what he calls "negative rites of passage" and "positive rites of passage." To the best of my knowledge, this is not a distinction made by Turner and, as I understand this anthropologist, represents something of a misunderstanding of what the liminal state is all about. It is certainly true, in the Bible (as Van Leeuwen documents) and elsewhere, that instruction is sometimes presented in terms of what must be avoided (cf. Gammie's "admonitions") and sometimes in terms of what should be adhered to (Gammie's "exhortations"). However, there is no reason to envision different rituals. Indeed, one definitive purpose of the liminal state is to effect a breakdown of the initiate's sense of "positive" and "negative" so that a new ethic can be created for and accepted by him or her. Thus, "positive" and "negative" instruction would be mixed, sometimes even paradoxically so, in the context of any given rite of passage, and the paradoxical mixture that appears in Prov 1:8–33, 7:6–27, and 9:1–18 may be a case in point. However, the whole function of the liminal state—indeed the whole definition of liminality—is undercut by the presentation of two apparently oppositely-valued ritual events.

1.2.3   This failure to ground Proverbs 1–9 in a more concrete social setting is closely related to the lack of feminist critique. On the one hand, Van Leeuwen argues that, as protrepsis, Proverbs 1–9 provides instruction to young men coming of age, a notion that would at first glance seem to provide part of what I am complaining is missing. On the other hand, however, he claims that, as paraenesis, this material confirms adult sages—male *or female*—in their wisdom. In the latter case, the teaching on sexual fidelity is to be understood primarily symbolically, with reference to wisdom and folly, rather than literally.

1.2.4   Already in the discussion of the protreptic function, however, Van Leeuwen subverts the significance of the literal meaning of the instructions on sexual and marital fidelity. These topics

> are not the heart of these chapters. Marriage and adultery, along with roads and houses, are taken up into an all encompassing symbol system whose basic purpose is to depict the lineaments of a world view. These instructions ultimately guide "sons" in a quest for cosmic Wisdom.

Here Van Leeuwen explicitly posits his idealizing abstraction of Turner's model: Proverbs 1–9 has to do with "religio-moral" limina and is "only in a second sense social." Such a statement is either confused or naive. What does "only in a second sense" mean? What is "moral" if it is not "social"? In Turner's work, the whole point of the liminal state is preparation for a new form of existence that is inherently, if not limitedly, social. The purpose of the new teaching given in the liminal state is "status eleva-tion." Liminal paraenesis, *including both its moral exhortation and its cosmic or mythic underpinnings and authorizations*, is given to allow the recipient to take a new place in society. Neither dimension can be subordinated in Proverbs 1–9. For this reason, the marriage and sexual imagery here must be understood as fundamentally (though not exclusively) literal. The young *man* is about to take a new place in society that involves in an essential way his understanding about the boundaries of sexuality and the appropriateness of faithful marriage as definitive, if not exhaustive, of the way of Wisdom. How women are initiated into this way we are left to imagine.

1.2.5   Whether one takes these instructions literally or symbolically (or, as I would suggest, as a mutually authorizing conjunction of the lan-guages of ethos and cosmos) the *communitas* of married love which they both authorize and draw authorization from must be critiqued as the sta-tus-supporting *communitas* that it was: one promulgated by the patriarchal power structure, whose effect (if not its purpose) was men's control of female access to the reins of power. Women receive no instruction here with respect to their own status elevation. Van Leeuwen's quotation from Lasine regarding the Sinai covenant applies certainly, but less sanguinely than I think he intended, to the relationship of marital *communitas* and social structure envisioned here: "structure is not opposed to communitas...but rather completes and guarantees it." Yes indeed, and in the form the male power structure has decided upon.

1.2.6   It is my view that the primary address to men, as opposed to women, which is implied by the sexual-marital imagery, persists even in what Van Leeuwen thinks of as its paraenetic function, its address to adult sages. In this context, the teaching on marriage involves the paradigm of status *reversal* as well. In marriage, the man will ritually "pretend" to exist in a non-hierarchical, "uncarved" environment. But the purpose of this experience is to reinforce the structures in which he otherwise participates. The woman's experience is seen here only second-hand, and through male eyes. Perhaps she also experienced some of the advantages of the "fluid abandonment" of marriage, which helped her get through her daytime subordination to men in the larger patriarchal power structure. For Turner, release of tension between members of different rungs in the power hierarchy is one of the major functions of status reversal (200–203). Or perhaps she was simply compelled by social convention to support the ritual pretense of her husband.

1.2.7   Over against this rather harsh reconstruction of social reality as experienced by women, I should indicate as well another possible scenario in which these instructions, though directed toward men, may have actually offered some support to women as well. I have argued elsewhere (1985: 255–82) that Proverbs 1–9 took shape in the early post-exilic period, a time when the contributions of women to society were visible enough that they could not have avoided notice and vital enough that it was in the larger social interest to support and authorize them. In this setting, the marriage scene imaged in Proverbs 5 may have truly represented the experience of women as well as men in the mutual give and take of the marital relationship. What cannot be ignored, however, is that, as "relatively equal" as men and women might have become for this brief historical moment, there is still no address here to women on the limits of their sexual activity or their role in the success of a faithful marriage. Thus, by implication, there is no instruction intended for them on the pursuit of wisdom as their men undertook it. If Proverbs 1–9 envisions a degree of female authority and equality, it is still authority and equality granted by men—and reclaimed by them not long thereafter. To put this in Turner's paradigm, as rendered by Perdue, the "status reversal" of Proverbs 5 is not the permanent liminality attempted by social marginals, but that enacted by the powerful in society to reinforce their power.

1.3.0   The introductory article by Perdue utilizes several other types of social analysis in addition to Turner, including an appropriate underlay of Berger and Luckman's social construction of reality, a *Gemeinschaft-Gesellschaft* distinction drawn from Toennies, and a characterization of the social models of order and conflict.

1.3.1   The *Gemeinschaft-Gesellschaft* distinction is a very interesting one that is applied more descriptively than analytically in Perdue's discussion. It is certainly useful in this regard, but I found myself wishing for further consideration of the surely varying nuances of relationship between these two social domains. The work of Rainer Albertz, for example, is a sustained study of the sometimes complementary, sometimes contradictory interactions of "personal piety" and "official religion" in ancient Israel. In wisdom scholarship, the question of the relative literalness of the "parent-child" metaphor in wisdom instructions might benefit from consideration of whether the school sages merely borrow this term from the family in an "imitative" manner, as Perdue suggests, or, on the other hand, whether they have *co-opted* family symbolism in the same way Albertz demonstrates that the monarchy did in the seventh century (169–78). At one point, Perdue mentions that tensions could arise from the competing requirements of society and community, but passes over this quickly with the statement that it was the moral philosophers' goal to integrate competing expectations and that "paraenesis provided the content for shaping and integrating the moral life." Acknowledgement of this concern to integrate, it seems to me, should not be seen as the resolution to this issue, but rather the point of departure for discussion of some of the significant workings of ancient society.

1.4.0   Perdue's "conflict vs. order" paradigms are also useful tools for analyzing ancient societies (as well as for analyzing the analysts who show a preference of one over the other!). His particular application of these paradigms to Israel's wisdom tradition, especially Job and Qoheleth, did, however, raise some questions for me as to whether this either-or choice of "order vs. conflict" really fits all situations. (Cf. Attridge's unsuccessful effort to locate Hebrews within Perdue's four paradigmatic functions of hortatory literature.)

1.4.1   He describes, for example, "the function of the poetry of Job" as that of "undermining traditional teaching in order to destabilize the oppressive institutions controlled and ordered by the power elite." Later on, he places Job in the social functional category of "legitimation," specifically of an alternative, subversive paraenesis which attacks the bankrupt deuteronomic dogma of retribution during the sixth century collapse of Judah, and replaces it with the vision of a social order constituted by the struggle for justice and the inevitable experience of suffering. I do not find Job so easily categorized, for two reasons: first, because the dating is so difficult and, second, because the author's exact point of view on Job's predicament is so hard to isolate. We cannot be sure, for example, that the poetry was ever intended to be read apart from the prose (cf. Fontaine, Janzen), and the comparable ancient Near Eastern problem literature suggests that specific political oppression is not required for such ruminations on unjust suffering and questioning of too-tidy theologies of retribution.

1.4.2   Further, we should note that Job is described as a member of the establishment and that he never relinquishes the notion that he functioned with justice in this position, even banking his life on that fact (27:1–6; 29:1–31:40). In spite of the increasing personal nastiness of his friends, moreover, there is never any indication that they behaved other than justly in their public dealings. There is certainly a crisis of some sort here, but I'm not sure we can make Job a subversive in a narrowly political sense. In fact, Perdue's *Gemeinschaft-Gesellschaft* framework shows some promise here. One of the critical dynamics in the book of Job is the refusal of the friends to be friends, i.e., to fulfill the loyalties demanded in the sphere of *Gemeinschaft*. Instead, they adhere to the requirements for socio-cosmic order and legitimation characteristic of the *Gesellschaft*. Now, this particular sort of conflict, combined as it is in Job with the issue of retribution, may possibly reflect a setting in Babylonian-controlled Judah. The struggle seems to be, however, between two *power* groups vying for control (Jeremiah's supporters vs. his enemies? and/or two factions struggling for control of the "wisdom" tradition, whatever that was at the time?), with no one speaking directly with the voice of the disenfranchised. Whatever the exact case, we need a more nuanced analysis of the societal dynamics represented in Job.

1.4.3   The example of Qoheleth as a representative of the conflict paradigm could also be more nuanced. Perdue argues that this book is an important example of subversive paraenesis because its objective

> is not to discover sapiential values and their required human institutions which are grounded in the order of creation, but rather to submit that human activity is analogous to the predetermined, tedious, cyclical movements of elements in nature.

It is certainly true that Qoheleth challenges some traditional values with these ideas, but I am leery to call him "subversive" (cf. Murphy, 1979). There is a strong sense in which his is just a cynical "upside-down" view of reigning ideas of the connection of nature and social institutions. Rather than arguing that the cosmos has a firm and right structure that undergirds the firm and right structures of society, he says that, just as the cosmos is paradoxically orderly but damnably and unknowably so, so is human activity and society. There remains, in other words, a definite, if maddening, connection between ethos and cosmos, the knowledge of which is requisite for proper living. As Perdue most insightfully observes, Qoheleth opts for the domain of *Gemeinschaft*, over the corrupt *Gesellschaft*, as the source of this proper living and, thus, of meaningful existence such as it can be found. But this observation, I think, reinforces my point that we are not dealing with outright "subversiveness" here. This book is certainly being written in a situation of stress, and is far from representative of a paradigm of "order." Rather than calling it "conflict," however, it seems to me that we need a third category that might be labelled "critical coping." As Perdue himself recognizes, for Qoheleth "change is impossible." This is, then, the paraenesis of a group seeking just to get by.

The Connection of Literature and Society

2.1.0   Although various aspects of the connection of paraenetic literature to society were discussed in the preceding section, here I shall focus specifically on the issue of form-criticism, which defines part of the purpose of this volume. I have been much influenced, as has the field of biblical studies as a whole (even those who are not committed practitioners of its methods), by the rise of sociological analysis in our discipline. Form-criticism has particularly benefited from this new interest insofar as the question of social setting has, in effect, forced it back to one of its original root concerns, the place of genres in social institutions. It was, therefore, something of a surprise to read John Gammie's extensive morphological analysis of paraenesis which proceeded with barely a nod to such questions. Within the structure of the volume as a whole, I understand that Perdue and he have divided up, as it were, the issue of genre and society in their respective introductory essays. There has been, however, no effort here to integrate the insights or conclusions of these two studies in any systematic way. Indeed, Gammie's "underlying principles of genre analysis" do not include any reference to social setting.

2.1.1   Given, then, my own presuppositions about the inseparability of genre analysis and social analysis, how to evaluate an essay that begins from a different presupposition? Gammie's work will certainly carry the authority of his command of an admirable depth and breadth of material, as well as the clarity and rigorous, consistent application of his methodological guidelines. The terminologically confusing but theoretically useful distinction between the "secondary genre of paraenetic literature" and the "subgenre of paraenesis" should also be noted. It has, to use the model Reese develops in the previous response, the quality of a dictionary, a reference tool to which scholars will turn time and time again to help shape our working vocabulary on a rich and complex form of literature. Even where disagreements emerge, as has already happened in two of the articles in this volume, a comprehensive touchstone such as this is always of value.

2.1.2   On one point, in particular, Gammie's work stresses a vital principle for morphological studies, namely, that taxonomy should provide a basis for comparison of works of literature, not exclusion of them from one's "curriculum of study" because they do not fit some ideal model for a given genre. Different genres often are put together in a single work, and the interaction of the parts and the whole bears exploration. Even where this is not the case, one might add, genres and sub-genres always function in relationship to each other within their larger cultural context. Thus, the teacher-scholar makes his methodological point from within the frame of reference of his paraenetic subject matter: comparison is the heart of the matter!

2.2.0   These important points made in the literary abstract by Gammie flow naturally into a consideration of social setting, of the persons who make the decisions about combining or adapting genres and of the contexts that create the need to do so. It is interesting that, of the two essays that address Gammie's introductory essay directly, Attridge finds modifications of his taxonomy necessary in order to meet the needs of "thicker" description whereas Williams levies a more general critique. Attridge anticipates Reese's response on which I will focus here.

2.2.1   Reese's thesis in the previous response is that "research in semiotics provides methodological tools" to explain the role of the Wisdom of Solomon in maintaining the identity of hellenistic Jews. I would suggest that it does both more and less than this. More, first of all, insofar as it serves as a useful model for connecting diachronic or socio-historical analysis with synchronic or literary-formal analysis. Reese is concerned to identify forms, but always with attention to their purpose in the settings in which they were written and read. Even the process of taxonomy itself is socially conditioned, as his discussion of Aristotle's now-"classic"-as-well-as-"classical" rhetorical distinctions shows. This point provides a qualification to one of Gammie's "underlying principles of genre analysis," which is to show the relationship of one's classifications to classical usage. If even "classical usage" is the result of social processes, then the modern taxonomer's attention is necessarily drawn to these considerations. The flexibility of taxonomy that Gammie calls for at the literary level is inherently related to the flexibility of changing social situations and, equally importantly, to the ideologies that the creators of moral exhortation take up in response to this flux. One might image this complex of relationships in literary form, as Reese does with his "inference model of encyclopedia," or more temporo-spatially, as a three-dimensional object (of form, ideas and social structure) moving through time. Gottwald's complicated, but comprehensive charting of Israel's "socio-literary-theological sectors within the frame of sociopolitical organizational domains" (602–6) is an excellent example of such an effort.

2.2.2   Given the work of Gottwald, which it seems to me addresses some of the same methodological concerns as Reese, it might be questioned whether "semiotics theory" as such is necessary to accomplish Reese's purposes. Although semiotics is designated here as a "theory," it functions in Reese's essay for the most part as simply descriptive of a historico-literary process, rather than as an effort to explain why this process came about. To put in another way, I find his basic methodological thesis on the socially determined flexibility of literary genres hard to contest. On the other hand, the semiotics perspective does not particularly work to "prove" that the labelling of the Wisdom of Solomon as "protreptic-with-a-dash-of-encomium-and-diatribe" is the correct one, or that it served the purpose Reese ascribes to it. These conclusions are based, rather, on a combination of form- and social-historical analysis that the semiotics approach apparently describes and allows for (though the author never explicitly says so), but whose results (or even procedures) it does not dictate. It remains to be seen whether semiotics as applied to biblical studies has more to offer than its (not to be discounted) function as a systematization of what I take to be good socio-literary common sense. Had Reese summarized at the outset his understanding of semiotics theory, its assumptions and methods, the reader might be clearer about its specific interpretive value. Instead, references to it are often either after-the-fact of a particular interpretation or focused on what it shows is not the case, rather than on its positive contributions. Most distressingly, a precise understanding of the key notion of "the inference model of the encyclopedia" is left very much to inference until § 7.

2.3   I believe, nonetheless, that some of the other articles in this volume would have been enhanced by a perspective along the lines of Reese's. In no case is one of the burning questions of Hebrew Scripture wisdom scholarship addressed, namely, the import of the variations in the social setting of the instructions—whether tribal village, royal court, or schools preparing persons either for the urban bureaucracy or for Torah piety. Would such a consideration have made a difference in Gammie's taxonomy? Would the liminality of Proverbs 1–9 (Van Leeuwen) have functioned differently in a pre-exilic court school than in a post-exilic synagogue? Was the death-of-the-sage literature (Perdue) limited to the educated upper classes, or did it have a place also among the poor and/or marginalized, and what difference would such a change in context mean to its function? Did this literature have the same function within Israel's monotheistic belief system and unified anthropology as it did in Egypt and Greece, with their polytheism and belief in an immortal soul? In general, closer attention to context-as-it-relates-to-form in this sort of comparative discussion might be able to provide us with data for further analysis of the relationship of wisdom forms to their varying social settings.

2.4   Finally, it must be noted that the primacy given to literary form over social act evident in several of these essays (even those with an expressed concern for social setting) has excluded from consideration what must have been a significant amount of society-shaping paraenetic activity—mostly delivered orally or else by those without the institutional connections to have writings preserved—namely, the moral exhortation given by mothers to their daughters.

The Role of Religious Symbolism in Paraenesis

3.0   From the point of view of social analysis, one of the most interesting questions that might be addressed is that of the source or sources of authority of moral instruction. Why do those who hear it listen? Why is a moral teacher acknowledged (by some, but undoubtedly always not by others) to be worth listening to? What constitutes the attractiveness of a given way of life? Four of these essays present some provocative reflections on these questions by analyzing the connection of what I will broadly call religious symbolism—including ritual, metaphor, myth and symbol—with paraenesis. Again, while two of the New Testament scholars, Williams and Quinn, have made worthwhile contributions on this issue, I will limit my remarks to the articles on the Hebrew Bible.

3.1.1   Although he does not formulate his thesis specifically in this way, I would suggest that Perdue's "Ritual Passage" essay generates a model for understanding the authorizing interconnection of the "literal" and "symbolic" aspects of a particular sort of paraenetic literature (cf. Geertz on the work of religious symbols, 87–141). On one level, the three aspects of death he identifies in this literature move from a more "literal" understanding of it (the "actual" death of the sage combined with a "record" of his last teachings) through a sociological extension of the idea (the passage of the sage's followers into a new, more responsible and independent state of existence), to a symbolic or mythic character of the death narrative which shapes and authenticates the group's perception of reality.

3.1.2   In fact, however, as Perdue's careful exposition makes clear, both the "literal" and the "symbolic" qualities of death are operative in all three of these aspects. The first aspect includes the ritual, liminal state of the sage's passing away, with whatever possibility his culture allows for immortality, as well as an implicit understanding of the symbol system that has authenticated his teachings in the past and brought his followers to participate in this final drama. Under aspect two, the disciples' state can also be understood within the ritual construct of liminality. Aspect three mythologizes not only the person of the sage and his death, but also his instructions, so that what was previously mundane becomes part and parcel of the social construction of reality for the ongoing group of disciples: in the narrative, the sage and his teachings become one and serve as the paradigm for all further life and thought.

3.2.1   One of the great values of Perdue's article, in this respect, is his carefully calibrated articulation of the more literal and more symbolic aspects of the death metaphor, and their interweaving. Greater sensitivity on this point would, I believe, have enhanced Van Leeuwen's work on the root metaphors of Proverbs 1–9. What is missing here, I would suggest, is an understanding of the way in which a root metaphor actually helps to *constitute* what it seeks to communicate. To say that *"underlying* the bipolar metaphorical system...in Proverbs 1–9 is a *yet more fundamental reality* which these images together portray" (my emphases) is to miss the point of the work of a root metaphor, which is to *create* this reality (cf., e.g., McFague, 1982: 42; Herzog, 1980: 101). The reality of the "Kingdom of God," for example, does not exist (at least to any sort of human intelligibility) apart from the words "Kingdom of God. " As feminists are well aware, to change the words is (at least to begin) to change the reality.

3.2.2   Van Leeuwen's own explication actually reinforces my point, as witnessed in his attempt to describe the "two fundamental characteristics" of the world presumably "underlying" these metaphors.

> First is its structure of boundaries or limits. Second is the bi-polar human *eros* for the beauty of Wisdom, who prescribes life within limits, or for the seeming beauty of Folly, who offers bogus delights in defiance of created limits.

At least in the second of these characteristics, Van Leeuwen has been forced back to the metaphorical language which he was seeking to get "underneath. " I would suggest this is because there is no where " lower" to go! There is, in fact, something inherently "female" about reality as perceived by these sages, among other things, its *epistemological* indeterminacy (cf. Lasine, 50–51). The problem is not acknowledging the existence of good and evil, but knowing which is which, especially when human language is involved (Camp 1987: 51–58; 1988: 22–25). While Van Leeuwen notes what he refers to as "moral indeterminacy" in the female imagery, he abstracts it to the problem of "being taken in by superficial resemblances." I would argue instead that, whether rightly or wrongly from a modern perspective, these ancient men discovered a definitive embodiment of the issue in their experience of men's relationships with women. Sexual relationships and their social fruits provide a paradigm in praxis for the necessary knowledge for dealing with indeterminacy, the irreducible female imagery bonding the ethos of marital fidelity to the metaphysic of love for Wisdom.

3.2.3   The same issue surfaces in Van Leeuwen's analysis of the water imagery. He notes both positive and negative applications of the imagery, but concludes with what appears to be an unqualifiedly positive interpretation of water imagery as a symbol of true *communitas* to be found in "the liquid abandonment of married love." He acknowledges no sense of the epistemological tension the sages creatively express when they use the same symbol to represent the rejected *communitas* of the Strange Woman as well.

3.3.1   Van Leeuwen's work on the boundary imagery also deserves attention. "Boundary," too, we should note at the outset, is a reality-constituting metaphor, and not some "deeper" level of reality itself. The author's explications of the root חקק and the expression עבר פי provide marvelous, culturally specific examples of how language creates and maintains the bond between the cosmic and moral realms. While he seems to assume that the bond is not *created*, but merely *expressed*, in language, one need only observe how the connection is lost once the occurrences of the key root חקק in Prov 8:27–29 and 8:15 are variously translated into "when he *drew* a circle," "when he assigned to the sea its *limit*," "when he *marked out* the foundations," and "the kings and rulers who *decree* what is just." Comparative data on other ancient Near Eastern usages of this root, if any, would have been informative, allowing assessment of Israel's relative uniqueness in this particular metaphor.

3.3.2   In general, however, I am less convinced by the connection he attempts to demonstrate between cosmic and moral boundaries. It is not that the ancient Israelites did not make such connections; surely every culture attempts to justify (and sometimes critique) its morality with its cosmogony, and the play on חקק shows one way the Israelites did too. The problem lies more in the generality of this connection, without any attempt to specify how the connection is drawn or who is drawing it and for what purpose.

3.3.3   The use of the idea of boundary markers is a case in point. Van Leeuwen cites an Egyptian example of an oath: "I have set such and such a boundary stone as firmly as the heavens are established," and then a presumably comparable example from Prov. 23:10–11, which warns against the removal of "the ancient boundary" or entry into the fields of orphans, "for their Redeemer is strong; he will wage their fight for them."

While the emphasis on boundaries is similar, I submit that there are fundamentally different understandings of reality in these two texts, brought forth in their respective metaphorical languagings of a cosmic guarantee based on an immutably established heaven as opposed to one offered by the warrior-god of Israel. As an hypothesis, I suggest that the former bespeaks the royal-hierarchical social reality of Egypt, while the latter echoes that sector of Israelite ideology that resisted such an institution. It is quite likely that *some* of the Hebrew Bible tradition—that supportive of the monarchy in its Solomonic form—would appeal to heavenly authority in a manner more akin to Egypt (e.g., Ps. 89:2–4).

3.3.4   There are several texts cited by Van Leeuwen, moreover, that include *national* boundaries in the metaphorical mix of cosmos and morality. But surely the concern of the just to protect the ancient heritage of the widow and orphan cannot be simply equated with the preservation of national boundaries or, if it is, there are manifest political (as well as religious) motivations behind the equation. One way or the other, there are almost certainly different understandings of the connection of ethos and world view in Israel's multi-layered tradition, and each of Van Leeuwen's examples needs a social-ideological analysis of the specific language of the boundary metaphor to discern the way in which it creates and authorizes its version of social reality.

3.4   Failure to do such an ideology critique results in (or perhaps results from?) his assumption that it could not have been the sages' intent to legitimate an unjust social order because "the cosmic order embodies a normativity that judges the status quo as an imperfect realization of the norms of justice." Van Leeuwen is clearly aware that the concept of divine order is sometimes used to rationalize injustice, and he has elsewhere done an insightful social-ideological analysis of the connection of cosmic and moral language (1986). Here, however, he offers no evidence for his claim that such rationalization could not have taken place among Israel's wisdom tradents. Even Proverbs' appeal to the language of justice cannot be taken as proof that these texts supported actual social justice. Oppressive regimes can use this language as handily as anyone else, as the royal psalms clearly show. The rhetoric of Ronald Reagan makes an excellent contemporary case in point. Assuming some sages worked in the royal court, they must have worked for "good" kings as well as "bad," even if they were not intentionally unjust in their personal lives. In the structures of institutional injustice, "intent" often has very little to do with the actual effect of one's language and actions. It is precisely this dilemma of unwitting self-deceit with respect to one's participation in injustice that the intimately related "good" and "bad" female metaphors of Proverbs 1–9 try to unmask. Unfortunately, understood historically at least, these metaphors do not unmask one of the greatest deceptions of all, namely the patriarchal power to define the good society in its own likeness and interests, a power exercised, I should repeat, even in a case like Proverbs, where it legitimates a relatively high status for women. Because the cosmic order attested by Proverbs assumes as inherent this situation of injustice, it can hardly embody the ultimate normativity that Van Leeuwen attributes to it, though of course the sages would have thought it did.

3.5.1   There is one final piece to this fascinating puzzle of metaphor, paraenesis and ideology on which I would like to comment. Again we turn to Perdue's provocative piece on the death of the sage. I suggested above that he works through a nuanced understanding of the relationship of symbolic and literal thought in this literature and how this contributes to the mutual validation of ethos and world view for the groups involved, a dynamic process of validation that does not simply reproduce the social status quo, but enables a transition to a new situation (cf. Geertz on the function of ideology, 193–233). In this context, we might now suggest that this process hinges on the function of "death" as a root metaphor. Perdue found a remarkable coherence in the three-fold understanding of death throughout the eastern Mediterranean world from early times through the beginning of the common era. In the background of these understandings is the fact that

> death, especially that of significant others as well as anticipation of one's own extinction, is the most powerful force leading one to question the normative structure in which everyday life functions. This is equally true of social groups and societies. Thus idealized legends of the death of sages and the paraenesis they give as death approaches provide a major means by which this most serious form of anomy is faced and overcome.

3.5.2   This role of death and the death metaphor in the questioning of normative structures leads me to reflect, however, on the fact that ancient Israel's view of death was quite different from that of its Egyptian neighbors and its Greco-Roman successors. Not only do the latter assume an after-life, but there is an interesting fuzziness on the borderline between life and death which Perdue points out in several of the Egyptian documents. It is not always clear whether the sage has already died or whether he is on the verge of death. This is quite different from the Israelite metaphorizing of death which, as Van Leeuwen's paper shows, is understood as the antithesis of life. Moreover, when the Hebrew Bible's most infamous sage of death, Qoheleth, considers the topic, it does not lead him to a paraenesis that would be particularly helpful in the establishment of a new reality. Thus, I want to ask if and how this difference in attitude toward death relates to the process of the questioning of structures that went on in Israel.

3.5.3   Although there are many lines of reflection that might conceivably be taken, my own work leads me to notice in particular that there is another metaphorical reality that Israel brings into systemic alignment with death (and its opposite, life). This is the metaphor "woman." Van Leeuwen's essay has already called our attention to the prominence of this connection in Proverbs 1–9, and Perdue describes the interesting possibility that Prov. 31:1–9, the words of Lemuel's mother, is a text of ritual instruction comparable to the other liminal-situational texts he analyzes. We might note, however, that unlike the instructions from the Egyptian "fathers," who are either on their deathbeds or perhaps even already dead, the instruction of Lemuel's mother comes very much from the land of the living. This is the only place from which it *could* come, in (orthodox) Israel's point of view, and here, at least, the voice of life is a woman's voice.

3.5.4   If one includes the narrative preceding the last testament of David in the unit to be analyzed, the role of women here is also striking. David—or the people around him, at any rate—do not accept his approaching death gracefully. The "good death" which characterizes so much of the literature analyzed by Perdue is notably absent in 1 Kings 1 (at least through v 31), and one of the means attempted to prevent it involves the effort to arouse David sexually with the charms of Abishag.

3.5.5   Placing this narrative in comparison to Prov. 31:1–9 shows how the metaphorical juxtaposition of women, life, and death in Proverbs 1–9 can be played out in different ways. In the Proverbs instruction, Lemuel's mother warns her "new-born" king not to spend his strength on women (which McCreesh interprets in a sexual manner, 40), while in 1 Kings 1, the re-vivification of the almost-dead king is attempted in precisely this manner! Moreover, the liminal state of the dying of David the sage and the passage to kingship of Solomon his son is attended—one might even say "mid-wifed"—by one of the Bible's preeminent "strange women," Bathsheba (cf. the Matthean genealogy for "the wife of Uriah" as one of the four foreign women in Jesus's heritage). When the sage who would not be dead in ch. 1 finally gives his parting instructions in ch. 2, they are peculiarly deadly ones. It is, however, a combination of Bathsheba and Abishag who provide the ultimate excuse for Solomon's execution of his father's death sentences (2:13–38).

3.5.6   If, then, death is the most powerful force leading to the questioning of normative structures, a force which yet also provides the opportunity for the construction of symbolic forms to face and overcome this anomy, then for Israel, woman in all her metaphorical aspects—as birth mother and queen mother, as giver and taker of sexual energy, as purveyor of paraenesis to the young adult and as instructor of the senile in his own politically potent "memory," as Woman Wisdom and as Woman Stranger—woman in all her aspects is part and parcel of the questioning and re-construction of reality that centers around death. As Proverbs 1–9 and 1 Kings 1–2 suggest, women's paraenesis may be life-giving or it may be deadly. Or, depending on how one evaluates the reign of Solomon, it may be quite ambiguous—indeterminate. It is for scholars to let the light of women's presence out from under its bushel basket, not for the purpose of blinding ourselves to patriarchal realities, but in order to shed light in the dark corners of both past and present.

WORKS CONSULTED

Albertz, Rainer.
1978   *Persönliche Frömmigkeit und offiziele Religion. Religionsinterner Pluralismus in Israel und Babylon.* Stuttgart: Calwerverlag.

Andreasen, Niels-Erik A.
1983   "The Role of the Queen Mother in Israelite Society." *CBQ* 45:179–94.

Camp, Claudia V.
1985   *Wisdom and the Feminine in the Book of Proverbs.* Bible and Literature Series 11. Sheffield: Almond/JSOT.
1987   "Woman Wisdom as Root Metaphor: A Theological Consideration." Pp. 45–76 in *The Listening Heart: Essays in Wisdom and the Psalms in Honor of Roland E. Murphy, O. Carm.* Ed. K. Hoglund, *et al.* Sheffield: JSOT.
1988   "Wise and Strange: An Interpretation of the Female Imagery in Proverbs in Light of Trickster Mythology." *Semeia* 42:14–36.

Fontaine, Carole.
1987   "Folktale Structure in the Book of Job: A Formalist Reading." Pp. 205–32 in *Directions in Biblical Hebrew Poetry.* JSOTSup 40. Ed. E. Follis. Sheffield: JSOT.

Geertz, Clifford
1973   *The Interpretation of Cultures.* New York: Basic Books.

Gottwald, Norman K.
1985   *The Hebrew Bible: A Socio-Literary Introduction.* Philadelphia: Fortress.

Herzog, Frederick.
1980   *Justice Church.* Maryknoll, NY: Orbis.

Janzen, J. Gerald.
1985   *Job.* Atlanta: John Knox.

Lasine, Stuart.
1986   "Indeterminancy and the Bible: A Review of Literary and Anthropological Theories and Their Application to Biblical Texts." *Hebrew Studies* 27:48–81.

McCreesh, T. P.
1985   "Wisdom as Wife: Proverbs 31:10–31." *RB* 92:25–46.

McFague, Sallie.
1982   *Metaphorical Theology.* Philadelphia: Fortress.

Murphy, Roland E.
1979   "Qohelet's 'Quarrel' with the Fathers." Pp. 235–45 in *From Faith to Faith.* Ed. D. Y. Hadidian Pittsburgh: Pickwick.
1981   *Wisdom Literature: Job, Proverbs, Ruth, Canticles, Ecclesiastes, Esther.* FOTL 13. Grand Rapids: Eerdmans.

Perdue, Leo G.
1981   "Liminality as a Social Setting for Wisdom Instructions." *ZAW* 93:114–26.

Turner, Victor.
1979   *The Ritual Process: Structure and Anti-Structure.* Ithaca, NY: Cornell University Press. (Aldine, 1969).

Van Leeuwen, Raymond C.
1986   "Proverbs 30:21–23 and the Biblical World Upside Down." *JBL* 105:599–610.

Wright, Christopher J. H.
1979   "The Israelite Background and the Decalogue: The Social Background and Significance of Some Commandments." *Tyndale Bulletin* 30:101–24.

A Socio-Rhetorical Response: Contexts of Interaction and Forms of Exhortation

Vernon K. Robbins

ABSTRACT

While the first essay raises the possibility for social-anthropological analysis of paraenetic literature, the second essay introduces grammatical-syntactical form analysis that virtually defies social analysis. Klaus Berger's taxonomy of forms based on topics and persuasive figures could have aided the authors of the succeeding essays in the volume.

Williams' essay introduces a creative moment when it talks about the Sermon on the Mount as sacrifice transformed into a rhetoric of excess, but the analysis is weakened by an absence of heuristic rhetorical categories oriented toward social situations and an ambiguous use of the phrase "a rhetoric of excess." Levine's essay could have probed more extensively the possible role of women in the environment of Q tradition if deliberative, epideictic, and judicial rhetoric had been available as heuristic socio-rhetorical categories. If Quinn's essay had used rhetorical categories for analysis, the social implications of the judicially-charged language about women may have come into view. Attridge's essay uses the classical rhetorical categories in a highly advantageous manner to explore social dynamics of the environment of the Epistle to the Hebrews.

During the opening moments of this volume, the reader is tantalized by the possibility of seeing social-anthropological analyses of paraenetic literature in the Hebrew Bible and the New Testament. Perdue's use of Turner's anthropological approach sets the stage for an exciting discussion, but the literary analysis does not carry the project as far as one might have hoped. Some good moments arise in the succeeding essays as Perdue himself and others take aspects of the first essay into their discussion, and Claudia Camp has explored many of the strengths and weaknesses of this aspect of the volume. Therefore, I shall not replay this theme. I shall turn directly to the taxonomy of forms Gammie introduces in the second essay and give some attention to the essays concerned with New Testament literature.

One of the biggest hurdles interpreters must overcome, if they wish to explore the social character of biblical literature, is a rich and powerful inheritance of taxonomies of forms based on grammar and syntax. Gammie hammers down as securely as he can the golden spike of grammatical-syntactial form analysis in his first essay, virtually defying anyone to touch these forms with social analysis. The most natural way to build on this positivistic taxonomy would be to use an anthropological system grounded in conceptual logic—perhaps one that could work with polar oppositions, mediations, and a logical square.

But Gammie's essay opens the door for a moment, so let us see if there is room enough to put a toe in it. Gammie merges terminology from Ancient Near Eastern literature, including the Hebrew Bible, with terminology from Greco-Roman literature to establish his taxonomy. Therefore, at the beginning he opens the door for "Instructions," a term from Egyptian literature, and for "Paraenesis" and "Protreptic," terms from Greek literature. Moreover, Gammie introduces the three types of rhetoric based on social situations in the Greek city-state—forensic or judicial (law court), deliberative or symbouleutic (political assembly), and epideictic (civil ceremony). Thus, we seem to be on our way towards a comprehensive taxonomy of Paraenetic Literature in the Mediterranean World based on conventional social situations.

Then, however, Gammie closes the door. Instead of developing a taxonomy oriented toward social situations, he gleans his list of forms from literary-historical criticism grounded in grammatical and syntactical analysis. There is no evidence in the essays that Gammie is aware of Klaus Berger's comprehensive taxonomy of *Gattungen* in the New Testament, which uses rhetorical categories and terminology that exhibit social contexts (1984a; 1984b). Instead, Gammie nails boards on a wall of defense against aspects of the social analysis of Stanley Stowers, Benjamin Fiore, and others with grammatical and syntactical observations—the solid data on which he thinks "formal" characteristics must be based (see, e.g., 3.2)

If Gammie would have introduced Klaus Berger's work, the reader (and the authors of the subsequent essays) might have encountered a taxonomy concerned with "topics" and "persuasive figures" rather than grammar and syntax. Topics are the places people look for something to say about their subject (Kennedy: 20), and persuasive figures are expressions, phrases, and sequences of thought and assertion that have some kind of argumentative quality (Perelman & Olbrechts-Tyteca: 167–79). The arenas of life from which people glean topics and figures they use to persuade others are social phenomena. Thus, Berger bases his taxonomy of paraenetic forms in the New Testament on topics and figures in various kinds of social situations. And he concludes that paraenesis is deliberative (symbouleutic or advisory) rhetoric. Paraenesis functions like advice in a political assembly rather than accusation or defense in a law court (judicial or forensic rhetoric) or praise and blame in a civil ceremony (epideictic rhetoric). Within this framework, Berger finds the following categories:

(a) general social duties (concerned with *Gesellschaft*, if we use Perdue's essay)
(b) inner community social duties (concerned with *Gemeinschaft*)
(c) community paraenesis concerning "one another" and "unity" (*Gemeinschaft*)
(d) property and sexual ethic
(e) self-subordination
    (1) for wives (to husbands)
    (2) for Christians (to civil authorities)
    (3) for slaves (to masters)
    (4) for Christians (to community leaders)
    (5) for Christians (to one another)
(f) renunciation of retaliation, payment, opposition and judicial procedures in this age
(g) metaphorical paraenesis about watchfulness and temperateness
(h) postconversion admonition
(i) *Haustafel* and duty list
(j) epistolary paraenetic conclusion
(k) heresy conclusion
(l) warning about false teachers
(m) martyrdom paraenesis (Berger 1984a: 121–48).

This taxonomy is guided by topics and figures, not by grammar and syntax. For this reason, the *Gattunqen* reach provocatively toward arenas of life constituted by order, conflict, transition, ritual, liminality, *Gesellschaft*, *Gemeinschaft*, and other good social and anthropological categories that call forth rich discussion and debate.

If *Gattungen* like Berger's had been introduced into the discussion, the authors of the subsequent essays could have taken their analysis much further into social and anthropological issues. And the reader also may have acquired a richer framework for evaluating various discussions in the volume. For example, there is a creative moment in Williams' essay where he argues that the Sermon on the Mount is sacrifice transformed into a rhetoric of excess. How did Williams draw this conclusion? What moves does his presentation hide from the reader? How can we judge if the rhetoric in the Sermon on the Mount is a rhetoric of excess? How can we judge if Williams' argument itself is a rhetoric of excess or a rhetoric grounded in some kind of reasonableness? Since Williams, like Gammie, abandons the categories of judicial, deliberative, and epideictic rhetoric, these categories function in a hidden manner, and without clarity, in his analysis. If he would keep them in view as heuristic social categories, greater clarity could accompany his analysis.

Williams, building on observations by Kermode, proposes that a rhetoric of excess is constitutive to the contrasts in Matthew 5:21–48 between the old Torah and the new commandments (3.2). Thus, the shift from killing to anger, adultery to lustfulness, etc. is a rhetoric of excess. In his words, as he comments on 5:38–42:

> To take this style of rhetoric literally would be just as foolish as trying to obey the teaching on adultery by engaging in self-mutilation (5:27–30). If someone hits me am I to say, "Now hit me again"? If I were to lose $1,000 in a lawsuit, should I offer the winning party another one thousand on Christian principles? (3.2)

What the reader never sees, because Williams does not bring heuristic social categories into view, is that the antitheses have changed judicial (forensic) rhetoric into deliberative rhetoric. In other words, commandments that could be perceived as laws triable in a law court are transformed into guidelines that function as advice for maintaining honor in a political arena where citizens assemble to make decisions about group action. The "new" commandments function like advice in a political assembly: members (*politai*) who do not follow the advice will bring dishonor upon themselves and find themselves removed from positions of power and influence in the community, because the majority has decided to act on the basis of the advice.

The shift from judicial to deliberative rhetoric appears to be accompanied by a shift from a social context in the *Gesellschaft* to a social context in the *Gemeinschaft*. Within first century Jewish institutions, i.e., the *Gesellschaft*, the ten commandments have legal status. The teaching in the Sermon on the Mount transforms the commandments into advice which provides the means to acquire and maintain honor among people who identify themselves as Christians, i.e., in the *Gemeinschaft*. Where will judgment occur for the one who looks at a woman lustfully? Not in a law court where a verdict on adultery could be sought. Rather, people in the community will disapprove of or publicly denounce the man who looks at a woman lustfully. Thus, to preserve his honor in the community, the man will not look at a woman lustfully, since his socially formed knowledge informs him that this is a matter of committing adultery with her in his heart. The concern about divorce, then, is not about what is legal, but about what is shameful: it is a guideline nurtured among the members of the community (5:32). The new commandment makes any action concerning divorce in an official law court incidental to the real issue: personal indictment among associates in the community. This means that divorce has been moved from a judicial social setting in a dominant form of culture (*Gesellschaft*) to a political social setting in a localized community

(*Gemeinschaft*), a setting of interaction and power where the majority of the members have decided to act according to a certain kind of advice.

Only one of the new commandments maintains judicial language: the antithesis about killing (5: 21–26), which refers to "legal liability" and a "council." But where is the council that will judge a person who is angry with a brother or insults a brother? This is not a law court in the *Gesellschaft*. At most, this is a council set up by the community. And what will the punishment be? The person will be liable to the fire of Gehenna (5:22). This council appears not to proceed in the usual manner with punishments! The issue is honor and shame among other members of the community. Who will associate with someone who is liable to the fire of Gehenna? That person will be pushed to the periphery and not be given a position of leadership. Other people who act according to the advice in the new commandments will acquire and maintain honor in the community and receive positions of leadership and influence. And the worst kind of shame will come to those who do something liable in a law court in the *Gesellschaft* (5:25–26). That person has taken himself or herself outside the domain of the new commandments which concern actions that members try to persuade other members to follow. That person simply will have to suffer the punishments meted out by the civil court (5: 26).

Now let us return to Williams' statement about turning the other cheek and giving an additional $1,000 to a person who has won a lawsuit against us. How are we to evaluate Williams' statement: "If someone hits me am I to say, 'Now hit me again'" (3.2)? Williams appears to presuppose a situation outside a community governed by social pressures of honor and shame. Can Williams not imagine that these actions would work in the setting of a church community? If not, he should try it. Who hits a person in a church setting, and what happens if someone does? I can testify that hitting happens at church camps. And the person who says, "Now hit me again," wins the respect of everyone while the one who hit is brought to shame. Thus, the issue is the social dynamics functioning in the setting.

Social anthropologists tell us that Mediterranean society during the rise of early Christianity was dominated by dynamics of honor and shame (Gilmore), and the Sermon on the Mount exhibits these dynamics. We see this kind of culture nurtured today in families, ethnic communities, and social and religious groups of various kinds. Thus at church camp, where the dynamics of honor and shame function very well, a person can say, "Now hit me again," and it will work very effectively. In later centuries in Western culture, and certainly in the context of the Protestant Reformation and the Catholic Counter-Reformation, guilt culture was becoming dominant in European society. Many of us are heirs of this well-developed guilt culture. Within these dynamics, if we hit back we indict ourselves. We ask, "Why did I not control myself? I wonder if I can be forgiven and if I can forgive myself." But now a major portion of our society appears to function in the dynamics of a "rights" culture, and Williams exhibits the presuppositions of a "rights" culture in his essay. The norms of this kind of culture suggest that everyone has the right either to resist the person who hits on the cheek or to hit the person back. Why? This appears to be presupposed by basic American mythology: even Matt Dillon hit "when he had to," and so does Rambo, Dirty Harry, and Ronald Reagan (see Jewett and Lawrence). Moreover, everyone has the right to "their own" money. This is "personal property," if it was acquired within the "rights" of the *Gesellschaft*. Thus, a person would be foolish, Williams says, to "offer the winning party another one thousand on Christian principles?" So where have "Christian principles" gone? From communities governed by honor and shame during the first century to modern or post-modern society governed by individual rights. The point in the Sermon on the Mount is that the person who has been invited to hit the other cheek has been shamed, and the shame of being naked when a person has given all one's clothes to the person who sued would be completely overcome by the honor attained by the action. But Williams has found no way to let the dynamics of an honor and shame culture influence the presuppositions of his rights culture.

So, is the rhetoric in the Sermon on the Mount a rhetoric of excess? When it talks about plucking out one's own eye or cutting off one's hand, the social situations in which we live and in which most early Christians lived suggest that this is hyperbole—exaggerated, excessive assertion. But those situations which Tannehill analyzed as "focal instances" are at work daily in communities throughout the world. There are people who regularly turn the other cheek, give the shirt off their back, go a second mile, and give to everyone who asks. The question is the social context, and we should distinguish among social contexts and seek to understand the differences among them. It would be informative to have a taxonomy that exhibits the range of social settings and dynamics presupposed by paraenetic literature in the Bible. Berger's list is a good start. If we expanded and refined his taxonomy, we could begin to engage in significantly new conversations about social environments exhibited by biblical texts.

Is there any substance to Williams' assertion that the Sermon on the Mount has transformed sacrifice into a rhetoric of excess? Perhaps the major issue is the meaning of the term "excess," since it has acquired special meanings in post-modern analysis. Among other things, we would need to clarify the relation of Kermode's use of the term to the use of the term in theories about violence and eroticism (Bataille 40–48). But this is not, I think, the appropriate place to pursue this matter. I would like to think that Williams has opened the door for a quite new discussion of the Sermon on the Mount as "sacrificial rhetoric." With the provocative studies of sacrifice by Girard, Burkert, and others as a resource (Hamerton-Kelly), we may acquire significantly new understandings of the social function of actions like turning the other cheek, going the extra mile, and giving the shirt off our back. In fact, my colleague Thee Smith has found evidence that in certain social situations black people have enacted "focal instances" that have called forth mimetic desire in their white overlords that caused them to free their slaves or engage in other activities motivated by self-sacrifice. Moreover, the demonstrations led by Mahatma Ghandi and Martin Luther King, Jr. suggest the possibility for the success of related actions in a national arena, again following the leads in Perdue's essay that distinguish between *Gesellschaft* and *Gemeinschaft* as places of human activity. Thus, perhaps the issue is "sacrificial" rhetoric, and we need to have a careful look at the meanings of the term "excess" before we will have clarity as we use it in relation to the Sermon on the Mount.

This brings us naturally to Amy-Jill Levine's essay, where the theme is that women may be present where we cannot see them. Levine's essay could have been aided by a taxonomy of paraenetic literature oriented toward social situations. She observes that women are not present in Q1, and when they appear in Q2 they are in a subordinate role. Then she asks: since women are not mentioned among the medicants but among the supporting network when they appear in the second stage, could women actually have had greater power among the support network at an earlier stage?

Using categories we have introduced previously, we could make the following observations. In Q1, deliberative rhetoric is dominant and epideictic rhetoric is generalized. The deliberative rhetoric tells people how to act in general and specific terms: love your enemies and pray for those who mistreat you (Q 6:27–28); turn the other cheek when hit and give your cloak as well as your tunic (Q 6:29); give to everyone who begs (Q 6:30); do to people as you wish them to do to you (Q 6:31); go out carrying no money or knapsack nor wearing sandals (Q 10:4); accept hospitality only in one house in a village (Q 10:10); do not be anxious about what to say when you are delivered up to courts (Q 12:11); do not worry about body, food, and clothes (Q 12:22–31); etc. The advice, i.e., deliberative rhetoric, in Q1 provides guidelines whereby a group can acquire its identity by engaging in common actions. The epideictic rhetoric which accompanies the deliberative rhetoric is directed toward the source of the advice and toward broad groups of people who do or do not respond to the advice: praise to the Father who has revealed hidden things to the Son (Q 10:21–22); blessed are the poor (Q 6:20–21); blessed are the eyes that see and the ears that hear (Q 10:23–24); woe to Chorazin, Bethsaida, and Capernaum, which are worse than Tyre and Sidon, for not repenting (Q 10:13–15); woe to Jerusalem for killing the prophets and stoning its messengers (Q 13: 34). In Q1, then, praise and blame, i.e., the ingredients of epideictic rhetoric, are directed towards entire cities and general groups who respond or do not respond.

The deliberative and epideictic rhetoric in Q1 calls for people to make the attitudes, precepts, and actions in the sayings public: the person who hears you hears me (Q 10:16); whatever is whispered in the dark or in secret rooms is to be made known (Q 12:2–3); every one who acknowledges the author of these sayings in public will be acknowledged by God and everyone who denies will be denied (Q 12:8–9). Thus, the public arena is the testing ground for group identity. And, as Levine argues, the people of Q1 are asked to become "more" marginal to fulfill their public role. Is it presupposed that women will have power in the household and that men must play "the public role" of mendicant marginality? In Q1, is the marginality of women based more on association with "publicly marginal" men than with a role of maintaining a household? Do we see here a manner in which men established the primary identity of the group by their public actions? The problem, as Levine states, is that women are not mentioned in Q1. Could their public action be as important as men's public action for the identity of the group? Of special interest may be the things whispered in secret rooms that are made public (Q 12:2–3), since older women often participate in the dispersal of information about "secret things" in traditional societies (Campbell: 313–314). Perhaps here we see a major "public" activity of women alongside the public activity of men. The women's "support" role may not be limited to maintaining households: they may be major communicators of the "secret things" in the public sphere and, thus, they may be active participants in "acknowledging in public" the one who speaks the sayings. Unfortunately, as Levine reminds us, these hunches have to be reconstructed from silence in the sayings.

In Q2, where women are mentioned, they are, as Levine observes, "in a support role." Men, through their public role, are becoming more and more dominant in this group. This, of course, is encouraged by the broader social structures, which are patriarchal in nature and form. Men appear now to have a political view of their role, as exhibited in Q 22:28–30: "You are those who will sit with me on thrones judging the twelve tribes of Israel." In the setting of these male political aspirations, there is very little new deliberative rhetoric. The noticeable characteristic of Q2 is the highly charged epideictic rhetoric. The sayings envision crowds of Jewish people addressed as a "brood of vipers" (Q 3:7), John the Baptist accused of possessing a demon and Jesus referred to as a glutton, drunk, and friend of tax collectors and sinners (Q 7:33–34). The sayings direct woes toward Pharisees, calling them blind fools (Q 11:39–41) and whitewashed tombs or unmarked graves (Q 11:44), and accuses them of loading people with heavy burdens (Q 11:46), loving front seats in synagogues and salutations in market places (Q 11:43), taking away the key to knowledge (Q 11:51), neglecting justice (Q 11:42), and being full of extortion and rapacity (Q 11:39). The epideictic rhetoric in sayings attributed to John the Baptist and Jesus attacks a specific group of Jewish leaders, namely Pharisees, and their power in synagogues and marketplaces. In this setting, most directives appear in negative form: do not neglect justice (Q 11:42) and do not overload people with heavy burdens of religious law (Q 11:46). Also, in this setting the issue of purity laws, washing of cups and plates, appears (Q 11: 39–40). Therefore, in Q2 the group is engaging in a public power play against Pharisees who are perceived to be dominating the religious domain. Undoubtedly this is perceived to be "men's" work. The men in the Q group have now moved beyond more generalized work in cities, accompanied by a mode of "staying in one house for a while." They have targeted a group of people who have influence in the synagogues and marketplaces.

Only in this stage of the Q tradition, as Levine observes, do women appear in a few sayings, and they appear in a support role, as mothers and workers in the household. If women had some kind of public role during the stage of Q1, it is now being replaced by the importance of men's attack on other men in the public sphere. During this stage there is reference to Woman Wisdom (Q 7:35), but she appears in a context that privileges men as wisdom comes from the Father to the Son (Q 10:21–22) to the disciple of the teacher (Q 6:40). In other words, I agree with Levine that Sophia's "direct association with Jesus may be less a 'feminizing" of the teacher than a 'masculinizing' of the mythical source of that teaching" (5.6). And we should observe where the masculinizing occurs: among children playing in the market place (Q 7:31–35). The negative personal attacks are located in the market place and the exemplary action is found in the faithful steward in the household (12:42b–46), the centurion who has authority and built the synagogue (7:1–10), and the strong man's house (11:14–28). The rhetoric is becoming domesticated: the images and locations exhibit power plays among established groups in cities rather than generalized attacks from mendicants who only stay awhile. In this more settled environment, men are playing the key public role *and* running the households. Women play a strictly supportive role even in the household.

In Jerome Quinn's essay, we see a later stage of Christianity where men's dominance both in public and in the household is given explicit organizational and ritual form. Quinn's essay does not say, as it should, that 1 Tim 2:11–15 is moving from deliberative rhetoric toward judicial rhetoric. The assertions are like legal statements:

> (1) Let a woman learn in silence with all submissiveness.
> (2) I *permit* no woman to teach or to have authority over men; she is to keep silent. For Adam was formed first, then Eve; and Adam was not deceived, but the woman was deceived and became a transgressor.

This is the introduction of a law with a rationale supported by an internal argument from the contrary. The assertion with the rationale forms a syllogistic argument (enthymeme), which is a strong way to formulate a law and defend it, and the argument from the contrary clarifies the law articulated in the enthymeme (see Mack and Robbins: 54–59, 120–21). The language has moved away from honor and shame to "what is permitted." *Gemeinschaft* is acquiring characteristics of *Gesellschaft*. Instead of a deliberative environment, this environment is highly judicial—non-compliance will be considered an infraction of what is permitted rather than simply an action that brings dishonor and moves a person from a position of power to a peripheral location in the community. Women now must submit to judicially-charged paraenesis or they will face consequences in an environment where people are told what is and is not permitted.

In contrast to the essays discussed above, the essay by Attridge probes the Epistle to the Hebrews with the heuristic social categories of judicial, deliberative, and epideictic rhetoric. At the beginning of the essay, he articulates the difficulty of using Gammie's essay, since New Testament literature is significantly absent within the horizons of Gammie's interests and the three types of rhetoric in the Hellenistic world are pushed out of sight. Thus, Attridge has to create his own way into a discussion of Hebrews with social and rhetorical categories, and he does this in an admirable way using the term "homily" or *logos parakleseos*.

Attridge shows us a context in early Christianity where the rhetoric is not primarily deliberative since the community has already been constructed, and not primarily judicial or filled with negative epideictic since any threat to the community appears not to come from an outside or inside attack on the symbol system of the community. Instead, Hebrews contains the kind of epideictic rhetoric enriched with deliberative images and exposition that "reinforce the identity of a social sub-group in such a way as not to isolate it from its environment." Whether or not all would agree with this analysis, it works with rhetorical categories and taxonomies in a manner that opens the door to social contexts in early Christianity.

Thus, the essays on first century literature in this volume contain openings toward new analysis of paraenesis in social contexts. Unfortunately, the grammatical and syntactical impulse at work in the taxonomy in the second essay created an obstacle that limited the possibilities in the succeeding essays.

WORKS CONSULTED

Berger, Klaus
    1984a   *Formgeschichte des Neuen Testaments*. Heidelberg: Quelle & Meyer.
    1984b   "Hellenistische Gattungen im Neuen Testament." *Aufstieg und Niederqang der römischen Welt* 25.2: 1032–1432.

Bataille, Georges
    1984   *Death and Sensuality*. Reprint edition. New York: Walker and Company.

Gilmore, David D., ed.
    1987   *Honor and Shame and the Unity of the Mediterranean*. Washington, D.C.: American Anthropological Association.

Hamerton-Kelly, Robert G., ed.
    1987   *Violent Origins*. Stanford: Stanford University Press.

Jewett, Robert and John Shelton Lawrence
    1977   *The American Monomyth*. Garden City, NY: Anchor Press.

Kennedy, George A.
    1984   *New Testament Interpretation through Rhetorical Criticism*. Chapel Hill and London: University of North Carolina Press.

Mack, Burton L. and Vernon K. Robbins
    1989   *Patterns of Persuasion in the Gospels*. Sonoma: Polebridge Press.

Perelman, Ch. and L. Olbrechts-Tyteca
    1969   *The New Rhetoric: A Treatise on Argumentation*. Notre Dame and London: University of Notre Dame Press.

Printed in the United States
1310600003B/173

9 781589 831131